Chef's Kiss

AN ONI PRESS PUBLICATION

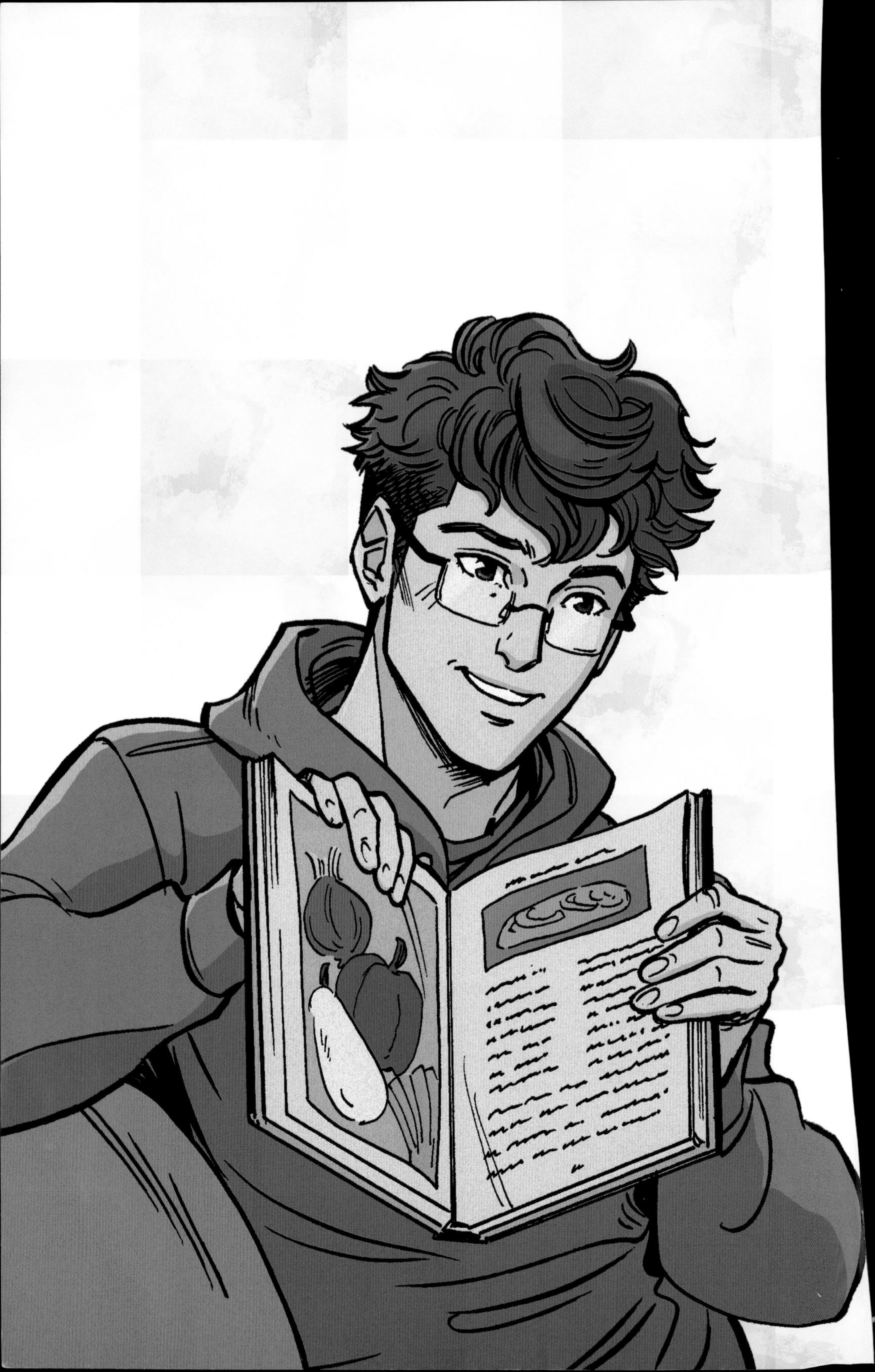

Chef's Kiss

Written by Jarrett Melendez
Illustrated by Danica Brine
Colored by Hank Jones
Lettered by Hassan Otsmane-Elhaou

Edited by Robin Herrera, Grace Scheipeter & Chris Cerasi
Designed by Sarah Rockwell
Consulting Reader: Jasmine Walls

PUBLISHED BY ONI-LION FORGE PUBLISHING GROUP, LLC.

James Lucas Jones, president & publisher • Charlie Chu, e.v.p. of creative & business development • Steve Ellis, s.v.p. of games & operations • Alex Segura, s.v.p of marketing & sales • Michelle Nguyen, associate publisher • Brad Rooks, director of operations • Amber O'Neill, special projects manager • Margot Wood, director of marketing & sales • Katie Sainz, marketing manager • Henry Barajas, sales manager • Tara Lehmann, publicist • Holly Aitchison, consumer marketing manager • Troy Look, director of design & production • Angie Knowles, production manager • Kate Z. Stone, senior graphic designer • Carey Hall, graphic designer • Sarah Rockwell, graphic designer • Hilary Thompson, graphic designer • Vincent Kukua, digital prepress technician • Chris Cerasi, managing editor • Jasmine Amiri, senior editor • Shawna Gore, senior editor • Amanda Meadows, senior editor • Robert Meyers, senior editor, licensing • Desiree Rodriguez, editor • Grace Scheipeter, editor • Zack Soto, editor • Ben Eisner, game developer • Jung Lee, logistics coordinator • Kuian Kellum, warehouse assistant • Joe Nozemack, publisher emeritus

onipress.com

@JarrettMelendez
@karibu_draws
@HankJonesColors
@HassanOE

Cover by Danica Brine
Oni Limited cover by Kevin Wada

First edition: March 2022

ISBN: 978-1-62010-904-5
Oni Limited ISBN: 978-1-63715-070-2
eISBN: 978-1-62010-910-6

Printed in China

Library of Congress Control Number: 2021941061

1 2 3 4 5 6 7 8 9 10

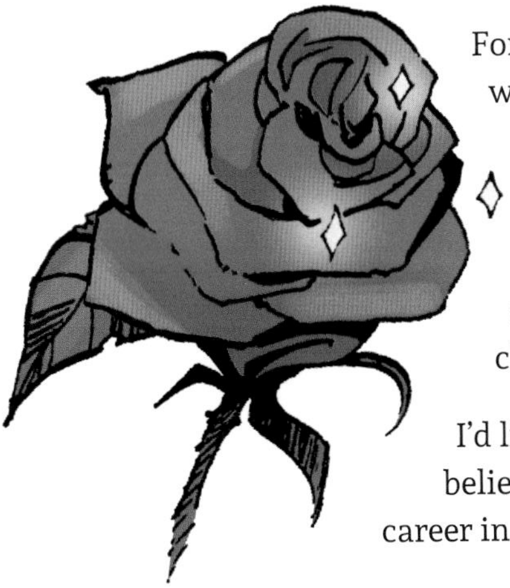

For Stuart,
who has been both the Liam to my Ben and the Ben to my Liam. Love you and, of course, the piggies. - Jarrett Melendez

This goes out to all my friends and family, as well as Nick, Dawn, and Jarrett for always cheering me on. - Danica Brine

I'd like to dedicate this to my parents, who believed in and supported me every step of my career in comics. - Hank Jones

Chapter One

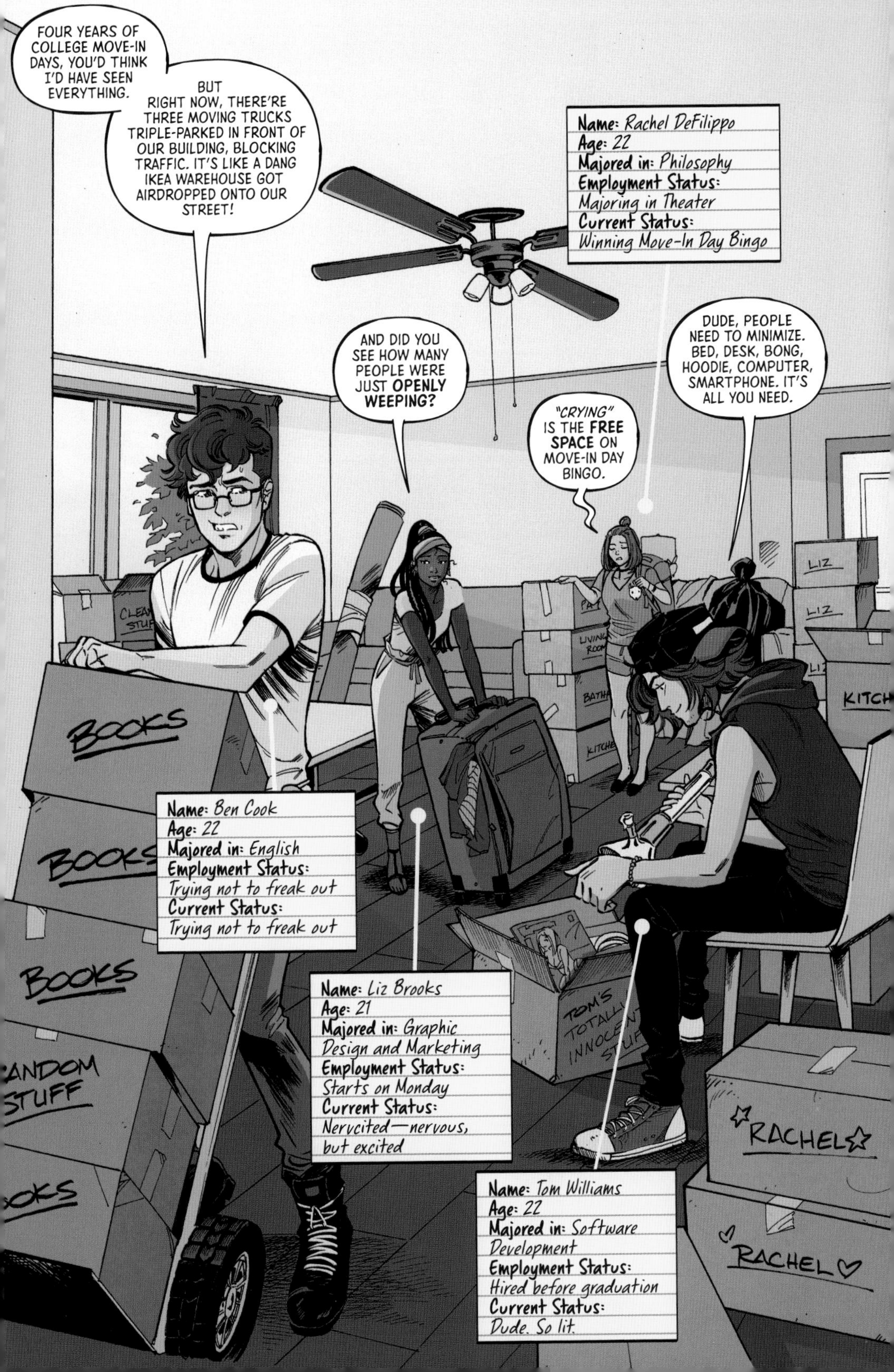
FOUR YEARS OF COLLEGE MOVE-IN DAYS, YOU'D THINK I'D HAVE SEEN EVERYTHING.
BUT RIGHT NOW, THERE'RE THREE MOVING TRUCKS TRIPLE-PARKED IN FRONT OF OUR BUILDING, BLOCKING TRAFFIC. IT'S LIKE A DANG IKEA WAREHOUSE GOT AIRDROPPED ONTO OUR STREET!
Name: Rachel DeFilippo
Age: 22
Majored in: Philosophy
Employment Status: Majoring in Theater
Current Status: Winning Move-In Day Bingo
AND DID YOU SEE HOW MANY PEOPLE WERE JUST OPENLY WEEPING?
"CRYING" IS THE FREE SPACE ON MOVE-IN DAY BINGO.
DUDE, PEOPLE NEED TO MINIMIZE. BED, DESK, BONG, HOODIE, COMPUTER, SMARTPHONE. IT'S ALL YOU NEED.
LIZ
LIZ
KITCH
BOOKS
BOOKS
BOOKS
RANDOM STUFF
BOOKS
Name: Ben Cook
Age: 22
Majored in: English
Employment Status: Trying not to freak out
Current Status: Trying not to freak out
Name: Liz Brooks
Age: 21
Majored in: Graphic Design and Marketing
Employment Status: Starts on Monday
Current Status: Nervcited—nervous, but excited
TOM'S TOTALLY INNOCENT STUFF
RACHEL
RACHEL
Name: Tom Williams
Age: 22
Majored in: Software Development
Employment Status: Hired before graduation
Current Status: Dude. So lit.

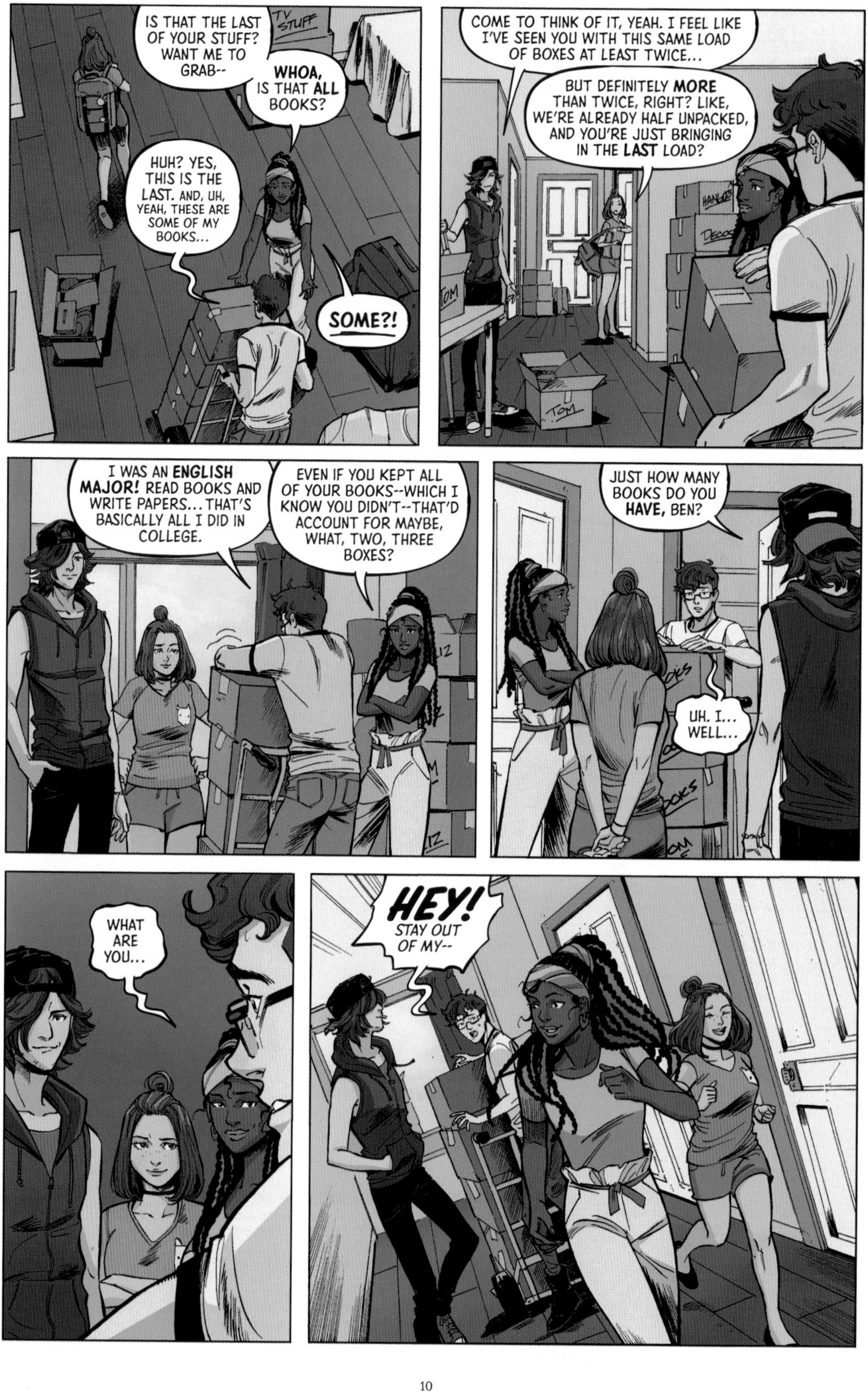

TV STUFF
IS THAT THE LAST OF YOUR STUFF? WANT ME TO GRAB--
WHOA, IS THAT ALL BOOKS?
HUH? YES, THIS IS THE LAST. AND, UH, YEAH, THESE ARE SOME OF MY BOOKS...
SOME?!
COME TO THINK OF IT, YEAH. I FEEL LIKE I'VE SEEN YOU WITH THIS SAME LOAD OF BOXES AT LEAST TWICE...
BUT DEFINITELY MORE THAN TWICE, RIGHT? LIKE, WE'RE ALREADY HALF UNPACKED, AND YOU'RE JUST BRINGING IN THE LAST LOAD?
TOM
I WAS AN ENGLISH MAJOR! READ BOOKS AND WRITE PAPERS... THAT'S BASICALLY ALL I DID IN COLLEGE.
EVEN IF YOU KEPT ALL OF YOUR BOOKS--WHICH I KNOW YOU DIDN'T--THAT'D ACCOUNT FOR MAYBE, WHAT, TWO, THREE BOXES?
JUST HOW MANY BOOKS DO YOU HAVE, BEN?
UH. I... WELL...
WHAT ARE YOU...
HEY! STAY OUT OF MY--

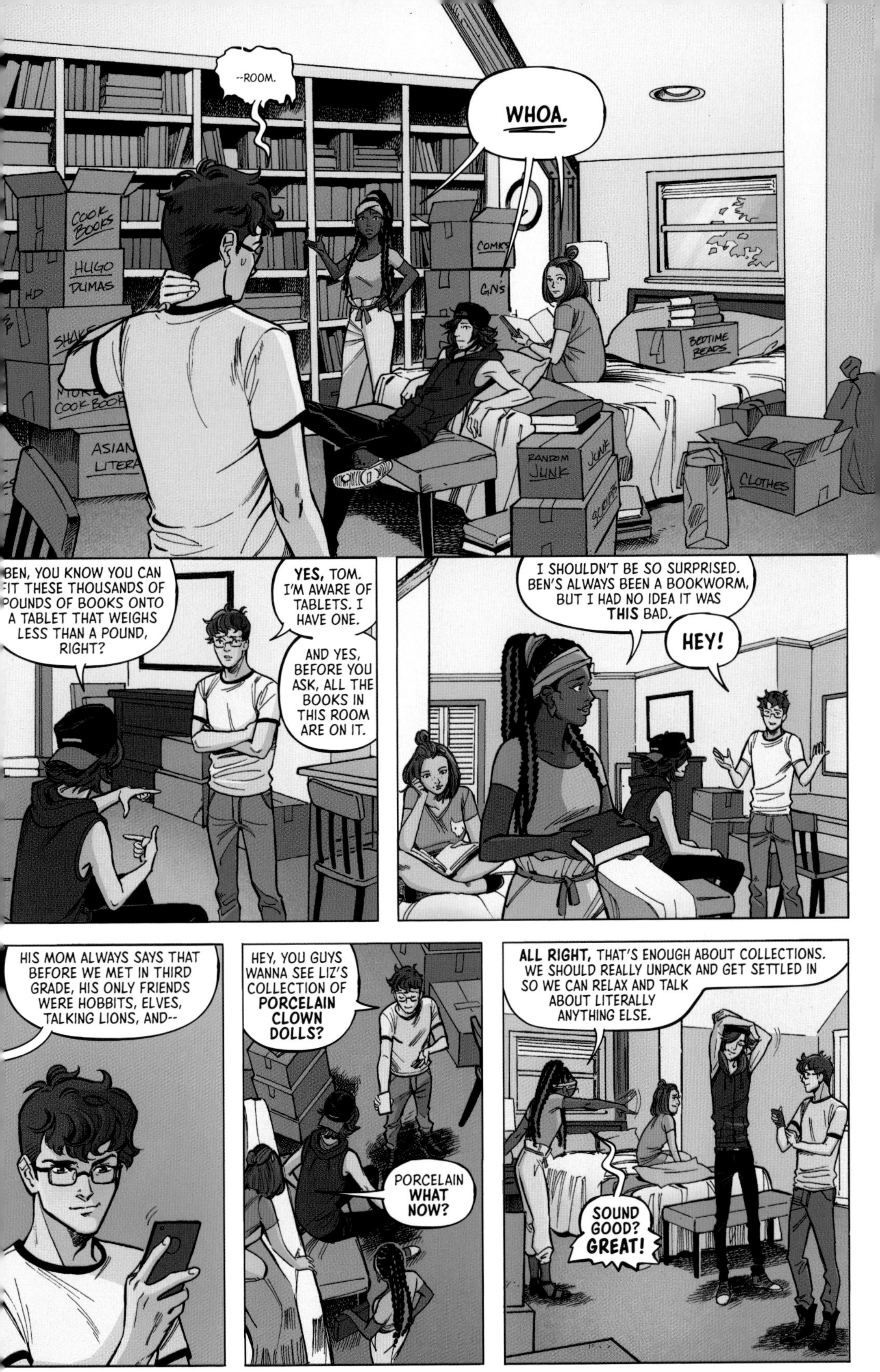
--ROOM.
WHOA.
COOK BOOKS
HUGO
DUMAS
HD
SHAKE
MORE COOKBOOK
ASIAN LITERA
COMICS
GN's
BEDTIME READS
RANDOM JUNK
JUNK
SCRIPTS
CLOTHES
BEN, YOU KNOW YOU CAN FIT THESE THOUSANDS OF POUNDS OF BOOKS ONTO A TABLET THAT WEIGHS LESS THAN A POUND, RIGHT?
YES, TOM. I'M AWARE OF TABLETS. I HAVE ONE.
AND YES, BEFORE YOU ASK, ALL THE BOOKS IN THIS ROOM ARE ON IT.
I SHOULDN'T BE SO SURPRISED. BEN'S ALWAYS BEEN A BOOKWORM, BUT I HAD NO IDEA IT WAS THIS BAD.
HEY!
HIS MOM ALWAYS SAYS THAT BEFORE WE MET IN THIRD GRADE, HIS ONLY FRIENDS WERE HOBBITS, ELVES, TALKING LIONS, AND--
HEY, YOU GUYS WANNA SEE LIZ'S COLLECTION OF PORCELAIN CLOWN DOLLS?
PORCELAIN WHAT NOW?
ALL RIGHT, THAT'S ENOUGH ABOUT COLLECTIONS. WE SHOULD REALLY UNPACK AND GET SETTLED IN SO WE CAN RELAX AND TALK ABOUT LITERALLY ANYTHING ELSE.
SOUND GOOD? GREAT!

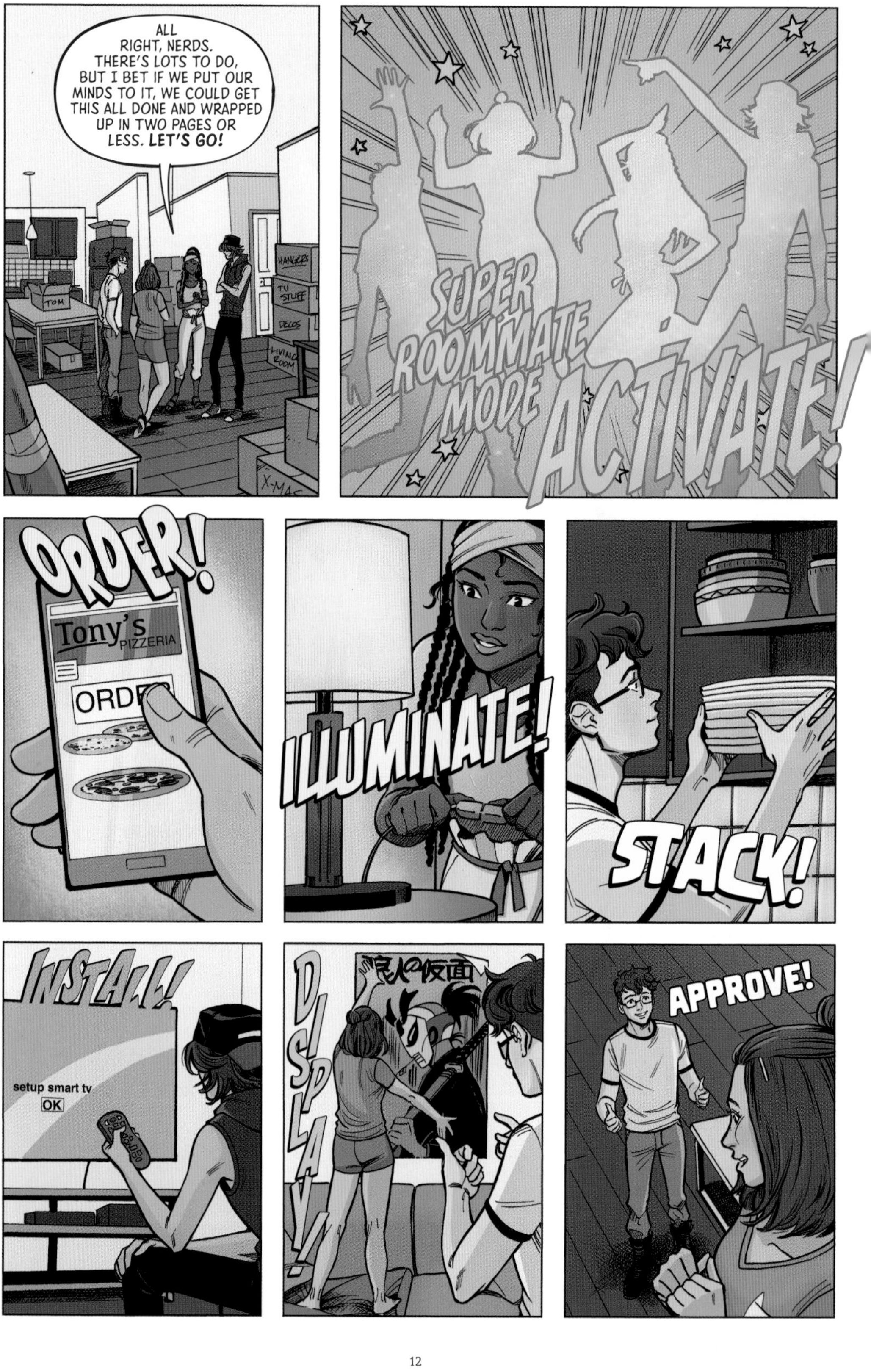
ALL RIGHT, NERDS. THERE'S LOTS TO DO, BUT I BET IF WE PUT OUR MINDS TO IT, WE COULD GET THIS ALL DONE AND WRAPPED UP IN TWO PAGES OR LESS. **LET'S GO!**
TOM
HANGERS
TV STUFF
DECOS
LIVING ROOM
X-MAS
SUPER ROOMMATE MODE ACTIVATE!
ORDER!
Tony's PIZZERIA
ILLUMINATE!
STACK!
INSTALL!
setup smart tv
OK
DISPLAY!
浪人の仮面
APPROVE!

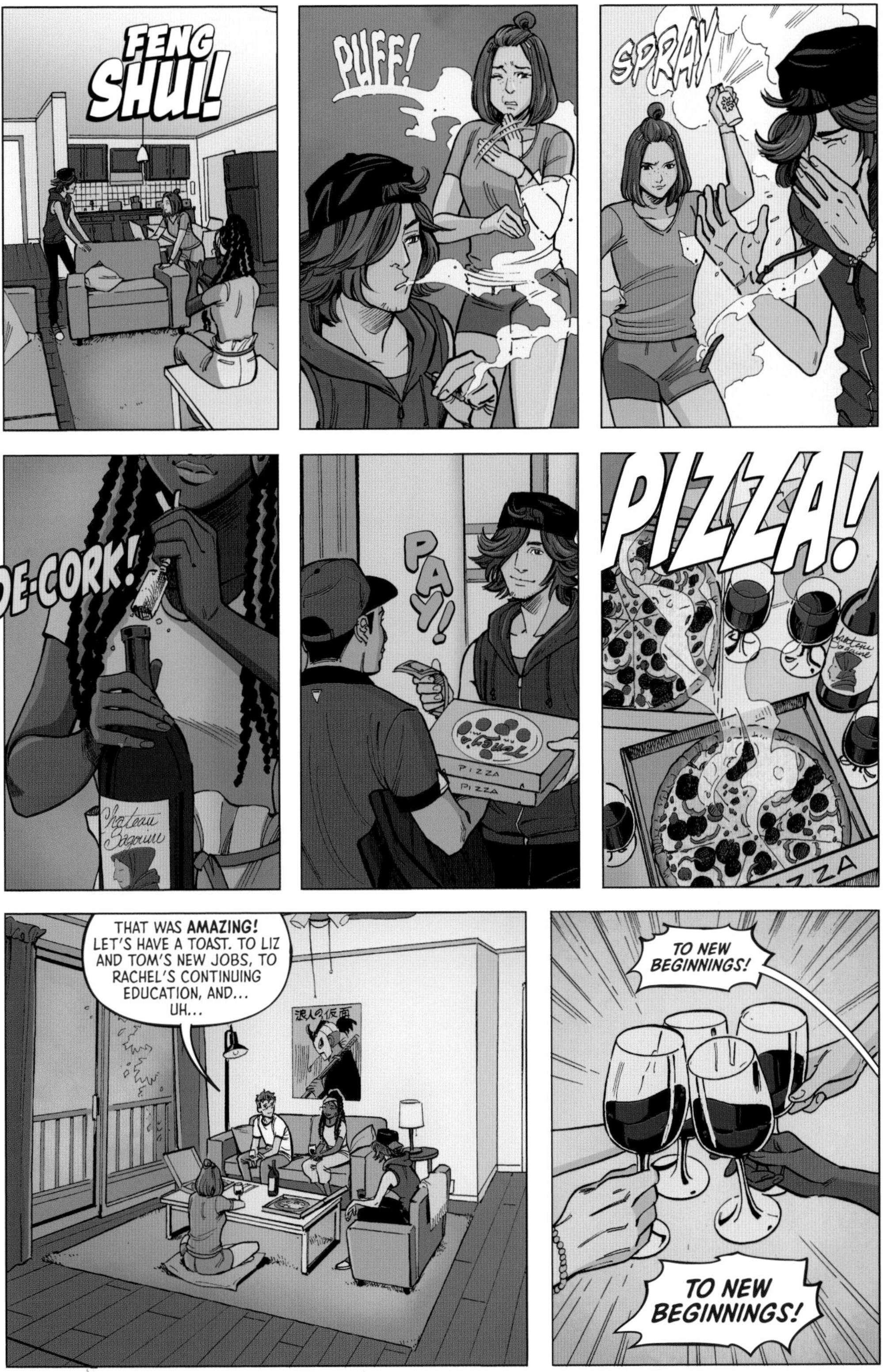
FENG SHUI!
PUFF!
SPRAY
DE-CORK!
PAY!
PIZZA!
THAT WAS AMAZING! LET'S HAVE A TOAST. TO LIZ AND TOM'S NEW JOBS, TO RACHEL'S CONTINUING EDUCATION, AND... UH...
TO NEW BEGINNINGS!
TO NEW BEGINNINGS!

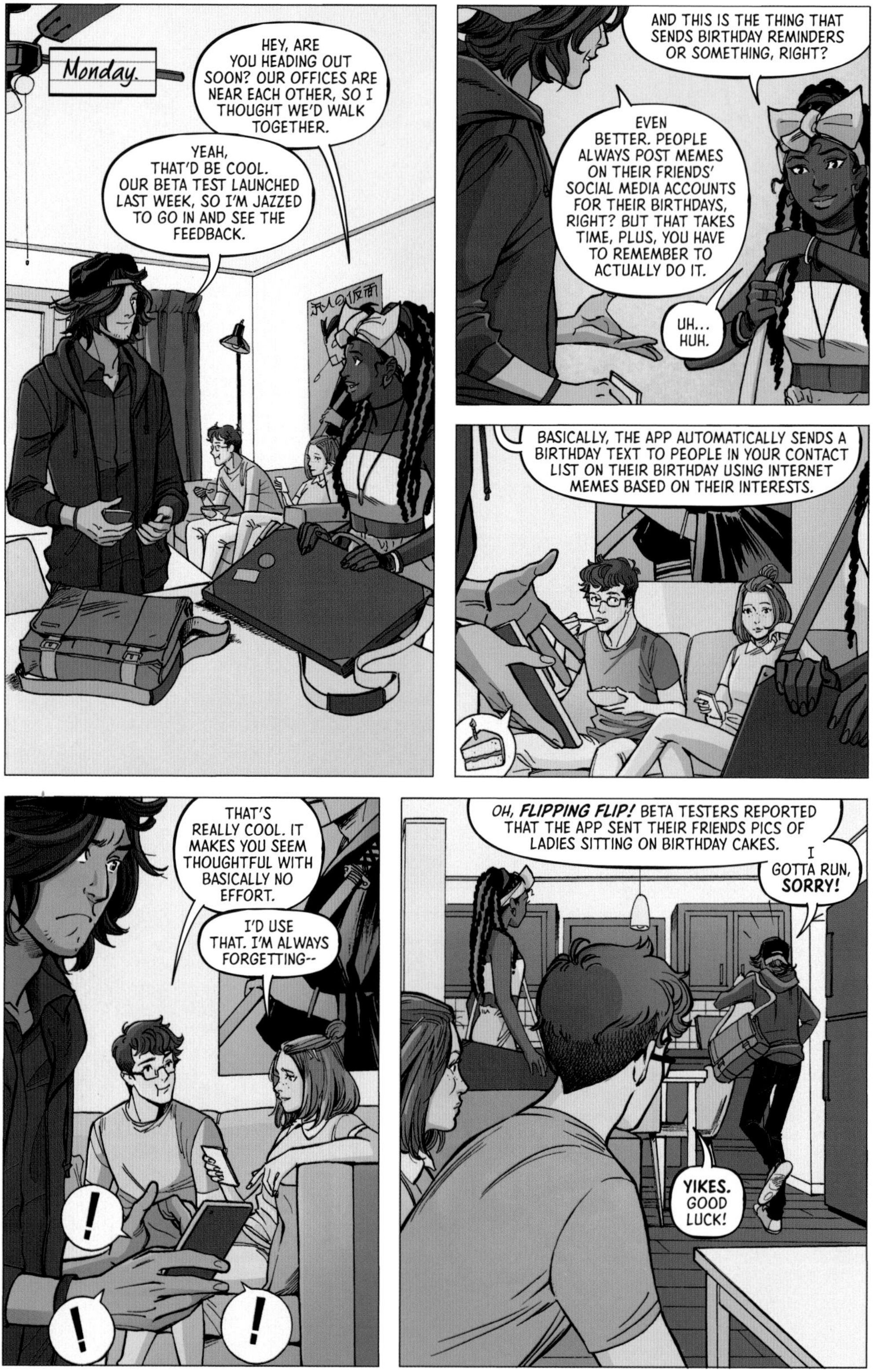
Monday.
HEY, ARE YOU HEADING OUT SOON? OUR OFFICES ARE NEAR EACH OTHER, SO I THOUGHT WE'D WALK TOGETHER.
YEAH, THAT'D BE COOL. OUR BETA TEST LAUNCHED LAST WEEK, SO I'M JAZZED TO GO IN AND SEE THE FEEDBACK.
AND THIS IS THE THING THAT SENDS BIRTHDAY REMINDERS OR SOMETHING, RIGHT?
EVEN BETTER. PEOPLE ALWAYS POST MEMES ON THEIR FRIENDS' SOCIAL MEDIA ACCOUNTS FOR THEIR BIRTHDAYS, RIGHT? BUT THAT TAKES TIME, PLUS, YOU HAVE TO REMEMBER TO ACTUALLY DO IT.
UH... HUH.
BASICALLY, THE APP AUTOMATICALLY SENDS A BIRTHDAY TEXT TO PEOPLE IN YOUR CONTACT LIST ON THEIR BIRTHDAY USING INTERNET MEMES BASED ON THEIR INTERESTS.
THAT'S REALLY COOL. IT MAKES YOU SEEM THOUGHTFUL WITH BASICALLY NO EFFORT.
I'D USE THAT. I'M ALWAYS FORGETTING--
!
!
!
OH, ***FLIPPING FLIP!*** BETA TESTERS REPORTED THAT THE APP SENT THEIR FRIENDS PICS OF LADIES SITTING ON BIRTHDAY CAKES.
I GOTTA RUN, **SORRY!**
YIKES. GOOD LUCK!

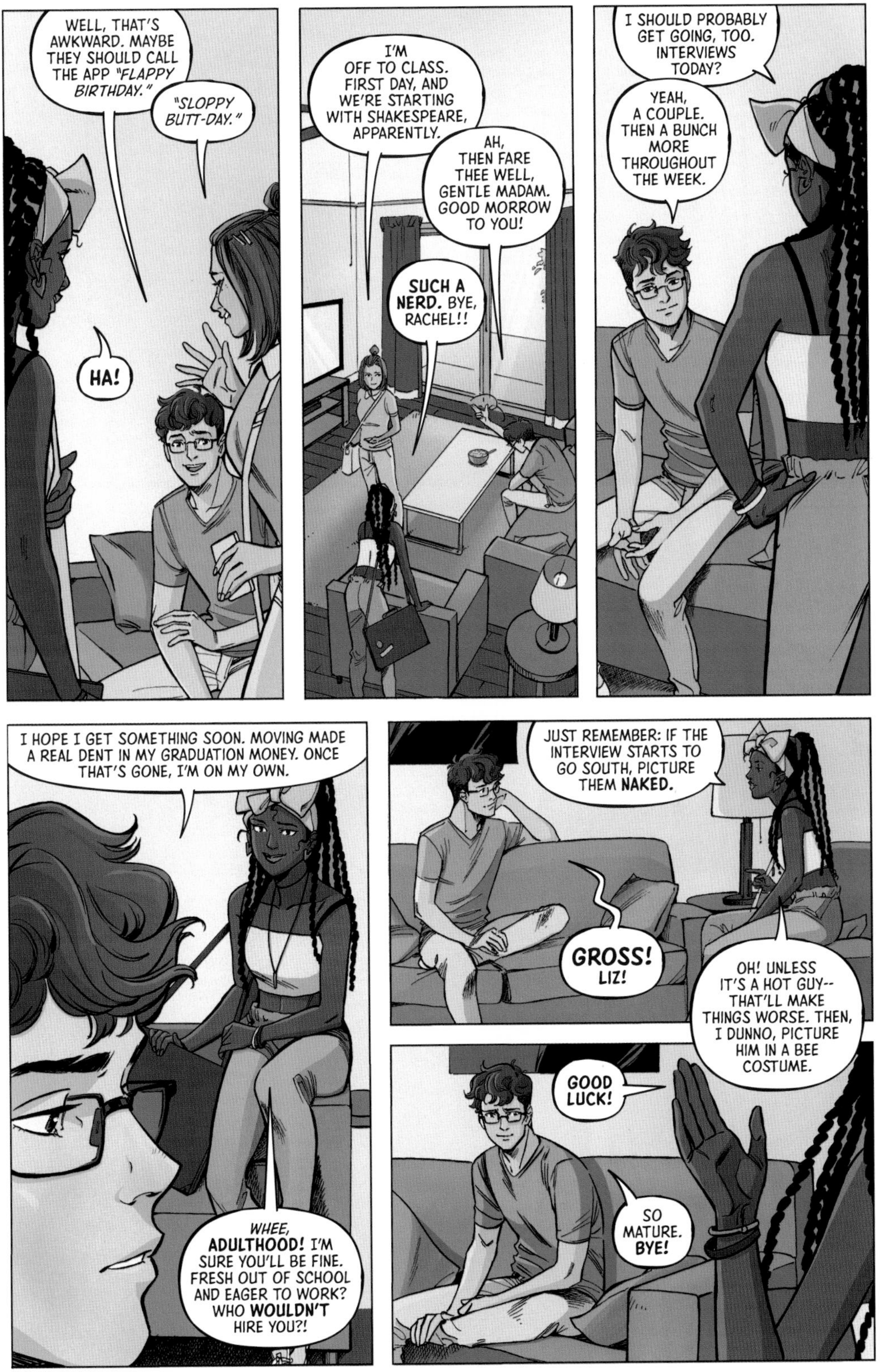
WELL, THAT'S AWKWARD. MAYBE THEY SHOULD CALL THE APP "FLAPPY BIRTHDAY."
"SLOPPY BUTT-DAY."
HA!
I'M OFF TO CLASS. FIRST DAY, AND WE'RE STARTING WITH SHAKESPEARE, APPARENTLY.
AH, THEN FARE THEE WELL, GENTLE MADAM. GOOD MORROW TO YOU!
SUCH A NERD. BYE, RACHEL!!
I SHOULD PROBABLY GET GOING, TOO. INTERVIEWS TODAY?
YEAH, A COUPLE. THEN A BUNCH MORE THROUGHOUT THE WEEK.
I HOPE I GET SOMETHING SOON. MOVING MADE A REAL DENT IN MY GRADUATION MONEY. ONCE THAT'S GONE, I'M ON MY OWN.
WHEE, ADULTHOOD! I'M SURE YOU'LL BE FINE. FRESH OUT OF SCHOOL AND EAGER TO WORK? WHO WOULDN'T HIRE YOU?!
JUST REMEMBER: IF THE INTERVIEW STARTS TO GO SOUTH, PICTURE THEM NAKED.
GROSS! LIZ!
OH! UNLESS IT'S A HOT GUY-- THAT'LL MAKE THINGS WORSE. THEN, I DUNNO, PICTURE HIM IN A BEE COSTUME.
GOOD LUCK!
SO MATURE. BYE!

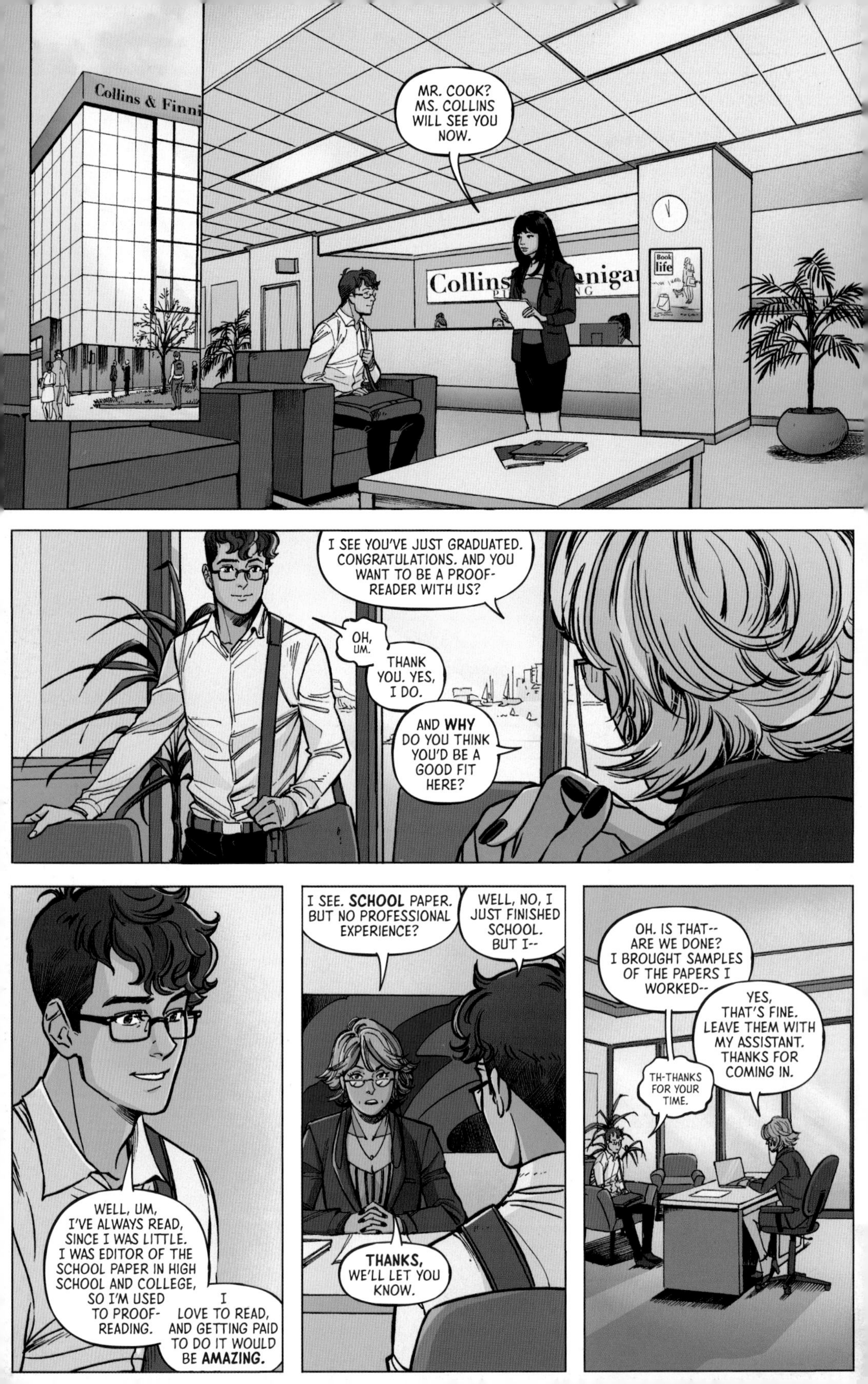
Collins & Finni
MR. COOK? MS. COLLINS WILL SEE YOU NOW.
Collins Flanigan PUBLISHING
Book life
I SEE YOU'VE JUST GRADUATED. CONGRATULATIONS. AND YOU WANT TO BE A PROOF-READER WITH US?
OH, UM.
THANK YOU. YES, I DO.
AND WHY DO YOU THINK YOU'D BE A GOOD FIT HERE?
WELL, UM, I'VE ALWAYS READ, SINCE I WAS LITTLE. I WAS EDITOR OF THE SCHOOL PAPER IN HIGH SCHOOL AND COLLEGE, SO I'M USED TO PROOF-READING.
I LOVE TO READ, AND GETTING PAID TO DO IT WOULD BE AMAZING.
I SEE. SCHOOL PAPER. BUT NO PROFESSIONAL EXPERIENCE?
WELL, NO, I JUST FINISHED SCHOOL. BUT I--
THANKS, WE'LL LET YOU KNOW.
OH. IS THAT-- ARE WE DONE? I BROUGHT SAMPLES OF THE PAPERS I WORKED--
YES, THAT'S FINE. LEAVE THEM WITH MY ASSISTANT. THANKS FOR COMING IN.
TH-THANKS FOR YOUR TIME.

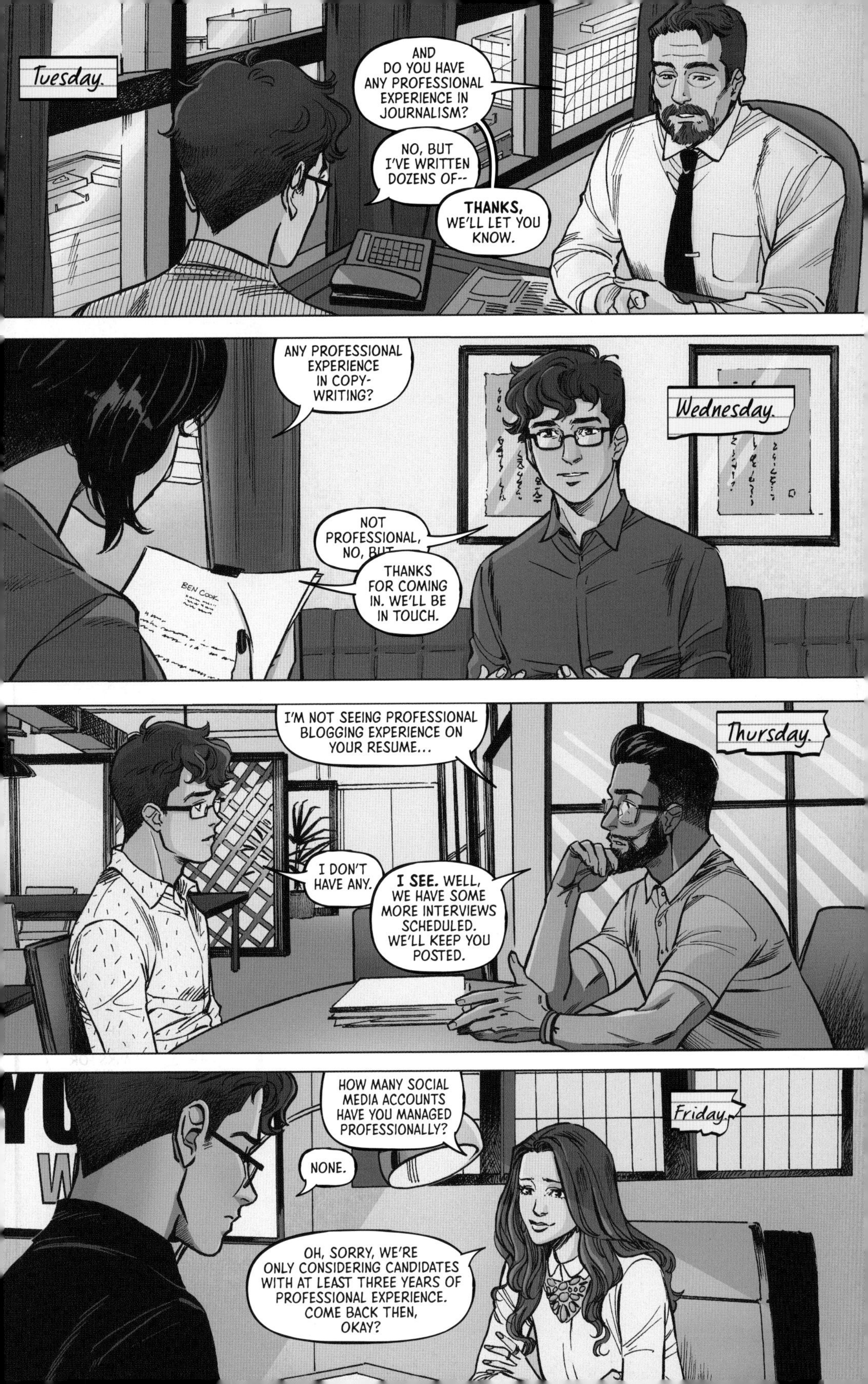
Tuesday.
AND DO YOU HAVE ANY PROFESSIONAL EXPERIENCE IN JOURNALISM?
NO, BUT I'VE WRITTEN DOZENS OF--
THANKS, WE'LL LET YOU KNOW.
ANY PROFESSIONAL EXPERIENCE IN COPY-WRITING?
Wednesday.
NOT PROFESSIONAL, NO, BUT
THANKS FOR COMING IN. WE'LL BE IN TOUCH.
BEN COOK
I'M NOT SEEING PROFESSIONAL BLOGGING EXPERIENCE ON YOUR RESUME...
Thursday.
I DON'T HAVE ANY.
I SEE. WELL, WE HAVE SOME MORE INTERVIEWS SCHEDULED. WE'LL KEEP YOU POSTED.
HOW MANY SOCIAL MEDIA ACCOUNTS HAVE YOU MANAGED PROFESSIONALLY?
Friday.
NONE.
OH, SORRY, WE'RE ONLY CONSIDERING CANDIDATES WITH AT LEAST THREE YEARS OF PROFESSIONAL EXPERIENCE. COME BACK THEN, OKAY?

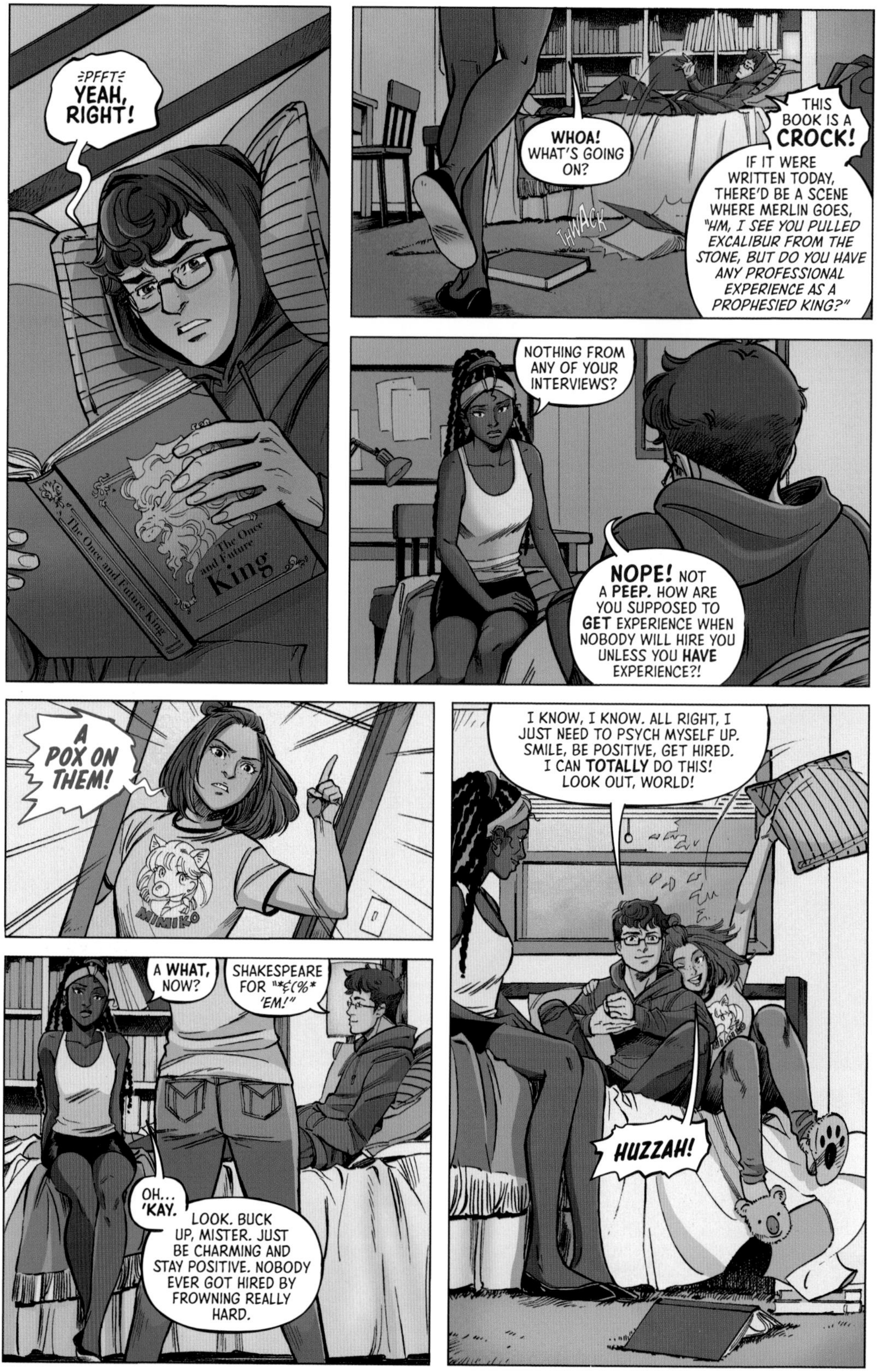
PFFT
YEAH, RIGHT!
The Once and Future King
The Once and Future King
WHOA! WHAT'S GOING ON?
THWACK
THIS BOOK IS A CROCK!
IF IT WERE WRITTEN TODAY, THERE'D BE A SCENE WHERE MERLIN GOES, "HM, I SEE YOU PULLED EXCALIBUR FROM THE STONE, BUT DO YOU HAVE ANY PROFESSIONAL EXPERIENCE AS A PROPHESIED KING?"
NOTHING FROM ANY OF YOUR INTERVIEWS?
NOPE! NOT A PEEP. HOW ARE YOU SUPPOSED TO GET EXPERIENCE WHEN NOBODY WILL HIRE YOU UNLESS YOU HAVE EXPERIENCE?!
A POX ON THEM!
MIMIKO
A WHAT, NOW?
SHAKESPEARE FOR "*£(%* 'EM!"
OH... 'KAY.
LOOK. BUCK UP, MISTER. JUST BE CHARMING AND STAY POSITIVE. NOBODY EVER GOT HIRED BY FROWNING REALLY HARD.
I KNOW, I KNOW. ALL RIGHT, I JUST NEED TO PSYCH MYSELF UP. SMILE, BE POSITIVE, GET HIRED. I CAN TOTALLY DO THIS! LOOK OUT, WORLD!
HUZZAH!

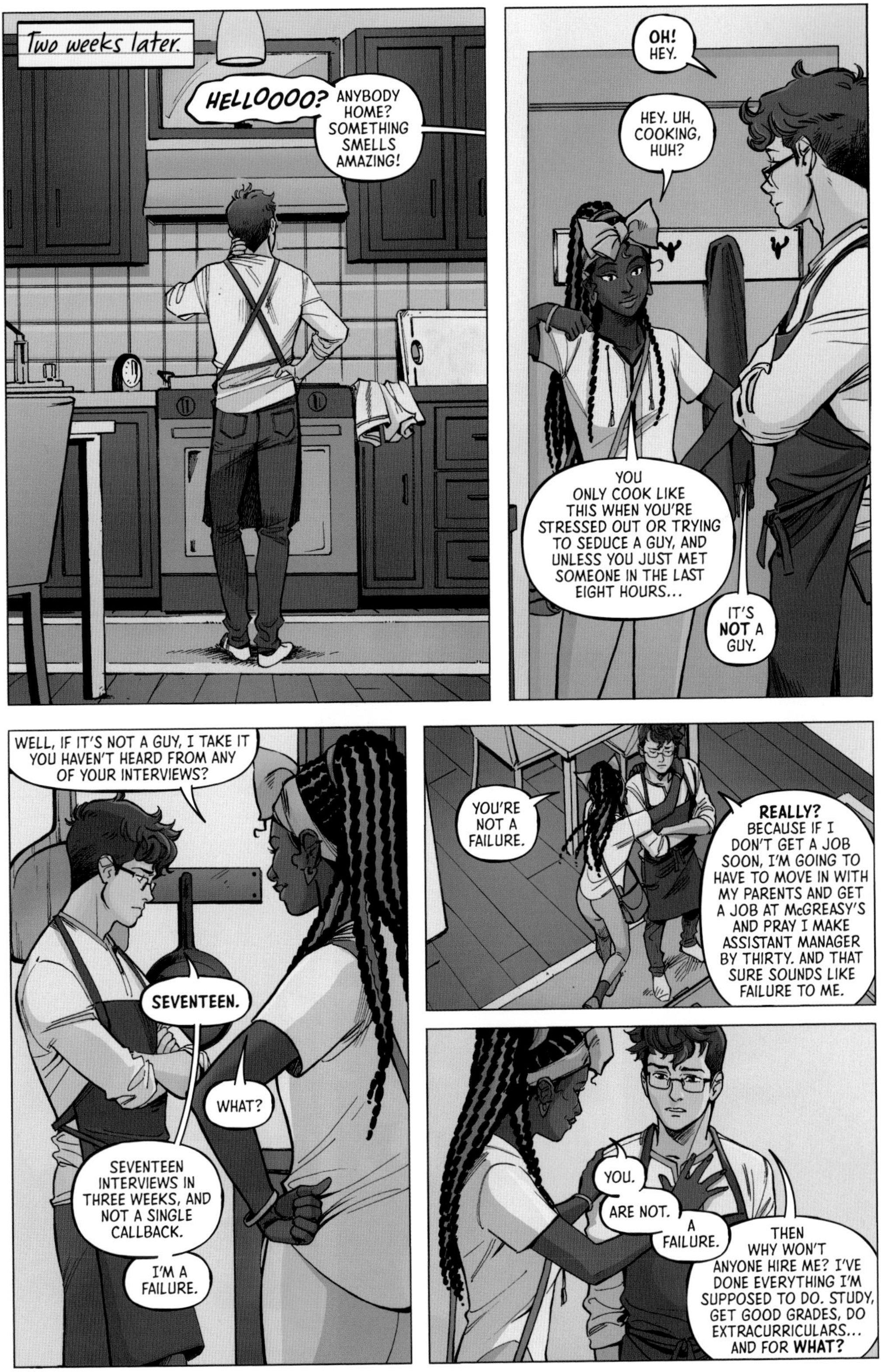
Two weeks later.
HELLOOOO? ANYBODY HOME? SOMETHING SMELLS AMAZING!
OH! HEY.
HEY. UH, COOKING, HUH?
YOU ONLY COOK LIKE THIS WHEN YOU'RE STRESSED OUT OR TRYING TO SEDUCE A GUY, AND UNLESS YOU JUST MET SOMEONE IN THE LAST EIGHT HOURS...
IT'S **NOT** A GUY.
WELL, IF IT'S NOT A GUY, I TAKE IT YOU HAVEN'T HEARD FROM ANY OF YOUR INTERVIEWS?
SEVENTEEN.
WHAT?
SEVENTEEN INTERVIEWS IN THREE WEEKS, AND NOT A SINGLE CALLBACK.
I'M A FAILURE.
YOU'RE NOT A FAILURE.
REALLY? BECAUSE IF I DON'T GET A JOB SOON, I'M GOING TO HAVE TO MOVE IN WITH MY PARENTS AND GET A JOB AT McGREASY'S AND PRAY I MAKE ASSISTANT MANAGER BY THIRTY. AND THAT SURE SOUNDS LIKE FAILURE TO ME.
YOU.
ARE NOT.
A FAILURE.
THEN WHY WON'T ANYONE HIRE ME? I'VE DONE EVERYTHING I'M SUPPOSED TO DO. STUDY, GET GOOD GRADES, DO EXTRACURRICULARS... AND FOR **WHAT?**

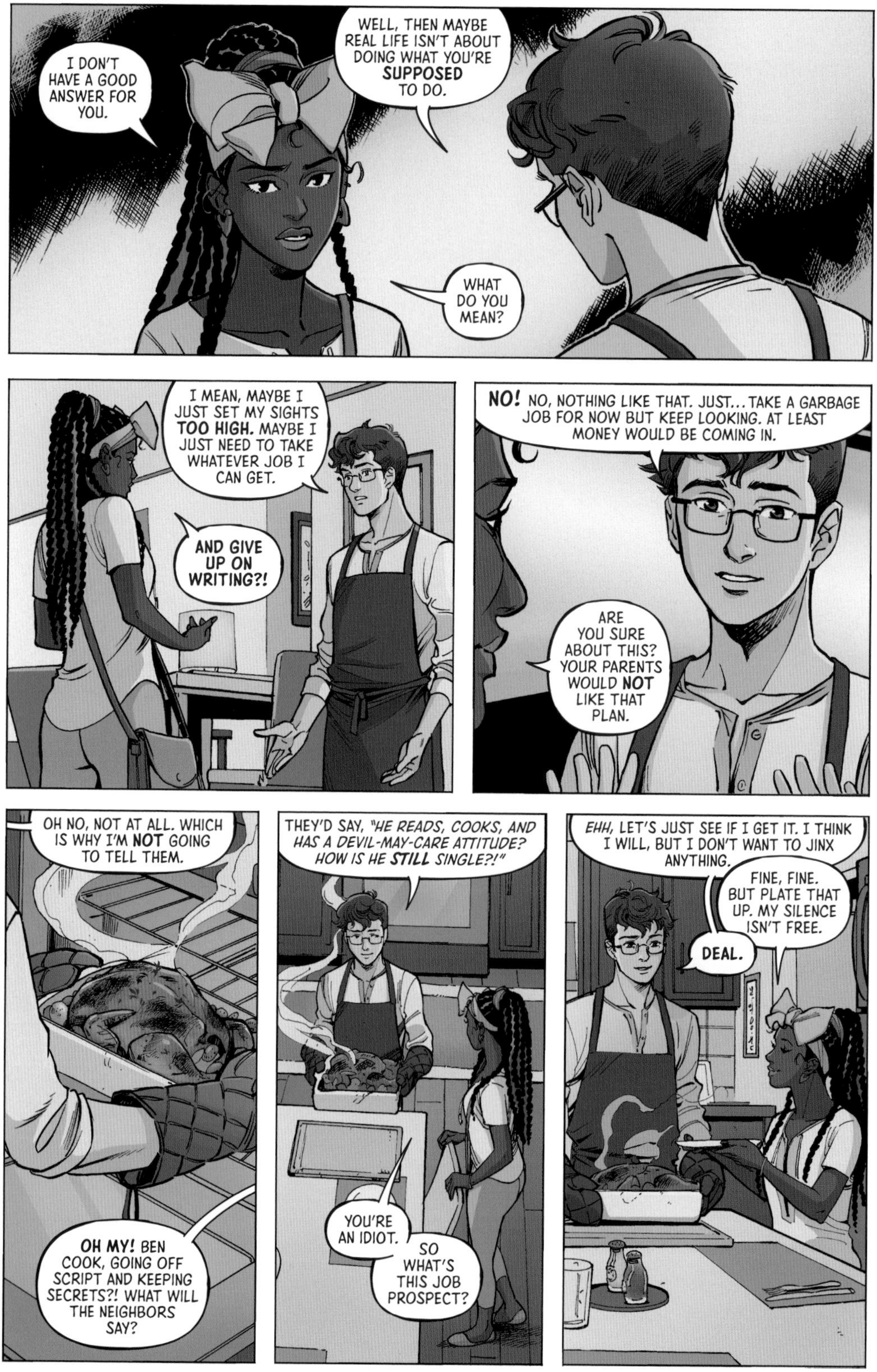
I DON'T HAVE A GOOD ANSWER FOR YOU.
WELL, THEN MAYBE REAL LIFE ISN'T ABOUT DOING WHAT YOU'RE **SUPPOSED** TO DO.
WHAT DO YOU MEAN?
I MEAN, MAYBE I JUST SET MY SIGHTS **TOO HIGH.** MAYBE I JUST NEED TO TAKE WHATEVER JOB I CAN GET.
AND GIVE UP ON WRITING?!
NO! NO, NOTHING LIKE THAT. JUST... TAKE A GARBAGE JOB FOR NOW BUT KEEP LOOKING. AT LEAST MONEY WOULD BE COMING IN.
ARE YOU SURE ABOUT THIS? YOUR PARENTS WOULD **NOT** LIKE THAT PLAN.
OH NO, NOT AT ALL. WHICH IS WHY I'M **NOT** GOING TO TELL THEM.
OH MY! BEN COOK, GOING OFF SCRIPT AND KEEPING SECRETS?! WHAT WILL THE NEIGHBORS SAY?
THEY'D SAY, *"HE READS, COOKS, AND HAS A DEVIL-MAY-CARE ATTITUDE? HOW IS HE **STILL** SINGLE?!"*
YOU'RE AN IDIOT.
SO WHAT'S THIS JOB PROSPECT?
EHH, LET'S JUST SEE IF I GET IT. I THINK I WILL, BUT I DON'T WANT TO JINX ANYTHING.
FINE, FINE. BUT PLATE THAT UP. MY SILENCE ISN'T FREE.
DEAL.

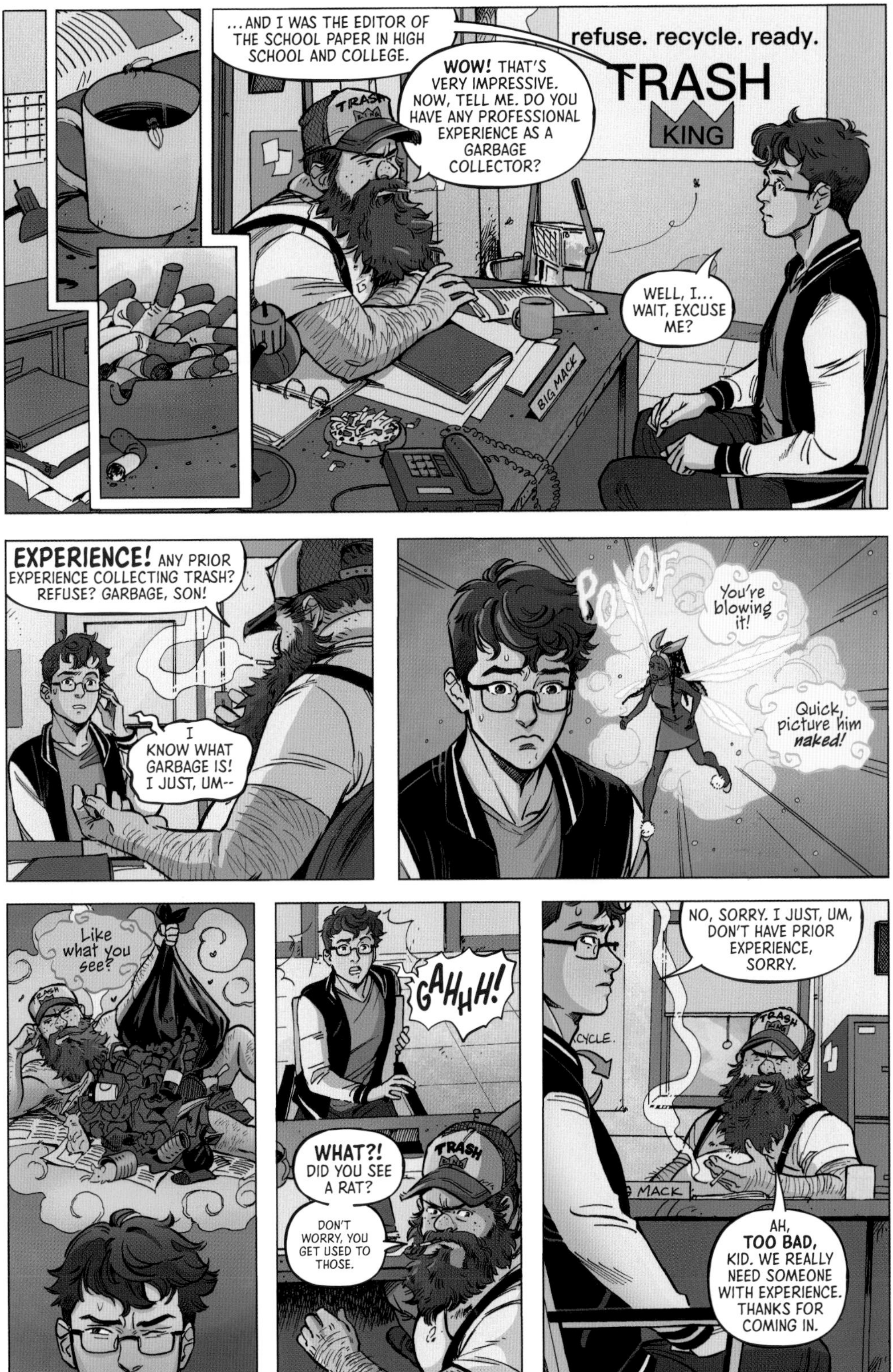
...AND I WAS THE EDITOR OF THE SCHOOL PAPER IN HIGH SCHOOL AND COLLEGE.
refuse. recycle. ready.
TRASH KING
WOW! THAT'S VERY IMPRESSIVE. NOW, TELL ME. DO YOU HAVE ANY PROFESSIONAL EXPERIENCE AS A GARBAGE COLLECTOR?
WELL, I... WAIT, EXCUSE ME?
BIG MACK
EXPERIENCE! ANY PRIOR EXPERIENCE COLLECTING TRASH? REFUSE? GARBAGE, SON!
I KNOW WHAT GARBAGE IS! I JUST, UM--
POOF
You're blowing it!
Quick, picture him naked!
Like what you see?
GAHHH!
WHAT?! DID YOU SEE A RAT?
DON'T WORRY, YOU GET USED TO THOSE.
NO, SORRY. I JUST, UM, DON'T HAVE PRIOR EXPERIENCE, SORRY.
AH, TOO BAD, KID. WE REALLY NEED SOMEONE WITH EXPERIENCE. THANKS FOR COMING IN.

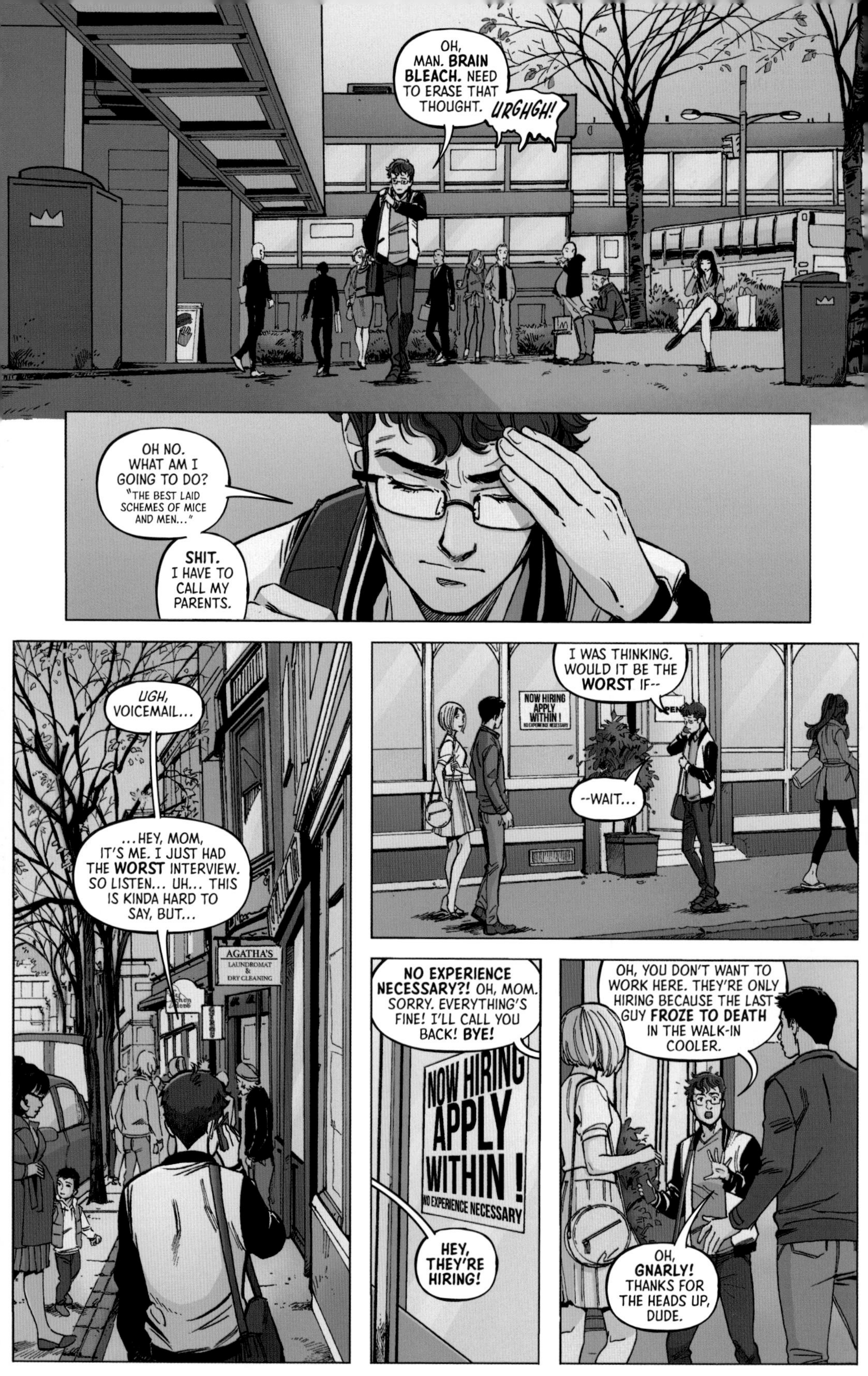
OH, MAN. **BRAIN BLEACH.** NEED TO ERASE THAT THOUGHT.
URGHGH!
OH NO. WHAT AM I GOING TO DO? "THE BEST LAID SCHEMES OF MICE AND MEN..."
SHIT. I HAVE TO CALL MY PARENTS.
UGH, VOICEMAIL...
...HEY, MOM, IT'S ME. I JUST HAD THE **WORST** INTERVIEW. SO LISTEN... UH... THIS IS KINDA HARD TO SAY, BUT...
AGATHA'S LAUNDROMAT & DRY CLEANING
I WAS THINKING. WOULD IT BE THE **WORST** IF--
NOW HIRING APPLY WITHIN! NO EXPERIENCE NECESSARY
--WAIT...
NO EXPERIENCE NECESSARY?! OH, MOM. SORRY. EVERYTHING'S FINE! I'LL CALL YOU BACK! **BYE!**
NOW HIRING APPLY WITHIN! NO EXPERIENCE NECESSARY
HEY, THEY'RE HIRING!
OH, YOU DON'T WANT TO WORK HERE. THEY'RE ONLY HIRING BECAUSE THE LAST GUY **FROZE TO DEATH** IN THE WALK-IN COOLER.
OH, **GNARLY!** THANKS FOR THE HEADS UP, DUDE.

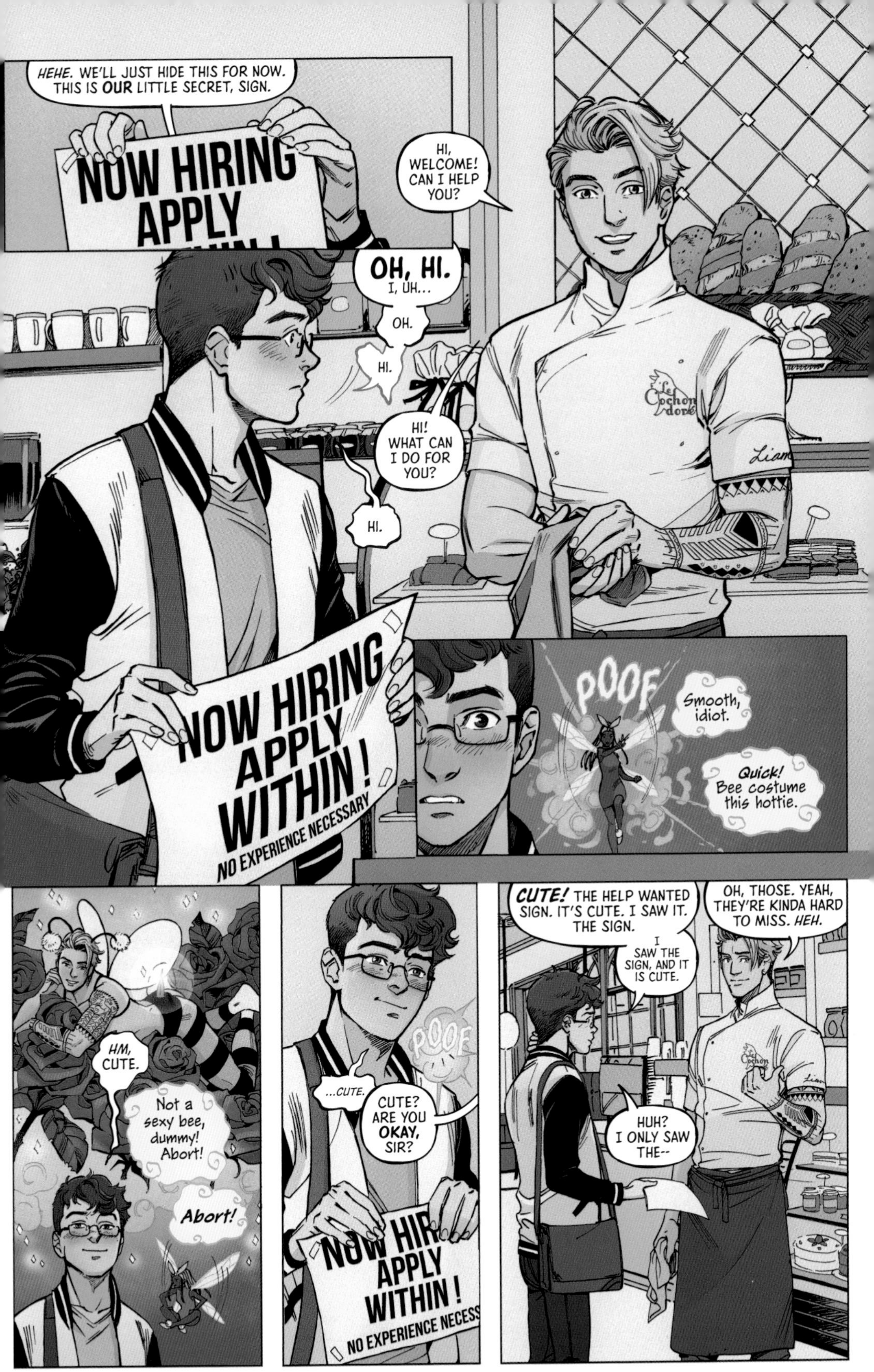

HEHE. WE'LL JUST HIDE THIS FOR NOW. THIS IS OUR LITTLE SECRET, SIGN.
NOW HIRING APPLY
HI, WELCOME! CAN I HELP YOU?
OH, HI. I, UH...
OH.
HI.
HI! WHAT CAN I DO FOR YOU?
HI.
Le Cochon doré
Liam
NOW HIRING APPLY WITHIN! NO EXPERIENCE NECESSARY
POOF
Smooth, idiot.
Quick! Bee costume this hottie.
HM, CUTE.
Not a sexy bee, dummy! Abort!
Abort!
...CUTE.
POOF
CUTE? ARE YOU OKAY, SIR?
NOW HIR APPLY WITHIN! NO EXPERIENCE NECESS
CUTE! THE HELP WANTED SIGN. IT'S CUTE. I SAW IT. THE SIGN.
I SAW THE SIGN, AND IT IS CUTE.
OH, THOSE. YEAH, THEY'RE KINDA HARD TO MISS. HEH.
HUH? I ONLY SAW THE--

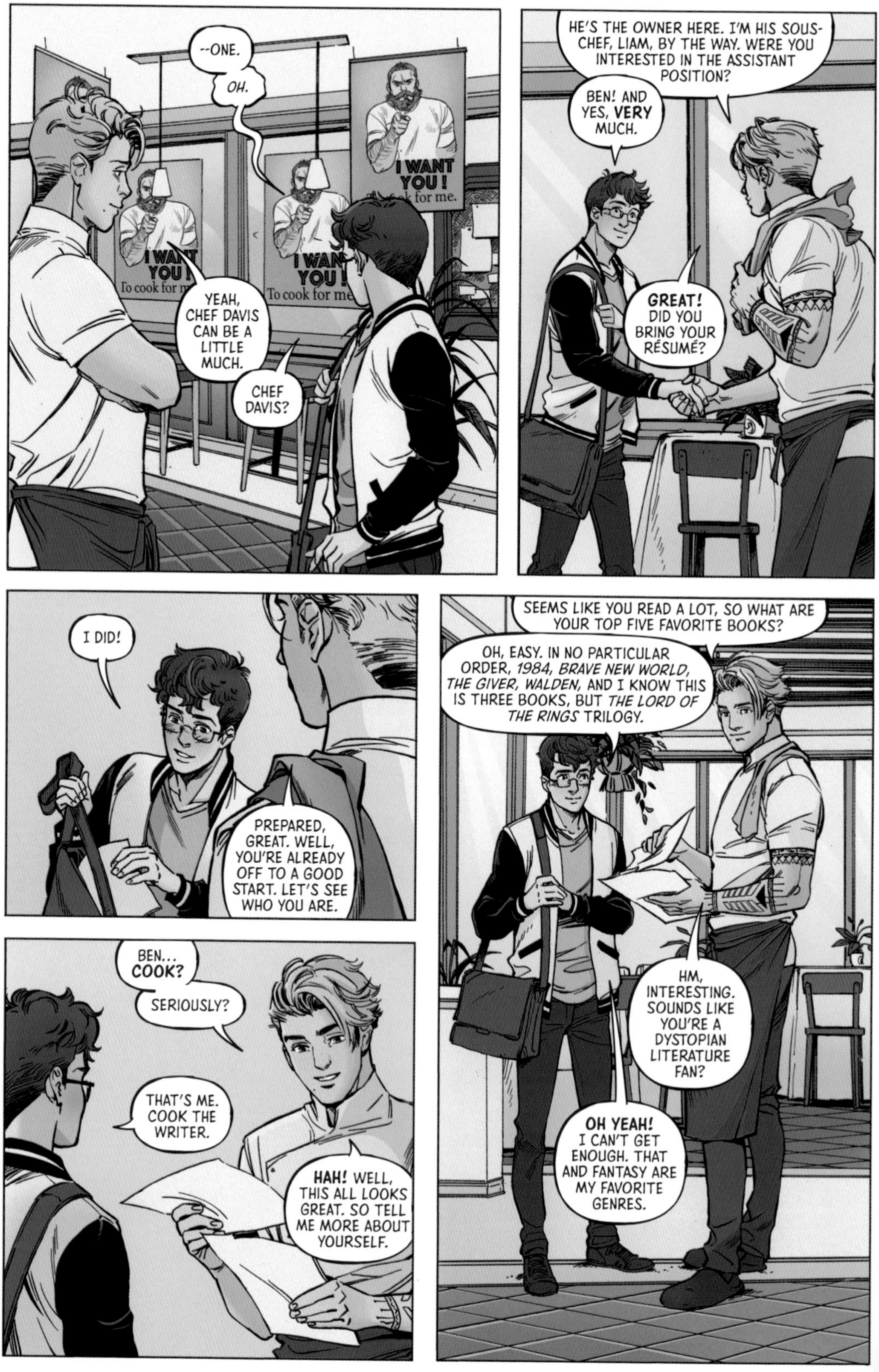

--ONE.
OH.
I WANT YOU ! To cook for me.
YEAH, CHEF DAVIS CAN BE A LITTLE MUCH.
CHEF DAVIS?
HE'S THE OWNER HERE. I'M HIS SOUS-CHEF, LIAM, BY THE WAY. WERE YOU INTERESTED IN THE ASSISTANT POSITION?
BEN! AND YES, **VERY** MUCH.
GREAT! DID YOU BRING YOUR RÉSUMÉ?
I DID!
PREPARED, GREAT. WELL, YOU'RE ALREADY OFF TO A GOOD START. LET'S SEE WHO YOU ARE.
BEN... **COOK?**
SERIOUSLY?
THAT'S ME. COOK THE WRITER.
HAH! WELL, THIS ALL LOOKS GREAT. SO TELL ME MORE ABOUT YOURSELF.
SEEMS LIKE YOU READ A LOT, SO WHAT ARE YOUR TOP FIVE FAVORITE BOOKS?
OH, EASY. IN NO PARTICULAR ORDER, *1984*, *BRAVE NEW WORLD*, *THE GIVER*, *WALDEN*, AND I KNOW THIS IS THREE BOOKS, BUT *THE LORD OF THE RINGS* TRILOGY.
HM, INTERESTING. SOUNDS LIKE YOU'RE A DYSTOPIAN LITERATURE FAN?
OH YEAH! I CAN'T GET ENOUGH. THAT AND FANTASY ARE MY FAVORITE GENRES.

ALL RIGHT, GREAT. SO COOK THE READER AND WRITER, WHY DO YOU WANT TO WORK HERE, AND WHY SHOULD I HIRE YOU?

HONESTLY? I **REALLY** NEED A JOB. I'M A HARD WORKER, I DON'T MIND LONG HOURS OR WORKING WEEKENDS. I'M GREAT AS PART OF A TEAM, AND I WORK WELL UNDER PRESSURE.

THAT'S GOOD. I LIKE AN HONEST ANSWER! WAY BETTER THAN THE PEOPLE WHO APPLY JUST FOR THE FREE FOOD.

DOES THAT REALLY HAPPEN?

OH, **ALL THE TIME!** IT'S THE WORST.

SO, DO YOU HAVE ANY EXPERIENCE WITH VEGETARIAN COOKING?

EXPERIENCE? I--BUT THE **SIGN** SAID--

IT'S OKAY IF YOU DON'T! WE JUST NEED TO KNOW FOR THE PRACTICAL EXAM PART OF THE INTERVIEW.

OH! WELL, I COOK AT HOME A LOT, BUT NO PROFESSIONAL EXPERIENCE. AND HARDLY EVER VEGETARIAN...

WAIT, **PRACTICAL** EXAM?

PERFECT! WE'LL PUT *"WORKS WELL UNDER PRESSURE"* TO THE TEST.

YOU'RE GOING TO COOK FOR ME!

BUT I ONLY COOK FOR GUYS I WANT... TO... UM...

YEAH, THAT SOUNDS GREAT!

ALL RIGHT! WE HAVE RECIPES YOU CAN USE, OR YOU CAN WORK FROM MEMORY IF YOU HAVE SOMETHING YOU LOVE TO COOK. UP TO YOU.

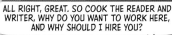

I CAN MAKE IT FROM MEMORY, I GUESS?

GREAT! LET'S GET YOU CHANGED. YOU'RE ABOUT MY SIZE, SO YOU CAN JUST BORROW ONE OF MY CHEF'S JACKETS.

CHANGED? ALL... ALL RIGHT?

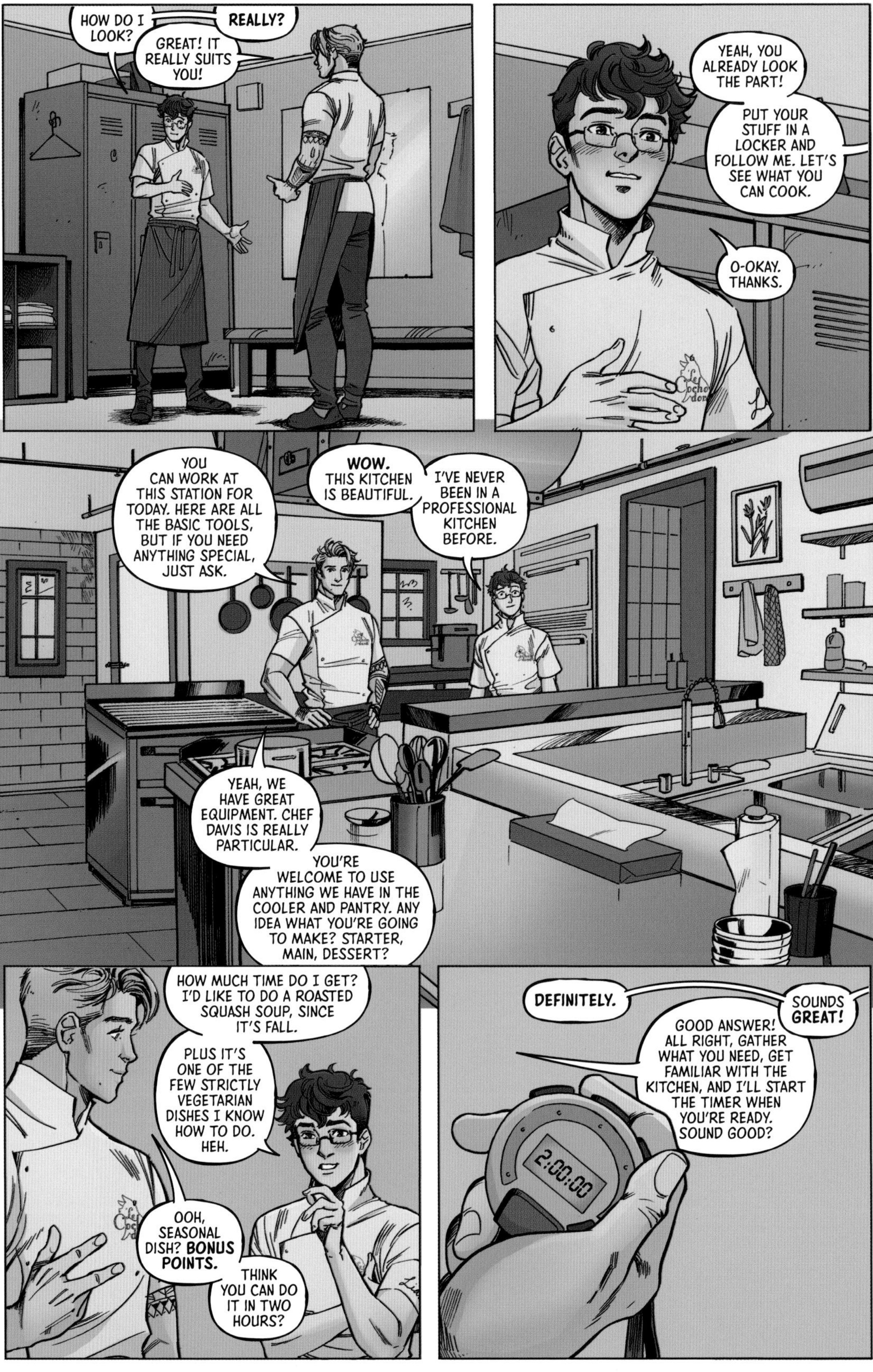
HOW DO I LOOK?
REALLY?
GREAT! IT REALLY SUITS YOU!
YEAH, YOU ALREADY LOOK THE PART!
PUT YOUR STUFF IN A LOCKER AND FOLLOW ME. LET'S SEE WHAT YOU CAN COOK.
O-OKAY. THANKS.
YOU CAN WORK AT THIS STATION FOR TODAY. HERE ARE ALL THE BASIC TOOLS, BUT IF YOU NEED ANYTHING SPECIAL, JUST ASK.
WOW. THIS KITCHEN IS BEAUTIFUL.
I'VE NEVER BEEN IN A PROFESSIONAL KITCHEN BEFORE.
YEAH, WE HAVE GREAT EQUIPMENT. CHEF DAVIS IS REALLY PARTICULAR.
YOU'RE WELCOME TO USE ANYTHING WE HAVE IN THE COOLER AND PANTRY. ANY IDEA WHAT YOU'RE GOING TO MAKE? STARTER, MAIN, DESSERT?
HOW MUCH TIME DO I GET? I'D LIKE TO DO A ROASTED SQUASH SOUP, SINCE IT'S FALL.
PLUS IT'S ONE OF THE FEW STRICTLY VEGETARIAN DISHES I KNOW HOW TO DO. HEH.
OOH, SEASONAL DISH? **BONUS POINTS.**
THINK YOU CAN DO IT IN TWO HOURS?
DEFINITELY.
SOUNDS **GREAT!**
GOOD ANSWER! ALL RIGHT, GATHER WHAT YOU NEED, GET FAMILIAR WITH THE KITCHEN, AND I'LL START THE TIMER WHEN YOU'RE READY. SOUND GOOD?
2:00:00

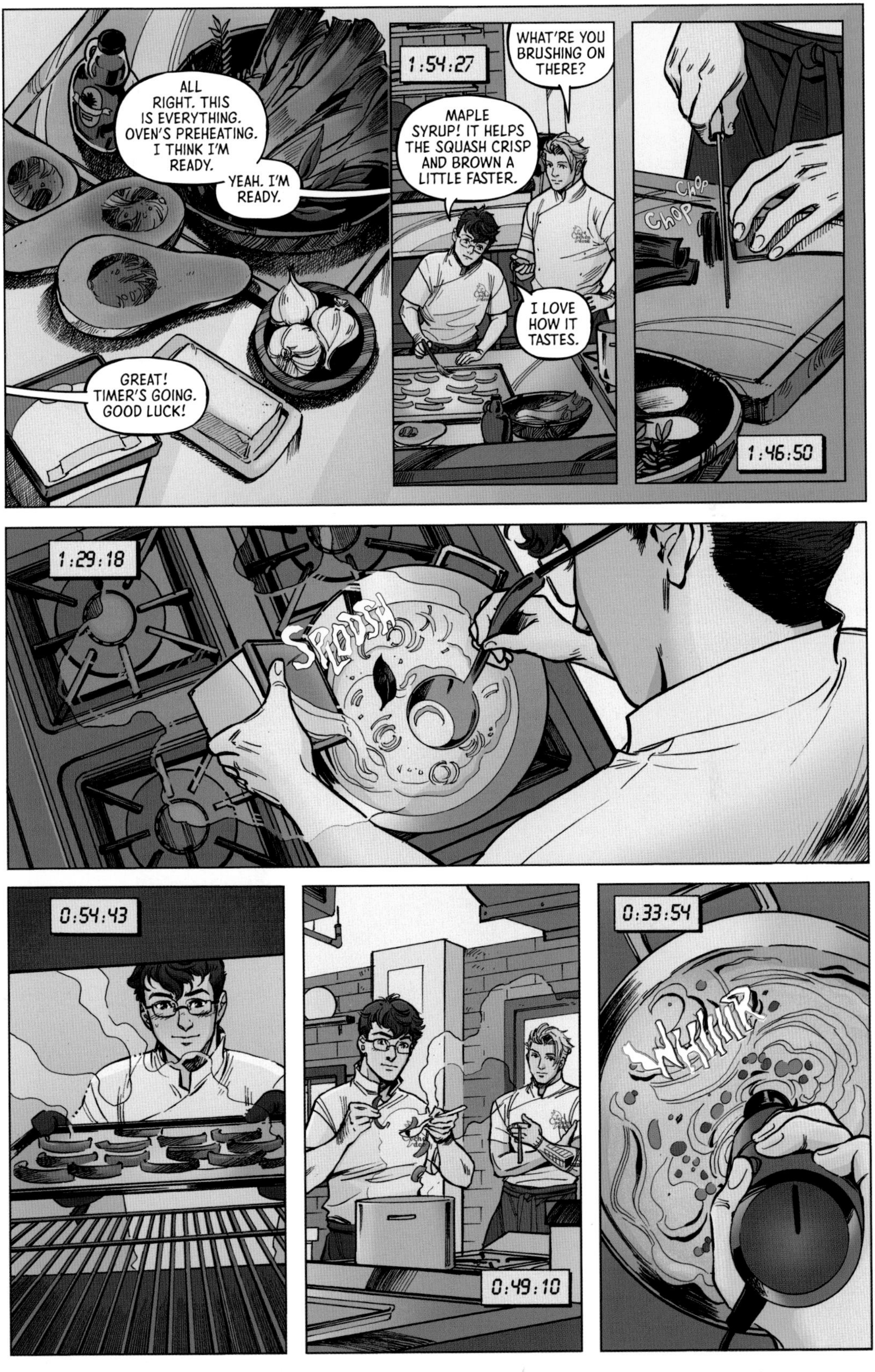
ALL RIGHT. THIS IS EVERYTHING. OVEN'S PREHEATING. I THINK I'M READY.
YEAH. I'M READY.
GREAT! TIMER'S GOING. GOOD LUCK!
1:54:27
WHAT'RE YOU BRUSHING ON THERE?
MAPLE SYRUP! IT HELPS THE SQUASH CRISP AND BROWN A LITTLE FASTER.
I LOVE HOW IT TASTES.
CHOP
CHOP
1:46:50
1:29:18
SPOOSH
0:54:43
0:49:10
0:33:54
WHIIIR

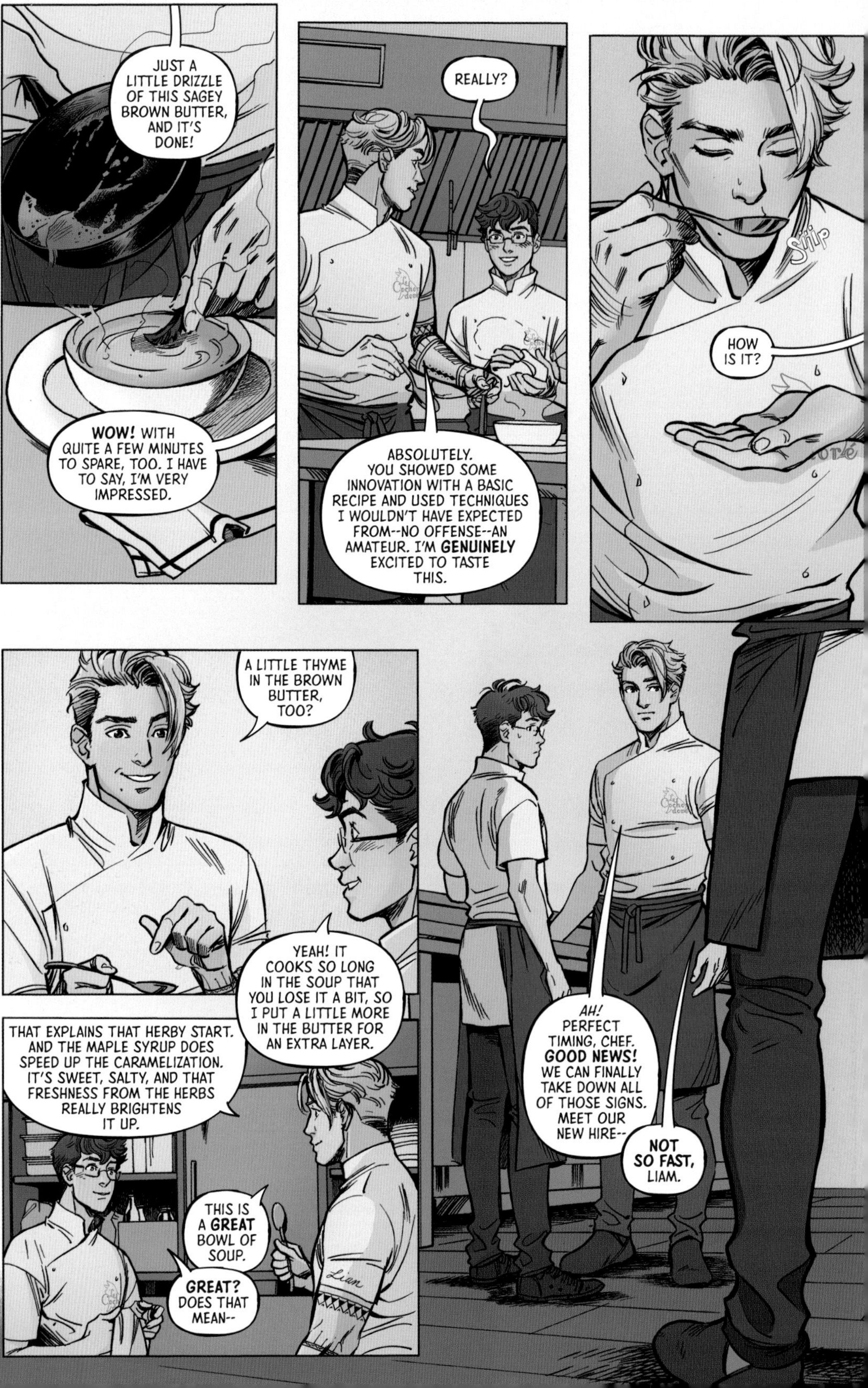
JUST A LITTLE DRIZZLE OF THIS SAGEY BROWN BUTTER, AND IT'S DONE!
WOW! WITH QUITE A FEW MINUTES TO SPARE, TOO. I HAVE TO SAY, I'M VERY IMPRESSED.
REALLY?
ABSOLUTELY. YOU SHOWED SOME INNOVATION WITH A BASIC RECIPE AND USED TECHNIQUES I WOULDN'T HAVE EXPECTED FROM--NO OFFENSE--AN AMATEUR. I'M GENUINELY EXCITED TO TASTE THIS.
SHLIP
HOW IS IT?
A LITTLE THYME IN THE BROWN BUTTER, TOO?
YEAH! IT COOKS SO LONG IN THE SOUP THAT YOU LOSE IT A BIT, SO I PUT A LITTLE MORE IN THE BUTTER FOR AN EXTRA LAYER.
THAT EXPLAINS THAT HERBY START. AND THE MAPLE SYRUP DOES SPEED UP THE CARAMELIZATION. IT'S SWEET, SALTY, AND THAT FRESHNESS FROM THE HERBS REALLY BRIGHTENS IT UP.
THIS IS A GREAT BOWL OF SOUP.
GREAT? DOES THAT MEAN--
AH! PERFECT TIMING, CHEF. GOOD NEWS! WE CAN FINALLY TAKE DOWN ALL OF THOSE SIGNS. MEET OUR NEW HIRE--
NOT SO FAST, LIAM.

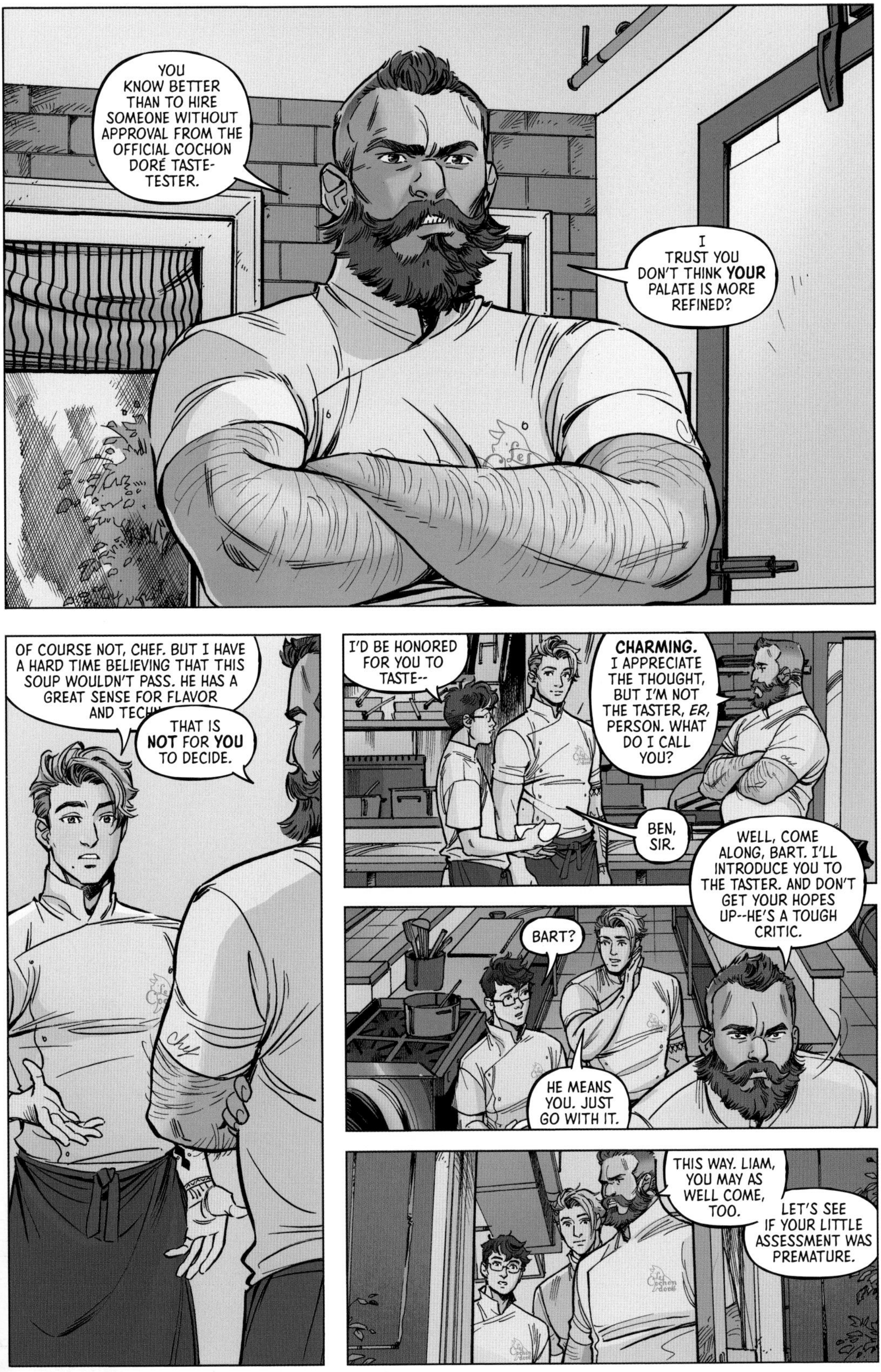
YOU KNOW BETTER THAN TO HIRE SOMEONE WITHOUT APPROVAL FROM THE OFFICIAL COCHON DORÉ TASTE-TESTER.
I TRUST YOU DON'T THINK **YOUR** PALATE IS MORE REFINED?
OF COURSE NOT, CHEF. BUT I HAVE A HARD TIME BELIEVING THAT THIS SOUP WOULDN'T PASS. HE HAS A GREAT SENSE FOR FLAVOR AND TECH
THAT IS **NOT** FOR **YOU** TO DECIDE.
I'D BE HONORED FOR YOU TO TASTE--
CHARMING. I APPRECIATE THE THOUGHT, BUT I'M NOT THE TASTER, *ER*, PERSON. WHAT DO I CALL YOU?
BEN, SIR.
WELL, COME ALONG, BART. I'LL INTRODUCE YOU TO THE TASTER. AND DON'T GET YOUR HOPES UP--HE'S A TOUGH CRITIC.
BART?
HE MEANS YOU. JUST GO WITH IT.
THIS WAY. LIAM, YOU MAY AS WELL COME, TOO.
LET'S SEE IF YOUR LITTLE ASSESSMENT WAS PREMATURE.

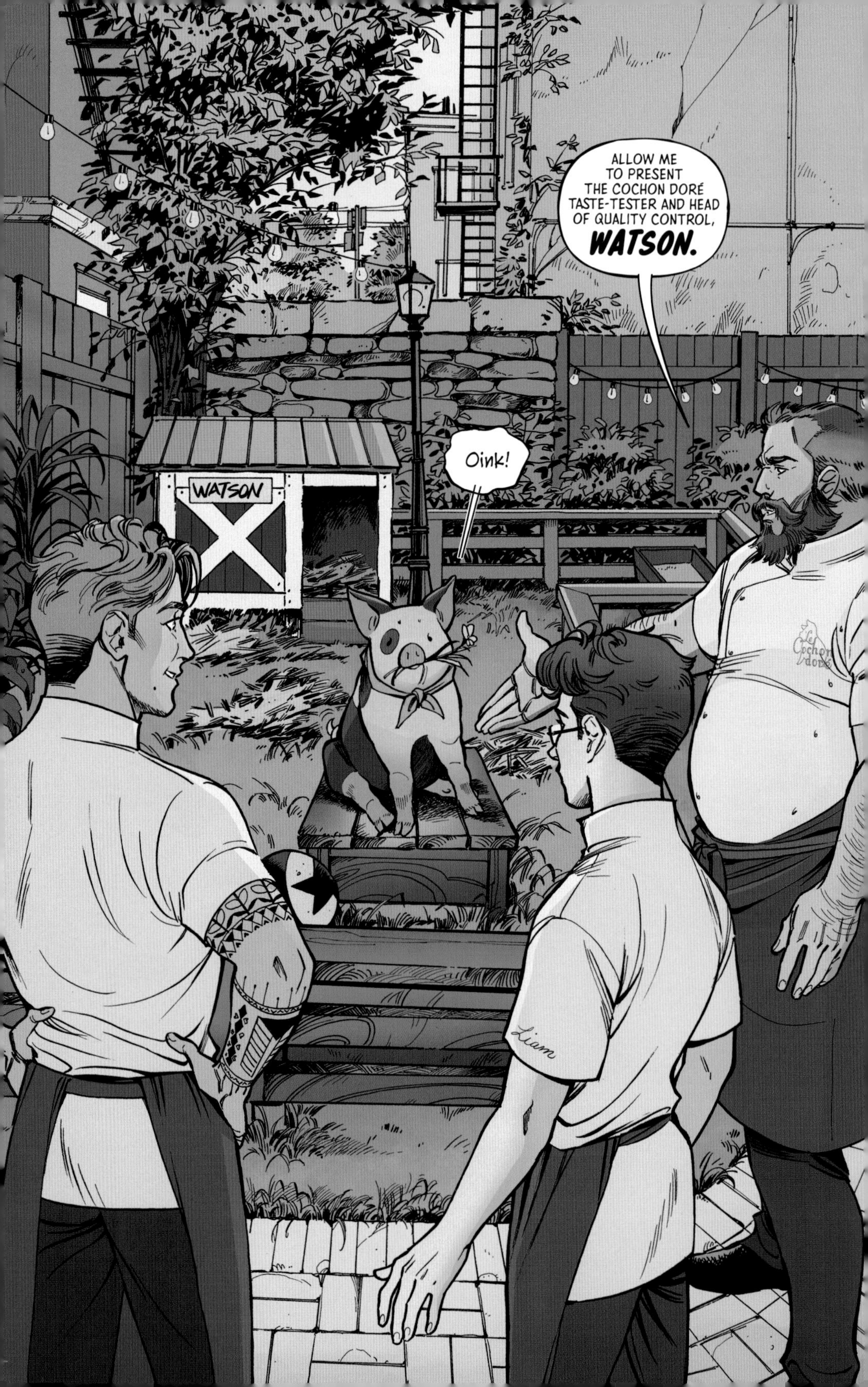
ALLOW ME TO PRESENT THE COCHON DORÉ TASTE-TESTER AND HEAD OF QUALITY CONTROL, **WATSON.**
WATSON
Oink!
Le Cochon doré
Liam

Chapter Two

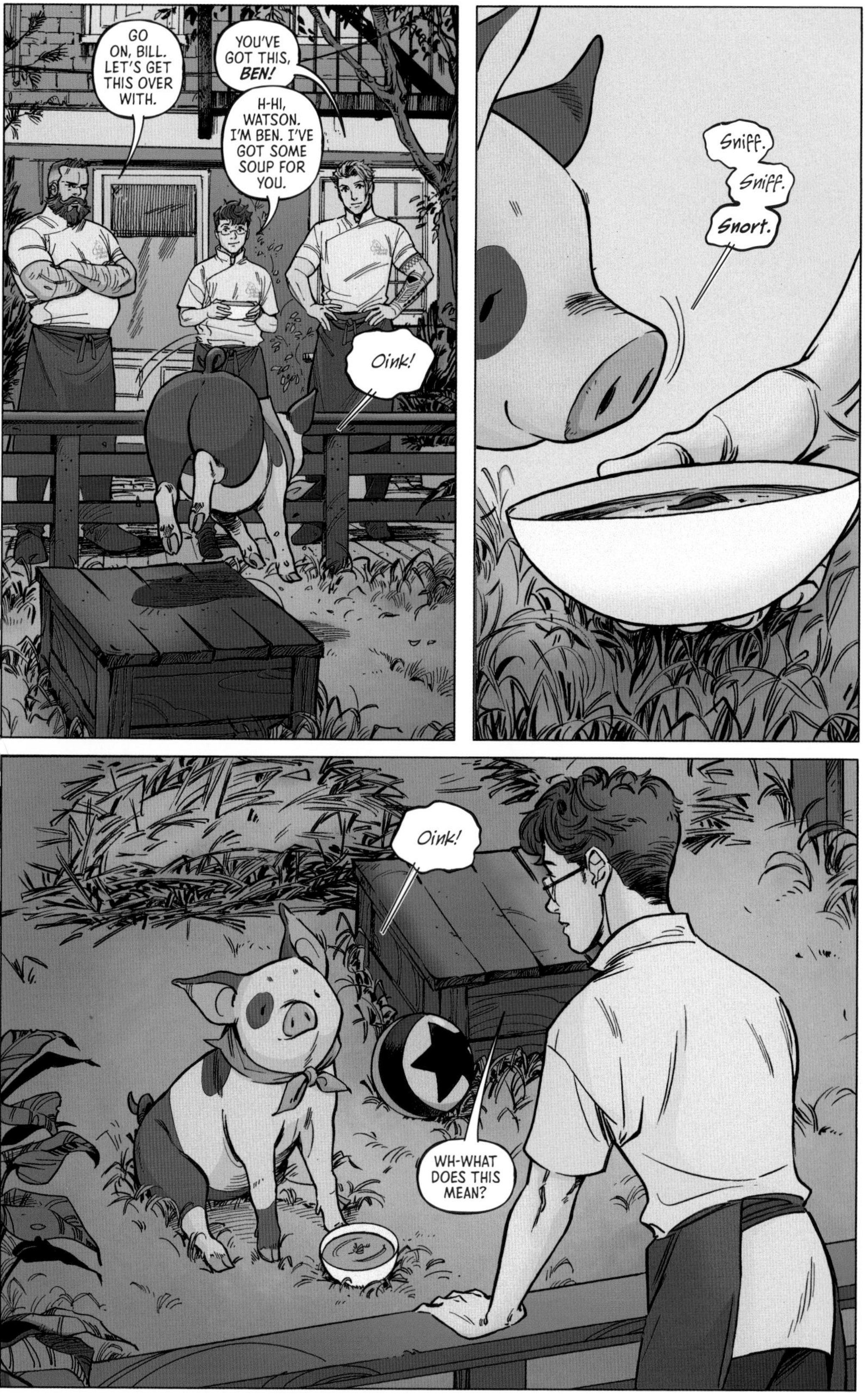
GO ON, BILL. LET'S GET THIS OVER WITH.
YOU'VE GOT THIS, *BEN!*
H-HI, WATSON. I'M BEN. I'VE GOT SOME SOUP FOR YOU.
Oink!
Sniff.
Sniff.
Snort.
Oink!
WH-WHAT DOES THIS MEAN?

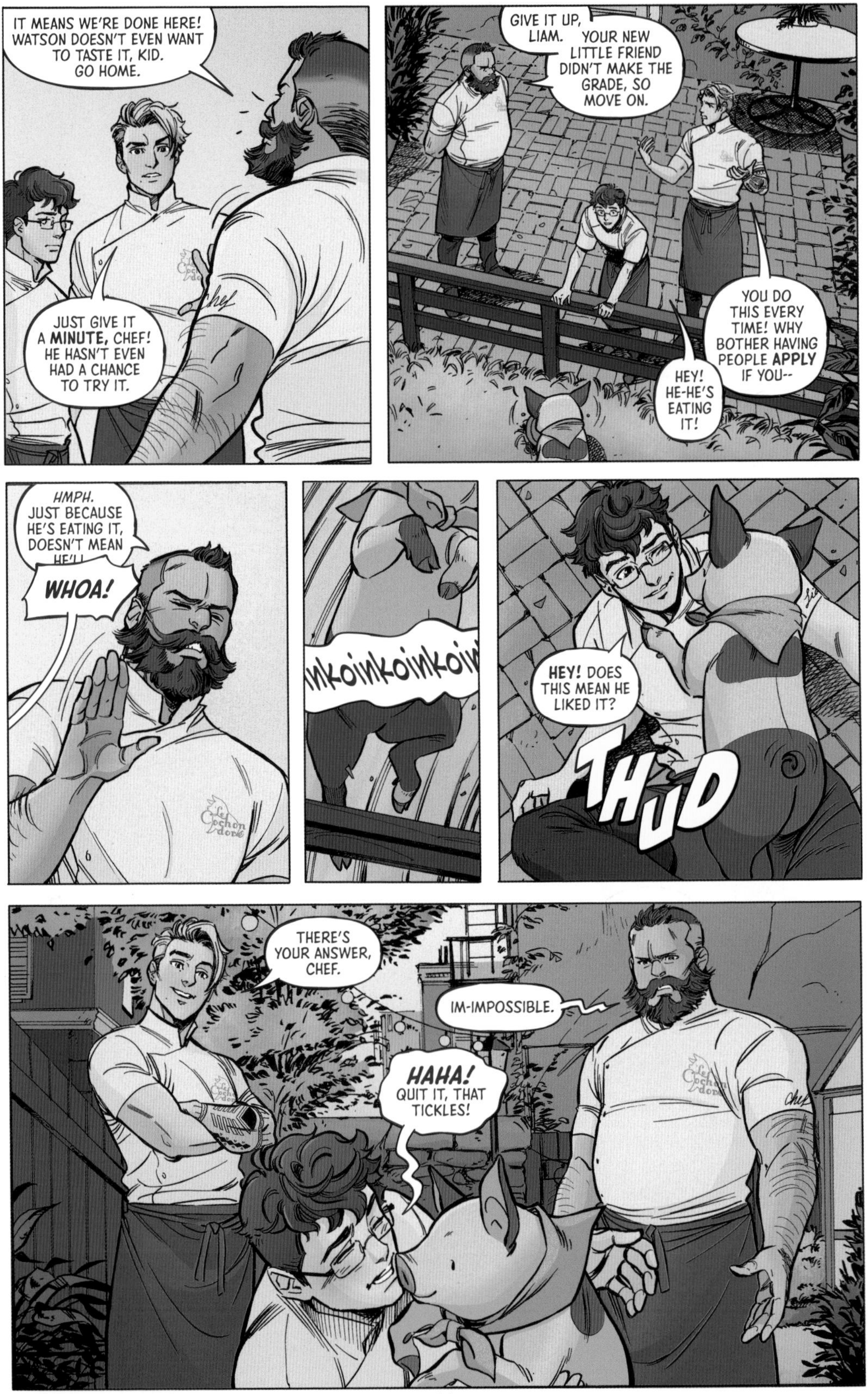
IT MEANS WE'RE DONE HERE! WATSON DOESN'T EVEN WANT TO TASTE IT, KID. GO HOME.
JUST GIVE IT A **MINUTE,** CHEF! HE HASN'T EVEN HAD A CHANCE TO TRY IT.
GIVE IT UP, LIAM.
YOUR NEW LITTLE FRIEND DIDN'T MAKE THE GRADE, SO MOVE ON.
YOU DO THIS EVERY TIME! WHY BOTHER HAVING PEOPLE **APPLY** IF YOU--
HEY! HE-HE'S EATING IT!
HMPH. JUST BECAUSE HE'S EATING IT, DOESN'T MEAN HE'LL
WHOA!
inkoinkoinkoinkoi
HEY! DOES THIS MEAN HE LIKED IT?
THUD
THERE'S YOUR ANSWER, CHEF.
IM-IMPOSSIBLE.
HAHA! QUIT IT, THAT TICKLES!

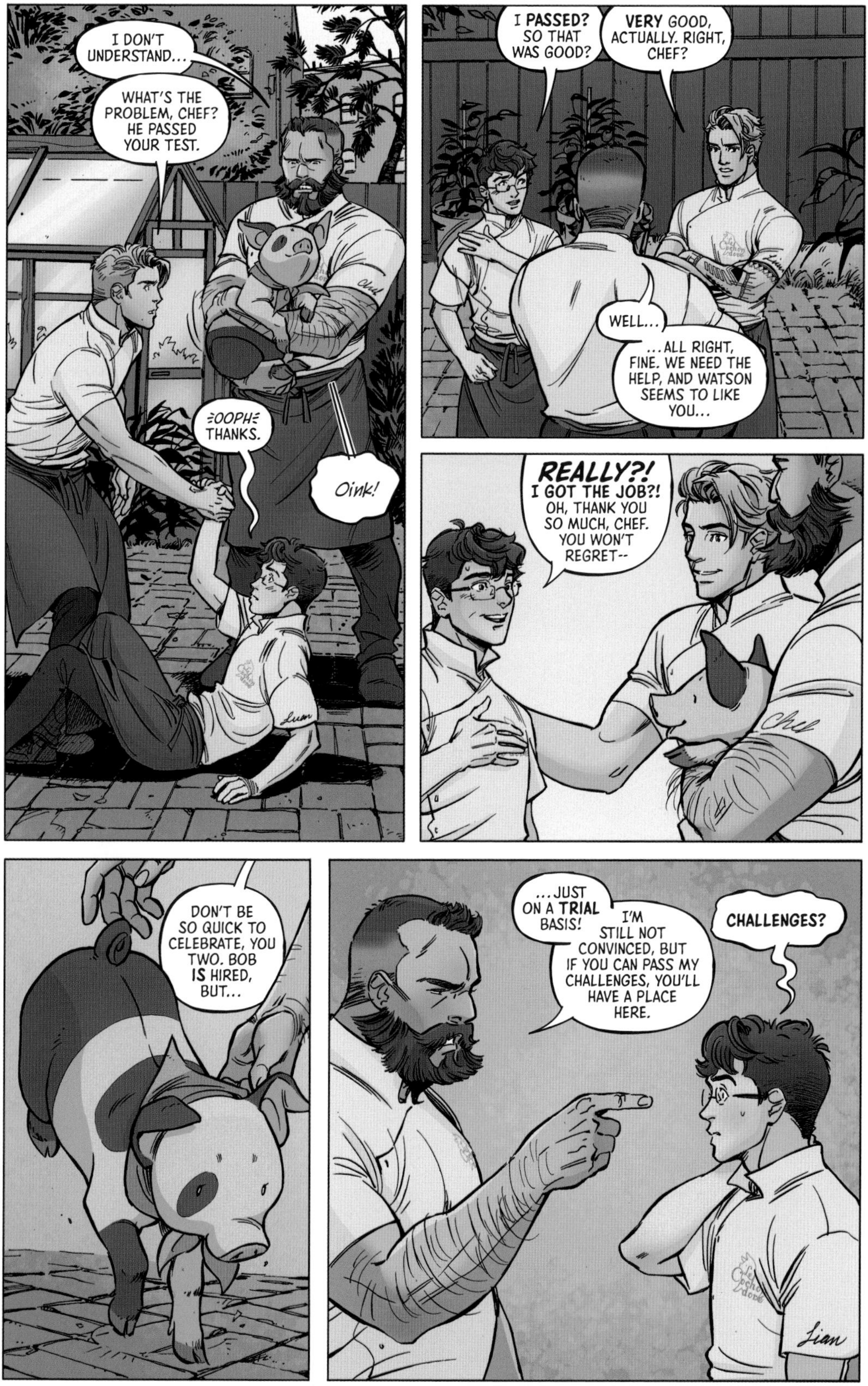
I DON'T UNDERSTAND...
WHAT'S THE PROBLEM, CHEF? HE PASSED YOUR TEST.
OOPH THANKS.
Oink!
I PASSED? SO THAT WAS GOOD?
VERY GOOD, ACTUALLY. RIGHT, CHEF?
WELL...
...ALL RIGHT, FINE. WE NEED THE HELP, AND WATSON SEEMS TO LIKE YOU...
REALLY?! I GOT THE JOB?! OH, THANK YOU SO MUCH, CHEF. YOU WON'T REGRET--
DON'T BE SO QUICK TO CELEBRATE, YOU TWO. BOB IS HIRED, BUT...
...JUST ON A TRIAL BASIS!
I'M STILL NOT CONVINCED, BUT IF YOU CAN PASS MY CHALLENGES, YOU'LL HAVE A PLACE HERE.
CHALLENGES?

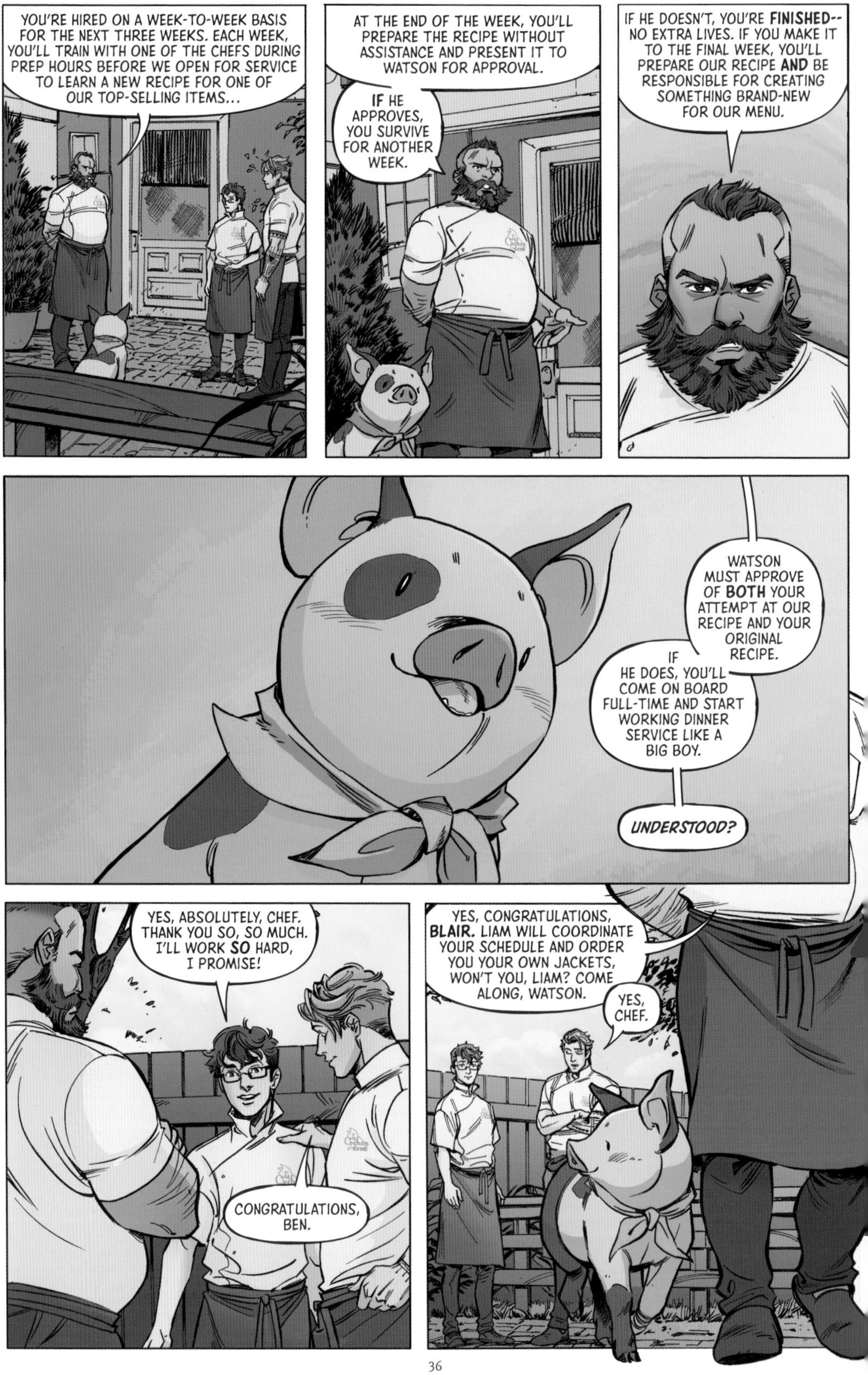
YOU'RE HIRED ON A WEEK-TO-WEEK BASIS FOR THE NEXT THREE WEEKS. EACH WEEK, YOU'LL TRAIN WITH ONE OF THE CHEFS DURING PREP HOURS BEFORE WE OPEN FOR SERVICE TO LEARN A NEW RECIPE FOR ONE OF OUR TOP-SELLING ITEMS...
AT THE END OF THE WEEK, YOU'LL PREPARE THE RECIPE WITHOUT ASSISTANCE AND PRESENT IT TO WATSON FOR APPROVAL.
IF HE APPROVES, YOU SURVIVE FOR ANOTHER WEEK.
IF HE DOESN'T, YOU'RE FINISHED-- NO EXTRA LIVES. IF YOU MAKE IT TO THE FINAL WEEK, YOU'LL PREPARE OUR RECIPE AND BE RESPONSIBLE FOR CREATING SOMETHING BRAND-NEW FOR OUR MENU.
WATSON MUST APPROVE OF BOTH YOUR ATTEMPT AT OUR RECIPE AND YOUR ORIGINAL RECIPE.
IF HE DOES, YOU'LL COME ON BOARD FULL-TIME AND START WORKING DINNER SERVICE LIKE A BIG BOY.
UNDERSTOOD?
YES, ABSOLUTELY, CHEF. THANK YOU SO, SO MUCH. I'LL WORK SO HARD, I PROMISE!
CONGRATULATIONS, BEN.
YES, CONGRATULATIONS, BLAIR. LIAM WILL COORDINATE YOUR SCHEDULE AND ORDER YOU YOUR OWN JACKETS, WON'T YOU, LIAM? COME ALONG, WATSON.
YES, CHEF.

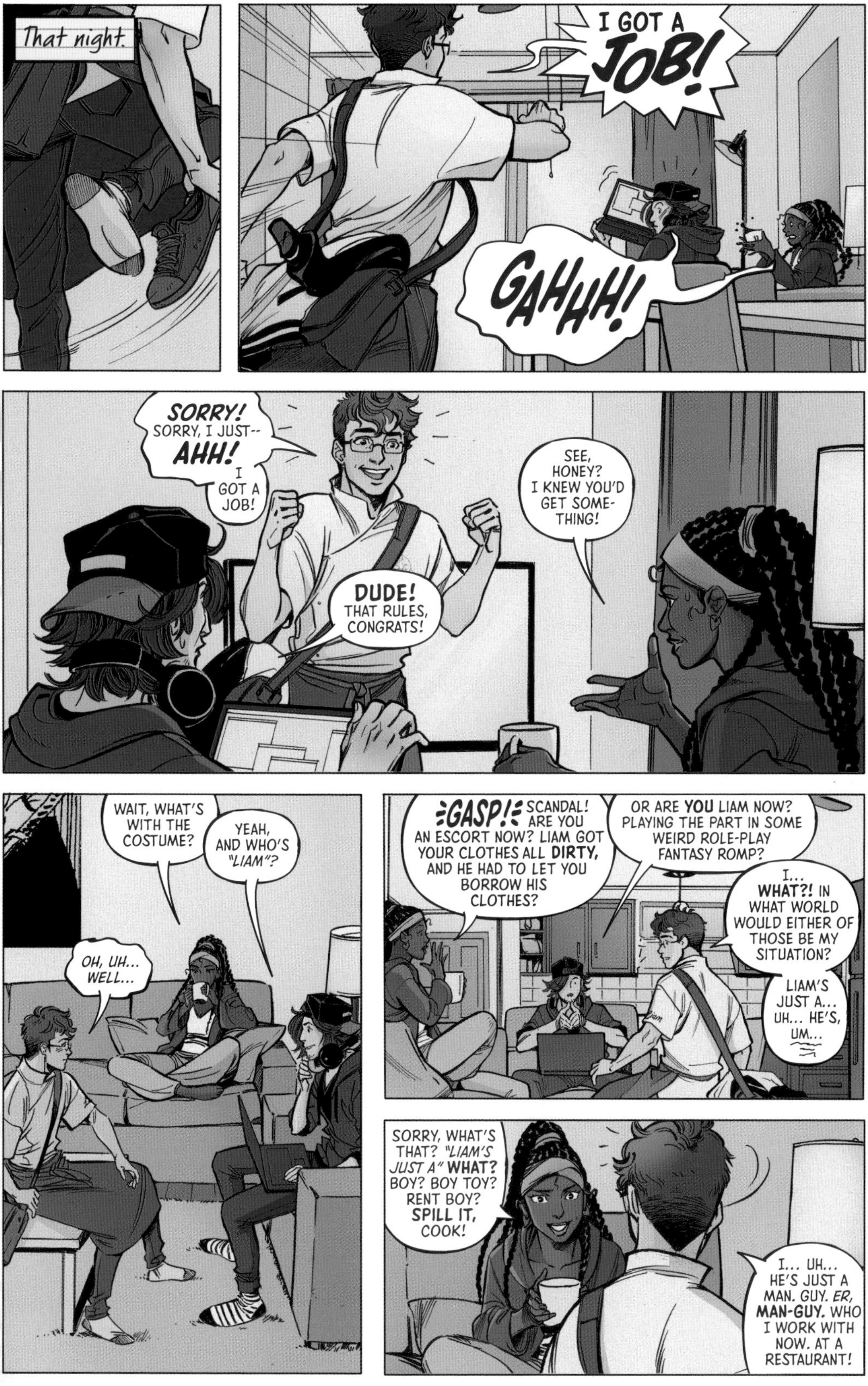
That night.
I GOT A JOB!
GAHHH!
SORRY! SORRY, I JUST-- AHH!
I GOT A JOB!
SEE, HONEY? I KNEW YOU'D GET SOME-THING!
DUDE! THAT RULES, CONGRATS!
WAIT, WHAT'S WITH THE COSTUME?
YEAH, AND WHO'S "LIAM"?
OH, UH... WELL...
GASP! SCANDAL! ARE YOU AN ESCORT NOW? LIAM GOT YOUR CLOTHES ALL DIRTY, AND HE HAD TO LET YOU BORROW HIS CLOTHES?
OR ARE YOU LIAM NOW? PLAYING THE PART IN SOME WEIRD ROLE-PLAY FANTASY ROMP?
I... WHAT?! IN WHAT WORLD WOULD EITHER OF THOSE BE MY SITUATION?
LIAM'S JUST A... UH... HE'S, UM...
SORRY, WHAT'S THAT? "LIAM'S JUST A" WHAT? BOY? BOY TOY? RENT BOY? SPILL IT, COOK!
I... UH... HE'S JUST A MAN. GUY. ER, MAN-GUY. WHO I WORK WITH NOW. AT A RESTAURANT!

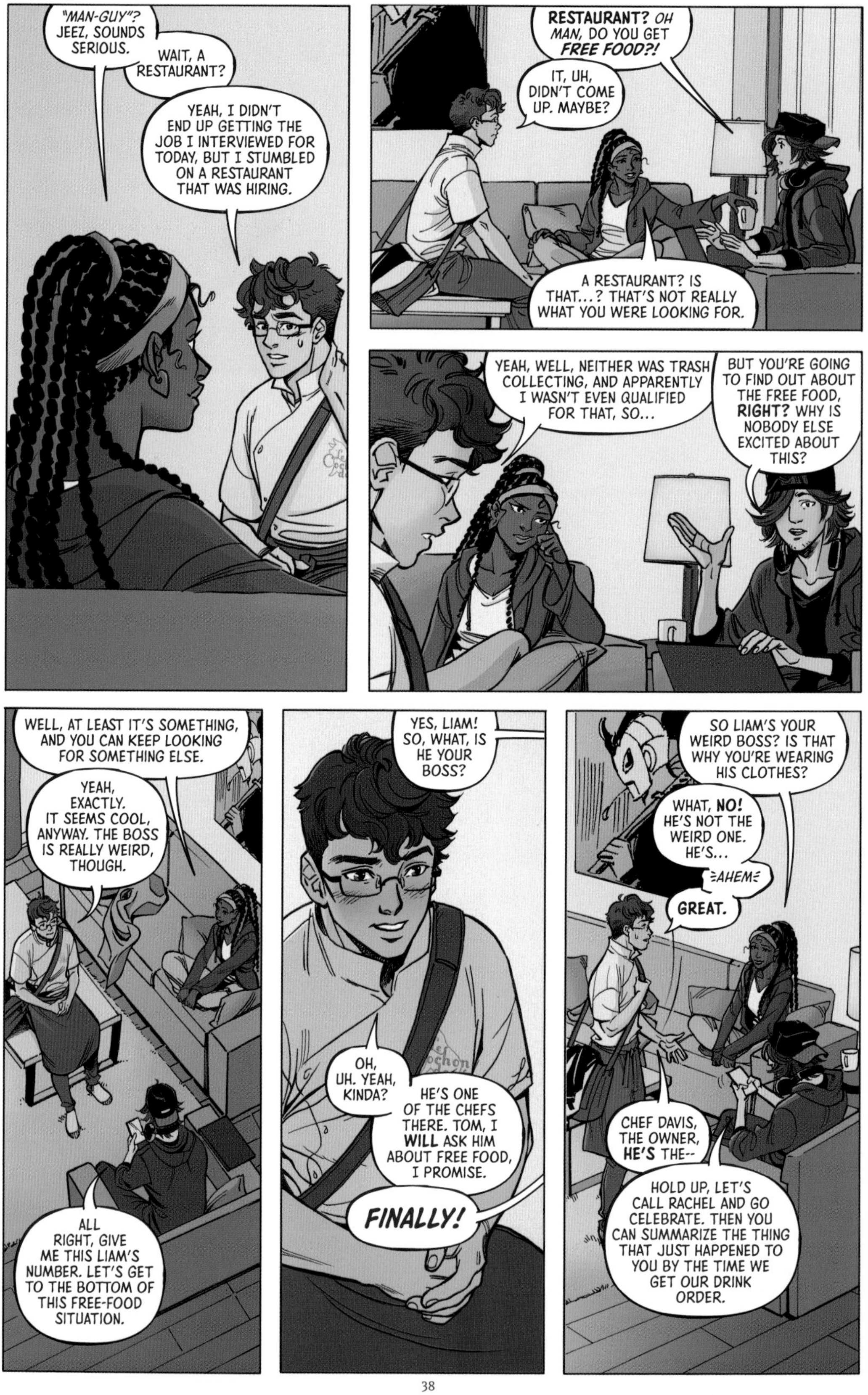
"MAN-GUY"? JEEZ, SOUNDS SERIOUS.
WAIT, A RESTAURANT?
YEAH, I DIDN'T END UP GETTING THE JOB I INTERVIEWED FOR TODAY, BUT I STUMBLED ON A RESTAURANT THAT WAS HIRING.
RESTAURANT? OH MAN, DO YOU GET FREE FOOD?!
IT, UH, DIDN'T COME UP. MAYBE?
A RESTAURANT? IS THAT...? THAT'S NOT REALLY WHAT YOU WERE LOOKING FOR.
YEAH, WELL, NEITHER WAS TRASH COLLECTING, AND APPARENTLY I WASN'T EVEN QUALIFIED FOR THAT, SO...
BUT YOU'RE GOING TO FIND OUT ABOUT THE FREE FOOD, RIGHT? WHY IS NOBODY ELSE EXCITED ABOUT THIS?
WELL, AT LEAST IT'S SOMETHING, AND YOU CAN KEEP LOOKING FOR SOMETHING ELSE.
YEAH, EXACTLY. IT SEEMS COOL, ANYWAY. THE BOSS IS REALLY WEIRD, THOUGH.
ALL RIGHT, GIVE ME THIS LIAM'S NUMBER. LET'S GET TO THE BOTTOM OF THIS FREE-FOOD SITUATION.
YES, LIAM! SO, WHAT, IS HE YOUR BOSS?
OH, UH. YEAH, KINDA?
HE'S ONE OF THE CHEFS THERE. TOM, I WILL ASK HIM ABOUT FREE FOOD, I PROMISE.
FINALLY!
SO LIAM'S YOUR WEIRD BOSS? IS THAT WHY YOU'RE WEARING HIS CLOTHES?
WHAT, NO! HE'S NOT THE WEIRD ONE. HE'S...
AHEM
GREAT.
CHEF DAVIS, THE OWNER, HE'S THE--
HOLD UP, LET'S CALL RACHEL AND GO CELEBRATE. THEN YOU CAN SUMMARIZE THE THING THAT JUST HAPPENED TO YOU BY THE TIME WE GET OUR DRINK ORDER.

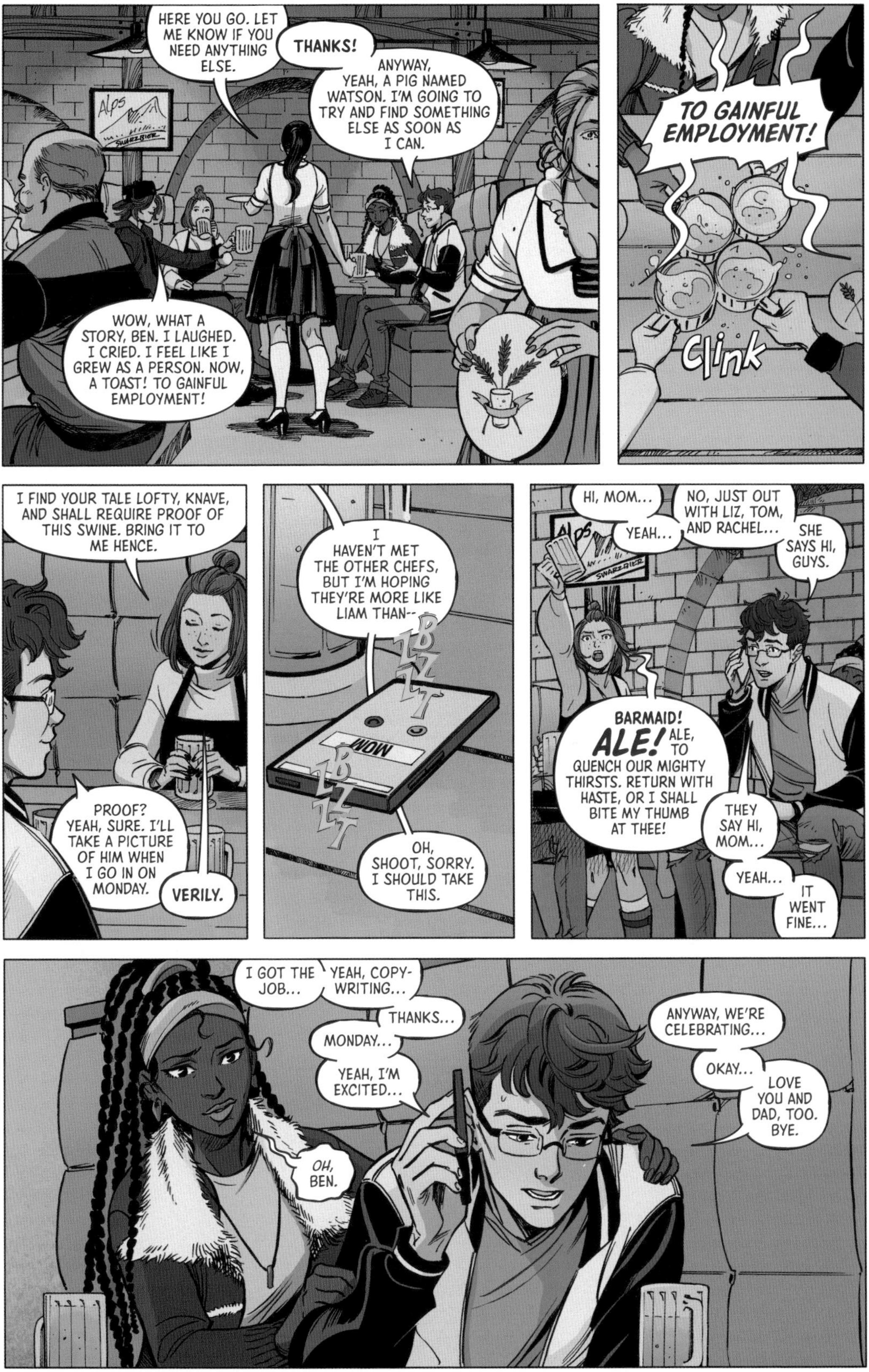
HERE YOU GO. LET ME KNOW IF YOU NEED ANYTHING ELSE.
THANKS!
ANYWAY, YEAH, A PIG NAMED WATSON. I'M GOING TO TRY AND FIND SOMETHING ELSE AS SOON AS I CAN.
WOW, WHAT A STORY, BEN. I LAUGHED. I CRIED. I FEEL LIKE I GREW AS A PERSON. NOW, A TOAST! TO GAINFUL EMPLOYMENT!
TO GAINFUL EMPLOYMENT!
CLINK
I FIND YOUR TALE LOFTY, KNAVE, AND SHALL REQUIRE PROOF OF THIS SWINE. BRING IT TO ME HENCE.
PROOF? YEAH, SURE. I'LL TAKE A PICTURE OF HIM WHEN I GO IN ON MONDAY.
VERILY.
I HAVEN'T MET THE OTHER CHEFS, BUT I'M HOPING THEY'RE MORE LIKE LIAM THAN--
BZZZT
MOM
BZZZT
OH, SHOOT, SORRY. I SHOULD TAKE THIS.
HI, MOM...
YEAH...
NO, JUST OUT WITH LIZ, TOM, AND RACHEL...
SHE SAYS HI, GUYS.
BARMAID! ALE! ALE, TO QUENCH OUR MIGHTY THIRSTS. RETURN WITH HASTE, OR I SHALL BITE MY THUMB AT THEE!
THEY SAY HI, MOM...
YEAH...
IT WENT FINE...
I GOT THE JOB...
YEAH, COPY-WRITING...
THANKS...
MONDAY...
YEAH, I'M EXCITED...
OH, BEN.
ANYWAY, WE'RE CELEBRATING...
OKAY...
LOVE YOU AND DAD, TOO. BYE.

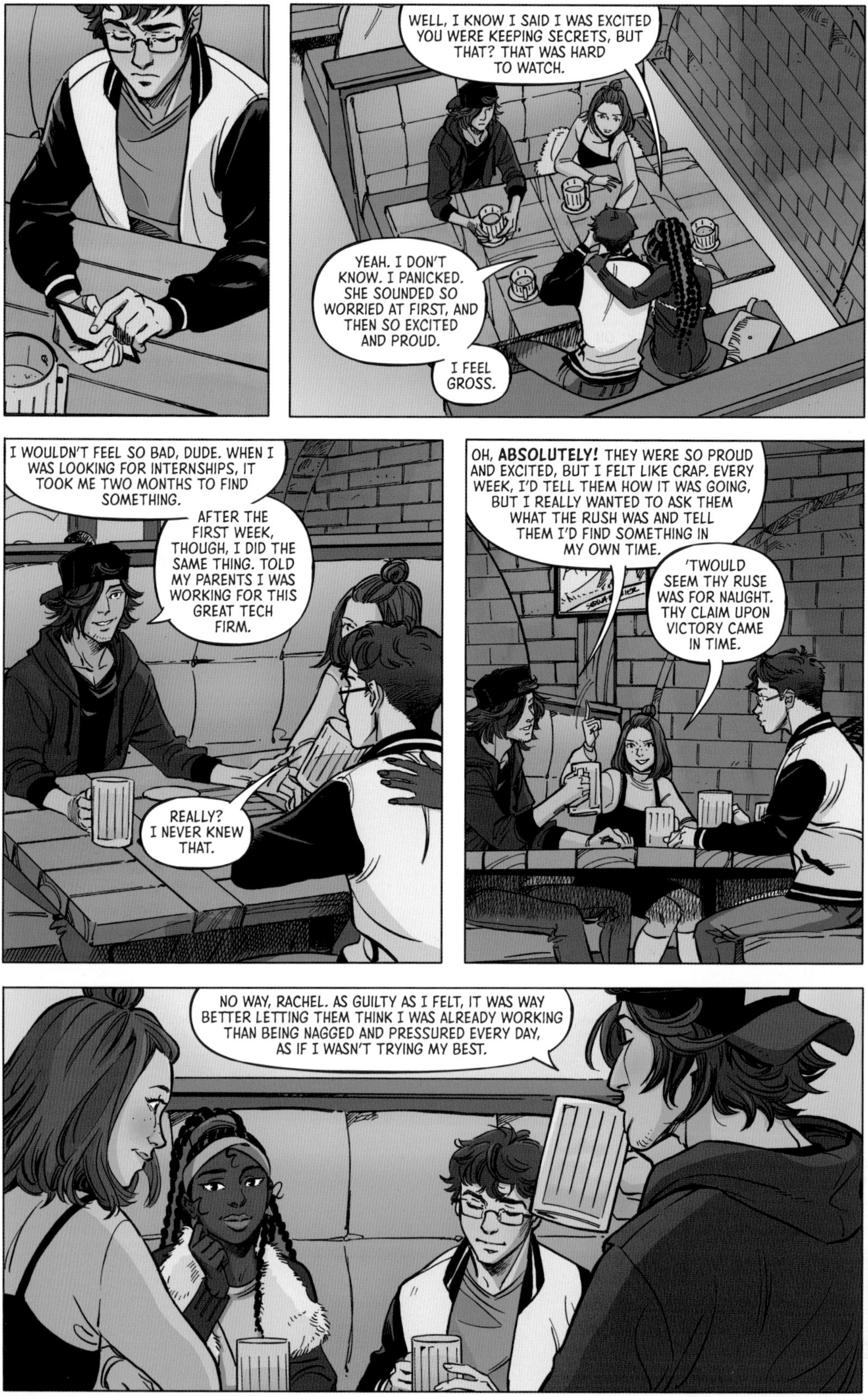
WELL, I KNOW I SAID I WAS EXCITED YOU WERE KEEPING SECRETS, BUT THAT? THAT WAS HARD TO WATCH.
YEAH. I DON'T KNOW. I PANICKED. SHE SOUNDED SO WORRIED AT FIRST, AND THEN SO EXCITED AND PROUD.
I FEEL GROSS.
I WOULDN'T FEEL SO BAD, DUDE. WHEN I WAS LOOKING FOR INTERNSHIPS, IT TOOK ME TWO MONTHS TO FIND SOMETHING.
AFTER THE FIRST WEEK, THOUGH, I DID THE SAME THING. TOLD MY PARENTS I WAS WORKING FOR THIS GREAT TECH FIRM.
REALLY? I NEVER KNEW THAT.
OH, **ABSOLUTELY!** THEY WERE SO PROUD AND EXCITED, BUT I FELT LIKE CRAP. EVERY WEEK, I'D TELL THEM HOW IT WAS GOING, BUT I REALLY WANTED TO ASK THEM WHAT THE RUSH WAS AND TELL THEM I'D FIND SOMETHING IN MY OWN TIME.
'TWOULD SEEM THY RUSE WAS FOR NAUGHT. THY CLAIM UPON VICTORY CAME IN TIME.
NO WAY, RACHEL. AS GUILTY AS I FELT, IT WAS WAY BETTER LETTING THEM THINK I WAS ALREADY WORKING THAN BEING NAGGED AND PRESSURED EVERY DAY, AS IF I WASN'T TRYING MY BEST.

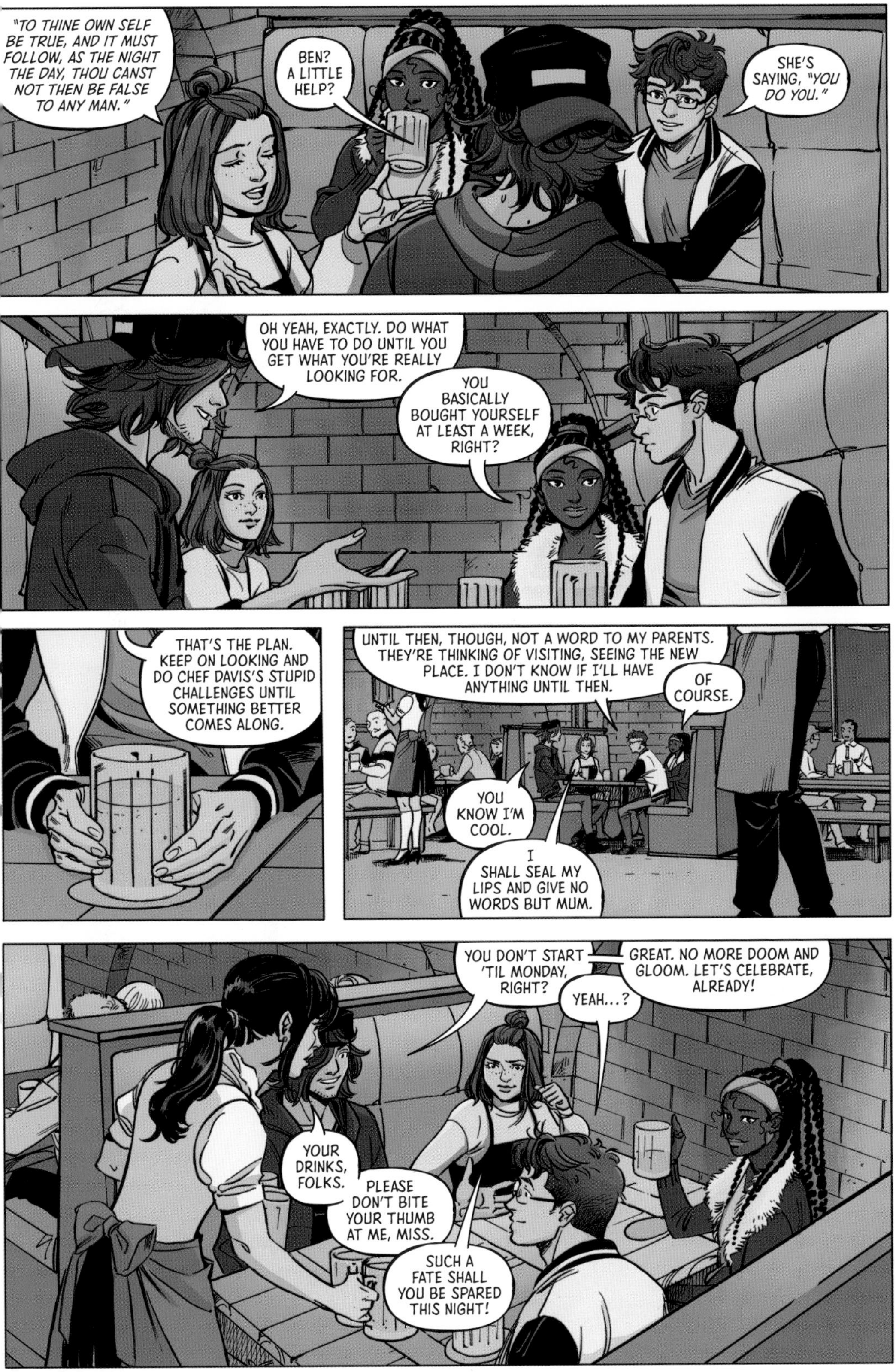
"TO THINE OWN SELF BE TRUE, AND IT MUST FOLLOW, AS THE NIGHT THE DAY, THOU CANST NOT THEN BE FALSE TO ANY MAN."
BEN? A LITTLE HELP?
SHE'S SAYING, "YOU DO YOU."
OH YEAH, EXACTLY. DO WHAT YOU HAVE TO DO UNTIL YOU GET WHAT YOU'RE REALLY LOOKING FOR.
YOU BASICALLY BOUGHT YOURSELF AT LEAST A WEEK, RIGHT?
THAT'S THE PLAN. KEEP ON LOOKING AND DO CHEF DAVIS'S STUPID CHALLENGES UNTIL SOMETHING BETTER COMES ALONG.
UNTIL THEN, THOUGH, NOT A WORD TO MY PARENTS. THEY'RE THINKING OF VISITING, SEEING THE NEW PLACE. I DON'T KNOW IF I'LL HAVE ANYTHING UNTIL THEN.
OF COURSE.
YOU KNOW I'M COOL.
I SHALL SEAL MY LIPS AND GIVE NO WORDS BUT MUM.
YOU DON'T START 'TIL MONDAY, RIGHT?
GREAT. NO MORE DOOM AND GLOOM. LET'S CELEBRATE, ALREADY!
YEAH...?
YOUR DRINKS, FOLKS.
PLEASE DON'T BITE YOUR THUMB AT ME, MISS.
SUCH A FATE SHALL YOU BE SPARED THIS NIGHT!

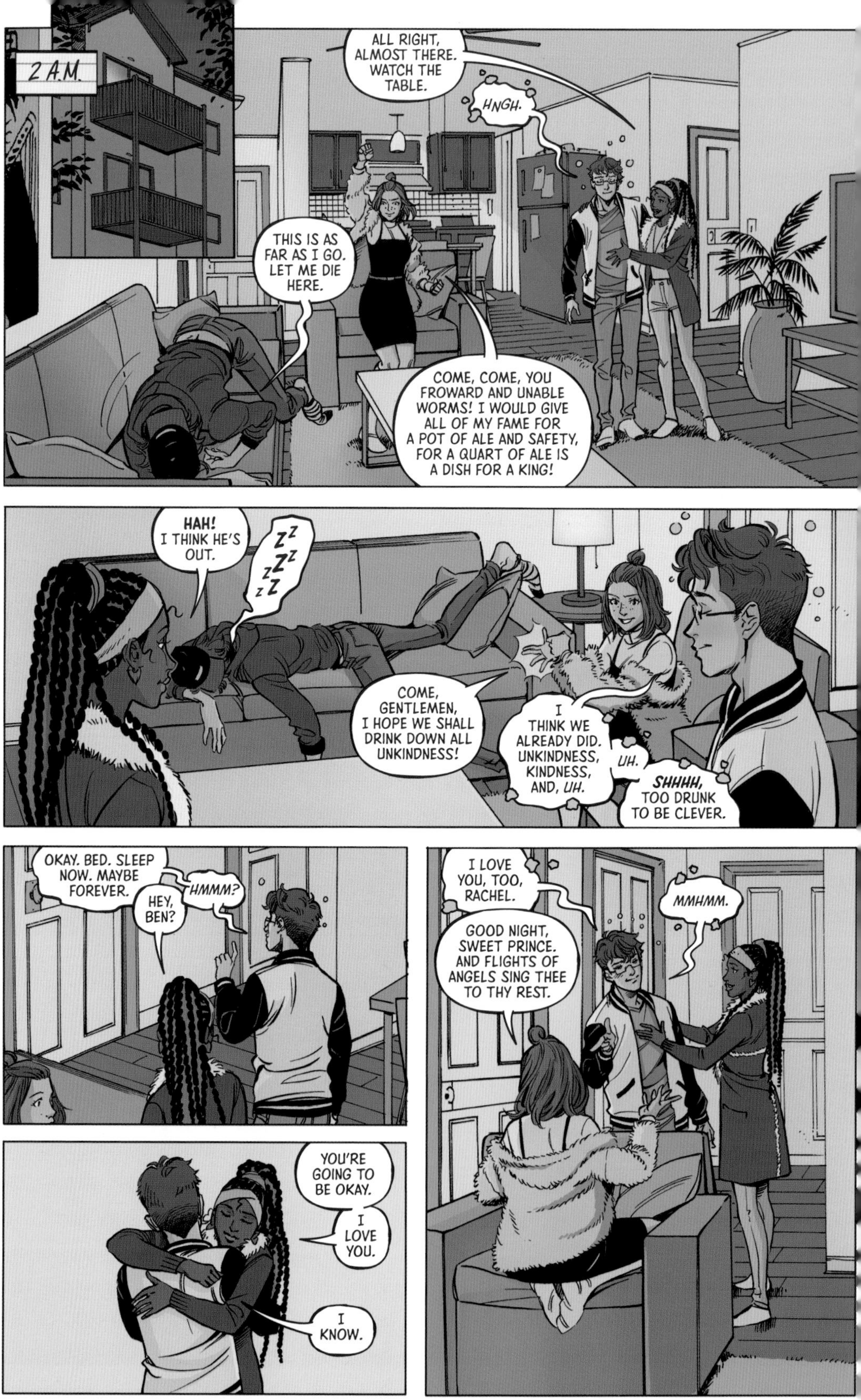
2 A.M.
ALL RIGHT, ALMOST THERE. WATCH THE TABLE.
HNGH.
THIS IS AS FAR AS I GO. LET ME DIE HERE.
COME, COME, YOU FROWARD AND UNABLE WORMS! I WOULD GIVE ALL OF MY FAME FOR A POT OF ALE AND SAFETY, FOR A QUART OF ALE IS A DISH FOR A KING!
HAH! I THINK HE'S OUT.
Z Z Z Z Z Z
COME, GENTLEMEN, I HOPE WE SHALL DRINK DOWN ALL UNKINDNESS!
I THINK WE ALREADY DID. UNKINDNESS, KINDNESS, AND, UH.
UH.
SHHHH, TOO DRUNK TO BE CLEVER.
OKAY. BED. SLEEP NOW. MAYBE FOREVER.
HMMM?
HEY, BEN?
YOU'RE GOING TO BE OKAY.
I LOVE YOU.
I KNOW.
I LOVE YOU, TOO, RACHEL.
MMHMM.
GOOD NIGHT, SWEET PRINCE. AND FLIGHTS OF ANGELS SING THEE TO THY REST.

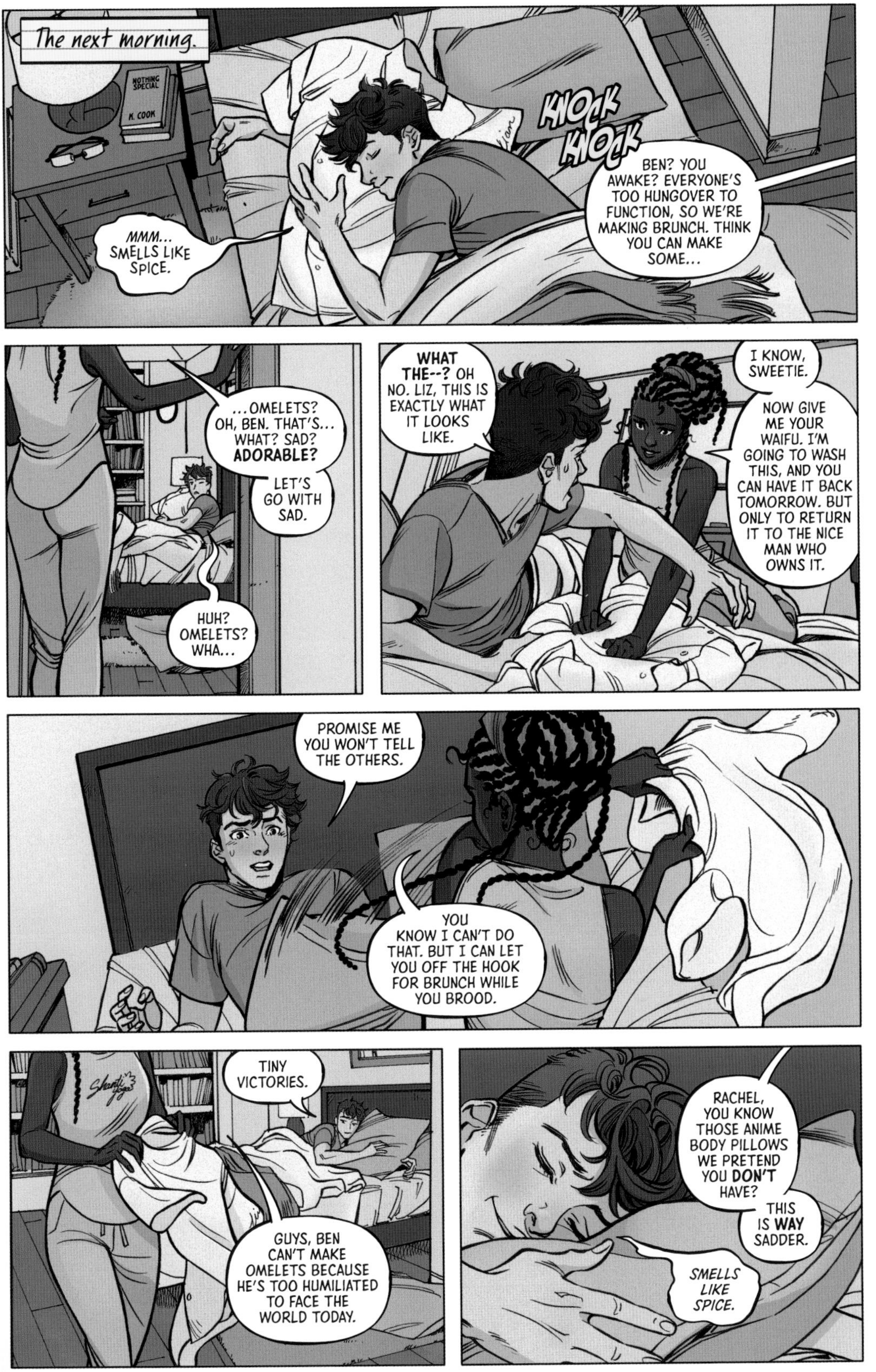

The next morning.
NOTHING SPECIAL
M. COOK
KNOCK KNOCK
BEN? YOU AWAKE? EVERYONE'S TOO HUNGOVER TO FUNCTION, SO WE'RE MAKING BRUNCH. THINK YOU CAN MAKE SOME...
MMM... SMELLS LIKE SPICE.
...OMELETS? OH, BEN. THAT'S... WHAT? SAD? **ADORABLE?**
LET'S GO WITH SAD.
HUH? OMELETS? WHA...
WHAT THE--? OH NO. LIZ, THIS IS EXACTLY WHAT IT LOOKS LIKE.
I KNOW, SWEETIE.
NOW GIVE ME YOUR WAIFU. I'M GOING TO WASH THIS, AND YOU CAN HAVE IT BACK TOMORROW. BUT ONLY TO RETURN IT TO THE NICE MAN WHO OWNS IT.
PROMISE ME YOU WON'T TELL THE OTHERS.
YOU KNOW I CAN'T DO THAT. BUT I CAN LET YOU OFF THE HOOK FOR BRUNCH WHILE YOU BROOD.
TINY VICTORIES.
GUYS, BEN CAN'T MAKE OMELETS BECAUSE HE'S TOO HUMILIATED TO FACE THE WORLD TODAY.
RACHEL, YOU KNOW THOSE ANIME BODY PILLOWS WE PRETEND YOU **DON'T** HAVE?
THIS IS **WAY** SADDER.
SMELLS LIKE SPICE.

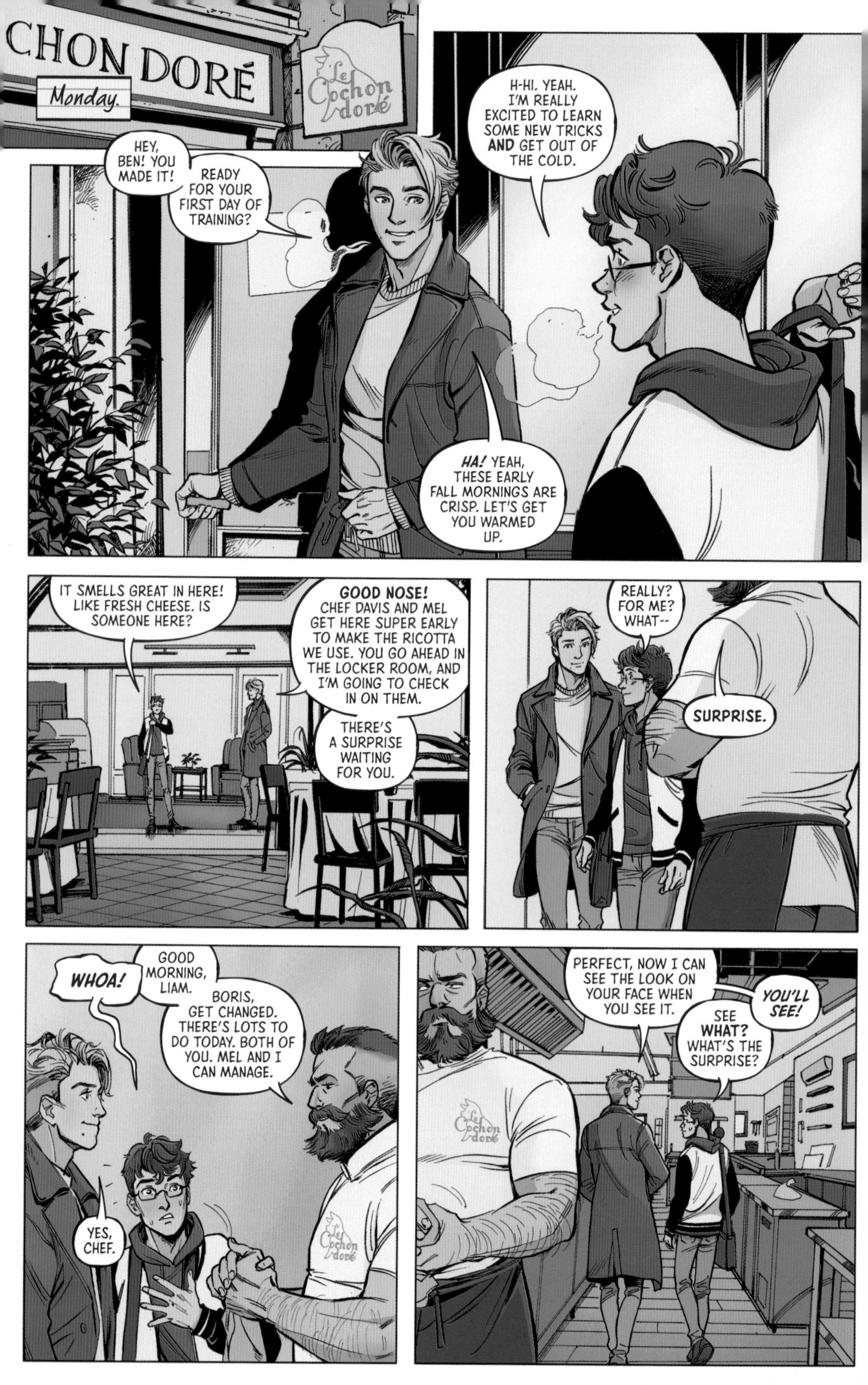
CHON DORÉ
Monday.
Le Cochon doré
HEY, BEN! YOU MADE IT!
READY FOR YOUR FIRST DAY OF TRAINING?
H-HI. YEAH. I'M REALLY EXCITED TO LEARN SOME NEW TRICKS AND GET OUT OF THE COLD.
HA! YEAH, THESE EARLY FALL MORNINGS ARE CRISP. LET'S GET YOU WARMED UP.
IT SMELLS GREAT IN HERE! LIKE FRESH CHEESE. IS SOMEONE HERE?
GOOD NOSE! CHEF DAVIS AND MEL GET HERE SUPER EARLY TO MAKE THE RICOTTA WE USE. YOU GO AHEAD IN THE LOCKER ROOM, AND I'M GOING TO CHECK IN ON THEM.
THERE'S A SURPRISE WAITING FOR YOU.
REALLY? FOR ME? WHAT--
SURPRISE.
WHOA!
GOOD MORNING, LIAM.
BORIS, GET CHANGED. THERE'S LOTS TO DO TODAY. BOTH OF YOU. MEL AND I CAN MANAGE.
YES, CHEF.
Le Cochon doré
PERFECT, NOW I CAN SEE THE LOOK ON YOUR FACE WHEN YOU SEE IT.
YOU'LL SEE!
SEE WHAT? WHAT'S THE SURPRISE?
Le Cochon doré

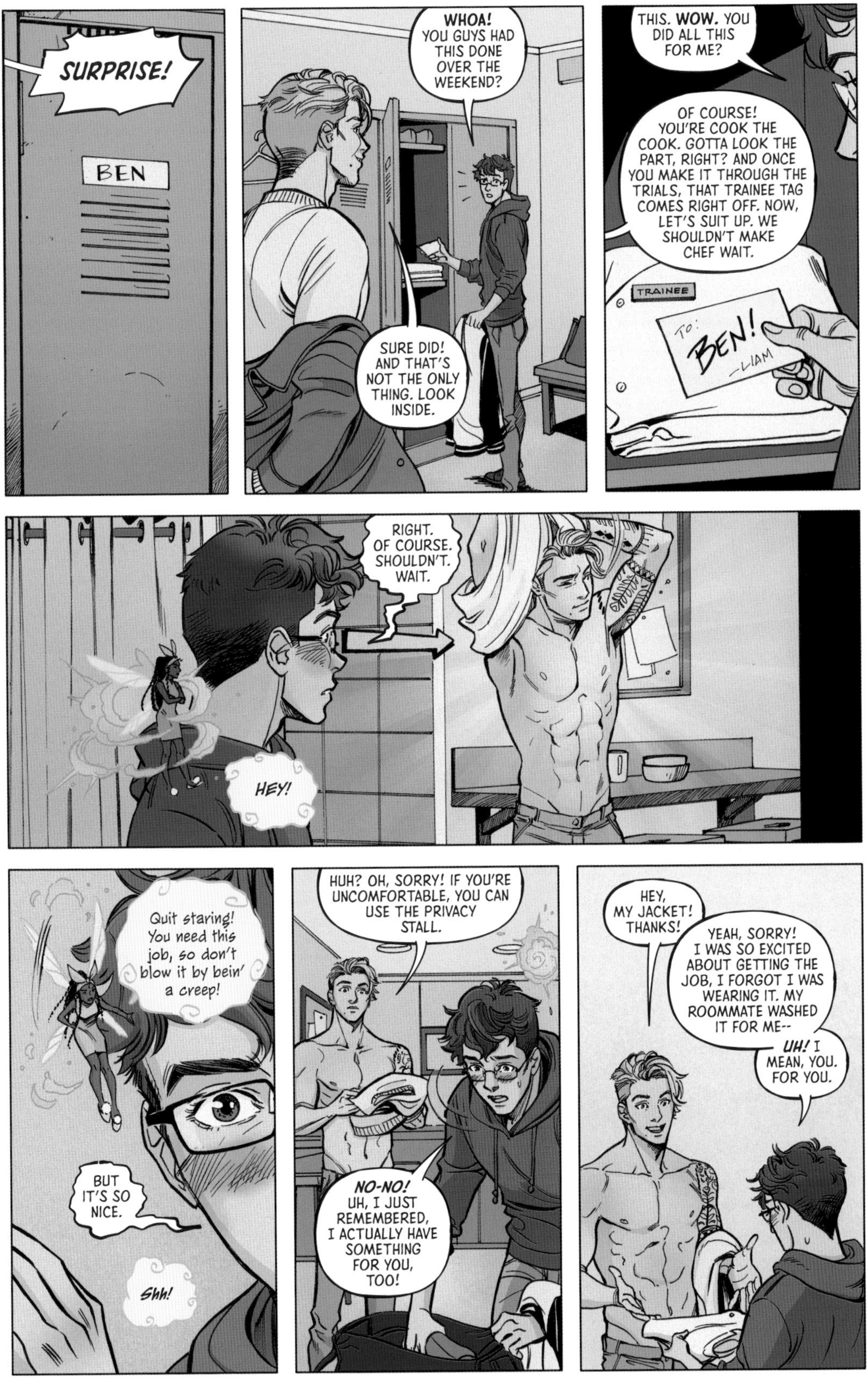
SURPRISE!
BEN
WHOA! YOU GUYS HAD THIS DONE OVER THE WEEKEND?
SURE DID! AND THAT'S NOT THE ONLY THING. LOOK INSIDE.
THIS. WOW. YOU DID ALL THIS FOR ME?
OF COURSE! YOU'RE COOK THE COOK. GOTTA LOOK THE PART, RIGHT? AND ONCE YOU MAKE IT THROUGH THE TRIALS, THAT TRAINEE TAG COMES RIGHT OFF. NOW, LET'S SUIT UP. WE SHOULDN'T MAKE CHEF WAIT.
TRAINEE
TO: BEN! —LIAM
RIGHT. OF COURSE. SHOULDN'T. WAIT.
HEY!
Quit staring! You need this job, so don't blow it by bein' a creep!
BUT IT'S SO NICE.
Shh!
HUH? OH, SORRY! IF YOU'RE UNCOMFORTABLE, YOU CAN USE THE PRIVACY STALL.
NO-NO! UH, I JUST REMEMBERED, I ACTUALLY HAVE SOMETHING FOR YOU, TOO!
HEY, MY JACKET! THANKS!
YEAH, SORRY! I WAS SO EXCITED ABOUT GETTING THE JOB, I FORGOT I WAS WEARING IT. MY ROOMMATE WASHED IT FOR ME--
UH! I MEAN, YOU. FOR YOU.

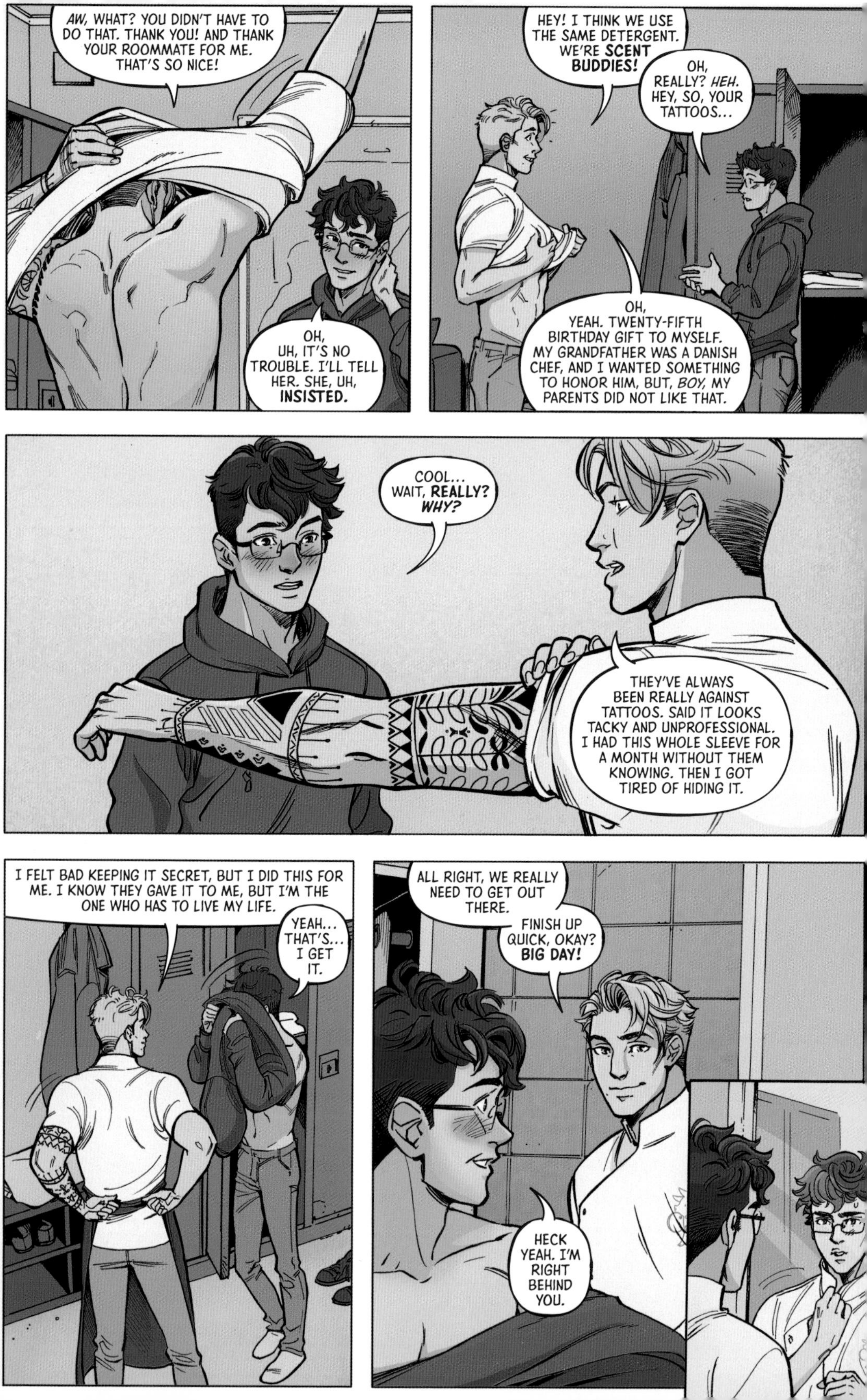
AW, WHAT? YOU DIDN'T HAVE TO DO THAT. THANK YOU! AND THANK YOUR ROOMMATE FOR ME. THAT'S SO NICE!
OH, UH, IT'S NO TROUBLE. I'LL TELL HER. SHE, UH, **INSISTED.**
HEY! I THINK WE USE THE SAME DETERGENT. WE'RE **SCENT BUDDIES!**
OH, REALLY? *HEH.* HEY, SO, YOUR TATTOOS...
OH, YEAH. TWENTY-FIFTH BIRTHDAY GIFT TO MYSELF. MY GRANDFATHER WAS A DANISH CHEF, AND I WANTED SOMETHING TO HONOR HIM, BUT, *BOY*, MY PARENTS DID NOT LIKE THAT.
COOL... WAIT, **REALLY?** ***WHY?***
THEY'VE ALWAYS BEEN REALLY AGAINST TATTOOS. SAID IT LOOKS TACKY AND UNPROFESSIONAL. I HAD THIS WHOLE SLEEVE FOR A MONTH WITHOUT THEM KNOWING. THEN I GOT TIRED OF HIDING IT.
I FELT BAD KEEPING IT SECRET, BUT I DID THIS FOR ME. I KNOW THEY GAVE IT TO ME, BUT I'M THE ONE WHO HAS TO LIVE MY LIFE.
YEAH... THAT'S... I GET IT.
ALL RIGHT, WE REALLY NEED TO GET OUT THERE.
FINISH UP QUICK, OKAY? **BIG DAY!**
HECK YEAH. I'M RIGHT BEHIND YOU.

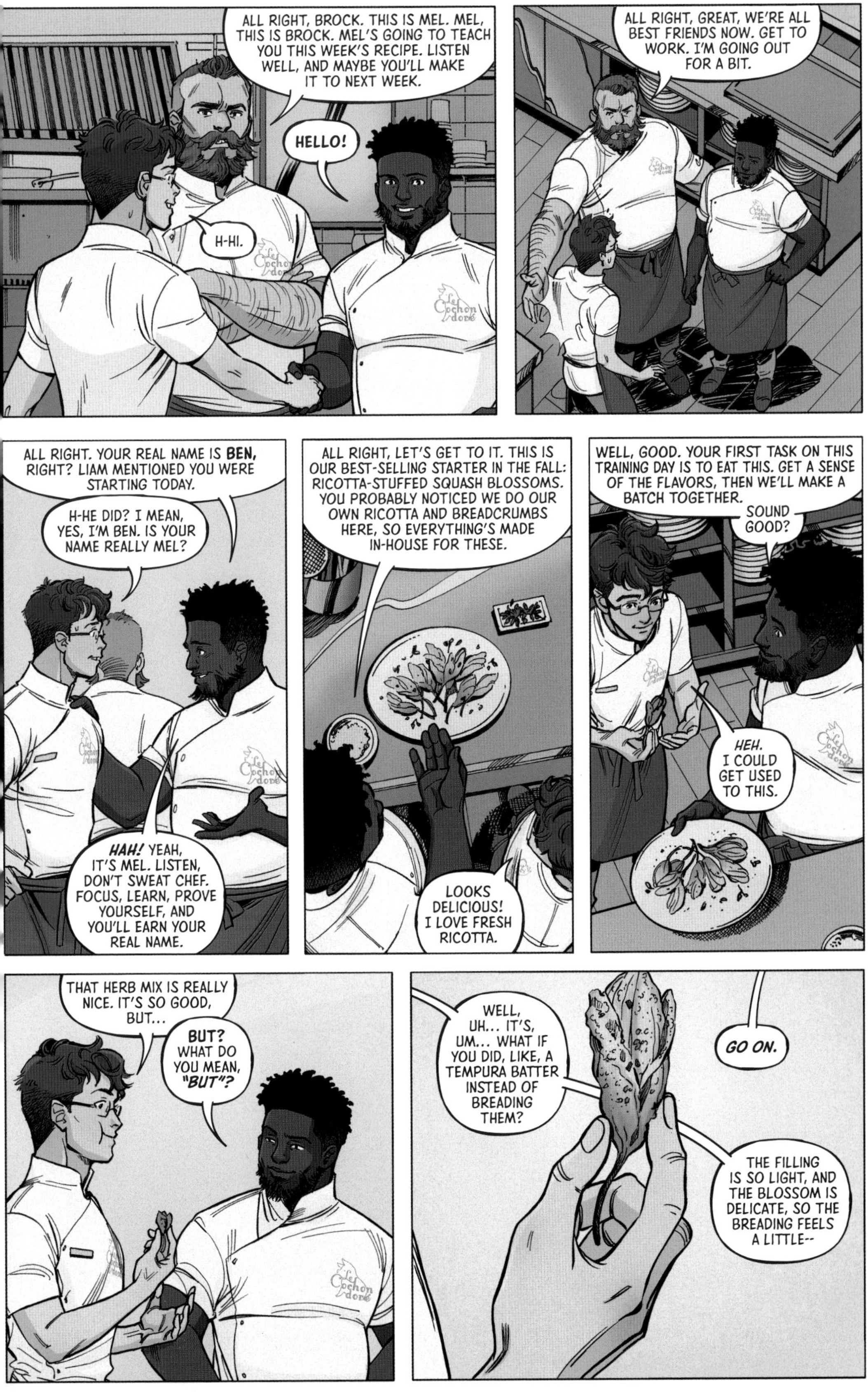
ALL RIGHT, BROCK. THIS IS MEL. MEL, THIS IS BROCK. MEL'S GOING TO TEACH YOU THIS WEEK'S RECIPE. LISTEN WELL, AND MAYBE YOU'LL MAKE IT TO NEXT WEEK.
HELLO!
H-HI.
ALL RIGHT, GREAT, WE'RE ALL BEST FRIENDS NOW. GET TO WORK. I'M GOING OUT FOR A BIT.
ALL RIGHT. YOUR REAL NAME IS BEN, RIGHT? LIAM MENTIONED YOU WERE STARTING TODAY.
H-HE DID? I MEAN, YES, I'M BEN. IS YOUR NAME REALLY MEL?
HAH! YEAH, IT'S MEL. LISTEN, DON'T SWEAT CHEF. FOCUS, LEARN, PROVE YOURSELF, AND YOU'LL EARN YOUR REAL NAME.
ALL RIGHT, LET'S GET TO IT. THIS IS OUR BEST-SELLING STARTER IN THE FALL: RICOTTA-STUFFED SQUASH BLOSSOMS. YOU PROBABLY NOTICED WE DO OUR OWN RICOTTA AND BREADCRUMBS HERE, SO EVERYTHING'S MADE IN-HOUSE FOR THESE.
LOOKS DELICIOUS! I LOVE FRESH RICOTTA.
WELL, GOOD. YOUR FIRST TASK ON THIS TRAINING DAY IS TO EAT THIS. GET A SENSE OF THE FLAVORS, THEN WE'LL MAKE A BATCH TOGETHER.
SOUND GOOD?
HEH. I COULD GET USED TO THIS.
THAT HERB MIX IS REALLY NICE. IT'S SO GOOD, BUT...
BUT? WHAT DO YOU MEAN, "BUT"?
WELL, UH... IT'S, UM... WHAT IF YOU DID, LIKE, A TEMPURA BATTER INSTEAD OF BREADING THEM?
GO ON.
THE FILLING IS SO LIGHT, AND THE BLOSSOM IS DELICATE, SO THE BREADING FEELS A LITTLE--

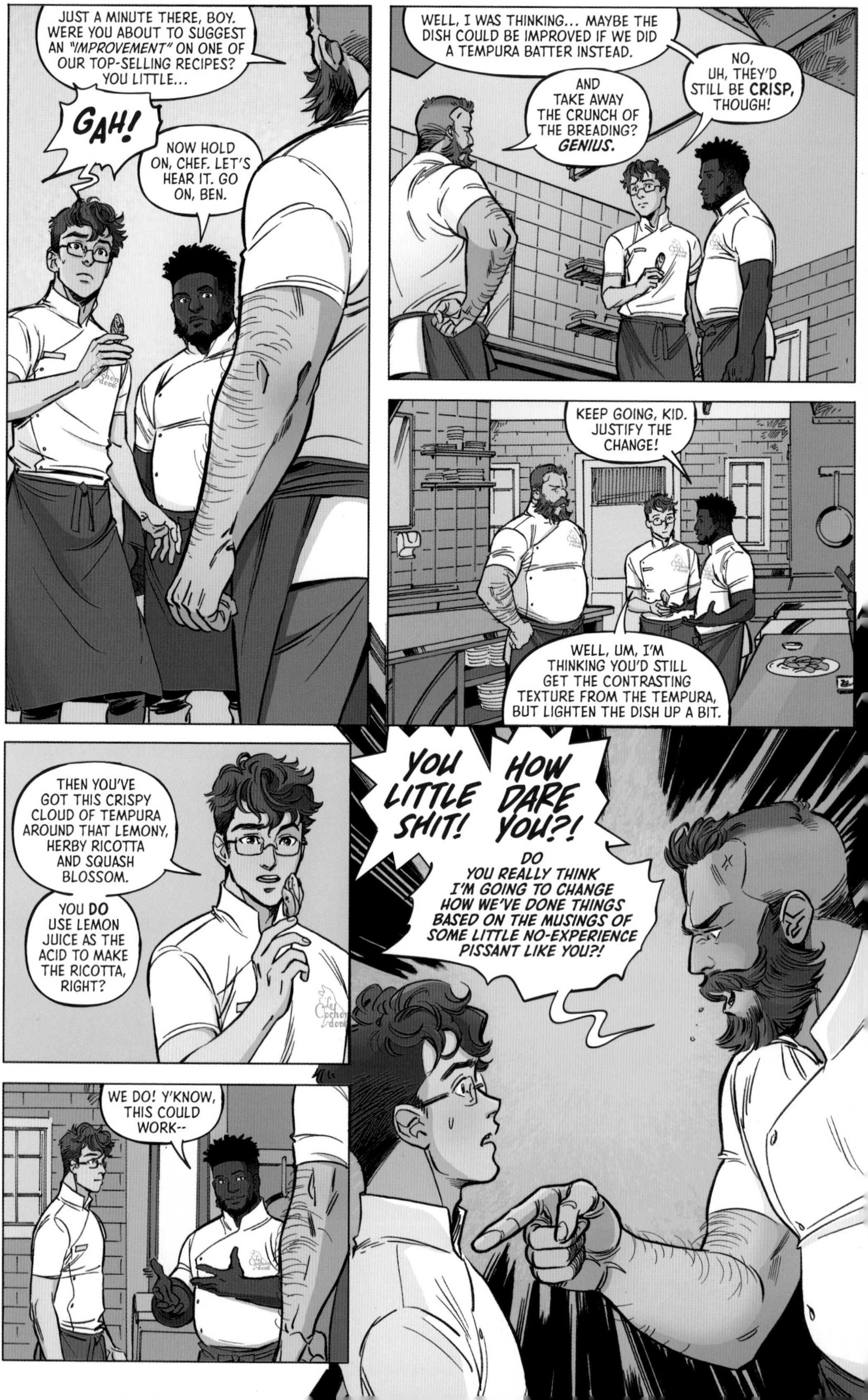

JUST A MINUTE THERE, BOY. WERE YOU ABOUT TO SUGGEST AN "IMPROVEMENT" ON ONE OF OUR TOP-SELLING RECIPES? YOU LITTLE...
GAH!
NOW HOLD ON, CHEF. LET'S HEAR IT. GO ON, BEN.
WELL, I WAS THINKING... MAYBE THE DISH COULD BE IMPROVED IF WE DID A TEMPURA BATTER INSTEAD.
AND TAKE AWAY THE CRUNCH OF THE BREADING? GENIUS.
NO, UH, THEY'D STILL BE CRISP, THOUGH!
KEEP GOING, KID. JUSTIFY THE CHANGE!
WELL, UM, I'M THINKING YOU'D STILL GET THE CONTRASTING TEXTURE FROM THE TEMPURA, BUT LIGHTEN THE DISH UP A BIT.
THEN YOU'VE GOT THIS CRISPY CLOUD OF TEMPURA AROUND THAT LEMONY, HERBY RICOTTA AND SQUASH BLOSSOM.
YOU DO USE LEMON JUICE AS THE ACID TO MAKE THE RICOTTA, RIGHT?
WE DO! Y'KNOW, THIS COULD WORK--
YOU LITTLE SHIT!
HOW DARE YOU?!
DO YOU REALLY THINK I'M GOING TO CHANGE HOW WE'VE DONE THINGS BASED ON THE MUSINGS OF SOME LITTLE NO-EXPERIENCE PISSANT LIKE YOU?!

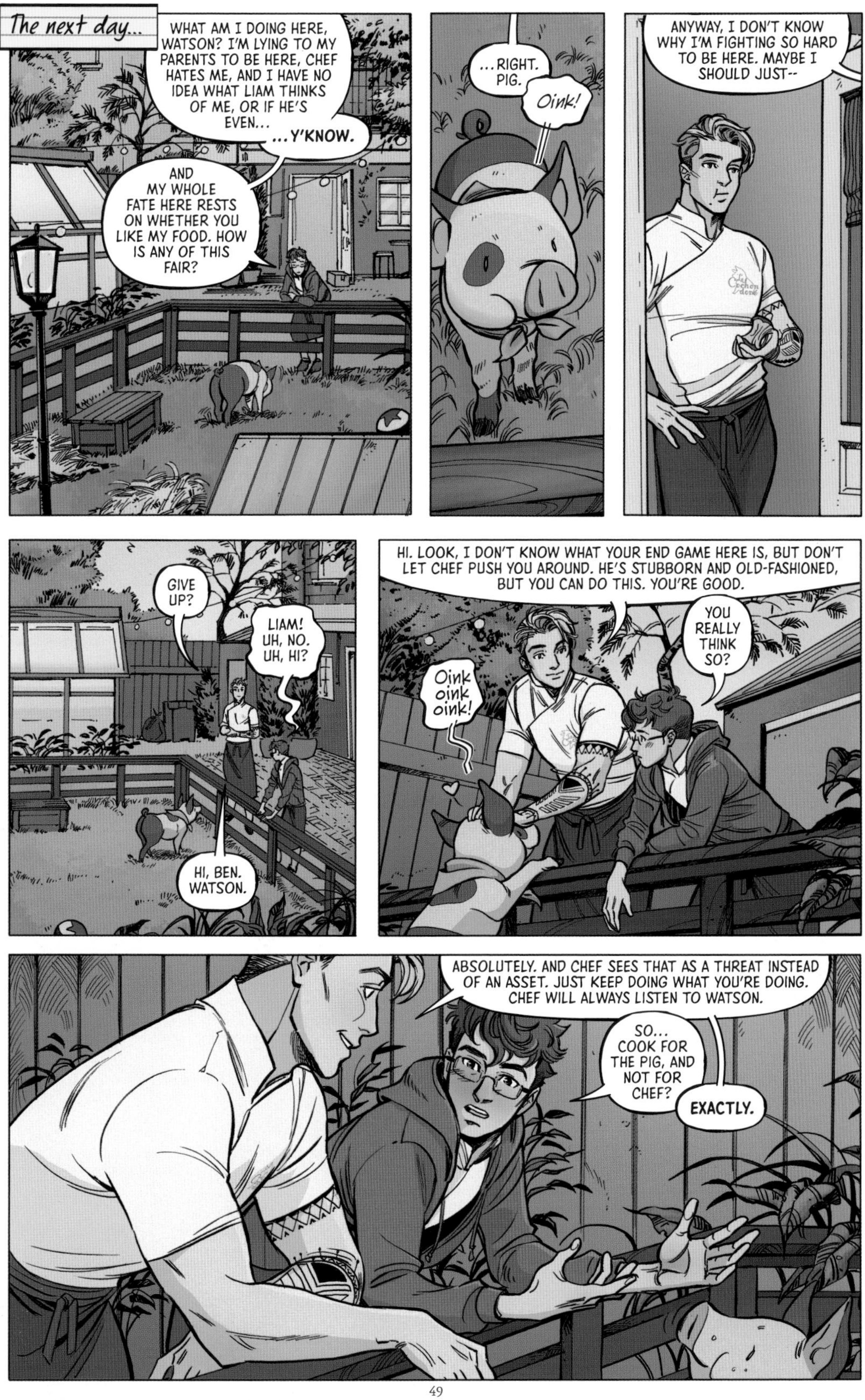
The next day...
WHAT AM I DOING HERE, WATSON? I'M LYING TO MY PARENTS TO BE HERE, CHEF HATES ME, AND I HAVE NO IDEA WHAT LIAM THINKS OF ME, OR IF HE'S EVEN...
...Y'KNOW.
AND MY WHOLE FATE HERE RESTS ON WHETHER YOU LIKE MY FOOD. HOW IS ANY OF THIS FAIR?
...RIGHT. PIG.
Oink!
ANYWAY, I DON'T KNOW WHY I'M FIGHTING SO HARD TO BE HERE. MAYBE I SHOULD JUST--
GIVE UP?
LIAM! UH, NO. UH, HI?
HI, BEN. WATSON.
HI. LOOK, I DON'T KNOW WHAT YOUR END GAME HERE IS, BUT DON'T LET CHEF PUSH YOU AROUND. HE'S STUBBORN AND OLD-FASHIONED, BUT YOU CAN DO THIS. YOU'RE GOOD.
Oink oink oink!
YOU REALLY THINK SO?
ABSOLUTELY. AND CHEF SEES THAT AS A THREAT INSTEAD OF AN ASSET. JUST KEEP DOING WHAT YOU'RE DOING. CHEF WILL ALWAYS LISTEN TO WATSON.
SO... COOK FOR THE PIG, AND NOT FOR CHEF?
EXACTLY.

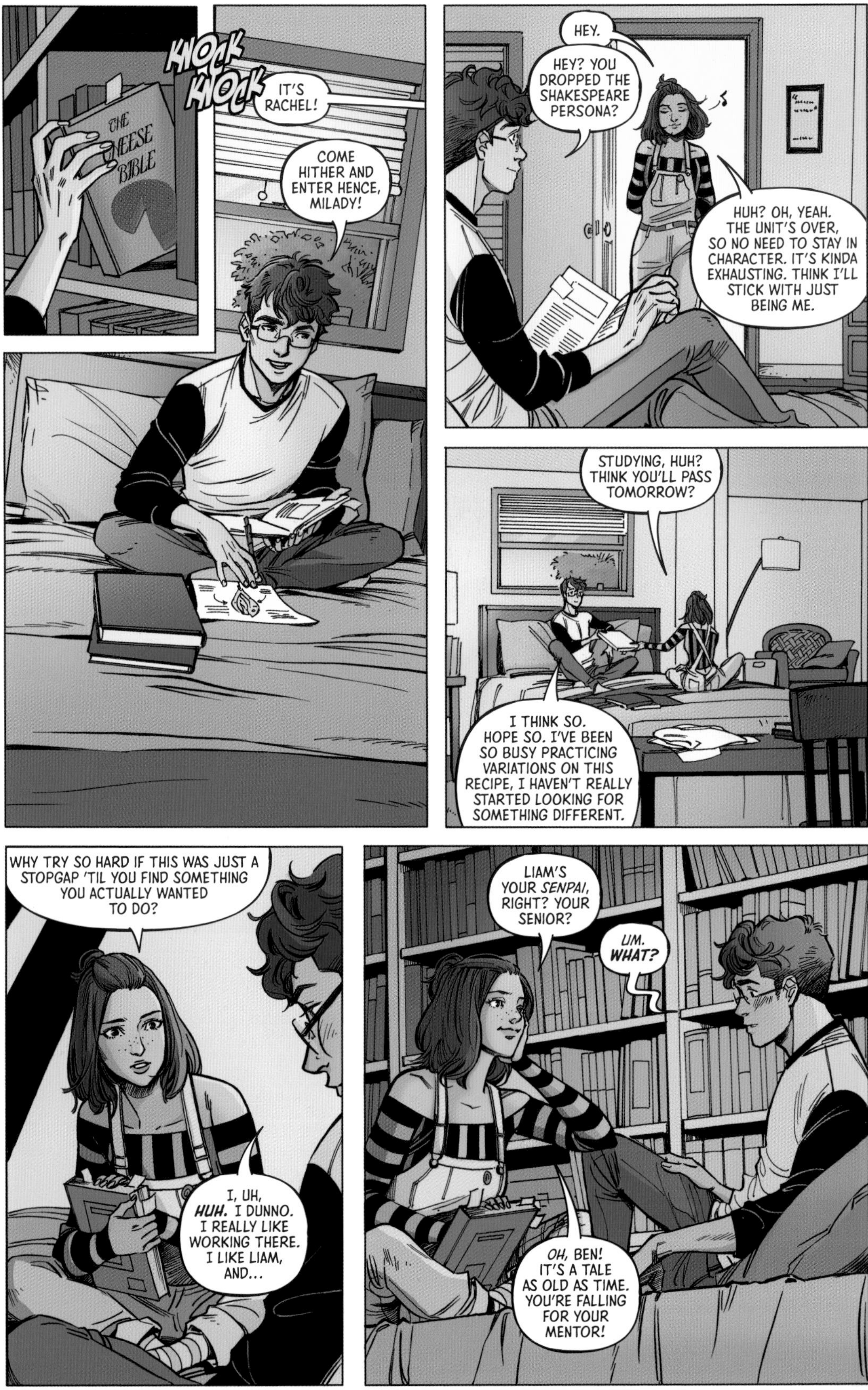
KNOCK KNOCK
IT'S RACHEL!
COME HITHER AND ENTER HENCE, MILADY!
HEY.
HEY? YOU DROPPED THE SHAKESPEARE PERSONA?
HUH? OH, YEAH. THE UNIT'S OVER, SO NO NEED TO STAY IN CHARACTER. IT'S KINDA EXHAUSTING. THINK I'LL STICK WITH JUST BEING ME.
STUDYING, HUH? THINK YOU'LL PASS TOMORROW?
I THINK SO. HOPE SO. I'VE BEEN SO BUSY PRACTICING VARIATIONS ON THIS RECIPE, I HAVEN'T REALLY STARTED LOOKING FOR SOMETHING DIFFERENT.
WHY TRY SO HARD IF THIS WAS JUST A STOPGAP 'TIL YOU FIND SOMETHING YOU ACTUALLY WANTED TO DO?
I, UH, HUH. I DUNNO. I REALLY LIKE WORKING THERE. I LIKE LIAM, AND...
LIAM'S YOUR SENPAI, RIGHT? YOUR SENIOR?
UM. WHAT?
OH, BEN! IT'S A TALE AS OLD AS TIME. YOU'RE FALLING FOR YOUR MENTOR!

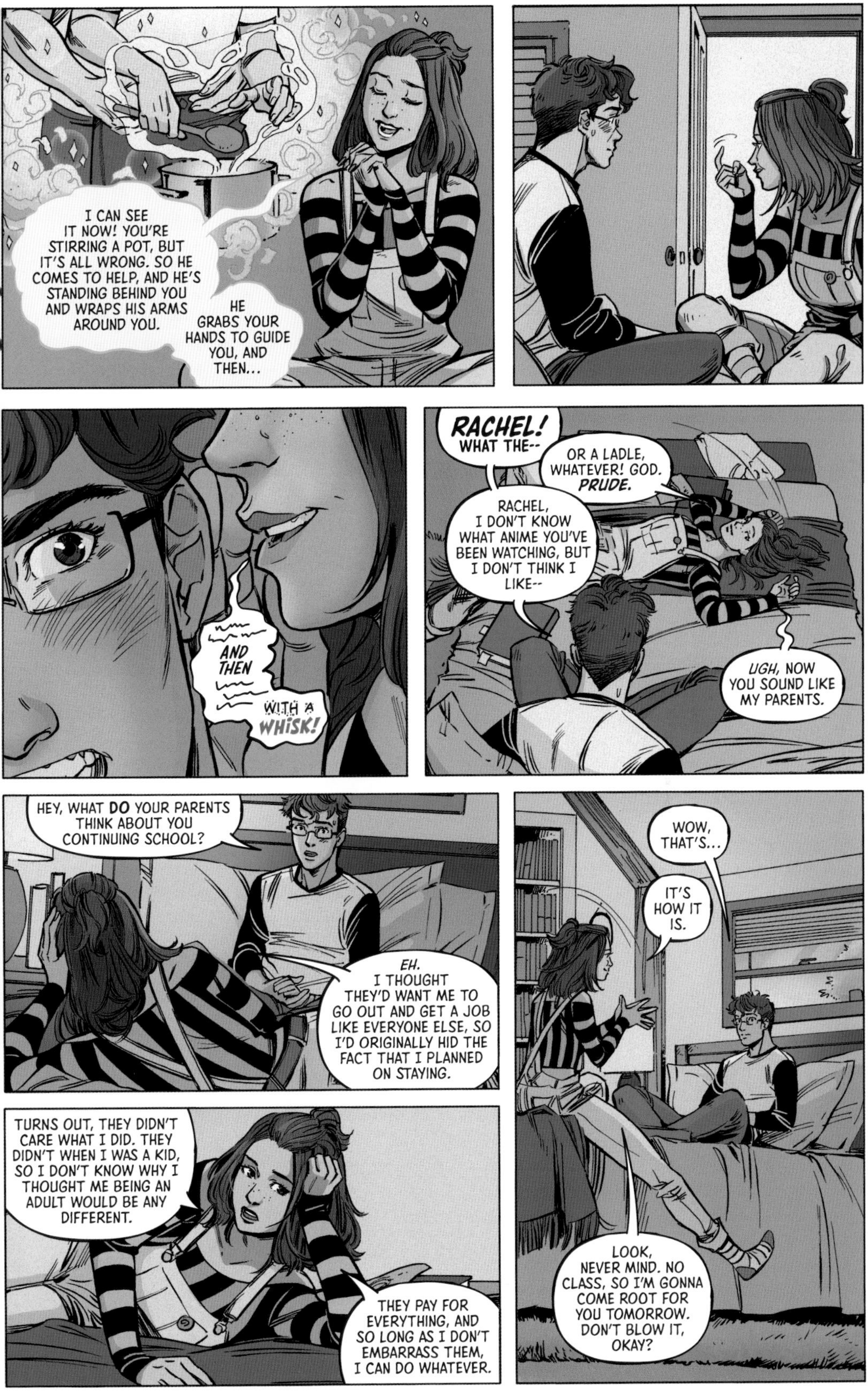

I CAN SEE IT NOW! YOU'RE STIRRING A POT, BUT IT'S ALL WRONG. SO HE COMES TO HELP, AND HE'S STANDING BEHIND YOU AND WRAPS HIS ARMS AROUND YOU.
HE GRABS YOUR HANDS TO GUIDE YOU, AND THEN...
AND THEN
WITH A WHISK!
RACHEL! WHAT THE--
OR A LADLE, WHATEVER! GOD. PRUDE.
RACHEL, I DON'T KNOW WHAT ANIME YOU'VE BEEN WATCHING, BUT I DON'T THINK I LIKE--
UGH, NOW YOU SOUND LIKE MY PARENTS.
HEY, WHAT DO YOUR PARENTS THINK ABOUT YOU CONTINUING SCHOOL?
EH. I THOUGHT THEY'D WANT ME TO GO OUT AND GET A JOB LIKE EVERYONE ELSE, SO I'D ORIGINALLY HID THE FACT THAT I PLANNED ON STAYING.
TURNS OUT, THEY DIDN'T CARE WHAT I DID. THEY DIDN'T WHEN I WAS A KID, SO I DON'T KNOW WHY I THOUGHT ME BEING AN ADULT WOULD BE ANY DIFFERENT.
THEY PAY FOR EVERYTHING, AND SO LONG AS I DON'T EMBARRASS THEM, I CAN DO WHATEVER.
WOW, THAT'S...
IT'S HOW IT IS.
LOOK, NEVER MIND. NO CLASS, SO I'M GONNA COME ROOT FOR YOU TOMORROW. DON'T BLOW IT, OKAY?

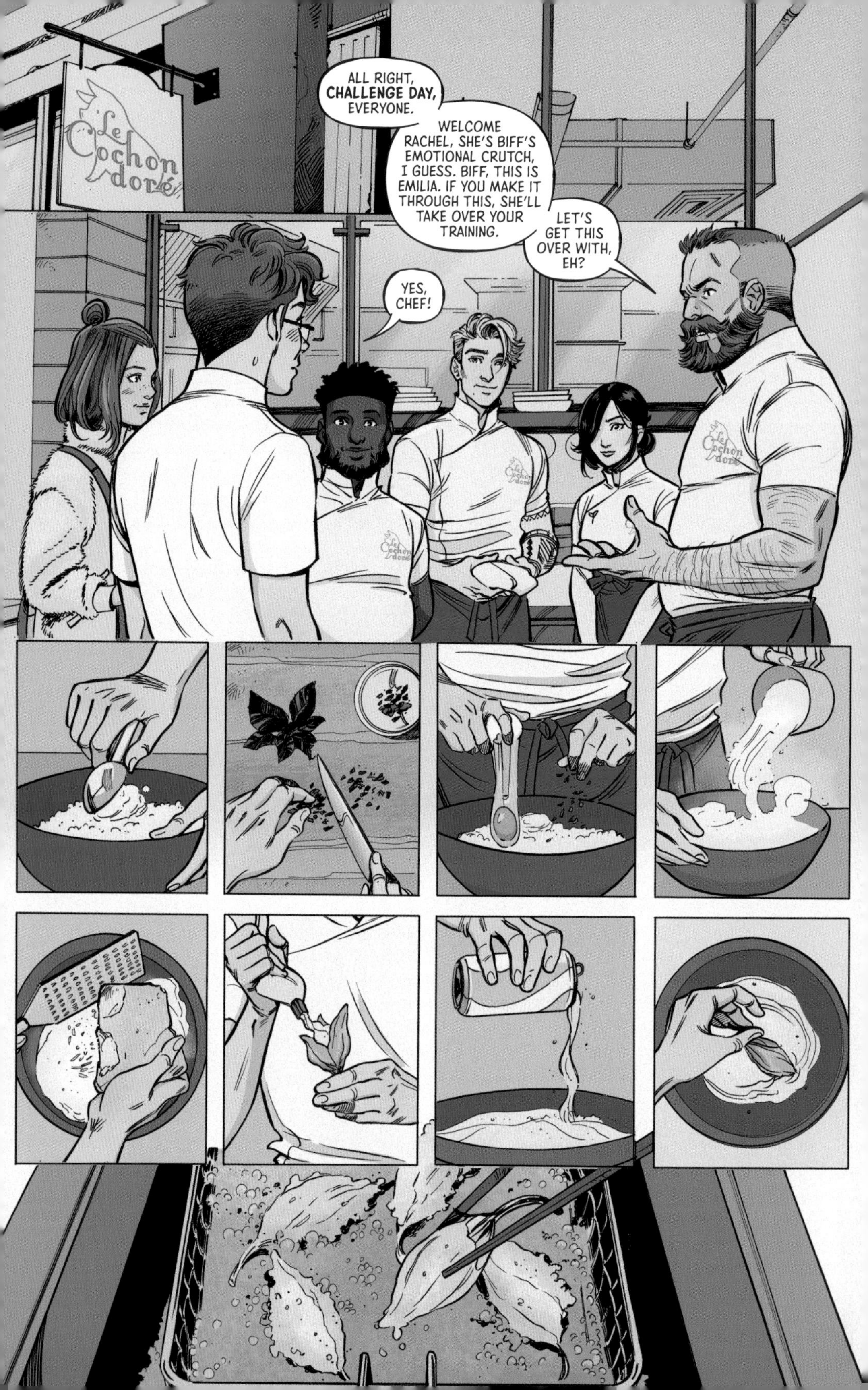
Le Cochon doré
ALL RIGHT, CHALLENGE DAY, EVERYONE.
WELCOME RACHEL, SHE'S BIFF'S EMOTIONAL CRUTCH, I GUESS. BIFF, THIS IS EMILIA. IF YOU MAKE IT THROUGH THIS, SHE'LL TAKE OVER YOUR TRAINING.
LET'S GET THIS OVER WITH, EH?
YES, CHEF!

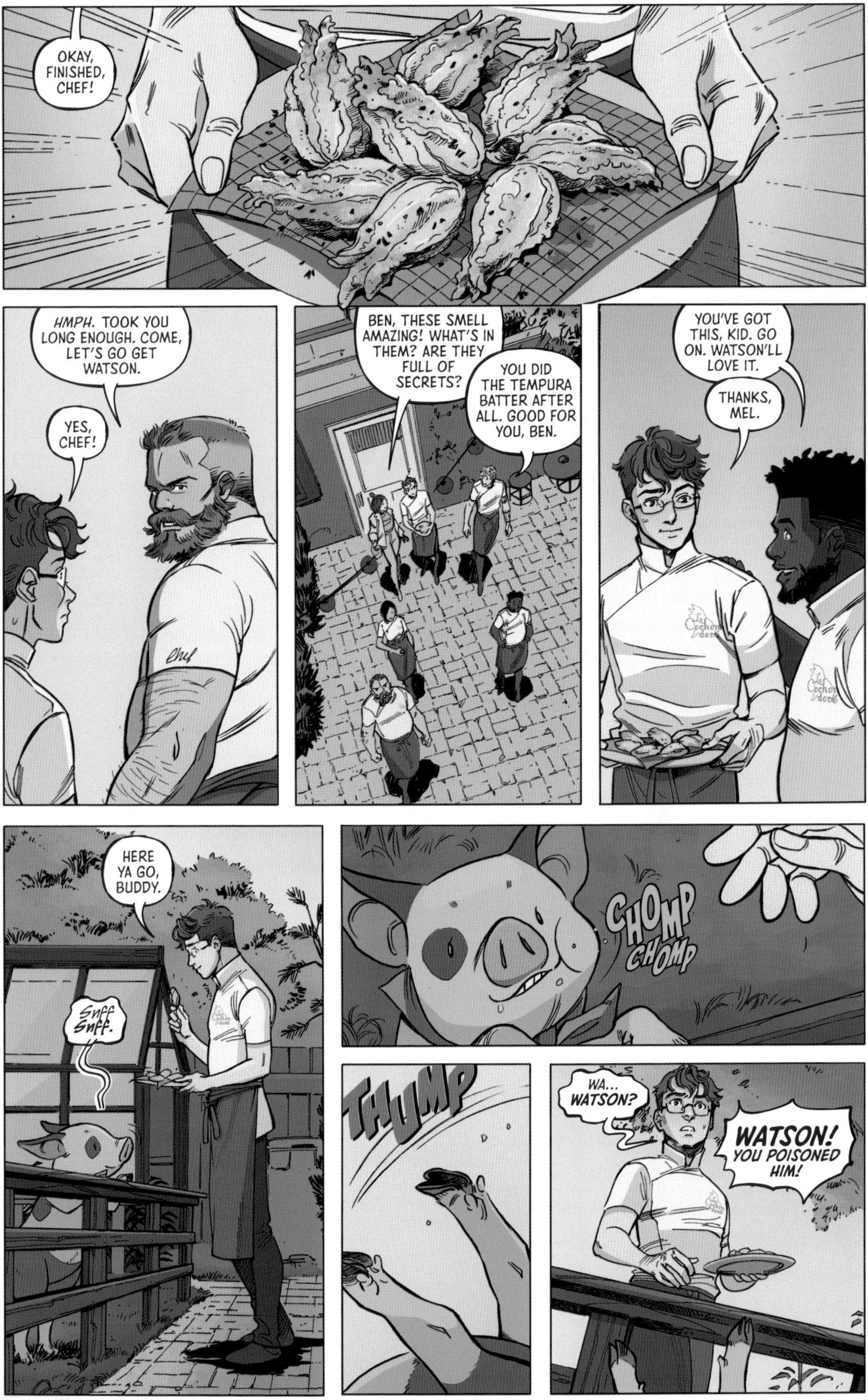
OKAY, FINISHED, CHEF!
HMPH. TOOK YOU LONG ENOUGH. COME, LET'S GO GET WATSON.
YES, CHEF!
BEN, THESE SMELL AMAZING! WHAT'S IN THEM? ARE THEY FULL OF SECRETS?
YOU DID THE TEMPURA BATTER AFTER ALL. GOOD FOR YOU, BEN.
YOU'VE GOT THIS, KID. GO ON. WATSON'LL LOVE IT.
THANKS, MEL.
HERE YA GO, BUDDY.
SNFF SNFF.
CHOMP CHOMP
THUMP
WA... WATSON?
WATSON! YOU POISONED HIM!

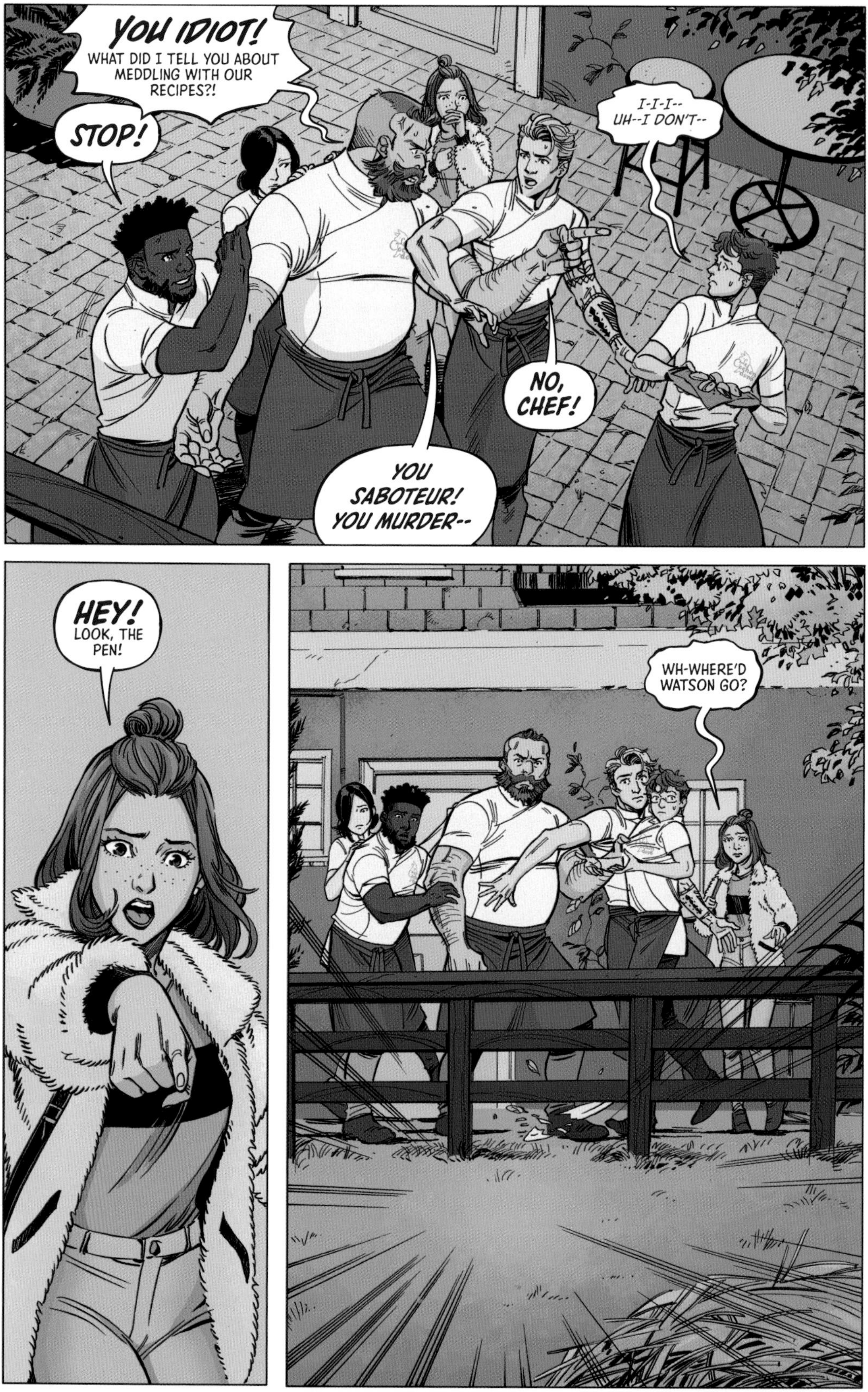
YOU IDIOT! WHAT DID I TELL YOU ABOUT MEDDLING WITH OUR RECIPES?!
STOP!
I-I-I-- UH--I DON'T--
NO, CHEF!
YOU SABOTEUR! YOU MURDER--
HEY! LOOK, THE PEN!
WH-WHERE'D WATSON GO?

Chapter Three

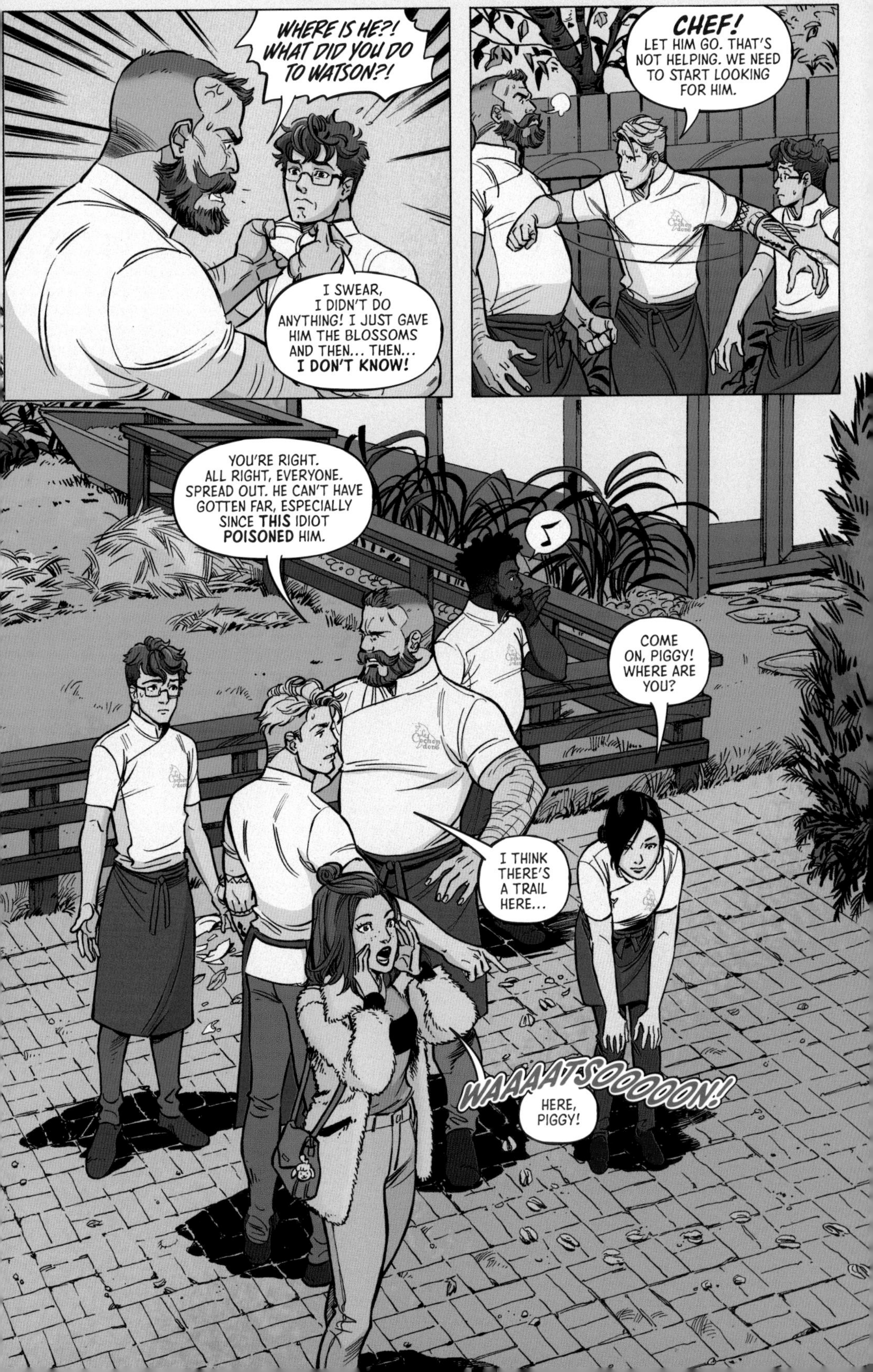
WHERE IS HE?! WHAT DID YOU DO TO WATSON?!
I SWEAR, I DIDN'T DO ANYTHING! I JUST GAVE HIM THE BLOSSOMS AND THEN... THEN... I DON'T KNOW!
CHEF! LET HIM GO. THAT'S NOT HELPING. WE NEED TO START LOOKING FOR HIM.
YOU'RE RIGHT. ALL RIGHT, EVERYONE. SPREAD OUT. HE CAN'T HAVE GOTTEN FAR, ESPECIALLY SINCE THIS IDIOT POISONED HIM.
COME ON, PIGGY! WHERE ARE YOU?
I THINK THERE'S A TRAIL HERE...
WAAAATSOOOOOON!
HERE, PIGGY!

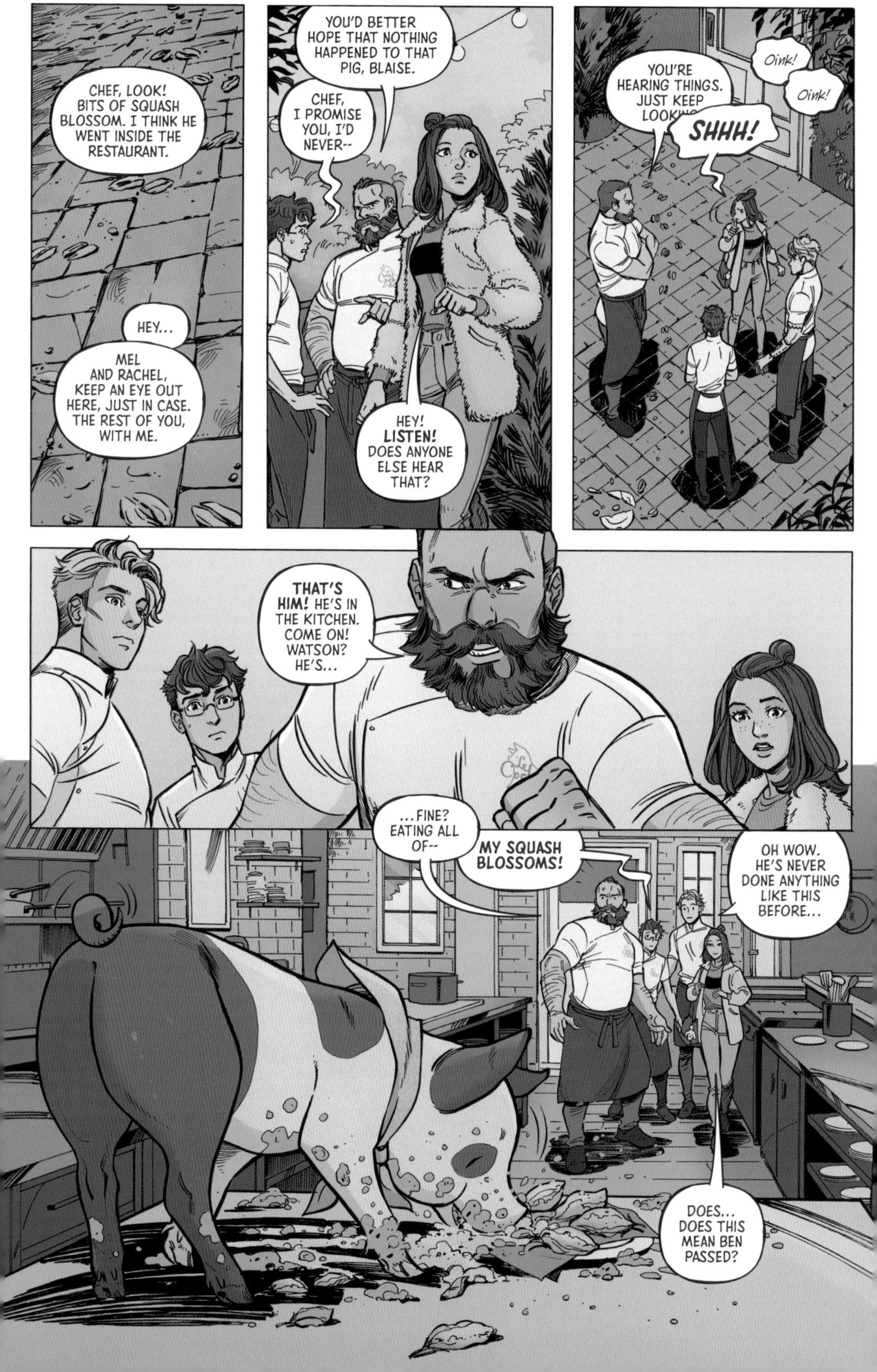
CHEF, LOOK! BITS OF SQUASH BLOSSOM. I THINK HE WENT INSIDE THE RESTAURANT.
HEY...
MEL AND RACHEL, KEEP AN EYE OUT HERE, JUST IN CASE. THE REST OF YOU, WITH ME.
YOU'D BETTER HOPE THAT NOTHING HAPPENED TO THAT PIG, BLAISE.
CHEF, I PROMISE YOU, I'D NEVER--
HEY! LISTEN! DOES ANYONE ELSE HEAR THAT?
Oink!
Oink!
YOU'RE HEARING THINGS. JUST KEEP LOOKING--
SHHH!
THAT'S HIM! HE'S IN THE KITCHEN. COME ON! WATSON? HE'S...
...FINE? EATING ALL OF--
MY SQUASH BLOSSOMS!
OH WOW. HE'S NEVER DONE ANYTHING LIKE THIS BEFORE...
DOES... DOES THIS MEAN BEN PASSED?

I THINK YOU OWE BEN AN APOLOGY, CHEF.

HMPH. SORRY FOR CALLING YOU A MURDERER.

IT'S OKAY, CHEF. I'M JUST GLAD WATSON'S OKAY. BUT I DON'T UNDERSTAND...

YES, SOME **DIRTY** PIG. I'M TAKING HIM HOME TO GIVE HIM A BATH.

LIAM, PAY BORT AND ISSUE NEXT WEEK'S CHALLENGE. BORT, YOU LIVE TO COOK ANOTHER DAY.

Oink!

HE WAS ACTING SICK, AS IF HE KNEW DAVIS WOULD FLIP OUT AND DISTRACT EVERYONE SO HE COULD SNEAK AWAY AND STEAL THE SQUASH BLOSSOMS. YOU'RE SOME PIG, WATSON.

YES, CHEF. CONGRATULATIONS, BEN. LOOKS LIKE—

AND SOMEBODY CLEAN UP THIS MESS! UNBELIEVABLE...

WELL, THAT WAS EXCITING. IS EVERY DAY LIKE THIS?

SORT OF. IT'S NOT YOUR USUAL RESTAURANT.

COME ON, LET'S LET THE OTHERS KNOW WATSON'S OKAY.

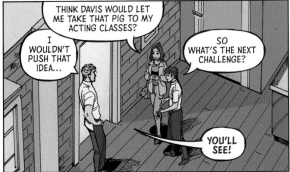

THINK DAVIS WOULD LET ME TAKE THAT PIG TO MY ACTING CLASSES?

I WOULDN'T PUSH THAT IDEA...

SO WHAT'S THE NEXT CHALLENGE?

YOU'LL SEE!

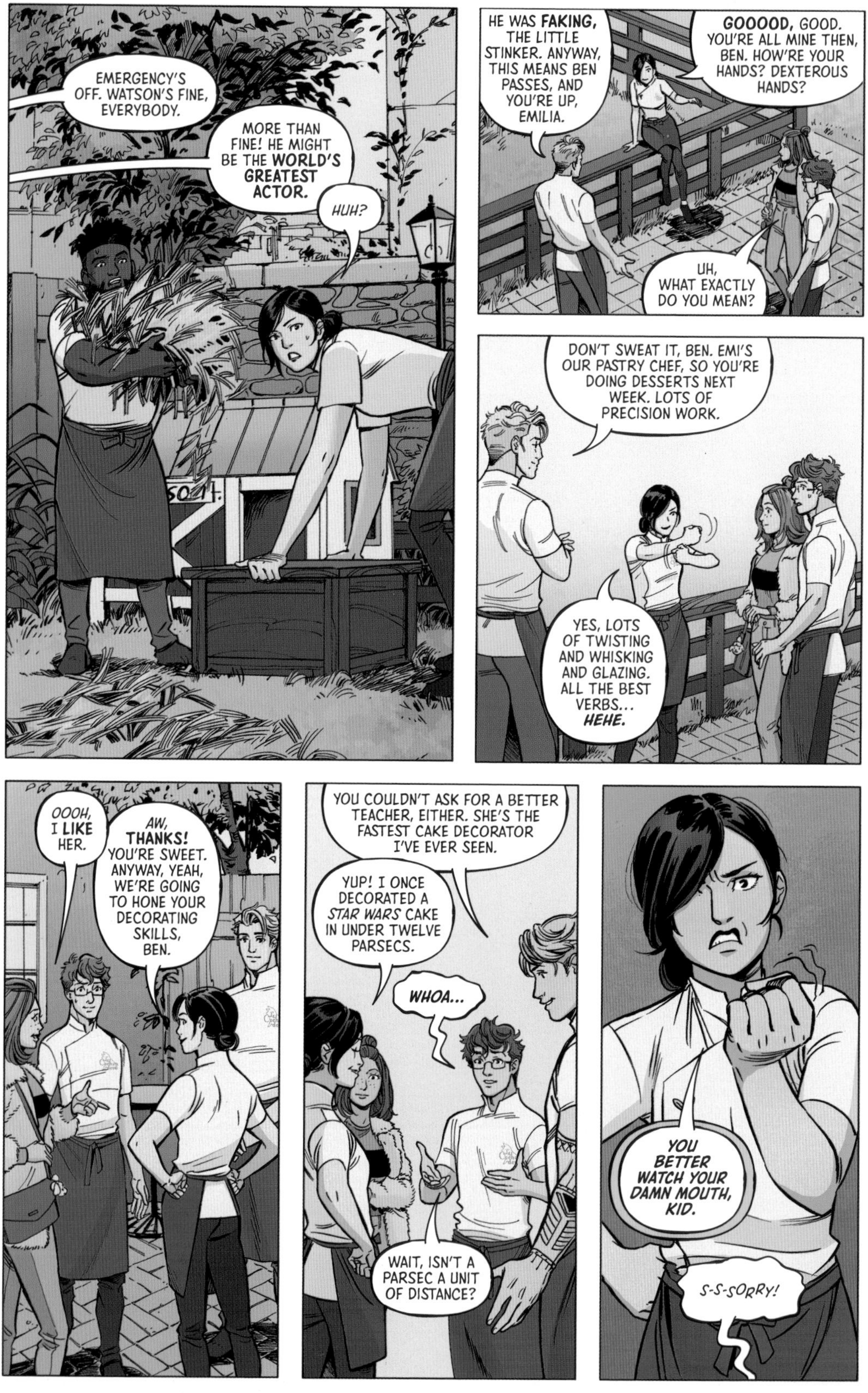
EMERGENCY'S OFF. WATSON'S FINE, EVERYBODY.
MORE THAN FINE! HE MIGHT BE THE WORLD'S GREATEST ACTOR.
HUH?
HE WAS FAKING, THE LITTLE STINKER. ANYWAY, THIS MEANS BEN PASSES, AND YOU'RE UP, EMILIA.
GOOOOD, GOOD. YOU'RE ALL MINE THEN, BEN. HOW'RE YOUR HANDS? DEXTEROUS HANDS?
UH, WHAT EXACTLY DO YOU MEAN?
DON'T SWEAT IT, BEN. EMI'S OUR PASTRY CHEF, SO YOU'RE DOING DESSERTS NEXT WEEK. LOTS OF PRECISION WORK.
YES, LOTS OF TWISTING AND WHISKING AND GLAZING. ALL THE BEST VERBS... HEHE.
OOOH, I LIKE HER.
AW, THANKS! YOU'RE SWEET. ANYWAY, YEAH, WE'RE GOING TO HONE YOUR DECORATING SKILLS, BEN.
YOU COULDN'T ASK FOR A BETTER TEACHER, EITHER. SHE'S THE FASTEST CAKE DECORATOR I'VE EVER SEEN.
YUP! I ONCE DECORATED A STAR WARS CAKE IN UNDER TWELVE PARSECS.
WHOA...
WAIT, ISN'T A PARSEC A UNIT OF DISTANCE?
YOU BETTER WATCH YOUR DAMN MOUTH, KID.
S-S-SORRY!

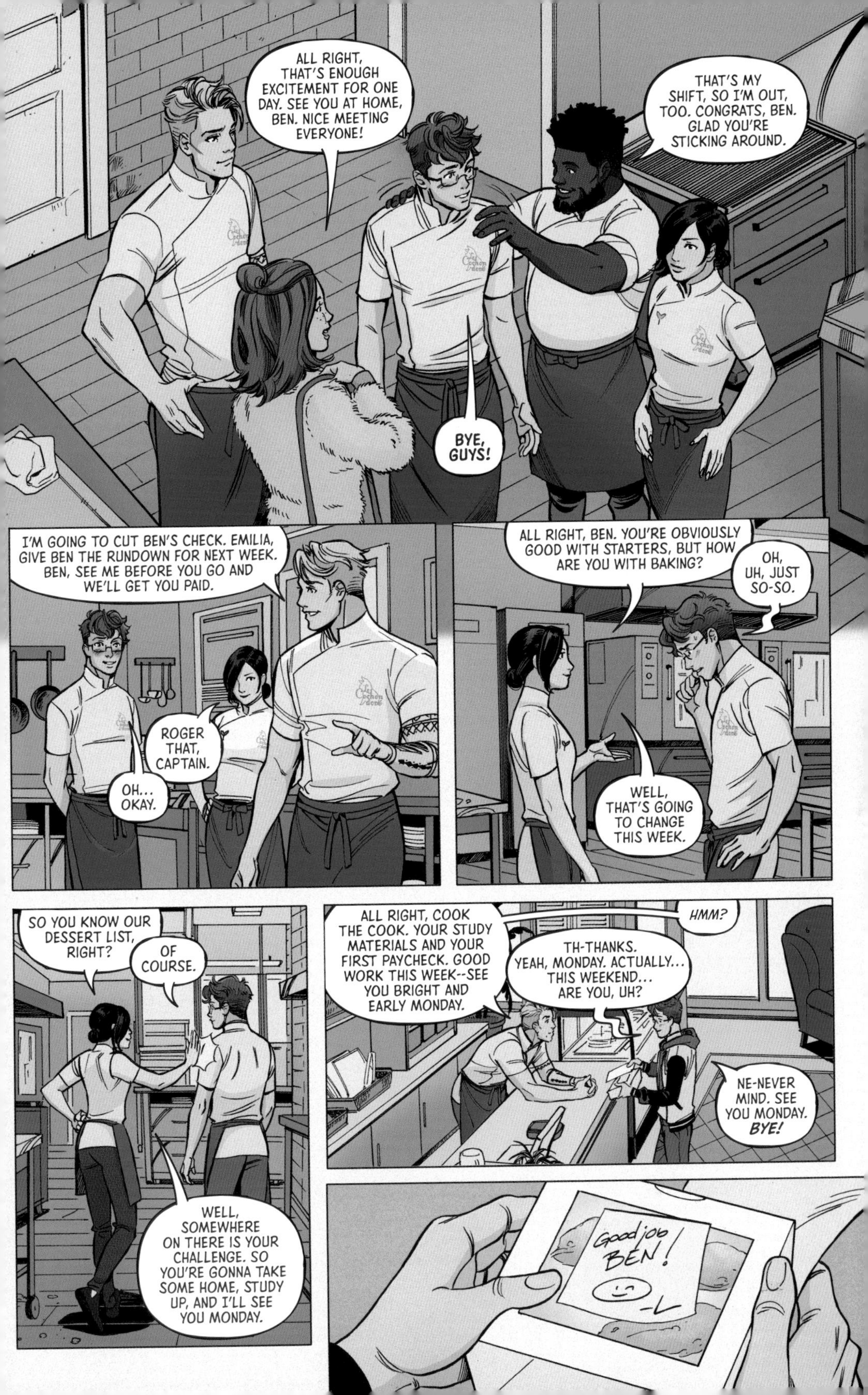
ALL RIGHT, THAT'S ENOUGH EXCITEMENT FOR ONE DAY. SEE YOU AT HOME, BEN. NICE MEETING EVERYONE!
THAT'S MY SHIFT, SO I'M OUT, TOO. CONGRATS, BEN. GLAD YOU'RE STICKING AROUND.
BYE, GUYS!
I'M GOING TO CUT BEN'S CHECK. EMILIA, GIVE BEN THE RUNDOWN FOR NEXT WEEK. BEN, SEE ME BEFORE YOU GO AND WE'LL GET YOU PAID.
ROGER THAT, CAPTAIN.
OH... OKAY.
ALL RIGHT, BEN. YOU'RE OBVIOUSLY GOOD WITH STARTERS, BUT HOW ARE YOU WITH BAKING?
OH, UH, JUST SO-SO.
WELL, THAT'S GOING TO CHANGE THIS WEEK.
SO YOU KNOW OUR DESSERT LIST, RIGHT?
OF COURSE.
WELL, SOMEWHERE ON THERE IS YOUR CHALLENGE. SO YOU'RE GONNA TAKE SOME HOME, STUDY UP, AND I'LL SEE YOU MONDAY.
ALL RIGHT, COOK THE COOK. YOUR STUDY MATERIALS AND YOUR FIRST PAYCHECK. GOOD WORK THIS WEEK--SEE YOU BRIGHT AND EARLY MONDAY.
HMM?
TH-THANKS. YEAH, MONDAY. ACTUALLY... THIS WEEKEND... ARE YOU, UH?
NE-NEVER MIND. SEE YOU MONDAY. BYE!
Good job BEN! -L

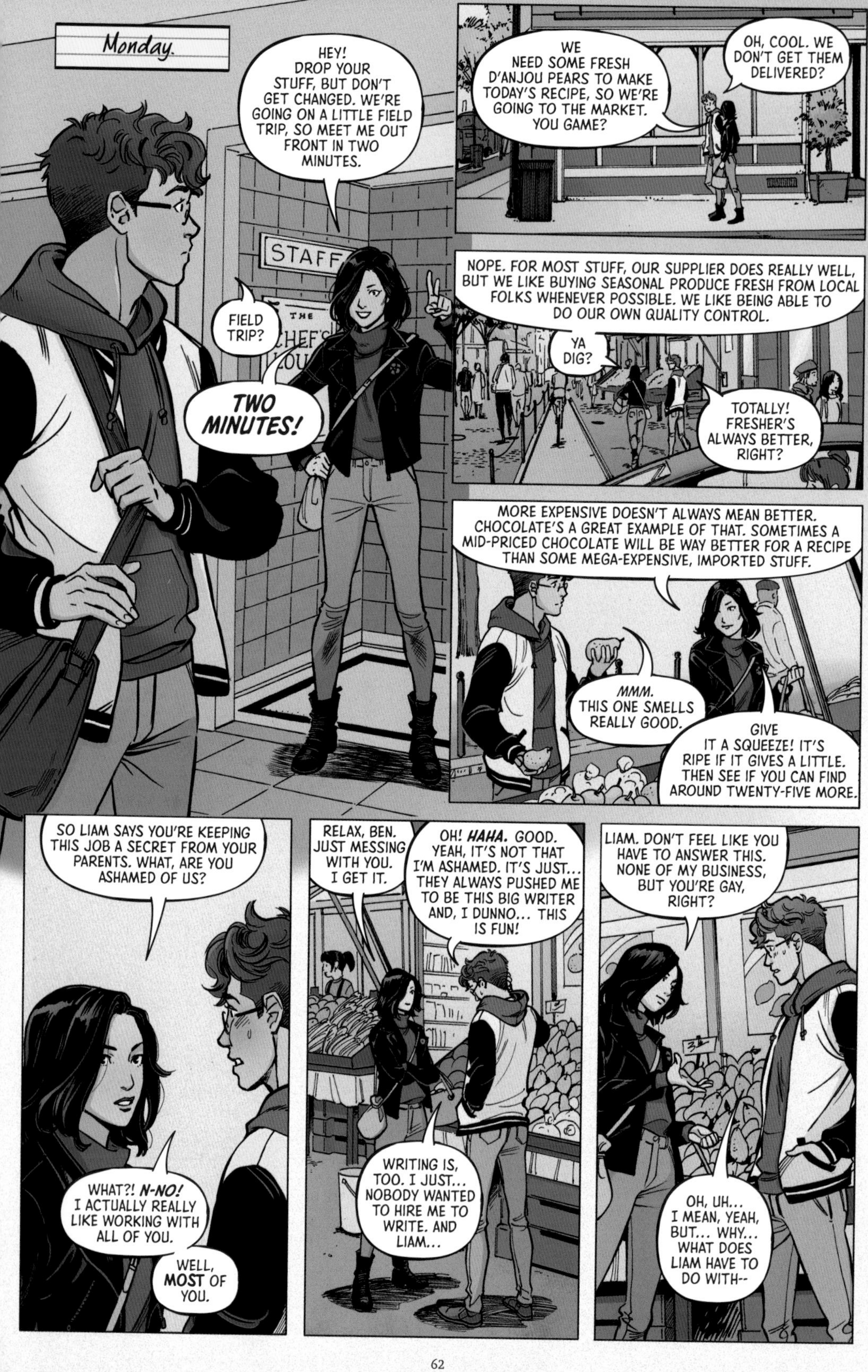
Monday.
HEY! DROP YOUR STUFF, BUT DON'T GET CHANGED. WE'RE GOING ON A LITTLE FIELD TRIP, SO MEET ME OUT FRONT IN TWO MINUTES.
STAFF
FIELD TRIP?
TWO MINUTES!
WE NEED SOME FRESH D'ANJOU PEARS TO MAKE TODAY'S RECIPE, SO WE'RE GOING TO THE MARKET. YOU GAME?
OH, COOL. WE DON'T GET THEM DELIVERED?
NOPE. FOR MOST STUFF, OUR SUPPLIER DOES REALLY WELL, BUT WE LIKE BUYING SEASONAL PRODUCE FRESH FROM LOCAL FOLKS WHENEVER POSSIBLE. WE LIKE BEING ABLE TO DO OUR OWN QUALITY CONTROL.
YA DIG?
TOTALLY! FRESHER'S ALWAYS BETTER, RIGHT?
MORE EXPENSIVE DOESN'T ALWAYS MEAN BETTER. CHOCOLATE'S A GREAT EXAMPLE OF THAT. SOMETIMES A MID-PRICED CHOCOLATE WILL BE WAY BETTER FOR A RECIPE THAN SOME MEGA-EXPENSIVE, IMPORTED STUFF.
MMM. THIS ONE SMELLS REALLY GOOD.
GIVE IT A SQUEEZE! IT'S RIPE IF IT GIVES A LITTLE. THEN SEE IF YOU CAN FIND AROUND TWENTY-FIVE MORE.
SO LIAM SAYS YOU'RE KEEPING THIS JOB A SECRET FROM YOUR PARENTS. WHAT, ARE YOU ASHAMED OF US?
WHAT?! N-NO! I ACTUALLY REALLY LIKE WORKING WITH ALL OF YOU.
WELL, MOST OF YOU.
RELAX, BEN. JUST MESSING WITH YOU. I GET IT.
OH! HAHA. GOOD. YEAH, IT'S NOT THAT I'M ASHAMED. IT'S JUST... THEY ALWAYS PUSHED ME TO BE THIS BIG WRITER AND, I DUNNO... THIS IS FUN!
WRITING IS, TOO. I JUST... NOBODY WANTED TO HIRE ME TO WRITE. AND LIAM...
LIAM. DON'T FEEL LIKE YOU HAVE TO ANSWER THIS. NONE OF MY BUSINESS, BUT YOU'RE GAY, RIGHT?
OH, UH... I MEAN, YEAH, BUT... WHY... WHAT DOES LIAM HAVE TO DO WITH--

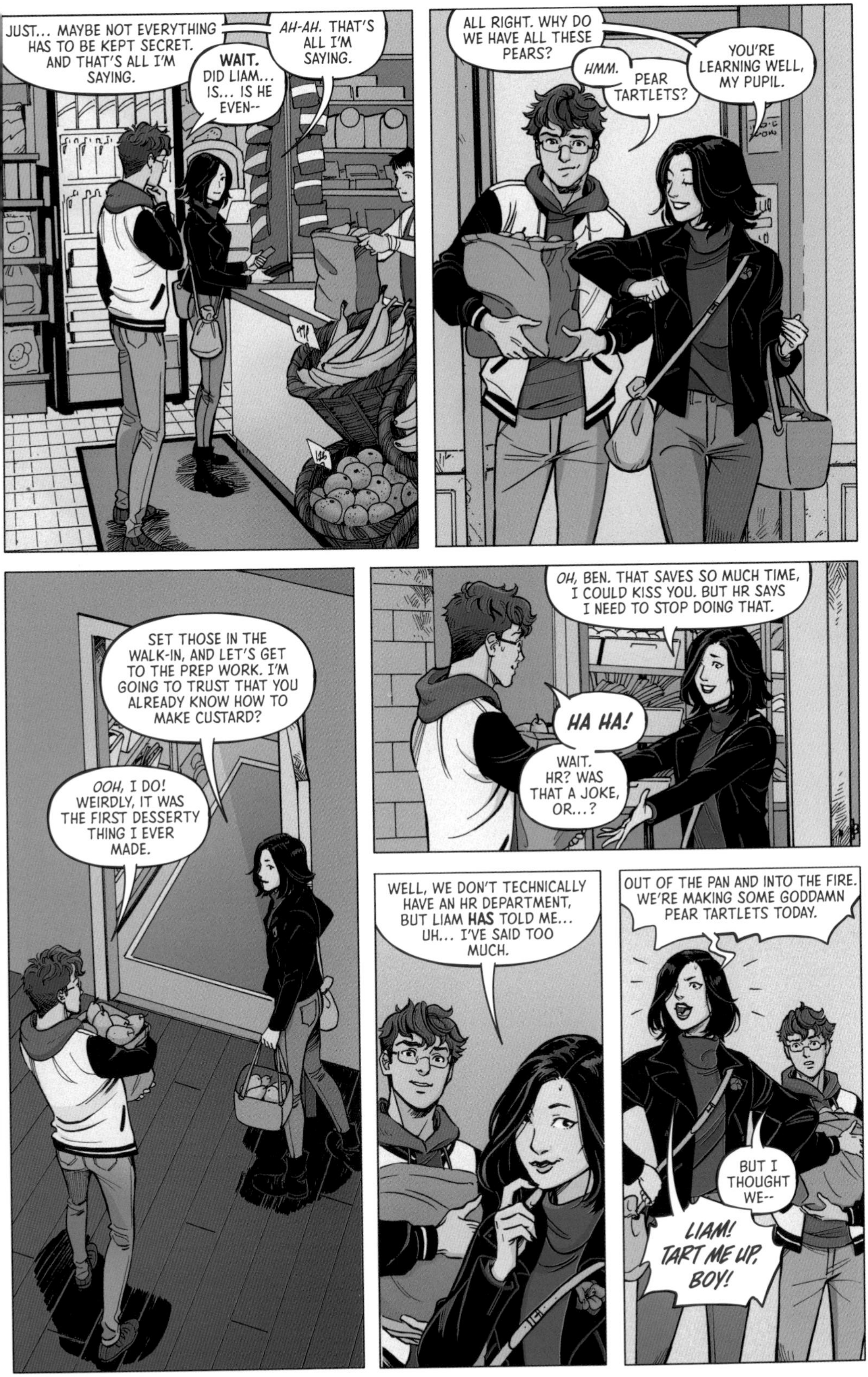

JUST... MAYBE NOT EVERYTHING HAS TO BE KEPT SECRET. AND THAT'S ALL I'M SAYING.
WAIT. DID LIAM... IS... IS HE EVEN--
AH-AH. THAT'S ALL I'M SAYING.
99¢
ALL RIGHT. WHY DO WE HAVE ALL THESE PEARS?
YOU'RE LEARNING WELL, MY PUPIL.
HMM. PEAR TARTLETS?
SET THOSE IN THE WALK-IN, AND LET'S GET TO THE PREP WORK. I'M GOING TO TRUST THAT YOU ALREADY KNOW HOW TO MAKE CUSTARD?
OOH, I DO! WEIRDLY, IT WAS THE FIRST DESSERTY THING I EVER MADE.
OH, BEN. THAT SAVES SO MUCH TIME, I COULD KISS YOU. BUT HR SAYS I NEED TO STOP DOING THAT.
HA HA!
WAIT. HR? WAS THAT A JOKE, OR...?
WELL, WE DON'T TECHNICALLY HAVE AN HR DEPARTMENT, BUT LIAM HAS TOLD ME... UH... I'VE SAID TOO MUCH.
OUT OF THE PAN AND INTO THE FIRE. WE'RE MAKING SOME GODDAMN PEAR TARTLETS TODAY.
BUT I THOUGHT WE--
LIAM! TART ME UP, BOY!

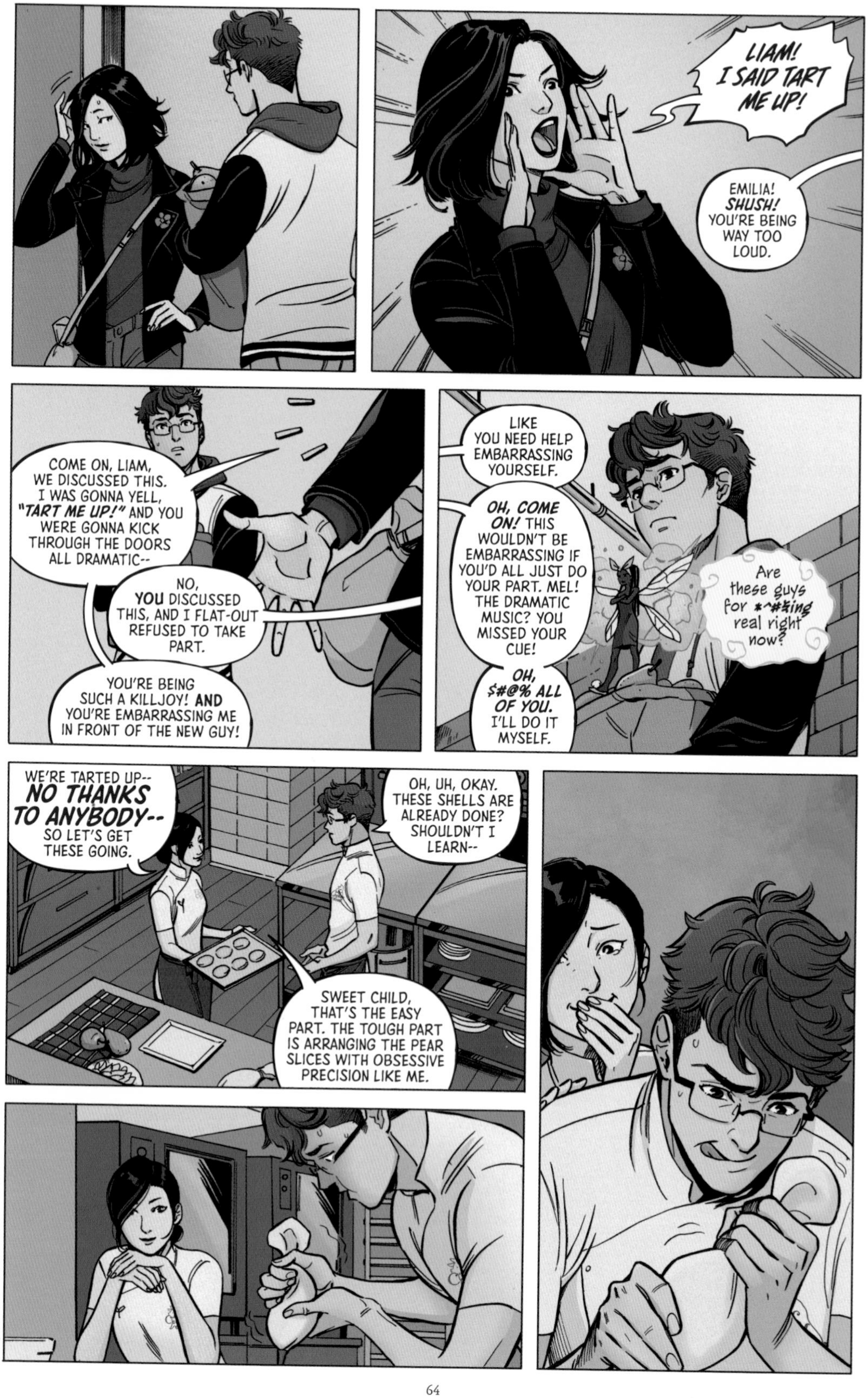
LIAM! I SAID TART ME UP!
EMILIA! SHUSH! YOU'RE BEING WAY TOO LOUD.
COME ON, LIAM, WE DISCUSSED THIS. I WAS GONNA YELL, "TART ME UP!" AND YOU WERE GONNA KICK THROUGH THE DOORS ALL DRAMATIC--
NO, YOU DISCUSSED THIS, AND I FLAT-OUT REFUSED TO TAKE PART.
YOU'RE BEING SUCH A KILLJOY! AND YOU'RE EMBARRASSING ME IN FRONT OF THE NEW GUY!
LIKE YOU NEED HELP EMBARRASSING YOURSELF.
OH, COME ON! THIS WOULDN'T BE EMBARRASSING IF YOU'D ALL JUST DO YOUR PART. MEL! THE DRAMATIC MUSIC? YOU MISSED YOUR CUE!
Are these guys for *^#%ing real right now?
OH, $#@% ALL OF YOU. I'LL DO IT MYSELF.
WE'RE TARTED UP-- NO THANKS TO ANYBODY-- SO LET'S GET THESE GOING.
OH, UH, OKAY. THESE SHELLS ARE ALREADY DONE? SHOULDN'T I LEARN--
SWEET CHILD, THAT'S THE EASY PART. THE TOUGH PART IS ARRANGING THE PEAR SLICES WITH OBSESSIVE PRECISION LIKE ME.

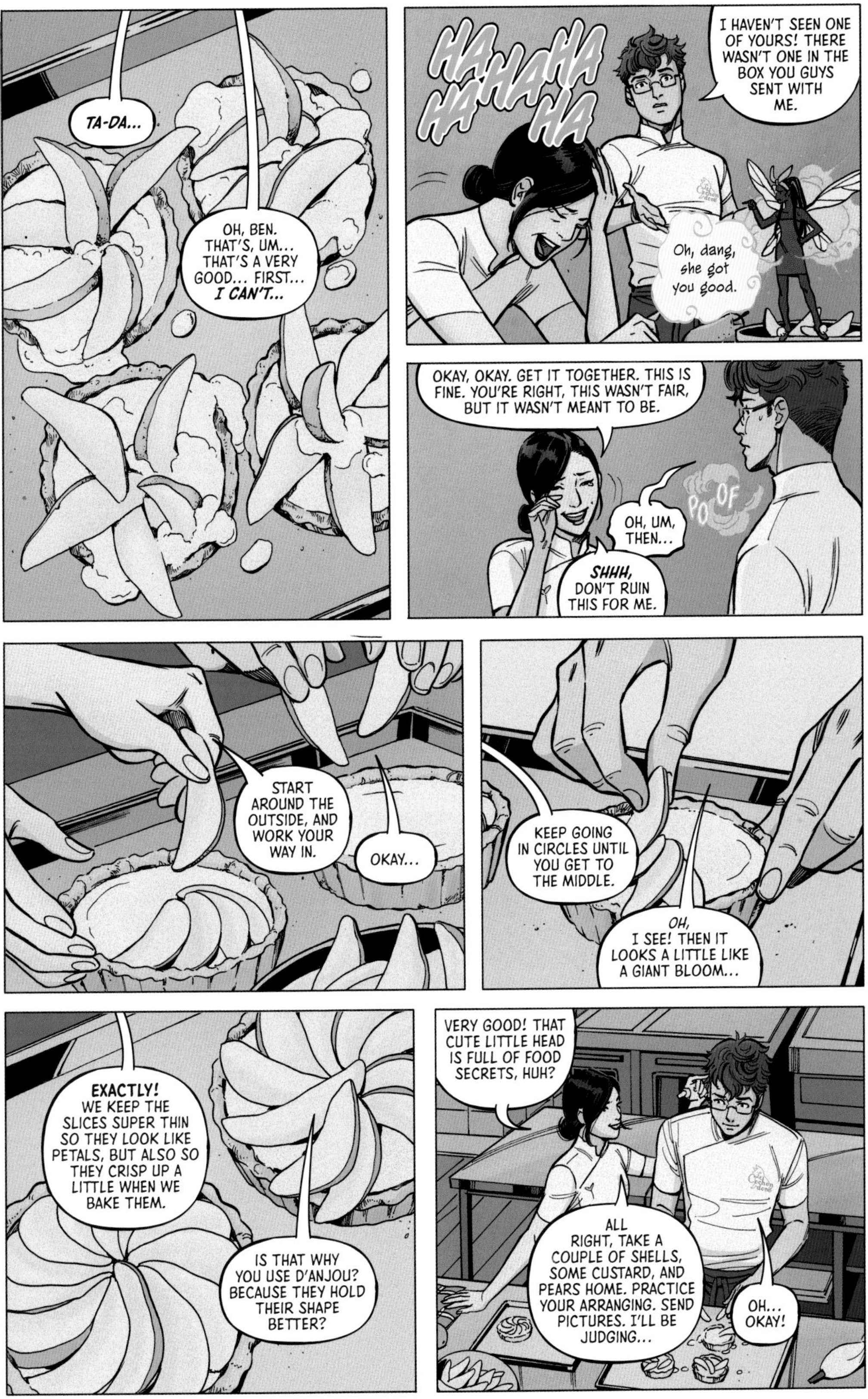
TA-DA...
OH, BEN. THAT'S, UM... THAT'S A VERY GOOD... FIRST... I CAN'T...
HAHAHAHA HAHAHA
I HAVEN'T SEEN ONE OF YOURS! THERE WASN'T ONE IN THE BOX YOU GUYS SENT WITH ME.
Oh, dang, she got you good.
OKAY, OKAY. GET IT TOGETHER. THIS IS FINE. YOU'RE RIGHT, THIS WASN'T FAIR, BUT IT WASN'T MEANT TO BE.
OH, UM, THEN...
POOF
SHHH, DON'T RUIN THIS FOR ME.
START AROUND THE OUTSIDE, AND WORK YOUR WAY IN.
OKAY...
KEEP GOING IN CIRCLES UNTIL YOU GET TO THE MIDDLE.
OH, I SEE! THEN IT LOOKS A LITTLE LIKE A GIANT BLOOM...
EXACTLY! WE KEEP THE SLICES SUPER THIN SO THEY LOOK LIKE PETALS, BUT ALSO SO THEY CRISP UP A LITTLE WHEN WE BAKE THEM.
IS THAT WHY YOU USE D'ANJOU? BECAUSE THEY HOLD THEIR SHAPE BETTER?
VERY GOOD! THAT CUTE LITTLE HEAD IS FULL OF FOOD SECRETS, HUH?
ALL RIGHT, TAKE A COUPLE OF SHELLS, SOME CUSTARD, AND PEARS HOME. PRACTICE YOUR ARRANGING. SEND PICTURES. I'LL BE JUDGING...
OH... OKAY!

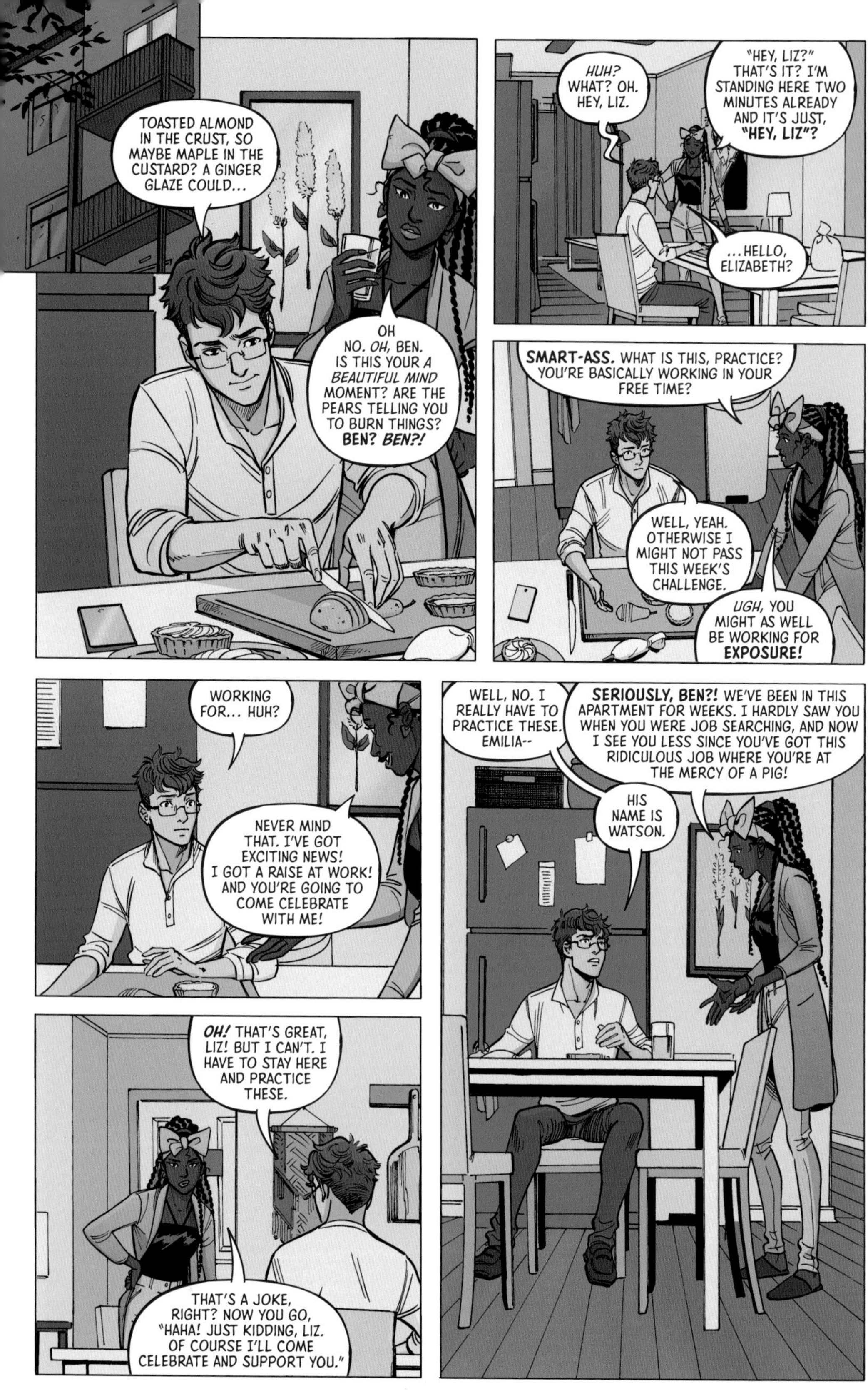
TOASTED ALMOND IN THE CRUST, SO MAYBE MAPLE IN THE CUSTARD? A GINGER GLAZE COULD...
OH NO. *OH*, BEN. IS THIS YOUR *A BEAUTIFUL MIND* MOMENT? ARE THE PEARS TELLING YOU TO BURN THINGS? **BEN? *BEN?!***
HUH? WHAT? OH. HEY, LIZ.
"HEY, LIZ?" THAT'S IT? I'M STANDING HERE TWO MINUTES ALREADY AND IT'S JUST, **"HEY, LIZ"?**
...HELLO, ELIZABETH?
SMART-ASS. WHAT IS THIS, PRACTICE? YOU'RE BASICALLY WORKING IN YOUR FREE TIME?
WELL, YEAH. OTHERWISE I MIGHT NOT PASS THIS WEEK'S CHALLENGE.
UGH, YOU MIGHT AS WELL BE WORKING FOR **EXPOSURE!**
WORKING FOR... HUH?
NEVER MIND THAT. I'VE GOT EXCITING NEWS! I GOT A RAISE AT WORK! AND YOU'RE GOING TO COME CELEBRATE WITH ME!
OH! THAT'S GREAT, LIZ! BUT I CAN'T. I HAVE TO STAY HERE AND PRACTICE THESE.
THAT'S A JOKE, RIGHT? NOW YOU GO, "HAHA! JUST KIDDING, LIZ. OF COURSE I'LL COME CELEBRATE AND SUPPORT YOU."
WELL, NO. I REALLY HAVE TO PRACTICE THESE. EMILIA--
SERIOUSLY, BEN?! WE'VE BEEN IN THIS APARTMENT FOR WEEKS. I HARDLY SAW YOU WHEN YOU WERE JOB SEARCHING, AND NOW I SEE YOU LESS SINCE YOU'VE GOT THIS RIDICULOUS JOB WHERE YOU'RE AT THE MERCY OF A PIG!
HIS NAME IS WATSON.

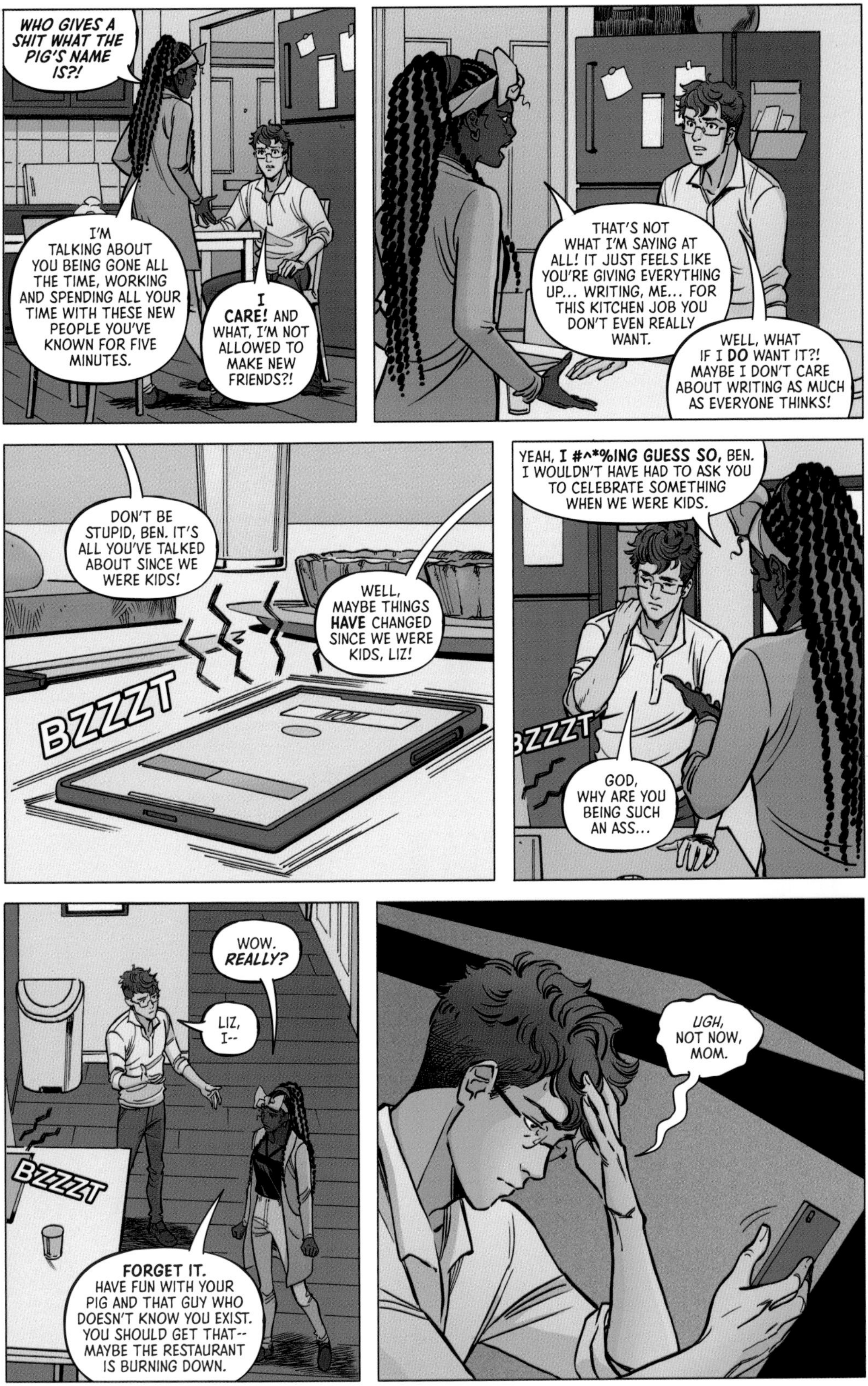
WHO GIVES A SHIT WHAT THE PIG'S NAME IS?!
I'M TALKING ABOUT YOU BEING GONE ALL THE TIME, WORKING AND SPENDING ALL YOUR TIME WITH THESE NEW PEOPLE YOU'VE KNOWN FOR FIVE MINUTES.
I CARE! AND WHAT, I'M NOT ALLOWED TO MAKE NEW FRIENDS?!
THAT'S NOT WHAT I'M SAYING AT ALL! IT JUST FEELS LIKE YOU'RE GIVING EVERYTHING UP... WRITING, ME... FOR THIS KITCHEN JOB YOU DON'T EVEN REALLY WANT.
WELL, WHAT IF I DO WANT IT?! MAYBE I DON'T CARE ABOUT WRITING AS MUCH AS EVERYONE THINKS!
DON'T BE STUPID, BEN. IT'S ALL YOU'VE TALKED ABOUT SINCE WE WERE KIDS!
WELL, MAYBE THINGS HAVE CHANGED SINCE WE WERE KIDS, LIZ!
BZZZT
YEAH, I #^*%ING GUESS SO, BEN. I WOULDN'T HAVE HAD TO ASK YOU TO CELEBRATE SOMETHING WHEN WE WERE KIDS.
BZZZT
GOD, WHY ARE YOU BEING SUCH AN ASS...
WOW. REALLY?
LIZ, I--
BZZZT
FORGET IT. HAVE FUN WITH YOUR PIG AND THAT GUY WHO DOESN'T KNOW YOU EXIST. YOU SHOULD GET THAT-- MAYBE THE RESTAURANT IS BURNING DOWN.
UGH, NOT NOW, MOM.

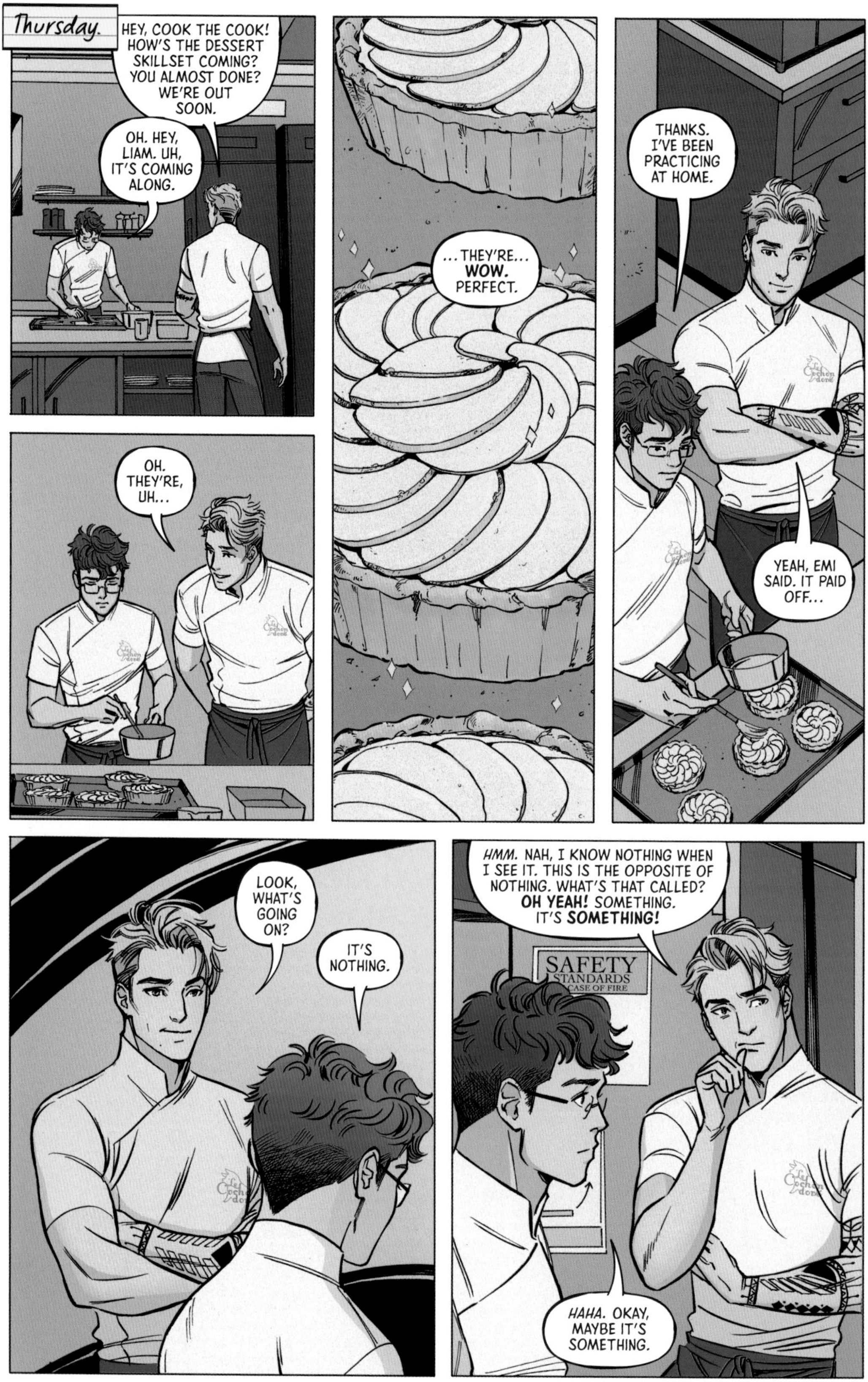
Thursday.
HEY, COOK THE COOK! HOW'S THE DESSERT SKILLSET COMING? YOU ALMOST DONE? WE'RE OUT SOON.
OH. HEY, LIAM. UH, IT'S COMING ALONG.
OH. THEY'RE, UH...
...THEY'RE... WOW. PERFECT.
THANKS. I'VE BEEN PRACTICING AT HOME.
YEAH, EMI SAID. IT PAID OFF...
LOOK, WHAT'S GOING ON?
IT'S NOTHING.
HMM. NAH, I KNOW NOTHING WHEN I SEE IT. THIS IS THE OPPOSITE OF NOTHING. WHAT'S THAT CALLED? OH YEAH! SOMETHING. IT'S SOMETHING!
SAFETY STANDARDS
CASE OF FIRE
HAHA. OKAY, MAYBE IT'S SOMETHING.

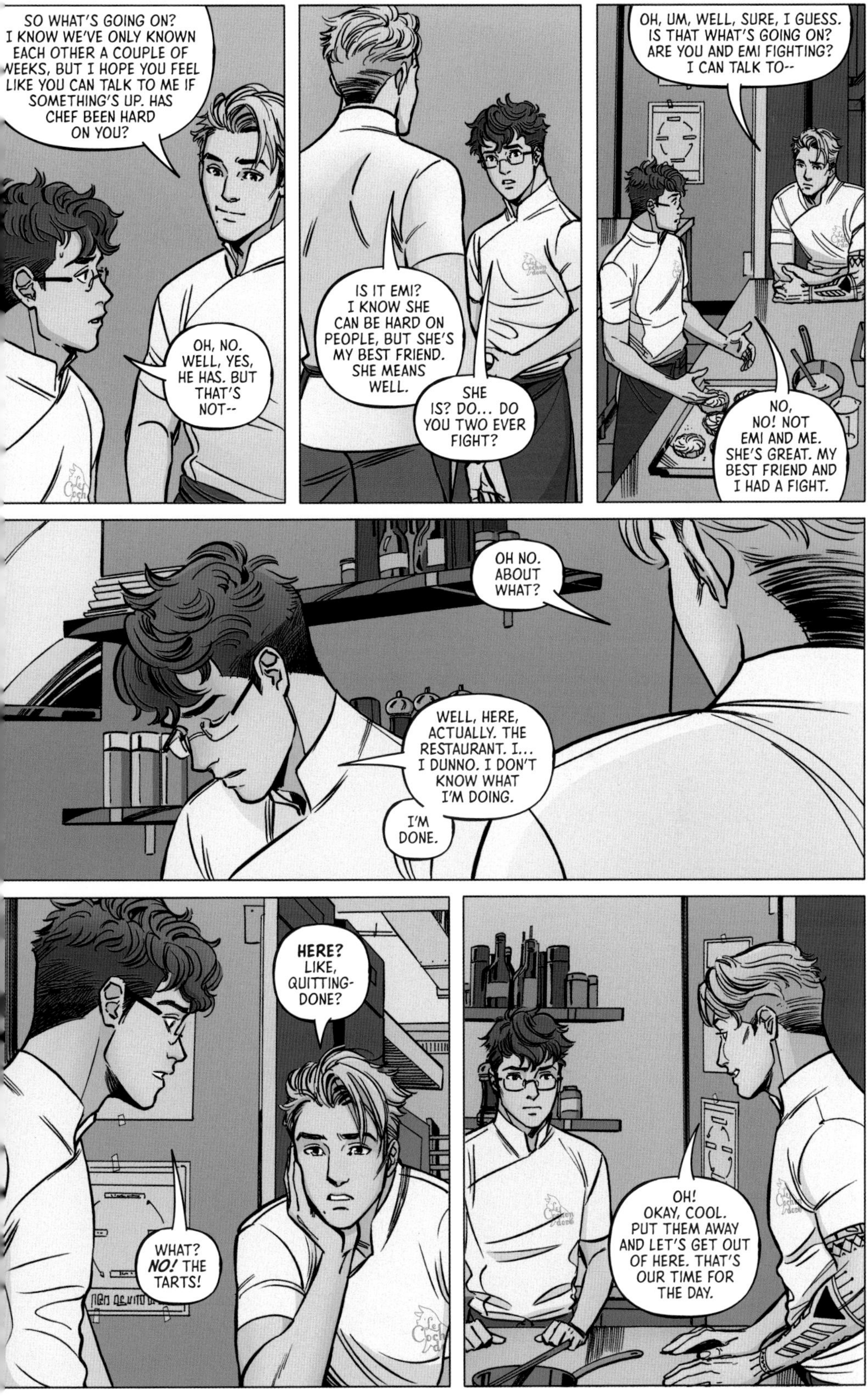
SO WHAT'S GOING ON? I KNOW WE'VE ONLY KNOWN EACH OTHER A COUPLE OF WEEKS, BUT I HOPE YOU FEEL LIKE YOU CAN TALK TO ME IF SOMETHING'S UP. HAS CHEF BEEN HARD ON YOU?
OH, NO. WELL, YES, HE HAS. BUT THAT'S NOT--
IS IT EMI? I KNOW SHE CAN BE HARD ON PEOPLE, BUT SHE'S MY BEST FRIEND. SHE MEANS WELL.
SHE IS? DO... DO YOU TWO EVER FIGHT?
OH, UM, WELL, SURE, I GUESS. IS THAT WHAT'S GOING ON? ARE YOU AND EMI FIGHTING? I CAN TALK TO--
NO, NO! NOT EMI AND ME. SHE'S GREAT. MY BEST FRIEND AND I HAD A FIGHT.
OH NO. ABOUT WHAT?
WELL, HERE, ACTUALLY. THE RESTAURANT. I... I DUNNO. I DON'T KNOW WHAT I'M DOING.
I'M DONE.
HERE? LIKE, QUITTING-DONE?
WHAT? NO! THE TARTS!
OH! OKAY, COOL. PUT THEM AWAY AND LET'S GET OUT OF HERE. THAT'S OUR TIME FOR THE DAY.

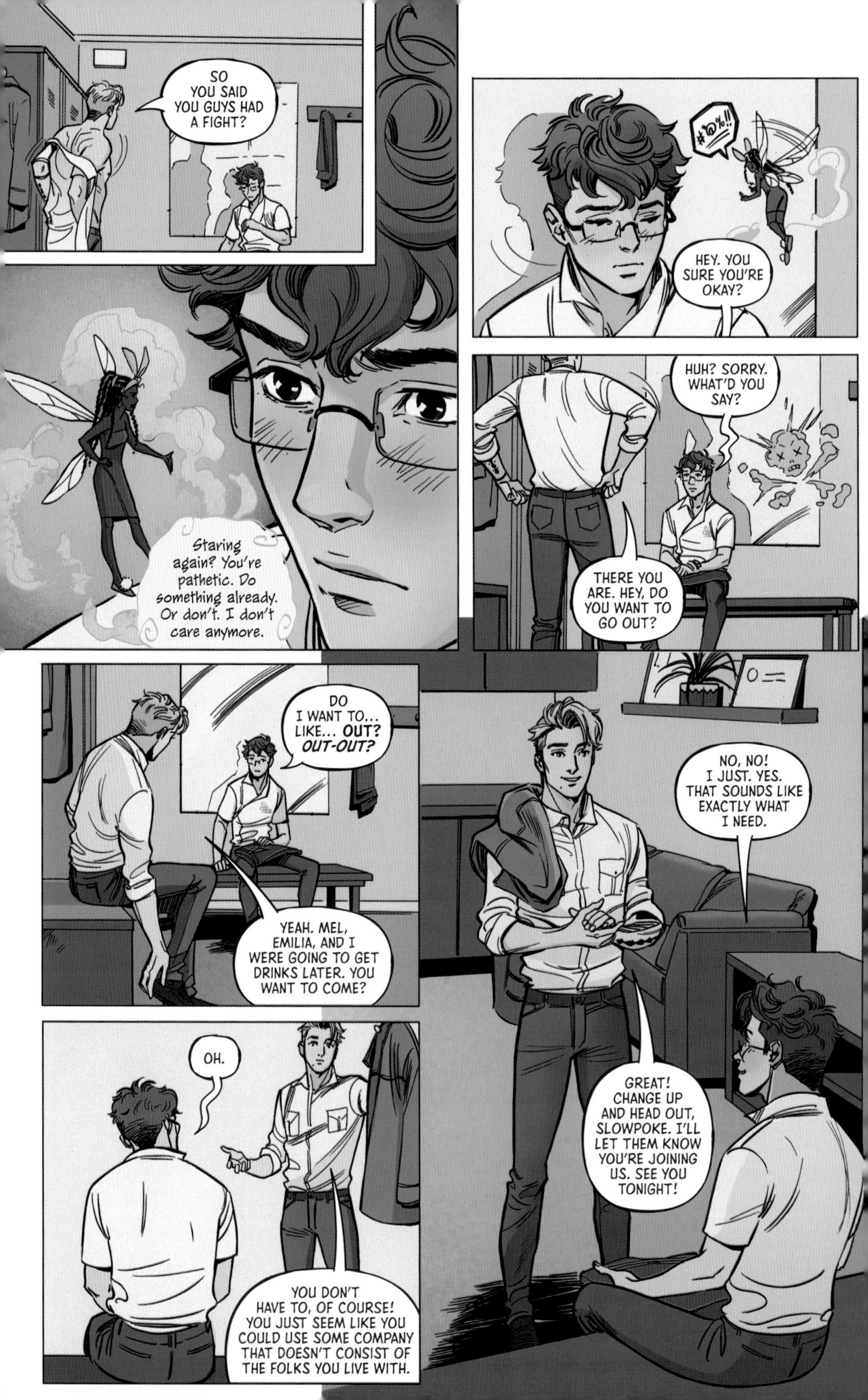
SO YOU SAID YOU GUYS HAD A FIGHT?
#@%!!
HEY. YOU SURE YOU'RE OKAY?
Staring again? You're pathetic. Do something already. Or don't. I don't care anymore.
HUH? SORRY. WHAT'D YOU SAY?
THERE YOU ARE. HEY, DO YOU WANT TO GO OUT?
DO I WANT TO... LIKE... **OUT? *OUT-OUT?***
YEAH. MEL, EMILIA, AND I WERE GOING TO GET DRINKS LATER. YOU WANT TO COME?
OH.
YOU DON'T HAVE TO, OF COURSE! YOU JUST SEEM LIKE YOU COULD USE SOME COMPANY THAT DOESN'T CONSIST OF THE FOLKS YOU LIVE WITH.
NO, NO! I JUST. YES. THAT SOUNDS LIKE EXACTLY WHAT I NEED.
GREAT! CHANGE UP AND HEAD OUT, SLOWPOKE. I'LL LET THEM KNOW YOU'RE JOINING US. SEE YOU TONIGHT!

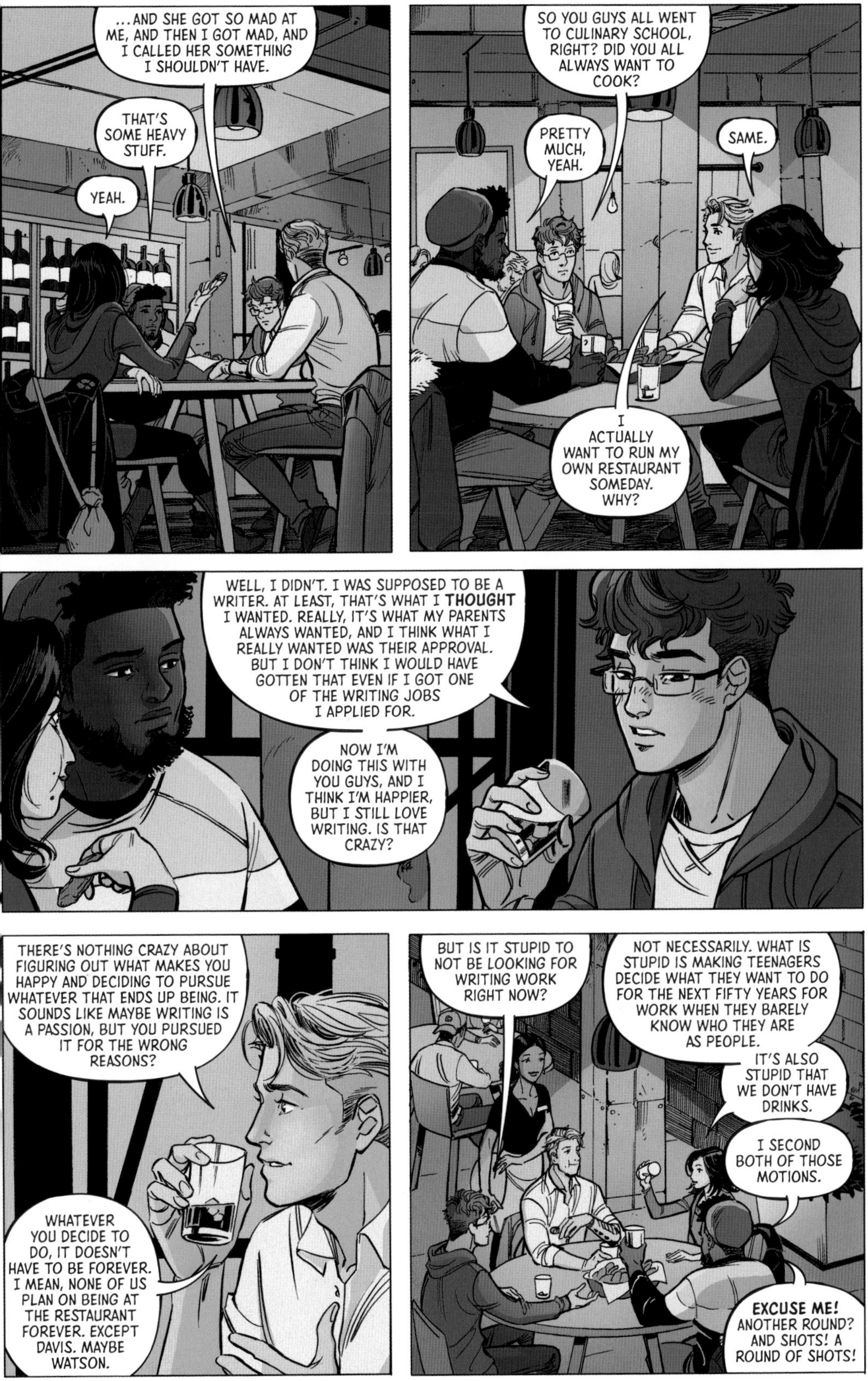
...AND SHE GOT SO MAD AT ME, AND THEN I GOT MAD, AND I CALLED HER SOMETHING I SHOULDN'T HAVE.
THAT'S SOME HEAVY STUFF.
YEAH.
SO YOU GUYS ALL WENT TO CULINARY SCHOOL, RIGHT? DID YOU ALL ALWAYS WANT TO COOK?
PRETTY MUCH, YEAH.
SAME.
I ACTUALLY WANT TO RUN MY OWN RESTAURANT SOMEDAY. WHY?
WELL, I DIDN'T. I WAS SUPPOSED TO BE A WRITER. AT LEAST, THAT'S WHAT I **THOUGHT** I WANTED. REALLY, IT'S WHAT MY PARENTS ALWAYS WANTED, AND I THINK WHAT I REALLY WANTED WAS THEIR APPROVAL. BUT I DON'T THINK I WOULD HAVE GOTTEN THAT EVEN IF I GOT ONE OF THE WRITING JOBS I APPLIED FOR.
NOW I'M DOING THIS WITH YOU GUYS, AND I THINK I'M HAPPIER, BUT I STILL LOVE WRITING. IS THAT CRAZY?
THERE'S NOTHING CRAZY ABOUT FIGURING OUT WHAT MAKES YOU HAPPY AND DECIDING TO PURSUE WHATEVER THAT ENDS UP BEING. IT SOUNDS LIKE MAYBE WRITING IS A PASSION, BUT YOU PURSUED IT FOR THE WRONG REASONS?
WHATEVER YOU DECIDE TO DO, IT DOESN'T HAVE TO BE FOREVER. I MEAN, NONE OF US PLAN ON BEING AT THE RESTAURANT FOREVER. EXCEPT DAVIS. MAYBE WATSON.
BUT IS IT STUPID TO NOT BE LOOKING FOR WRITING WORK RIGHT NOW?
NOT NECESSARILY. WHAT IS STUPID IS MAKING TEENAGERS DECIDE WHAT THEY WANT TO DO FOR THE NEXT FIFTY YEARS FOR WORK WHEN THEY BARELY KNOW WHO THEY ARE AS PEOPLE.
IT'S ALSO STUPID THAT WE DON'T HAVE DRINKS.
I SECOND BOTH OF THOSE MOTIONS.
EXCUSE ME! ANOTHER ROUND? AND SHOTS! A ROUND OF SHOTS!

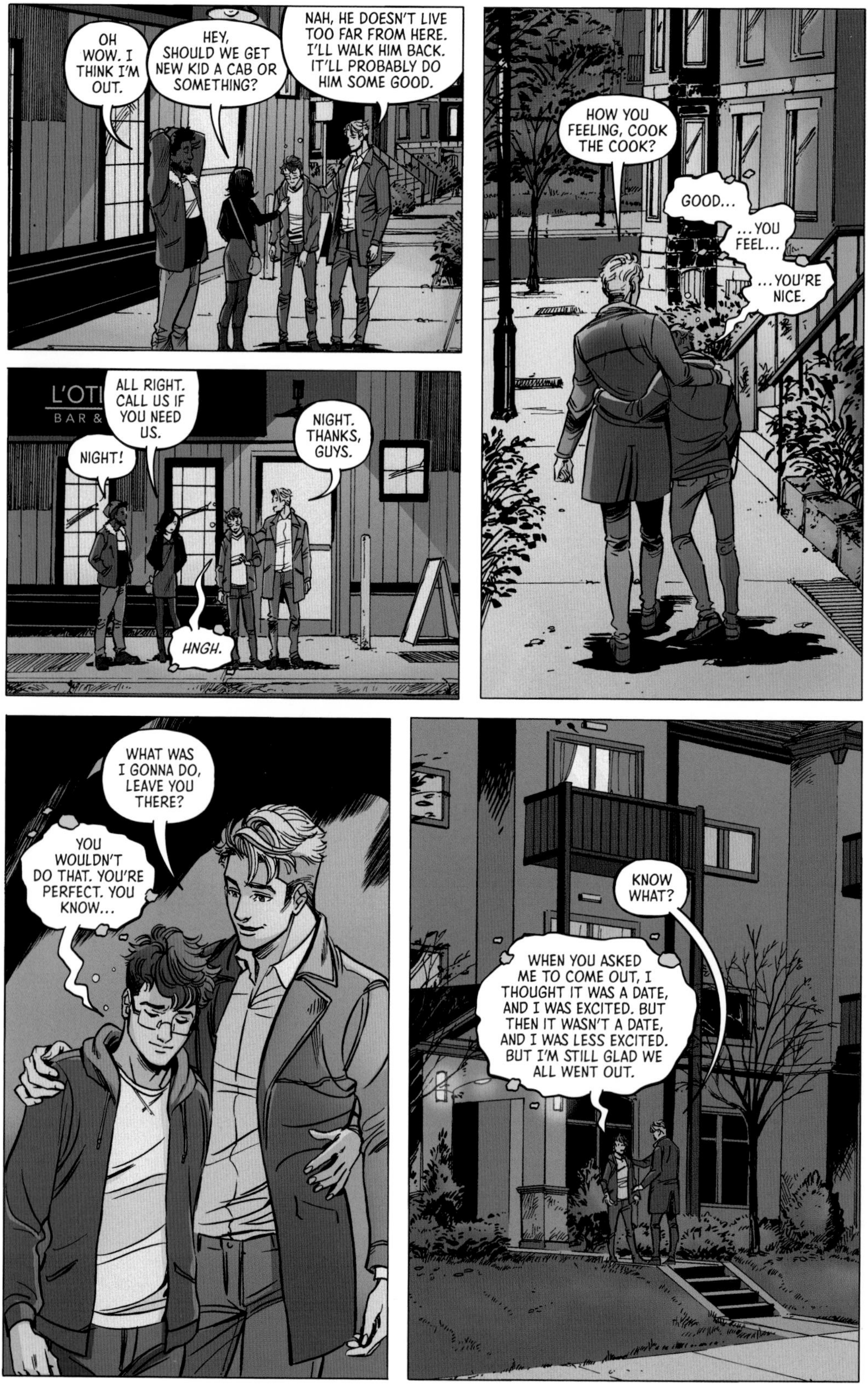
OH WOW. I THINK I'M OUT.
HEY, SHOULD WE GET NEW KID A CAB OR SOMETHING?
NAH, HE DOESN'T LIVE TOO FAR FROM HERE. I'LL WALK HIM BACK. IT'LL PROBABLY DO HIM SOME GOOD.
L'OTI
BAR &
ALL RIGHT. CALL US IF YOU NEED US.
NIGHT!
NIGHT. THANKS, GUYS.
HNGH.
HOW YOU FEELING, COOK THE COOK?
GOOD...
...YOU FEEL...
...YOU'RE NICE.
WHAT WAS I GONNA DO, LEAVE YOU THERE?
YOU WOULDN'T DO THAT. YOU'RE PERFECT. YOU KNOW...
KNOW WHAT?
WHEN YOU ASKED ME TO COME OUT, I THOUGHT IT WAS A DATE, AND I WAS EXCITED. BUT THEN IT WASN'T A DATE, AND I WAS LESS EXCITED. BUT I'M STILL GLAD WE ALL WENT OUT.

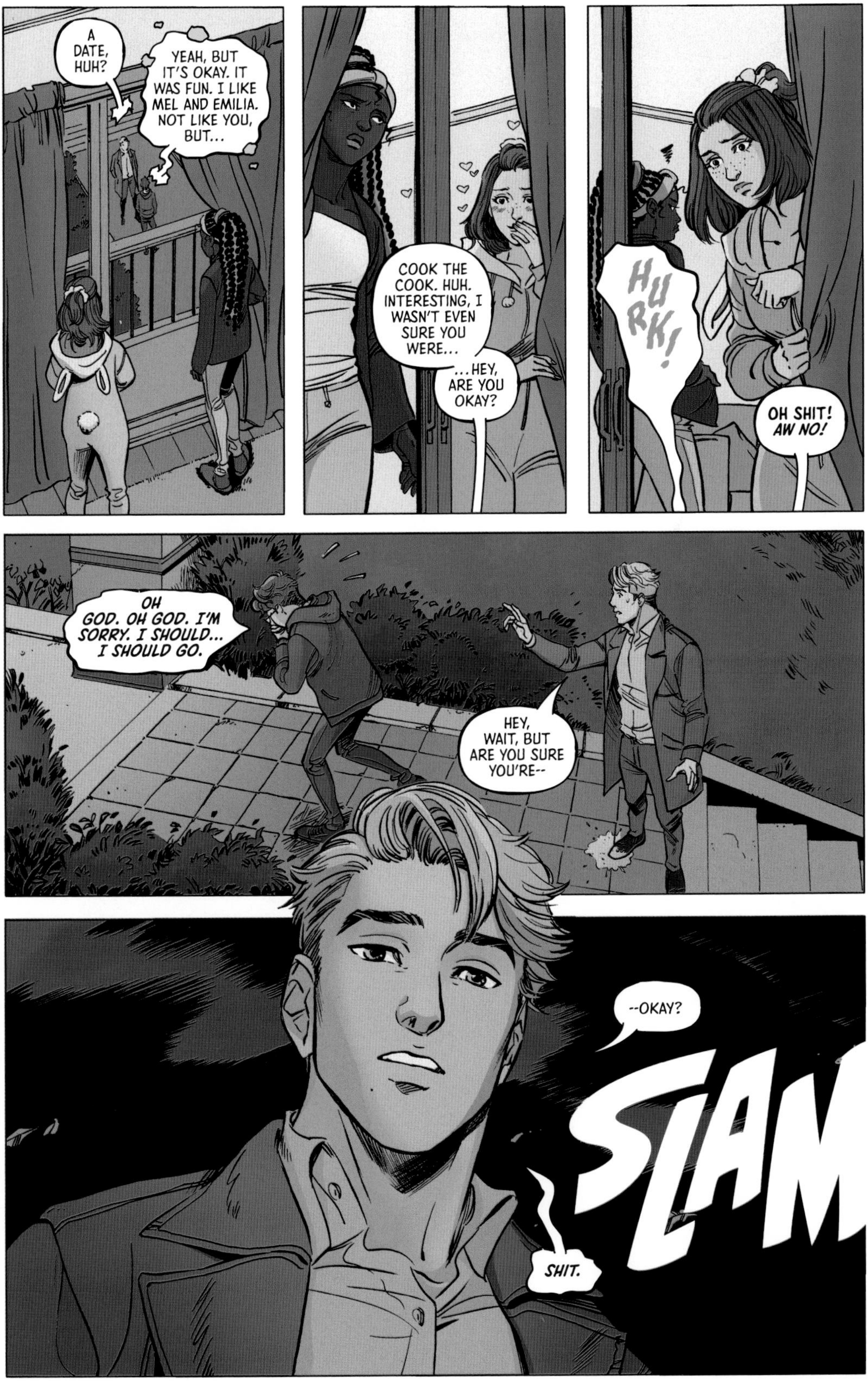
A DATE, HUH?
YEAH, BUT IT'S OKAY. IT WAS FUN. I LIKE MEL AND EMILIA. NOT LIKE YOU, BUT...
COOK THE COOK. HUH. INTERESTING, I WASN'T EVEN SURE YOU WERE...
...HEY, ARE YOU OKAY?
HURK!
OH SHIT! AW NO!
OH GOD. OH GOD. I'M SORRY. I SHOULD... I SHOULD GO.
HEY, WAIT, BUT ARE YOU SURE YOU'RE--
--OKAY?
SLAM
SHIT.

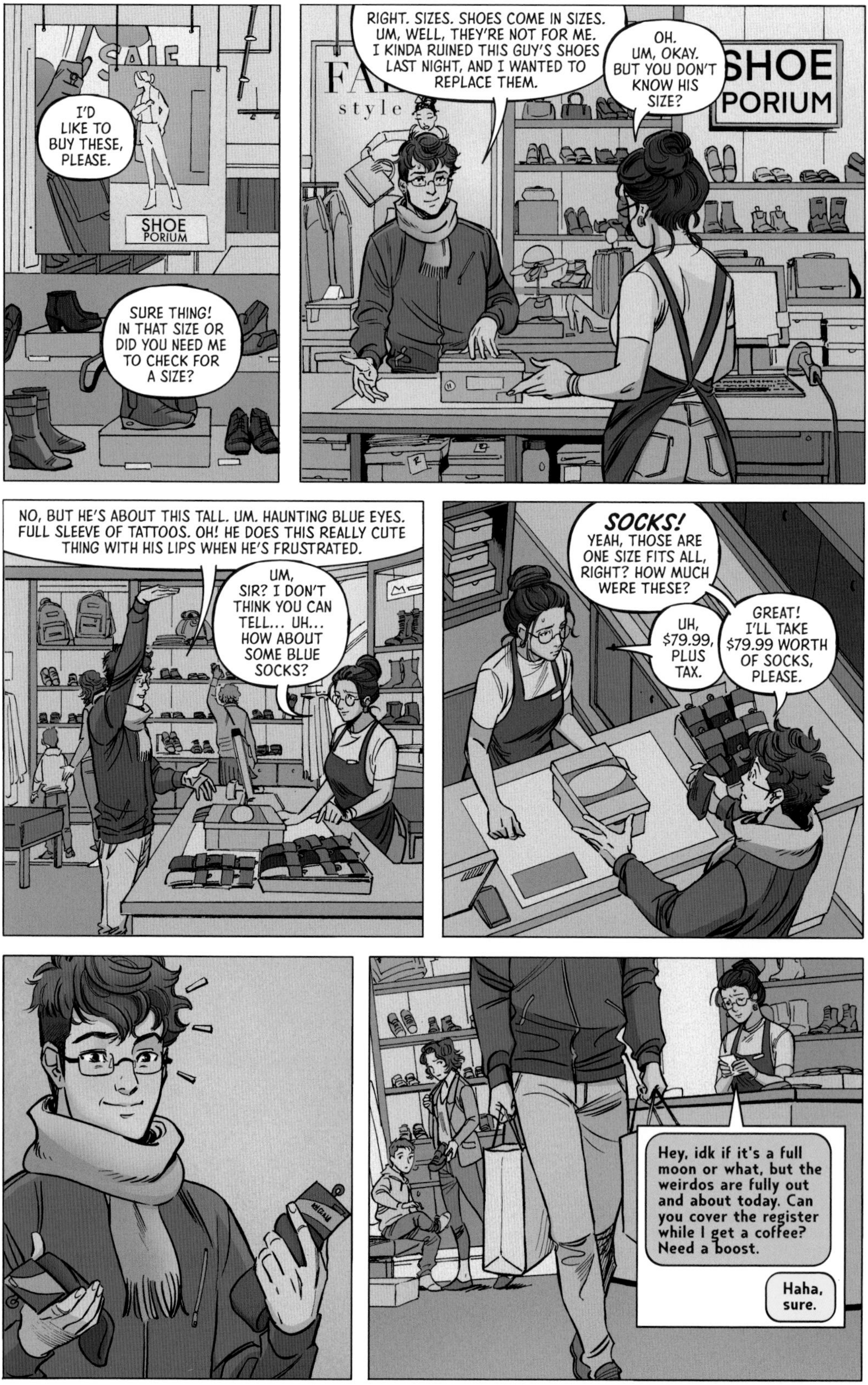
SALE
I'D LIKE TO BUY THESE, PLEASE.
SHOE PORIUM
SURE THING! IN THAT SIZE OR DID YOU NEED ME TO CHECK FOR A SIZE?
RIGHT. SIZES. SHOES COME IN SIZES. UM, WELL, THEY'RE NOT FOR ME. I KINDA RUINED THIS GUY'S SHOES LAST NIGHT, AND I WANTED TO REPLACE THEM.
OH. UM, OKAY. BUT YOU DON'T KNOW HIS SIZE?
SHOE PORIUM
NO, BUT HE'S ABOUT THIS TALL. UM. HAUNTING BLUE EYES. FULL SLEEVE OF TATTOOS. OH! HE DOES THIS REALLY CUTE THING WITH HIS LIPS WHEN HE'S FRUSTRATED.
UM, SIR? I DON'T THINK YOU CAN TELL... UH... HOW ABOUT SOME BLUE SOCKS?
SOCKS! YEAH, THOSE ARE ONE SIZE FITS ALL, RIGHT? HOW MUCH WERE THESE?
UH, $79.99, PLUS TAX.
GREAT! I'LL TAKE $79.99 WORTH OF SOCKS, PLEASE.
Hey, idk if it's a full moon or what, but the weirdos are fully out and about today. Can you cover the register while I get a coffee? Need a boost.
Haha, sure.

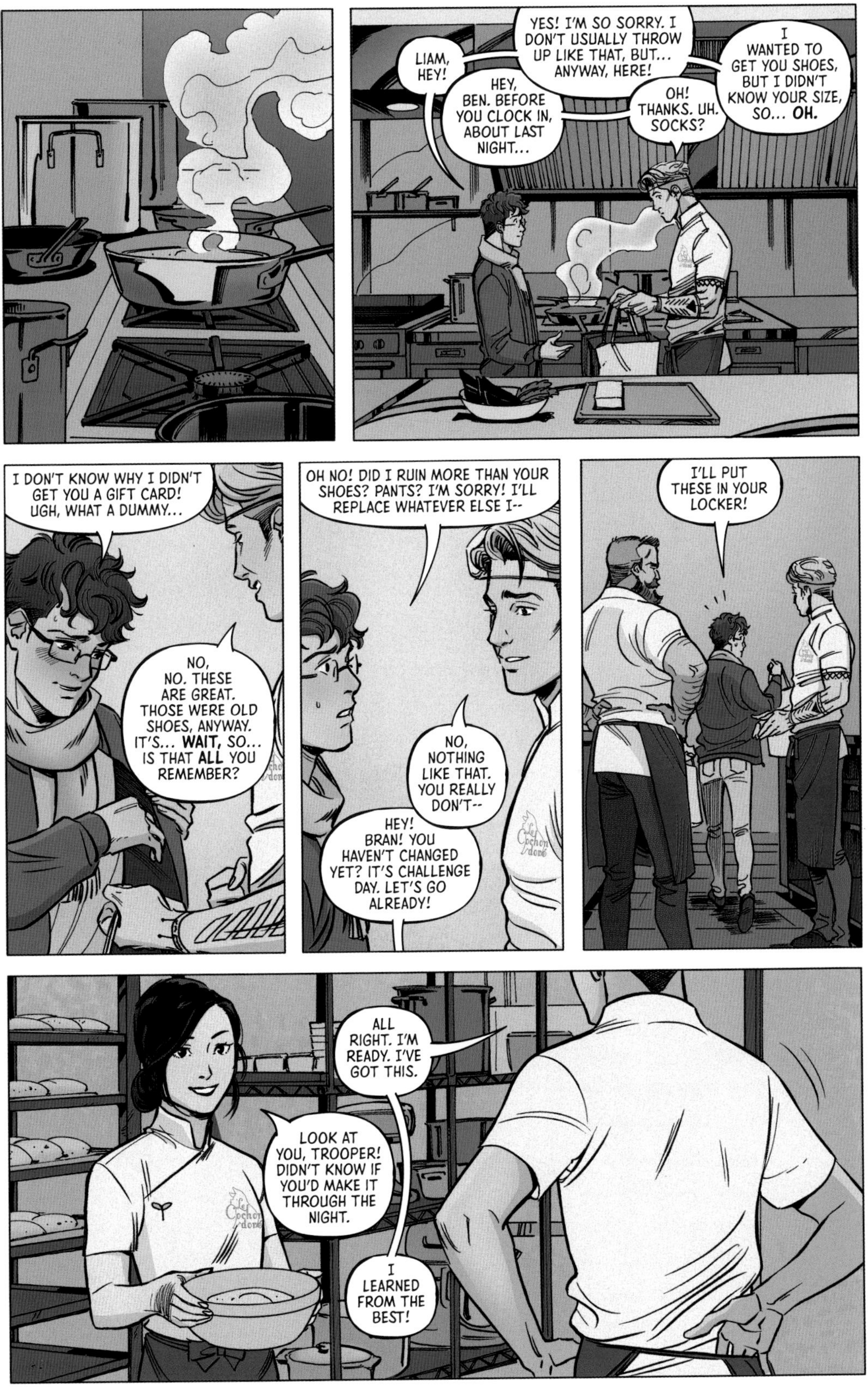
LIAM, HEY!
HEY, BEN. BEFORE YOU CLOCK IN, ABOUT LAST NIGHT...
YES! I'M SO SORRY. I DON'T USUALLY THROW UP LIKE THAT, BUT... ANYWAY, HERE!
OH! THANKS. UH. SOCKS?
I WANTED TO GET YOU SHOES, BUT I DIDN'T KNOW YOUR SIZE, SO... OH.
I DON'T KNOW WHY I DIDN'T GET YOU A GIFT CARD! UGH, WHAT A DUMMY...
NO, NO. THESE ARE GREAT. THOSE WERE OLD SHOES, ANYWAY. IT'S... WAIT, SO... IS THAT ALL YOU REMEMBER?
OH NO! DID I RUIN MORE THAN YOUR SHOES? PANTS? I'M SORRY! I'LL REPLACE WHATEVER ELSE I--
NO, NOTHING LIKE THAT. YOU REALLY DON'T--
HEY! BRAN! YOU HAVEN'T CHANGED YET? IT'S CHALLENGE DAY. LET'S GO ALREADY!
I'LL PUT THESE IN YOUR LOCKER!
ALL RIGHT. I'M READY. I'VE GOT THIS.
LOOK AT YOU, TROOPER! DIDN'T KNOW IF YOU'D MAKE IT THROUGH THE NIGHT.
I LEARNED FROM THE BEST!

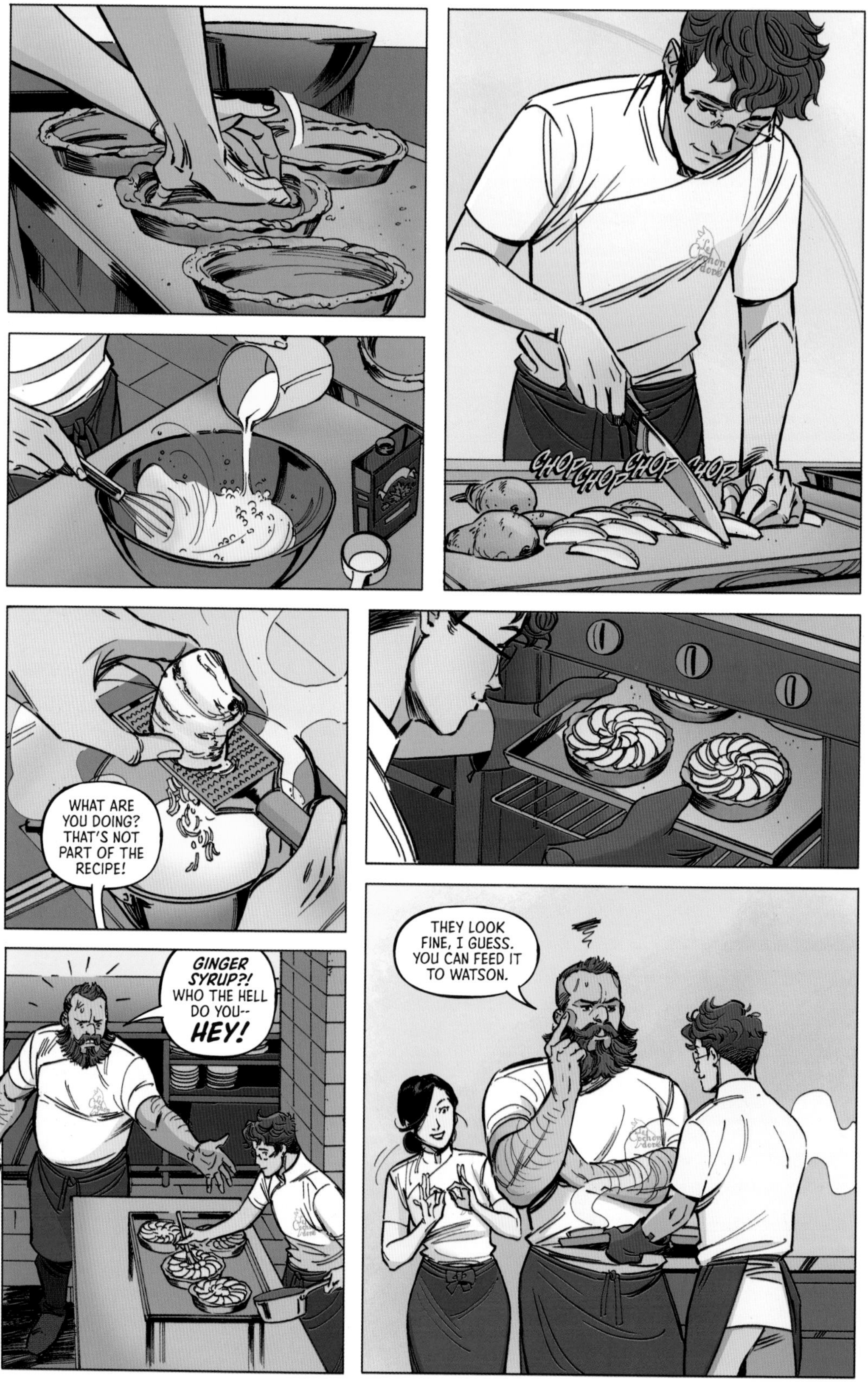
CHOP CHOP CHOP CHOP
WHAT ARE YOU DOING? THAT'S NOT PART OF THE RECIPE!
GINGER SYRUP?! WHO THE HELL DO YOU-- HEY!
THEY LOOK FINE, I GUESS. YOU CAN FEED IT TO WATSON.

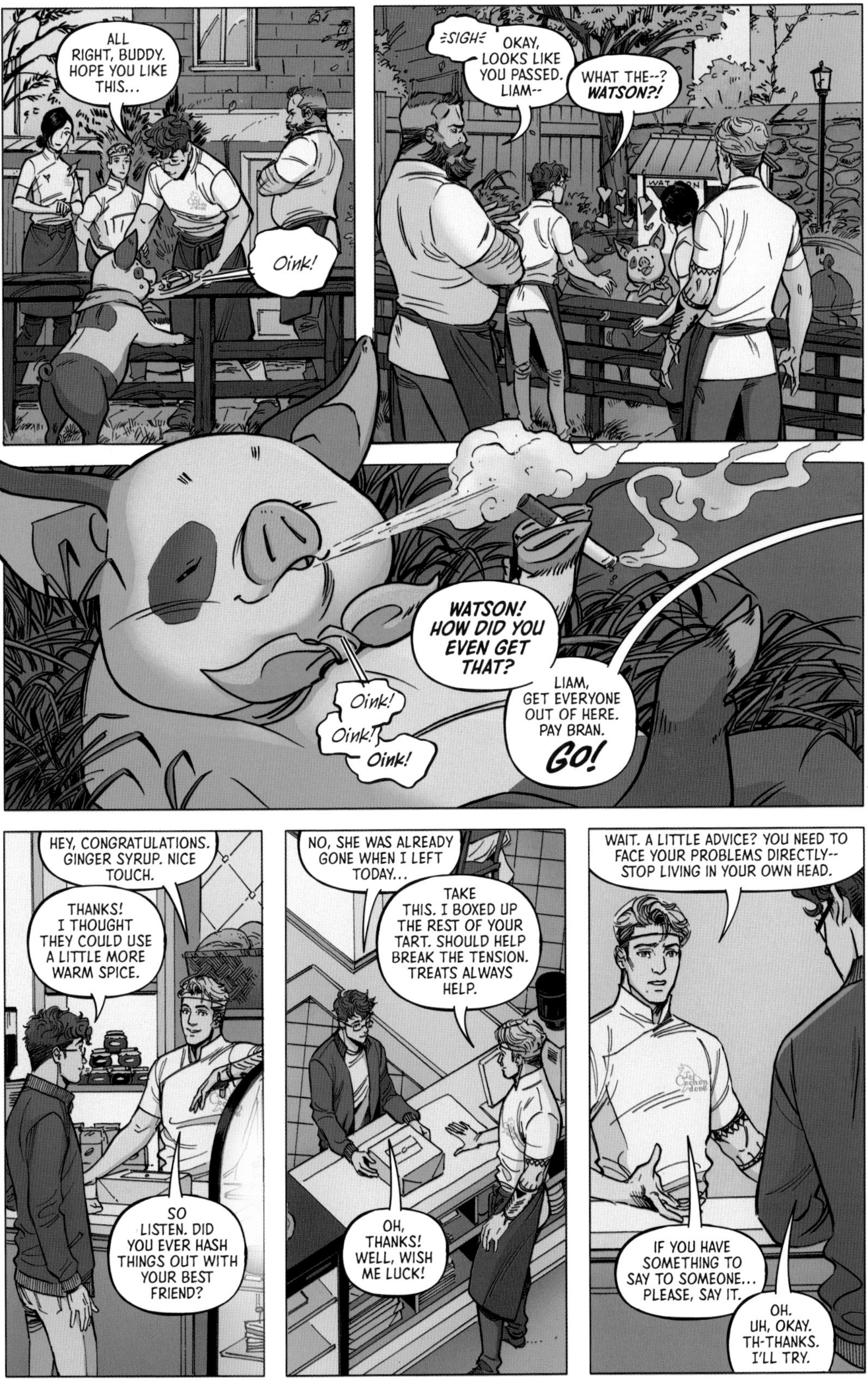
ALL RIGHT, BUDDY. HOPE YOU LIKE THIS...
Oink!
SIGH
OKAY, LOOKS LIKE YOU PASSED. LIAM--
WHAT THE--? WATSON?!
WATSON! HOW DID YOU EVEN GET THAT?
Oink! Oink! Oink!
LIAM, GET EVERYONE OUT OF HERE. PAY BRAN. GO!
HEY, CONGRATULATIONS. GINGER SYRUP. NICE TOUCH.
THANKS! I THOUGHT THEY COULD USE A LITTLE MORE WARM SPICE.
SO LISTEN. DID YOU EVER HASH THINGS OUT WITH YOUR BEST FRIEND?
NO, SHE WAS ALREADY GONE WHEN I LEFT TODAY...
TAKE THIS. I BOXED UP THE REST OF YOUR TART. SHOULD HELP BREAK THE TENSION. TREATS ALWAYS HELP.
OH, THANKS! WELL, WISH ME LUCK!
WAIT. A LITTLE ADVICE? YOU NEED TO FACE YOUR PROBLEMS DIRECTLY--STOP LIVING IN YOUR OWN HEAD.
IF YOU HAVE SOMETHING TO SAY TO SOMEONE... PLEASE, SAY IT.
OH. UH, OKAY. TH-THANKS. I'LL TRY.

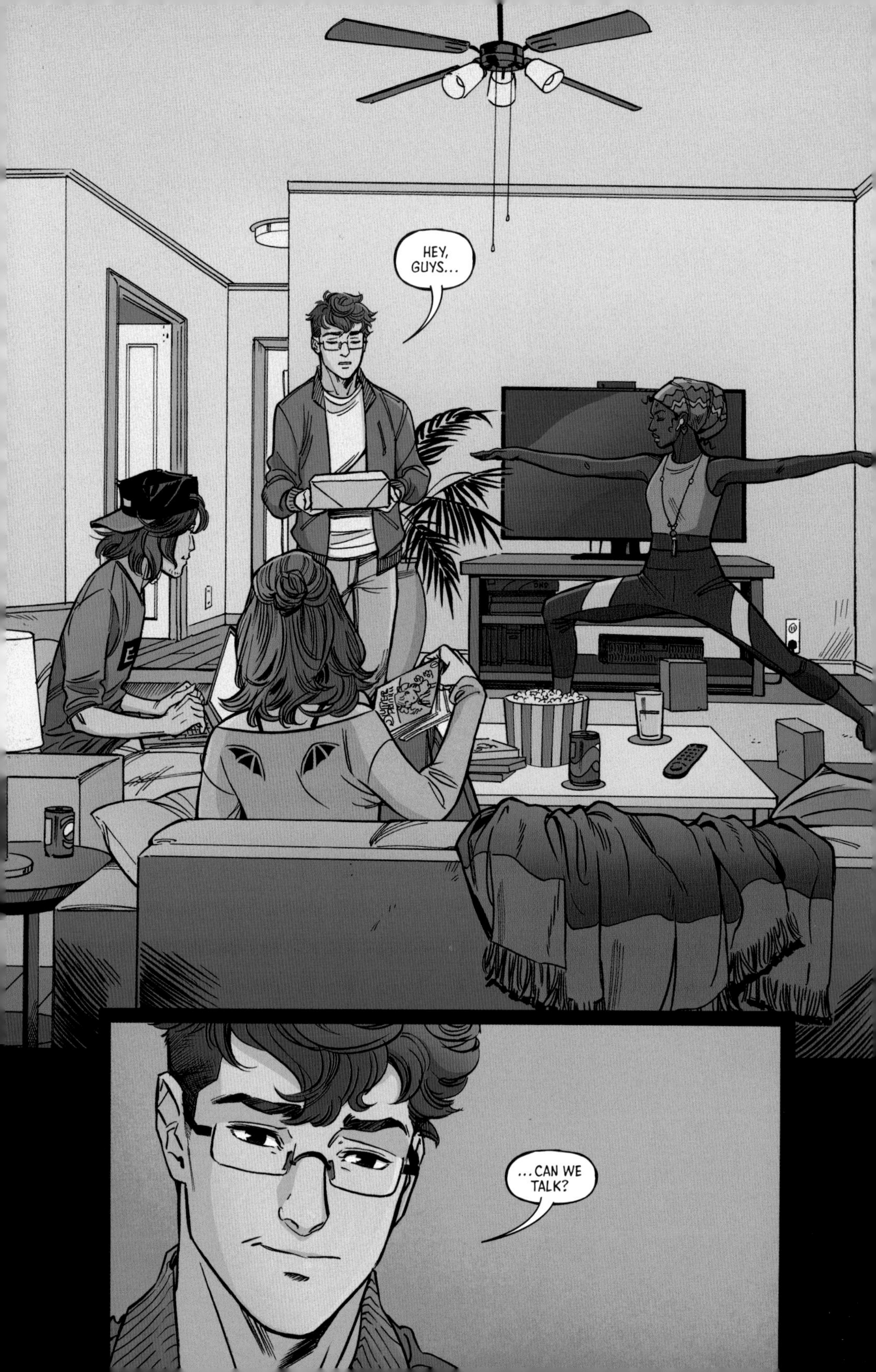
HEY, GUYS...
...CAN WE TALK?

Chapter Four

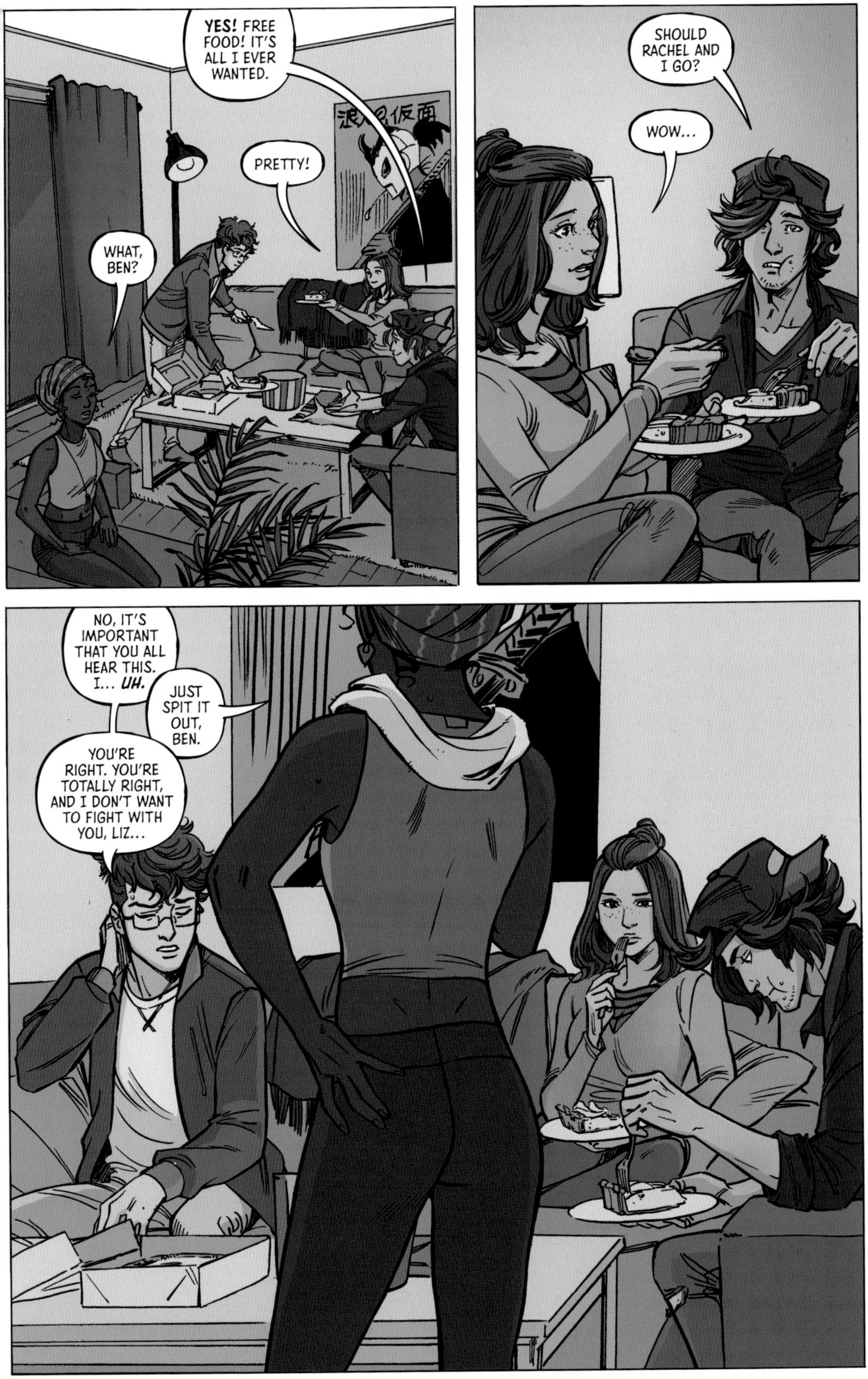
YES! FREE FOOD! IT'S ALL I EVER WANTED.
PRETTY!
WHAT, BEN?
SHOULD RACHEL AND I GO?
WOW...
NO, IT'S IMPORTANT THAT YOU ALL HEAR THIS. I... ***UH.***
JUST SPIT IT OUT, BEN.
YOU'RE RIGHT. YOU'RE TOTALLY RIGHT, AND I DON'T WANT TO FIGHT WITH YOU, LIZ...

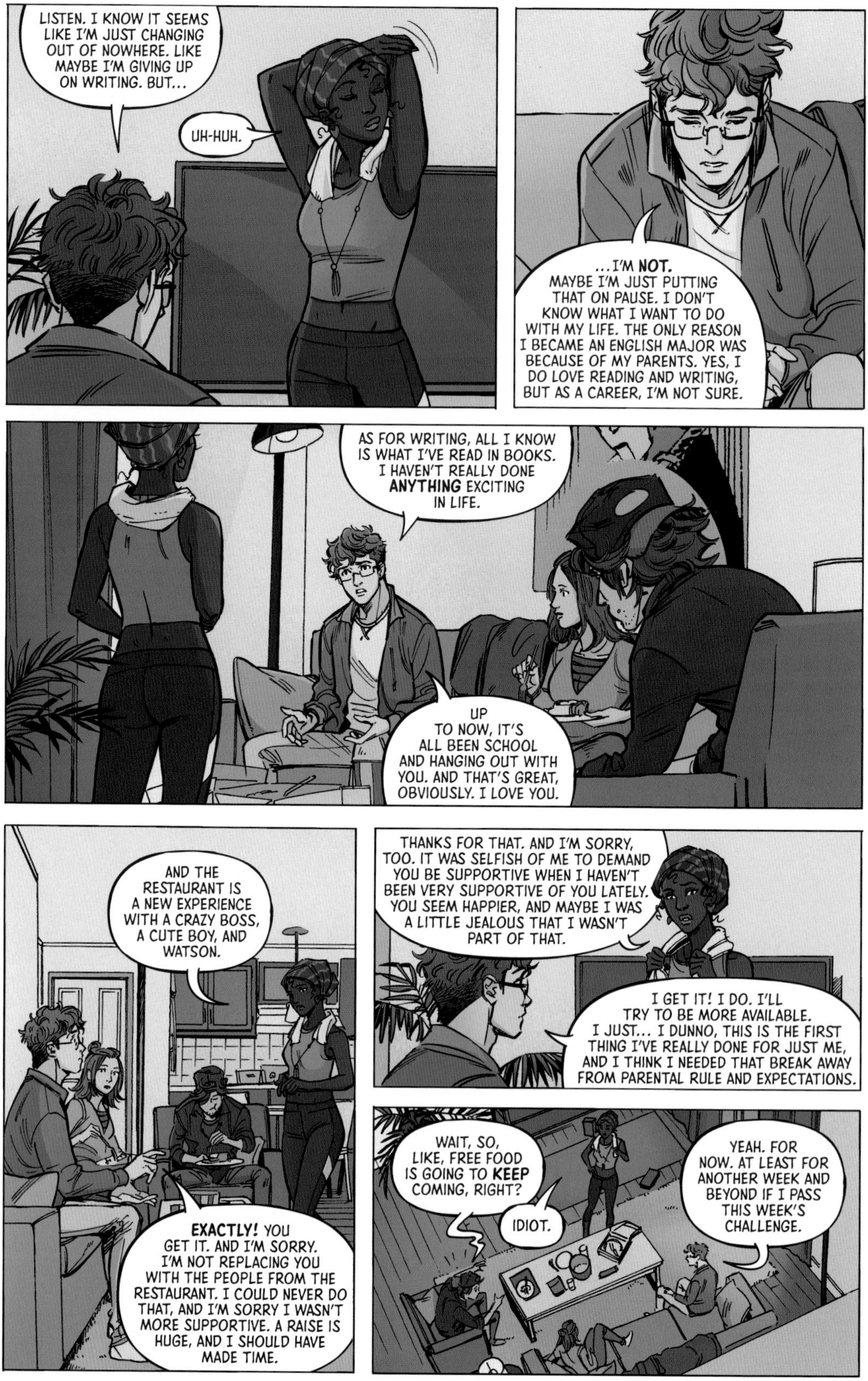
LISTEN. I KNOW IT SEEMS LIKE I'M JUST CHANGING OUT OF NOWHERE. LIKE MAYBE I'M GIVING UP ON WRITING. BUT...
UH-HUH.
...I'M **NOT.** MAYBE I'M JUST PUTTING THAT ON PAUSE. I DON'T KNOW WHAT I WANT TO DO WITH MY LIFE. THE ONLY REASON I BECAME AN ENGLISH MAJOR WAS BECAUSE OF MY PARENTS. YES, I DO LOVE READING AND WRITING, BUT AS A CAREER, I'M NOT SURE.
AS FOR WRITING, ALL I KNOW IS WHAT I'VE READ IN BOOKS. I HAVEN'T REALLY DONE **ANYTHING** EXCITING IN LIFE.
UP TO NOW, IT'S ALL BEEN SCHOOL AND HANGING OUT WITH YOU. AND THAT'S GREAT, OBVIOUSLY. I LOVE YOU.
AND THE RESTAURANT IS A NEW EXPERIENCE WITH A CRAZY BOSS, A CUTE BOY, AND WATSON.
EXACTLY! YOU GET IT. AND I'M SORRY. I'M NOT REPLACING YOU WITH THE PEOPLE FROM THE RESTAURANT. I COULD NEVER DO THAT, AND I'M SORRY I WASN'T MORE SUPPORTIVE. A RAISE IS HUGE, AND I SHOULD HAVE MADE TIME.
THANKS FOR THAT. AND I'M SORRY, TOO. IT WAS SELFISH OF ME TO DEMAND YOU BE SUPPORTIVE WHEN I HAVEN'T BEEN VERY SUPPORTIVE OF YOU LATELY. YOU SEEM HAPPIER, AND MAYBE I WAS A LITTLE JEALOUS THAT I WASN'T PART OF THAT.
I GET IT! I DO. I'LL TRY TO BE MORE AVAILABLE. I JUST... I DUNNO, THIS IS THE FIRST THING I'VE REALLY DONE FOR JUST ME, AND I THINK I NEEDED THAT BREAK AWAY FROM PARENTAL RULE AND EXPECTATIONS.
WAIT, SO, LIKE, FREE FOOD IS GOING TO **KEEP** COMING, RIGHT?
IDIOT.
YEAH. FOR NOW. AT LEAST FOR ANOTHER WEEK AND BEYOND IF I PASS THIS WEEK'S CHALLENGE.

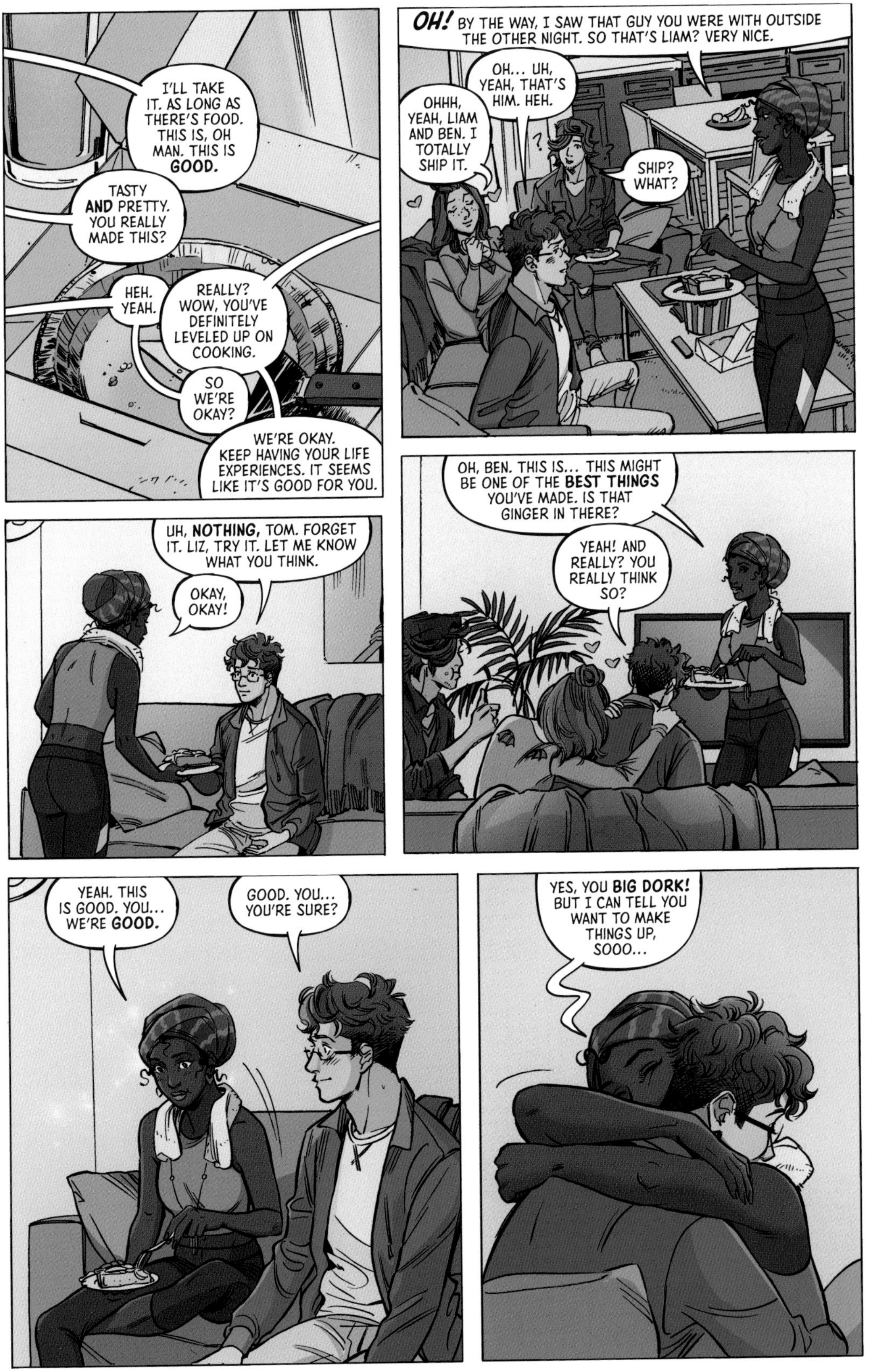
I'LL TAKE IT. AS LONG AS THERE'S FOOD. THIS IS, OH MAN. THIS IS **GOOD.**
TASTY **AND** PRETTY. YOU REALLY MADE THIS?
HEH. YEAH.
REALLY? WOW, YOU'VE DEFINITELY LEVELED UP ON COOKING.
SO WE'RE OKAY?
WE'RE OKAY. KEEP HAVING YOUR LIFE EXPERIENCES. IT SEEMS LIKE IT'S GOOD FOR YOU.
OH! BY THE WAY, I SAW THAT GUY YOU WERE WITH OUTSIDE THE OTHER NIGHT. SO THAT'S LIAM? VERY NICE.
OH... UH, YEAH, THAT'S HIM. HEH.
OHHH, YEAH, LIAM AND BEN. I TOTALLY SHIP IT.
SHIP? WHAT?
UH, **NOTHING,** TOM. FORGET IT. LIZ, TRY IT. LET ME KNOW WHAT YOU THINK.
OKAY, OKAY!
OH, BEN. THIS IS... THIS MIGHT BE ONE OF THE **BEST THINGS** YOU'VE MADE. IS THAT GINGER IN THERE?
YEAH! AND REALLY? YOU REALLY THINK SO?
YEAH. THIS IS GOOD. YOU... WE'RE **GOOD.**
GOOD. YOU... YOU'RE SURE?
YES, YOU **BIG DORK!** BUT I CAN TELL YOU WANT TO MAKE THINGS UP, SOOO...

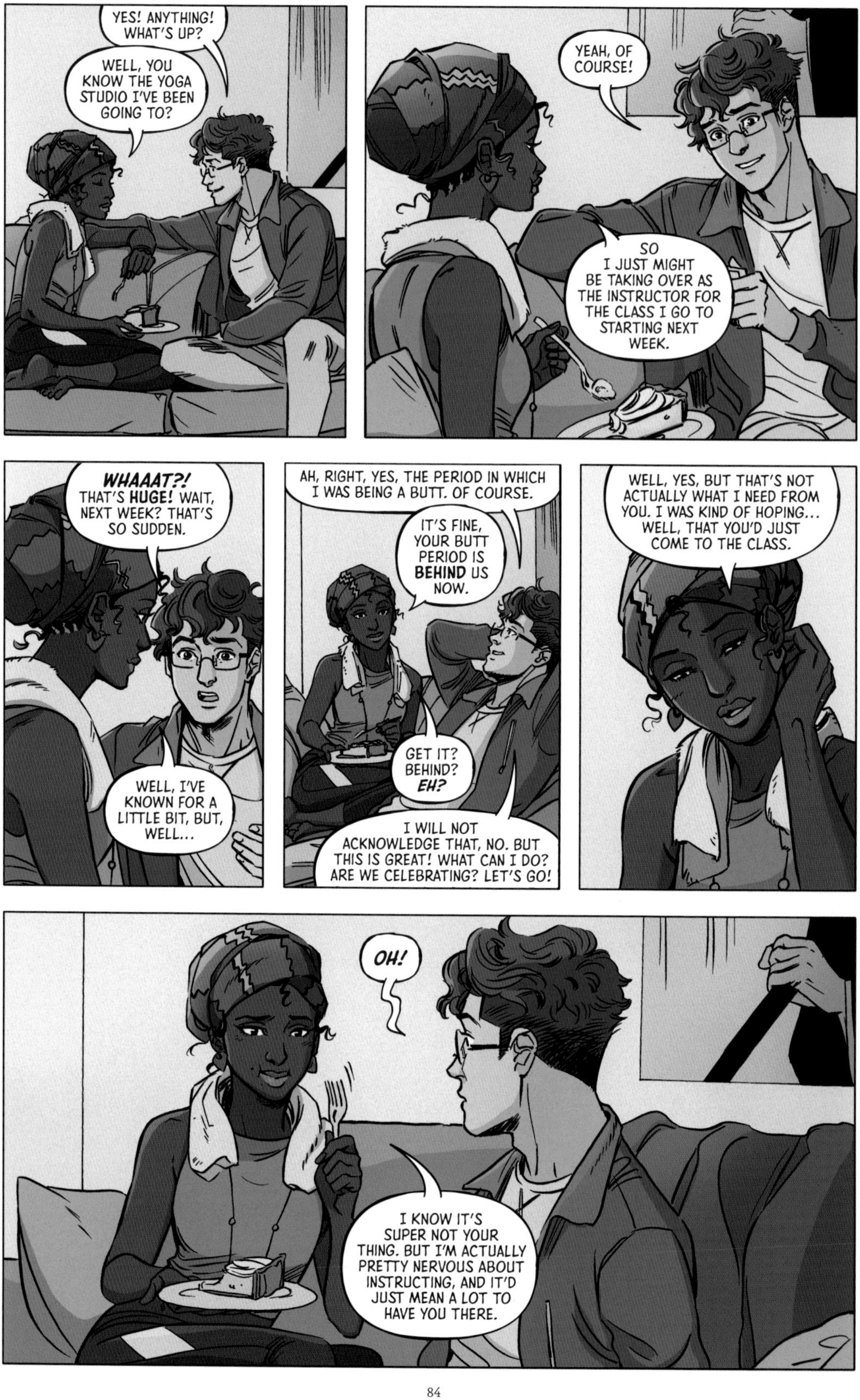
YES! ANYTHING! WHAT'S UP?
WELL, YOU KNOW THE YOGA STUDIO I'VE BEEN GOING TO?
YEAH, OF COURSE!
SO I JUST MIGHT BE TAKING OVER AS THE INSTRUCTOR FOR THE CLASS I GO TO STARTING NEXT WEEK.
WHAAAT?! THAT'S HUGE! WAIT, NEXT WEEK? THAT'S SO SUDDEN.
WELL, I'VE KNOWN FOR A LITTLE BIT, BUT, WELL...
AH, RIGHT, YES, THE PERIOD IN WHICH I WAS BEING A BUTT. OF COURSE.
IT'S FINE, YOUR BUTT PERIOD IS BEHIND US NOW.
GET IT? BEHIND? EH?
I WILL NOT ACKNOWLEDGE THAT, NO. BUT THIS IS GREAT! WHAT CAN I DO? ARE WE CELEBRATING? LET'S GO!
WELL, YES, BUT THAT'S NOT ACTUALLY WHAT I NEED FROM YOU. I WAS KIND OF HOPING... WELL, THAT YOU'D JUST COME TO THE CLASS.
OH!
I KNOW IT'S SUPER NOT YOUR THING. BUT I'M ACTUALLY PRETTY NERVOUS ABOUT INSTRUCTING, AND IT'D JUST MEAN A LOT TO HAVE YOU THERE.

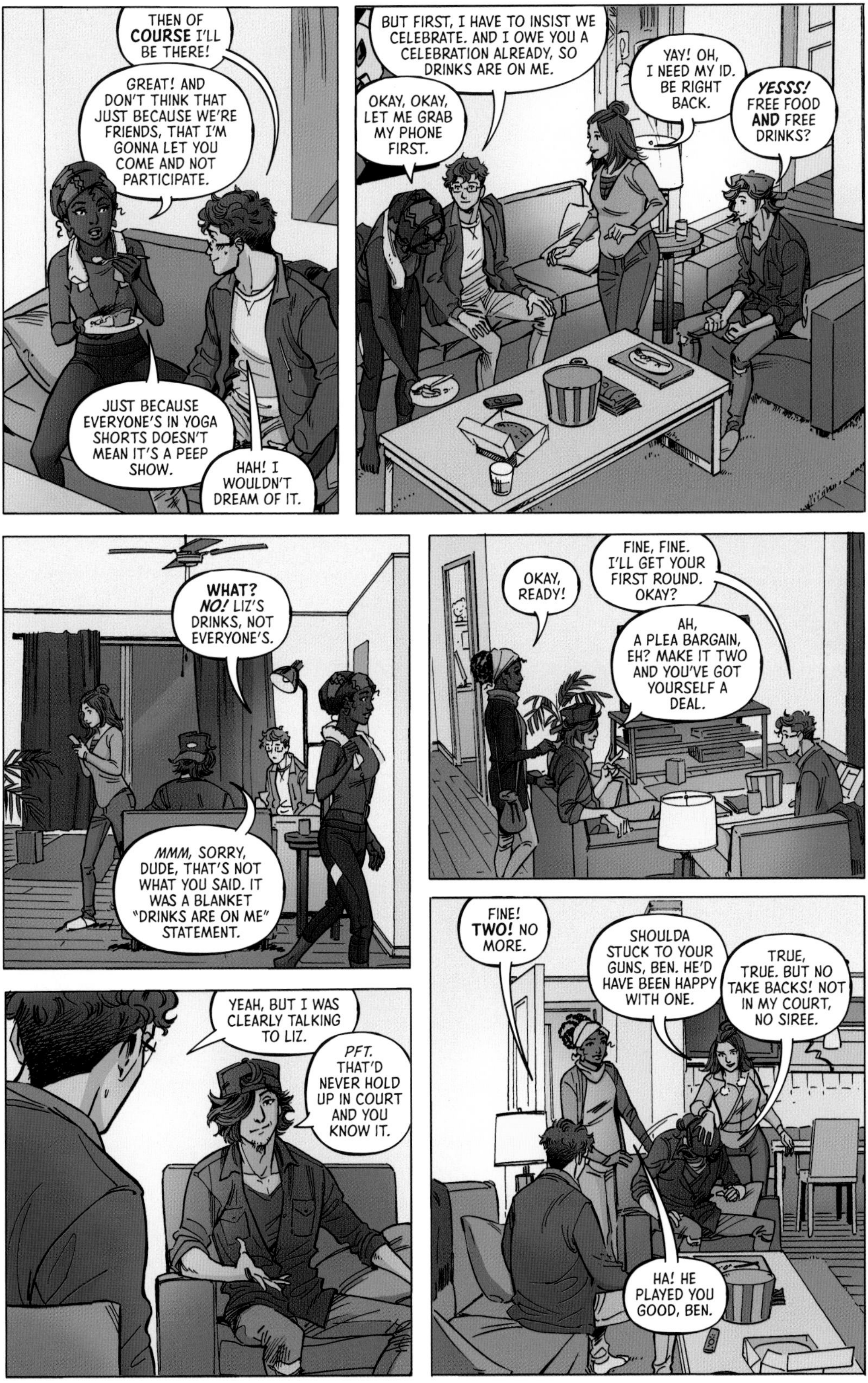
THEN OF **COURSE** I'LL BE THERE!
GREAT! AND DON'T THINK THAT JUST BECAUSE WE'RE FRIENDS, THAT I'M GONNA LET YOU COME AND NOT PARTICIPATE.
JUST BECAUSE EVERYONE'S IN YOGA SHORTS DOESN'T MEAN IT'S A PEEP SHOW.
HAH! I WOULDN'T DREAM OF IT.
BUT FIRST, I HAVE TO INSIST WE CELEBRATE. AND I OWE YOU A CELEBRATION ALREADY, SO DRINKS ARE ON ME.
OKAY, OKAY, LET ME GRAB MY PHONE FIRST.
YAY! OH, I NEED MY ID. BE RIGHT BACK.
YESSS! FREE FOOD **AND** FREE DRINKS?
WHAT? *NO!* LIZ'S DRINKS, NOT EVERYONE'S.
MMM, SORRY, DUDE, THAT'S NOT WHAT YOU SAID. IT WAS A BLANKET "DRINKS ARE ON ME" STATEMENT.
OKAY, READY!
FINE, FINE. I'LL GET YOUR FIRST ROUND. OKAY?
AH, A PLEA BARGAIN, EH? MAKE IT TWO AND YOU'VE GOT YOURSELF A DEAL.
YEAH, BUT I WAS CLEARLY TALKING TO LIZ.
PFT. THAT'D NEVER HOLD UP IN COURT AND YOU KNOW IT.
FINE! **TWO!** NO MORE.
SHOULDA STUCK TO YOUR GUNS, BEN. HE'D HAVE BEEN HAPPY WITH ONE.
TRUE, TRUE. BUT NO TAKE BACKS! NOT IN MY COURT, NO SIREE.
HA! HE PLAYED YOU GOOD, BEN.

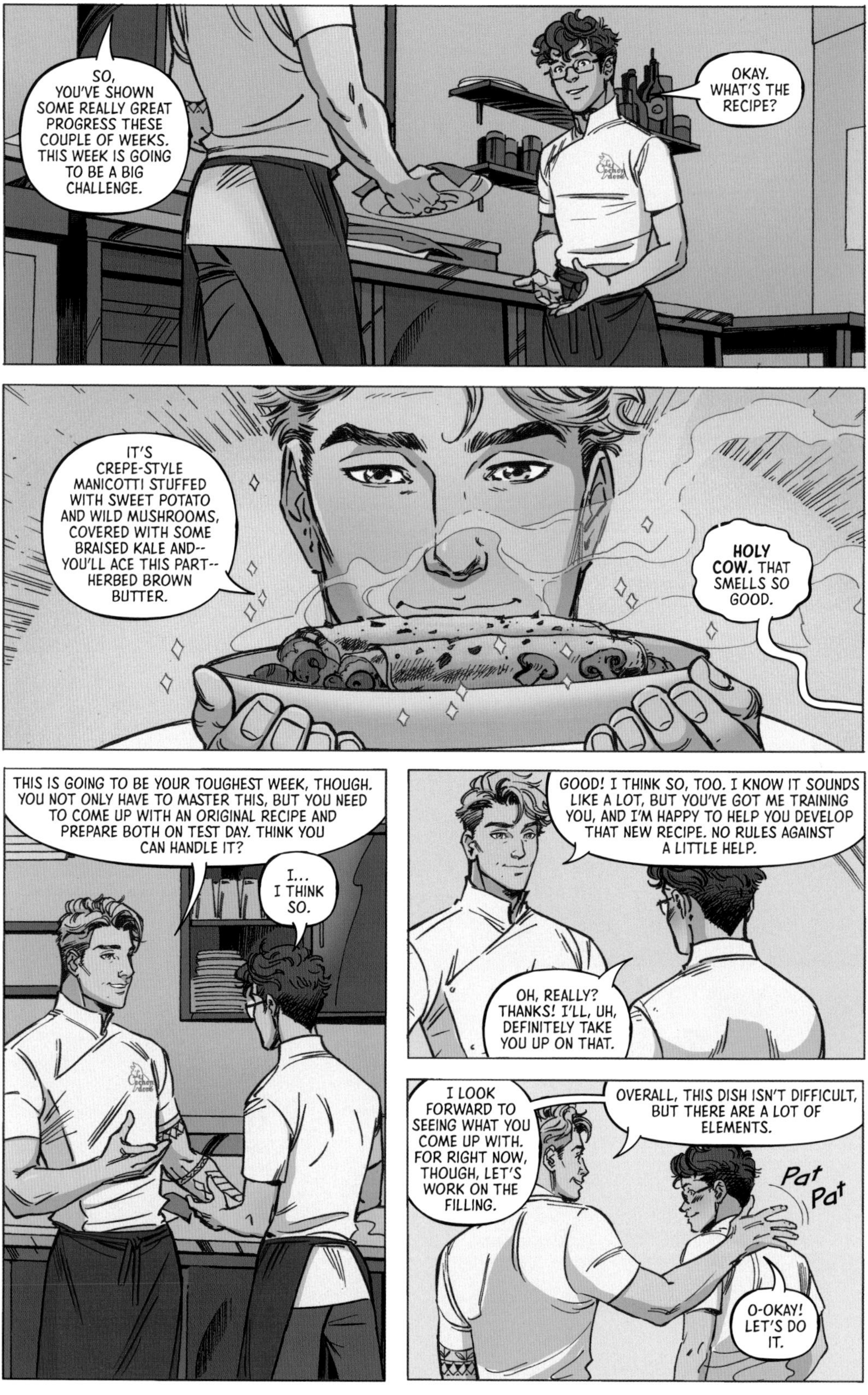
SO, YOU'VE SHOWN SOME REALLY GREAT PROGRESS THESE COUPLE OF WEEKS. THIS WEEK IS GOING TO BE A BIG CHALLENGE.
OKAY. WHAT'S THE RECIPE?
IT'S CREPE-STYLE MANICOTTI STUFFED WITH SWEET POTATO AND WILD MUSHROOMS, COVERED WITH SOME BRAISED KALE AND-- YOU'LL ACE THIS PART-- HERBED BROWN BUTTER.
HOLY COW. THAT SMELLS SO GOOD.
THIS IS GOING TO BE YOUR TOUGHEST WEEK, THOUGH. YOU NOT ONLY HAVE TO MASTER THIS, BUT YOU NEED TO COME UP WITH AN ORIGINAL RECIPE AND PREPARE BOTH ON TEST DAY. THINK YOU CAN HANDLE IT?
I... I THINK SO.
GOOD! I THINK SO, TOO. I KNOW IT SOUNDS LIKE A LOT, BUT YOU'VE GOT ME TRAINING YOU, AND I'M HAPPY TO HELP YOU DEVELOP THAT NEW RECIPE. NO RULES AGAINST A LITTLE HELP.
OH, REALLY? THANKS! I'LL, UH, DEFINITELY TAKE YOU UP ON THAT.
OVERALL, THIS DISH ISN'T DIFFICULT, BUT THERE ARE A LOT OF ELEMENTS.
I LOOK FORWARD TO SEEING WHAT YOU COME UP WITH. FOR RIGHT NOW, THOUGH, LET'S WORK ON THE FILLING.
Pat Pat
O-OKAY! LET'S DO IT.

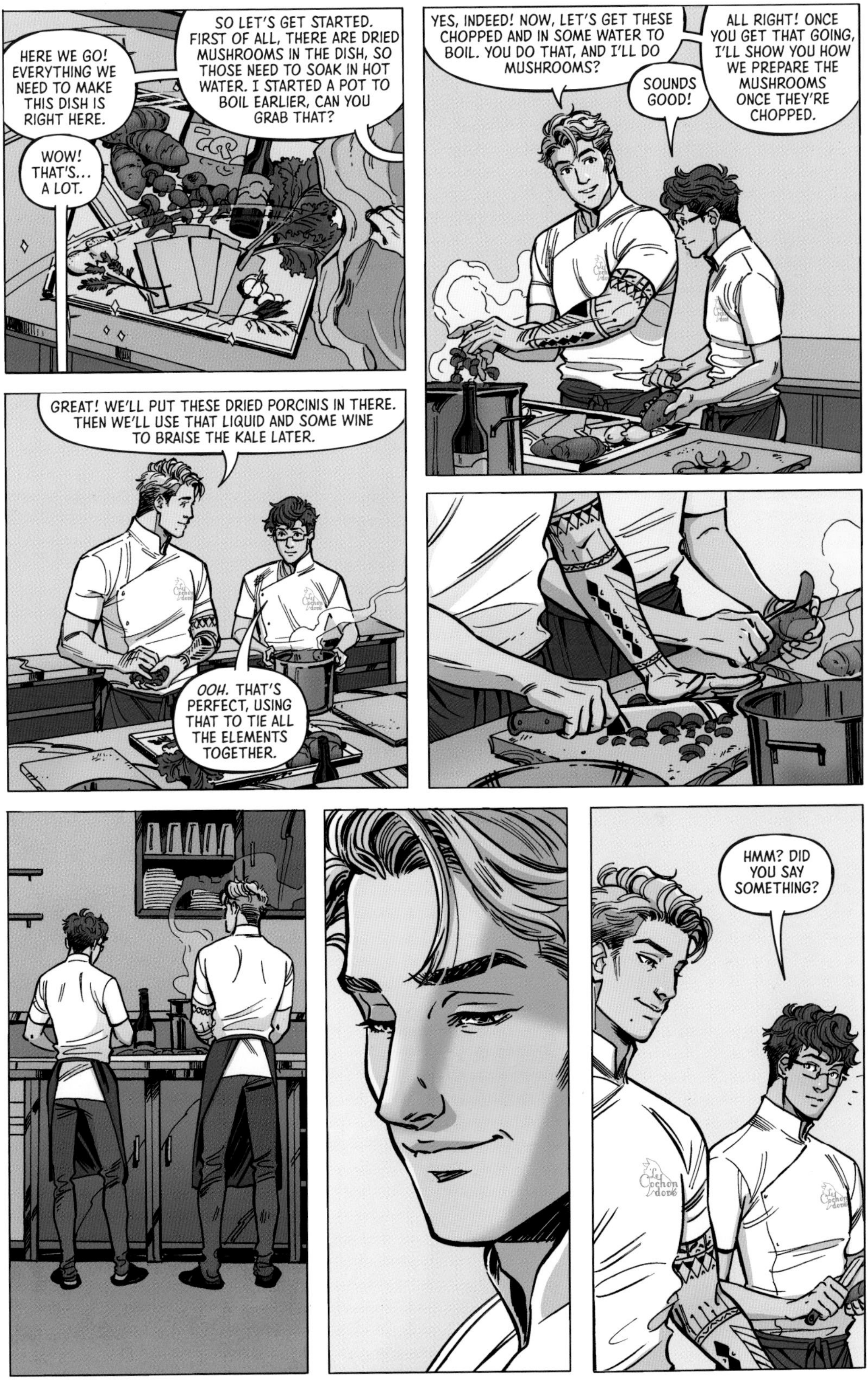
HERE WE GO! EVERYTHING WE NEED TO MAKE THIS DISH IS RIGHT HERE.
SO LET'S GET STARTED. FIRST OF ALL, THERE ARE DRIED MUSHROOMS IN THE DISH, SO THOSE NEED TO SOAK IN HOT WATER. I STARTED A POT TO BOIL EARLIER, CAN YOU GRAB THAT?
WOW! THAT'S... A LOT.
YES, INDEED! NOW, LET'S GET THESE CHOPPED AND IN SOME WATER TO BOIL. YOU DO THAT, AND I'LL DO MUSHROOMS?
SOUNDS GOOD!
ALL RIGHT! ONCE YOU GET THAT GOING, I'LL SHOW YOU HOW WE PREPARE THE MUSHROOMS ONCE THEY'RE CHOPPED.
GREAT! WE'LL PUT THESE DRIED PORCINIS IN THERE. THEN WE'LL USE THAT LIQUID AND SOME WINE TO BRAISE THE KALE LATER.
OOH. THAT'S PERFECT, USING THAT TO TIE ALL THE ELEMENTS TOGETHER.
HMM? DID YOU SAY SOMETHING?

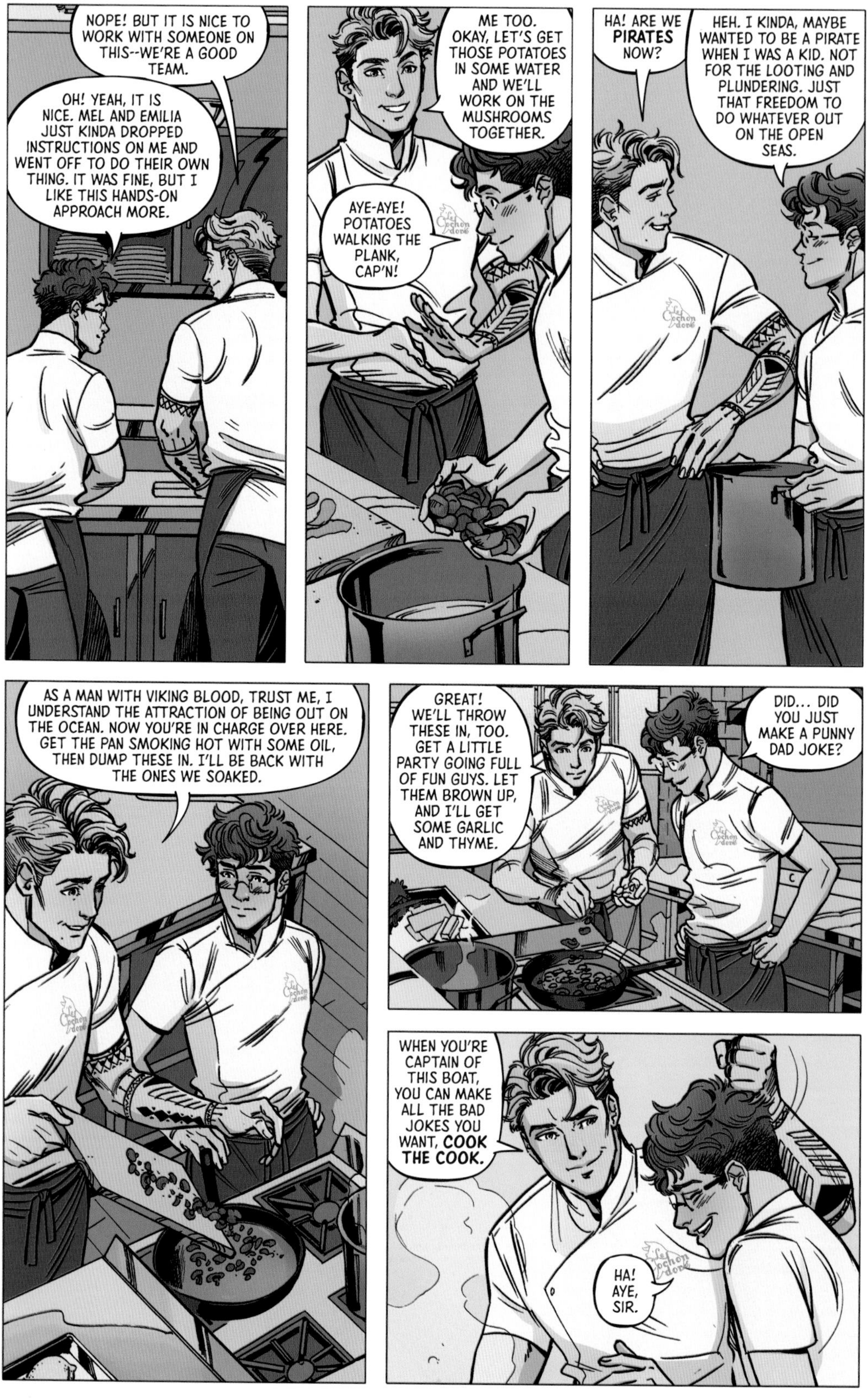
NOPE! BUT IT IS NICE TO WORK WITH SOMEONE ON THIS--WE'RE A GOOD TEAM.
OH! YEAH, IT IS NICE. MEL AND EMILIA JUST KINDA DROPPED INSTRUCTIONS ON ME AND WENT OFF TO DO THEIR OWN THING. IT WAS FINE, BUT I LIKE THIS HANDS-ON APPROACH MORE.
ME TOO. OKAY, LET'S GET THOSE POTATOES IN SOME WATER AND WE'LL WORK ON THE MUSHROOMS TOGETHER.
AYE-AYE! POTATOES WALKING THE PLANK, CAP'N!
HA! ARE WE **PIRATES** NOW?
HEH. I KINDA, MAYBE WANTED TO BE A PIRATE WHEN I WAS A KID. NOT FOR THE LOOTING AND PLUNDERING. JUST THAT FREEDOM TO DO WHATEVER OUT ON THE OPEN SEAS.
AS A MAN WITH VIKING BLOOD, TRUST ME, I UNDERSTAND THE ATTRACTION OF BEING OUT ON THE OCEAN. NOW YOU'RE IN CHARGE OVER HERE. GET THE PAN SMOKING HOT WITH SOME OIL, THEN DUMP THESE IN. I'LL BE BACK WITH THE ONES WE SOAKED.
GREAT! WE'LL THROW THESE IN, TOO. GET A LITTLE PARTY GOING FULL OF FUN GUYS. LET THEM BROWN UP, AND I'LL GET SOME GARLIC AND THYME.
DID... DID YOU JUST MAKE A PUNNY DAD JOKE?
WHEN YOU'RE CAPTAIN OF THIS BOAT, YOU CAN MAKE ALL THE BAD JOKES YOU WANT, **COOK THE COOK.**
HA! AYE, SIR.

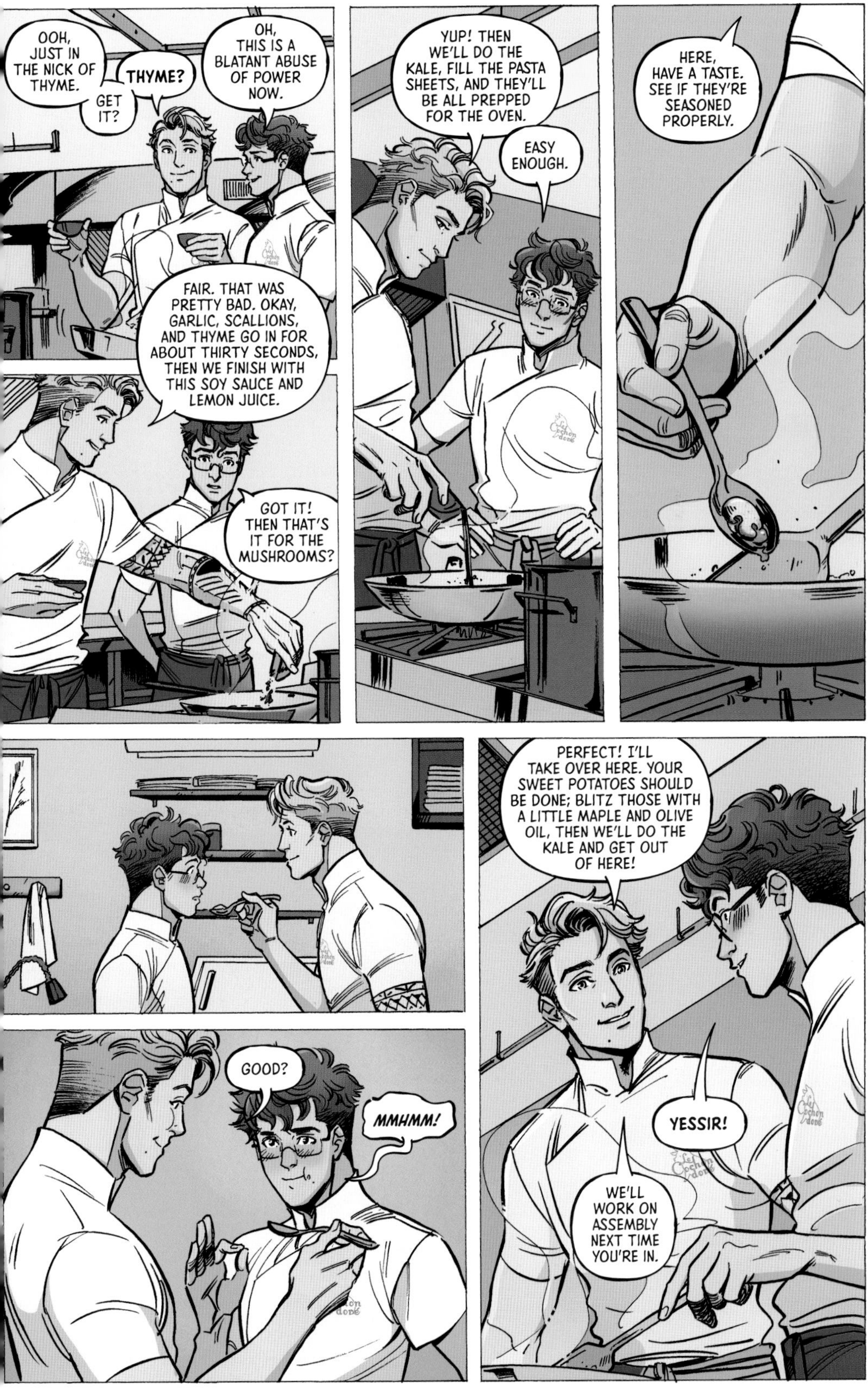
OOH, JUST IN THE NICK OF THYME.
GET IT?
THYME?
OH, THIS IS A BLATANT ABUSE OF POWER NOW.
FAIR. THAT WAS PRETTY BAD. OKAY, GARLIC, SCALLIONS, AND THYME GO IN FOR ABOUT THIRTY SECONDS, THEN WE FINISH WITH THIS SOY SAUCE AND LEMON JUICE.
GOT IT! THEN THAT'S IT FOR THE MUSHROOMS?
YUP! THEN WE'LL DO THE KALE, FILL THE PASTA SHEETS, AND THEY'LL BE ALL PREPPED FOR THE OVEN.
EASY ENOUGH.
HERE, HAVE A TASTE. SEE IF THEY'RE SEASONED PROPERLY.
GOOD?
MMHMM!
PERFECT! I'LL TAKE OVER HERE. YOUR SWEET POTATOES SHOULD BE DONE; BLITZ THOSE WITH A LITTLE MAPLE AND OLIVE OIL, THEN WE'LL DO THE KALE AND GET OUT OF HERE!
YESSIR!
WE'LL WORK ON ASSEMBLY NEXT TIME YOU'RE IN.

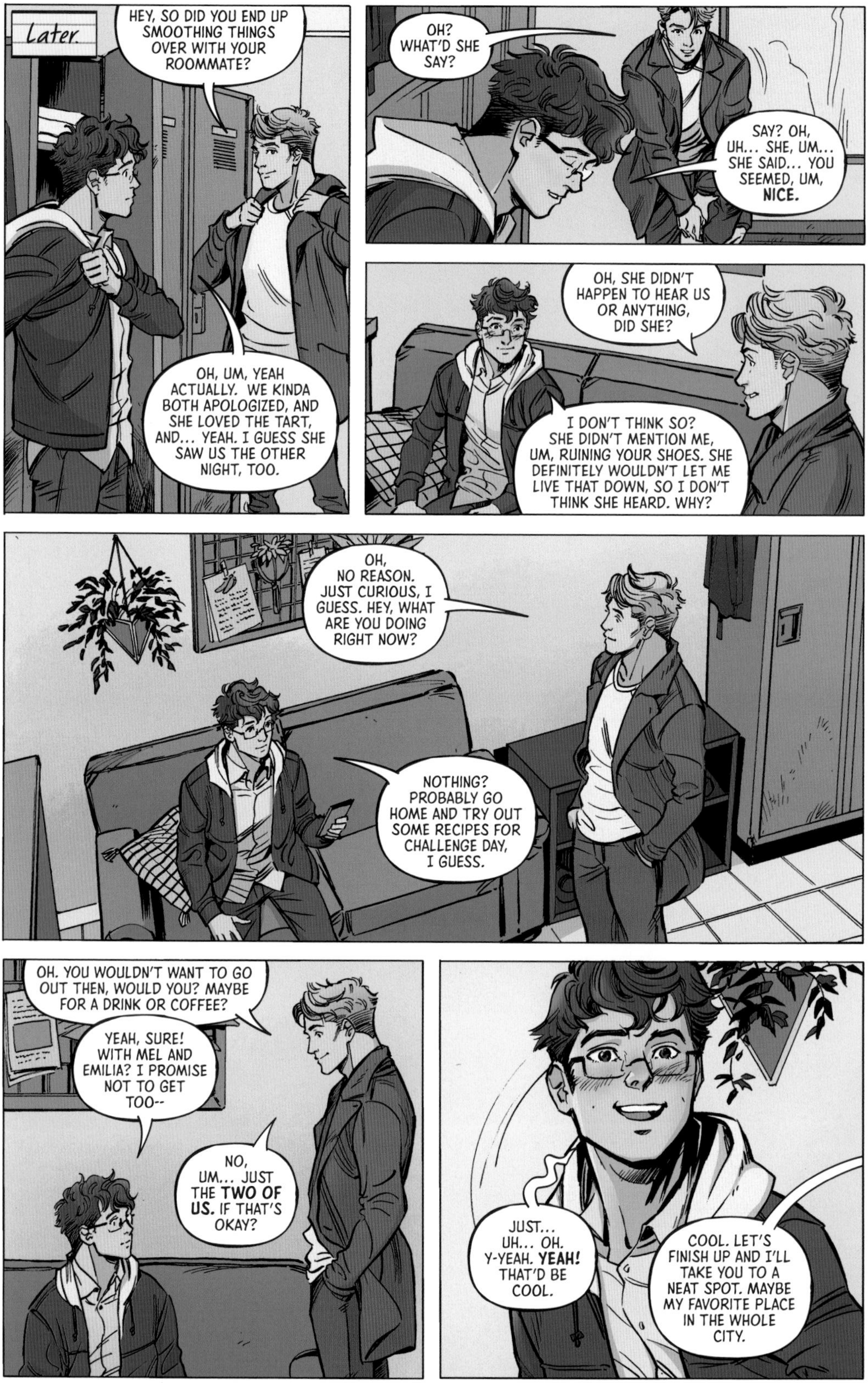

Later.
HEY, SO DID YOU END UP SMOOTHING THINGS OVER WITH YOUR ROOMMATE?
OH, UM, YEAH ACTUALLY. WE KINDA BOTH APOLOGIZED, AND SHE LOVED THE TART, AND... YEAH. I GUESS SHE SAW US THE OTHER NIGHT, TOO.
OH? WHAT'D SHE SAY?
SAY? OH, UH... SHE, UM... SHE SAID... YOU SEEMED, UM, NICE.
OH, SHE DIDN'T HAPPEN TO HEAR US OR ANYTHING, DID SHE?
I DON'T THINK SO? SHE DIDN'T MENTION ME, UM, RUINING YOUR SHOES. SHE DEFINITELY WOULDN'T LET ME LIVE THAT DOWN, SO I DON'T THINK SHE HEARD. WHY?
OH, NO REASON. JUST CURIOUS, I GUESS. HEY, WHAT ARE YOU DOING RIGHT NOW?
NOTHING? PROBABLY GO HOME AND TRY OUT SOME RECIPES FOR CHALLENGE DAY, I GUESS.
OH. YOU WOULDN'T WANT TO GO OUT THEN, WOULD YOU? MAYBE FOR A DRINK OR COFFEE?
YEAH, SURE! WITH MEL AND EMILIA? I PROMISE NOT TO GET TOO--
NO, UM... JUST THE TWO OF US. IF THAT'S OKAY?
JUST... UH... OH. Y-YEAH. YEAH! THAT'D BE COOL.
COOL. LET'S FINISH UP AND I'LL TAKE YOU TO A NEAT SPOT. MAYBE MY FAVORITE PLACE IN THE WHOLE CITY.

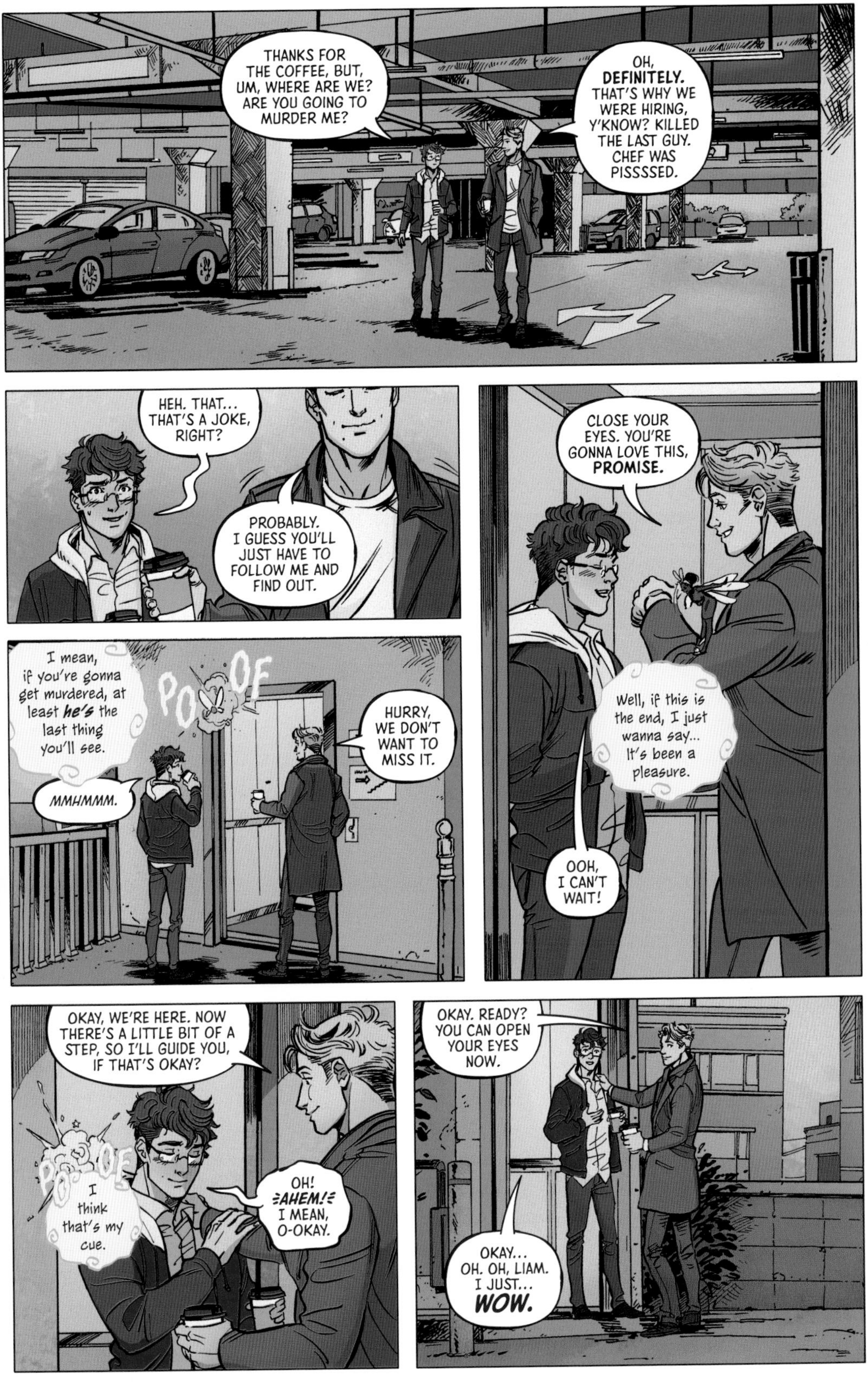
THANKS FOR THE COFFEE, BUT, UM, WHERE ARE WE? ARE YOU GOING TO MURDER ME?
OH, DEFINITELY. THAT'S WHY WE WERE HIRING, Y'KNOW? KILLED THE LAST GUY. CHEF WAS PISSSSED.
HEH. THAT... THAT'S A JOKE, RIGHT?
PROBABLY. I GUESS YOU'LL JUST HAVE TO FOLLOW ME AND FIND OUT.
CLOSE YOUR EYES. YOU'RE GONNA LOVE THIS, PROMISE.
Well, if this is the end, I just wanna say... It's been a pleasure.
OOH, I CAN'T WAIT!
I mean, if you're gonna get murdered, at least he's the last thing you'll see.
POOF
HURRY, WE DON'T WANT TO MISS IT.
MMHMMM.
OKAY, WE'RE HERE. NOW THERE'S A LITTLE BIT OF A STEP, SO I'LL GUIDE YOU, IF THAT'S OKAY?
POOF
I think that's my cue.
OH! AHEM! I MEAN, O-OKAY.
OKAY. READY? YOU CAN OPEN YOUR EYES NOW.
OKAY... OH. OH, LIAM. I JUST... WOW.

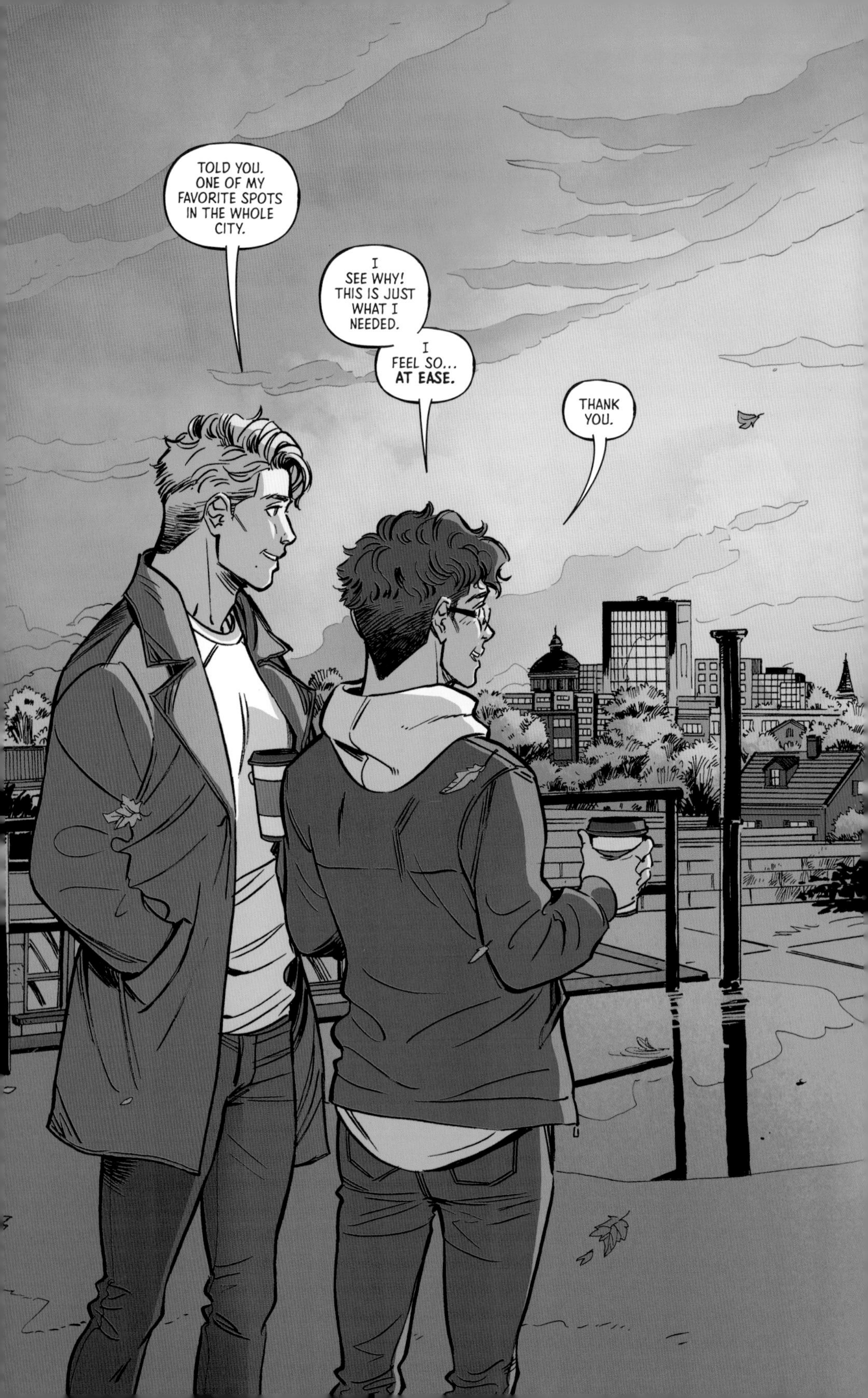
TOLD YOU. ONE OF MY FAVORITE SPOTS IN THE WHOLE CITY.
I SEE WHY! THIS IS JUST WHAT I NEEDED.
I FEEL SO... **AT EASE.**
THANK YOU.

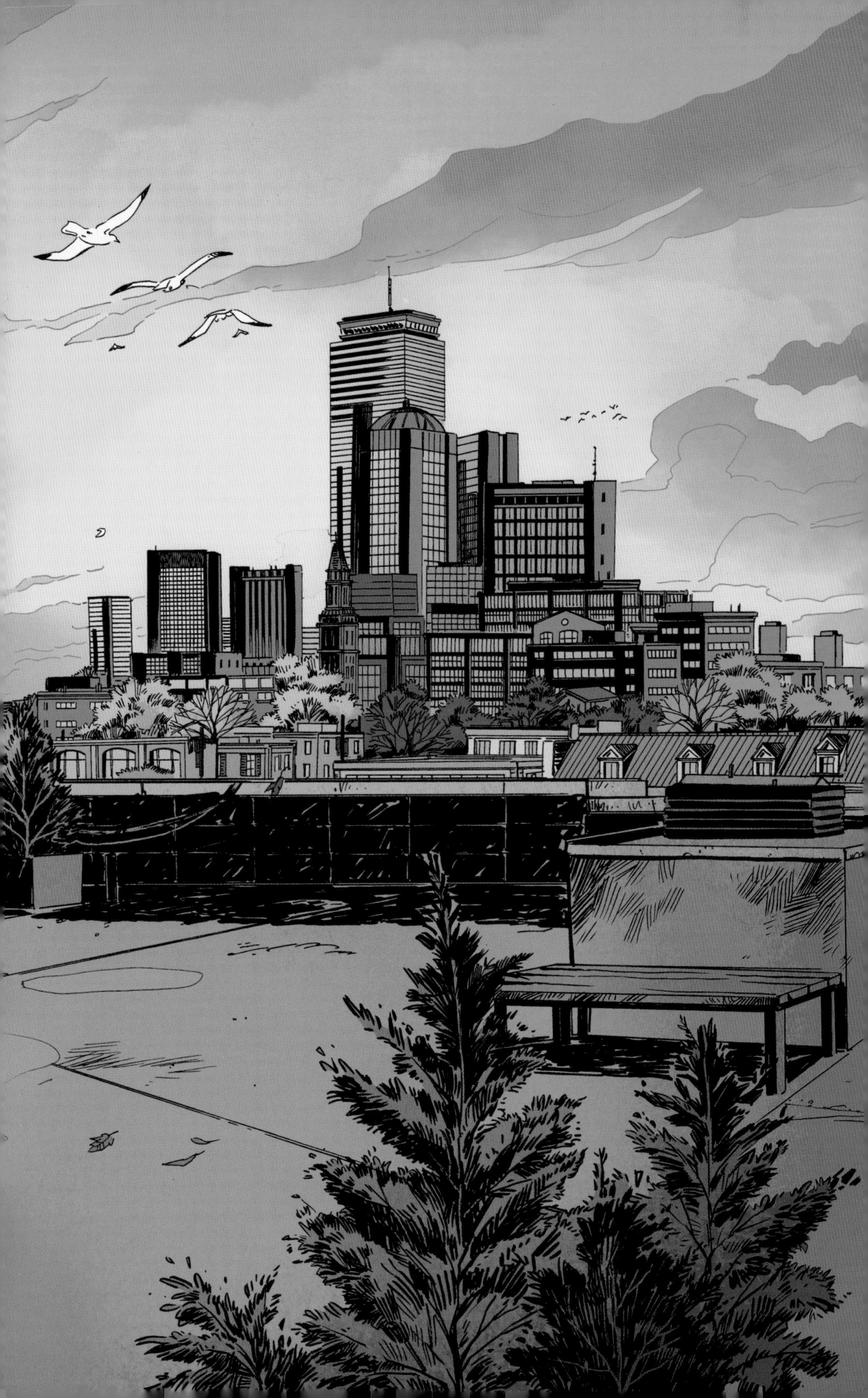

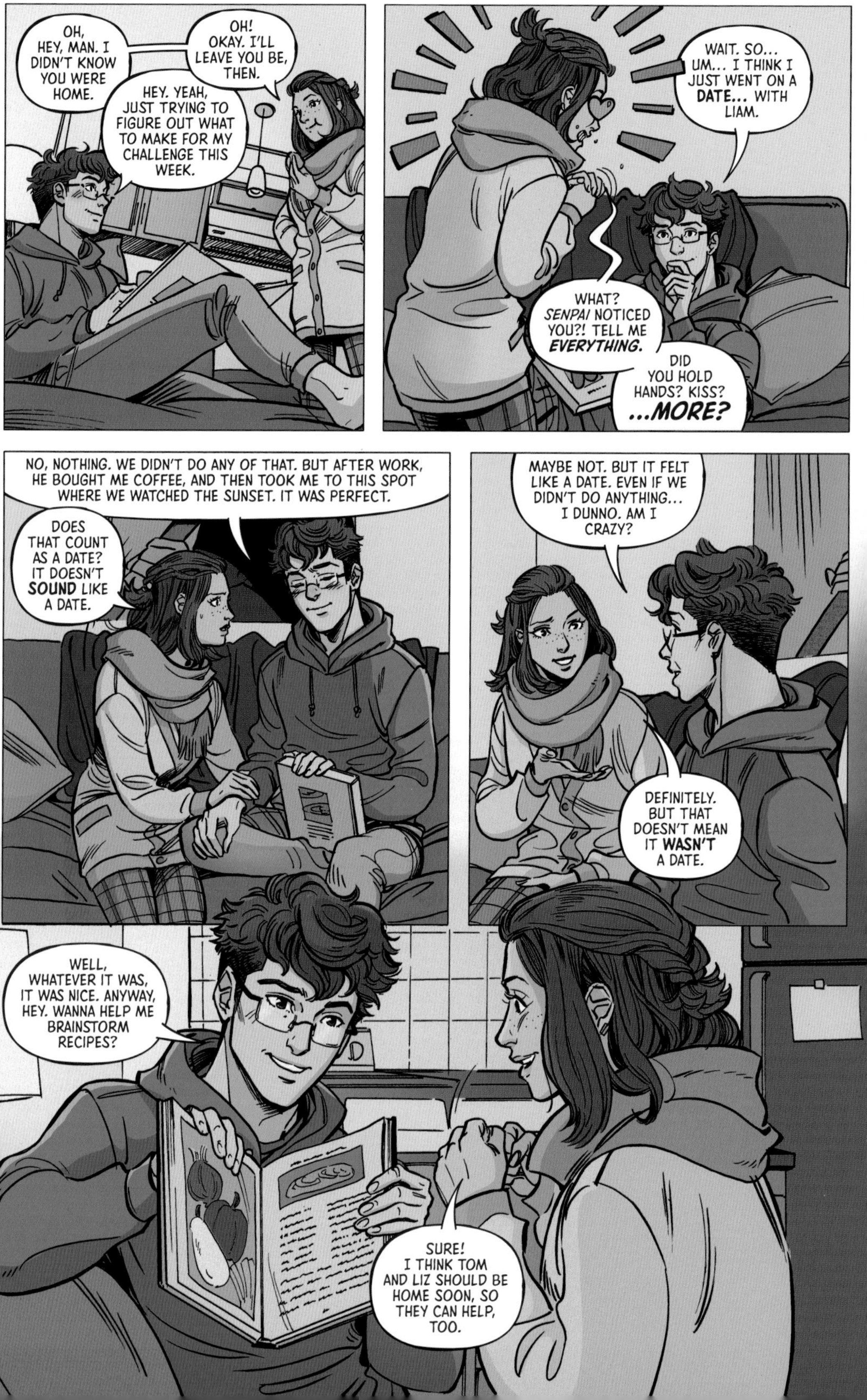
OH, HEY, MAN. I DIDN'T KNOW YOU WERE HOME.
OH! OKAY. I'LL LEAVE YOU BE, THEN.
HEY. YEAH, JUST TRYING TO FIGURE OUT WHAT TO MAKE FOR MY CHALLENGE THIS WEEK.
WAIT. SO... UM... I THINK I JUST WENT ON A **DATE...** WITH LIAM.
WHAT? *SENPAI* NOTICED YOU?! TELL ME ***EVERYTHING.***
DID YOU HOLD HANDS? KISS? ***...MORE?***
NO, NOTHING. WE DIDN'T DO ANY OF THAT. BUT AFTER WORK, HE BOUGHT ME COFFEE, AND THEN TOOK ME TO THIS SPOT WHERE WE WATCHED THE SUNSET. IT WAS PERFECT.
DOES THAT COUNT AS A DATE? IT DOESN'T **SOUND** LIKE A DATE.
MAYBE NOT. BUT IT FELT LIKE A DATE. EVEN IF WE DIDN'T DO ANYTHING... I DUNNO. AM I CRAZY?
DEFINITELY. BUT THAT DOESN'T MEAN IT **WASN'T** A DATE.
WELL, WHATEVER IT WAS, IT WAS NICE. ANYWAY, HEY. WANNA HELP ME BRAINSTORM RECIPES?
SURE! I THINK TOM AND LIZ SHOULD BE HOME SOON, SO THEY CAN HELP, TOO.

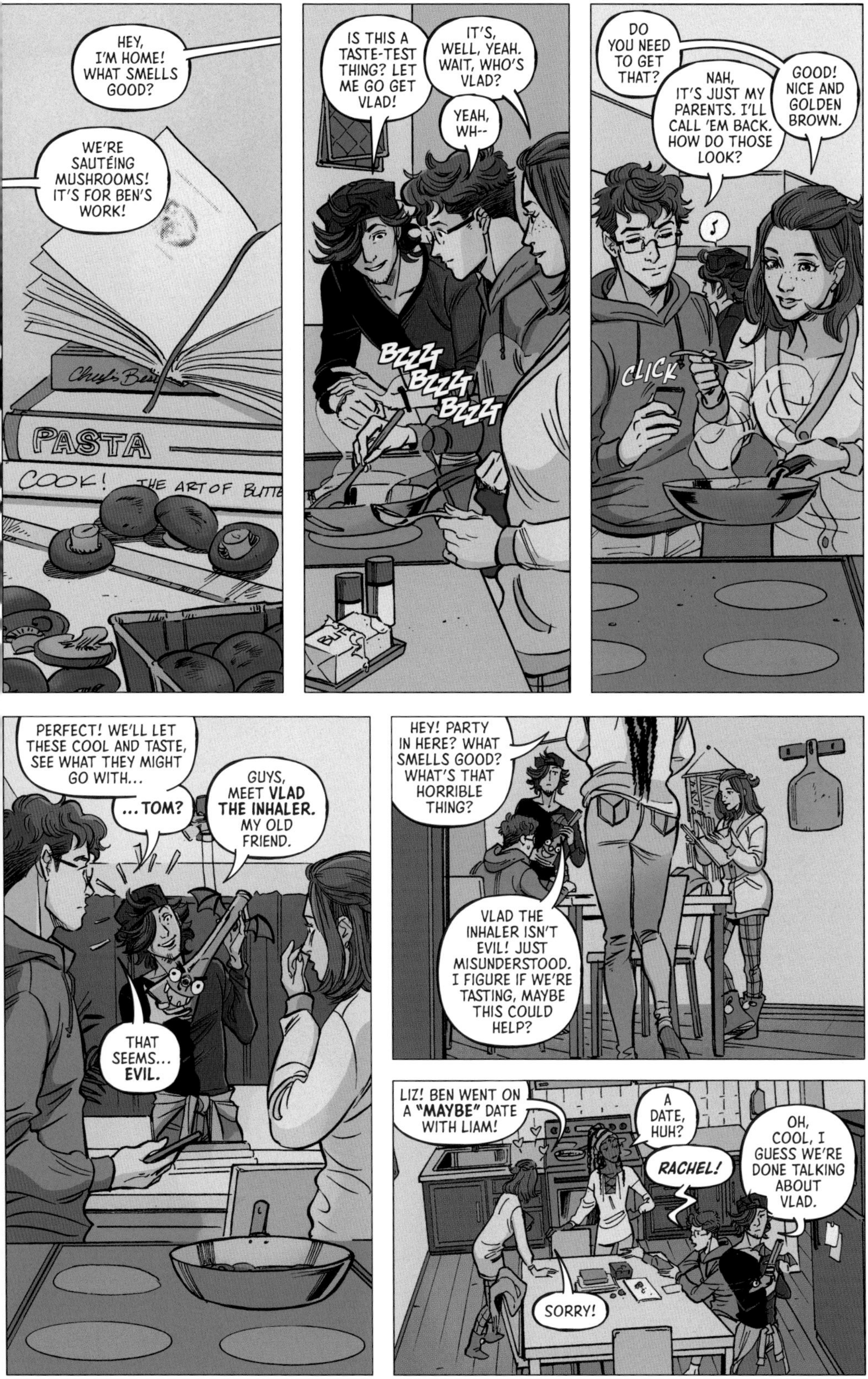
HEY, I'M HOME! WHAT SMELLS GOOD?
WE'RE SAUTÉING MUSHROOMS! IT'S FOR BEN'S WORK!
PASTA
COOK!
THE ART OF BUTTE
IS THIS A TASTE-TEST THING? LET ME GO GET VLAD!
IT'S, WELL, YEAH. WAIT, WHO'S VLAD?
YEAH, WH--
BZZZT BZZZT BZZZT
DO YOU NEED TO GET THAT?
NAH, IT'S JUST MY PARENTS. I'LL CALL 'EM BACK. HOW DO THOSE LOOK?
GOOD! NICE AND GOLDEN BROWN.
CLICK
PERFECT! WE'LL LET THESE COOL AND TASTE, SEE WHAT THEY MIGHT GO WITH...
...TOM?
GUYS, MEET **VLAD THE INHALER.** MY OLD FRIEND.
THAT SEEMS... **EVIL.**
HEY! PARTY IN HERE? WHAT SMELLS GOOD? WHAT'S THAT HORRIBLE THING?
VLAD THE INHALER ISN'T EVIL! JUST MISUNDERSTOOD. I FIGURE IF WE'RE TASTING, MAYBE THIS COULD HELP?
LIZ! BEN WENT ON A **"MAYBE"** DATE WITH LIAM!
A DATE, HUH?
RACHEL!
OH, COOL, I GUESS WE'RE DONE TALKING ABOUT VLAD.
SORRY!

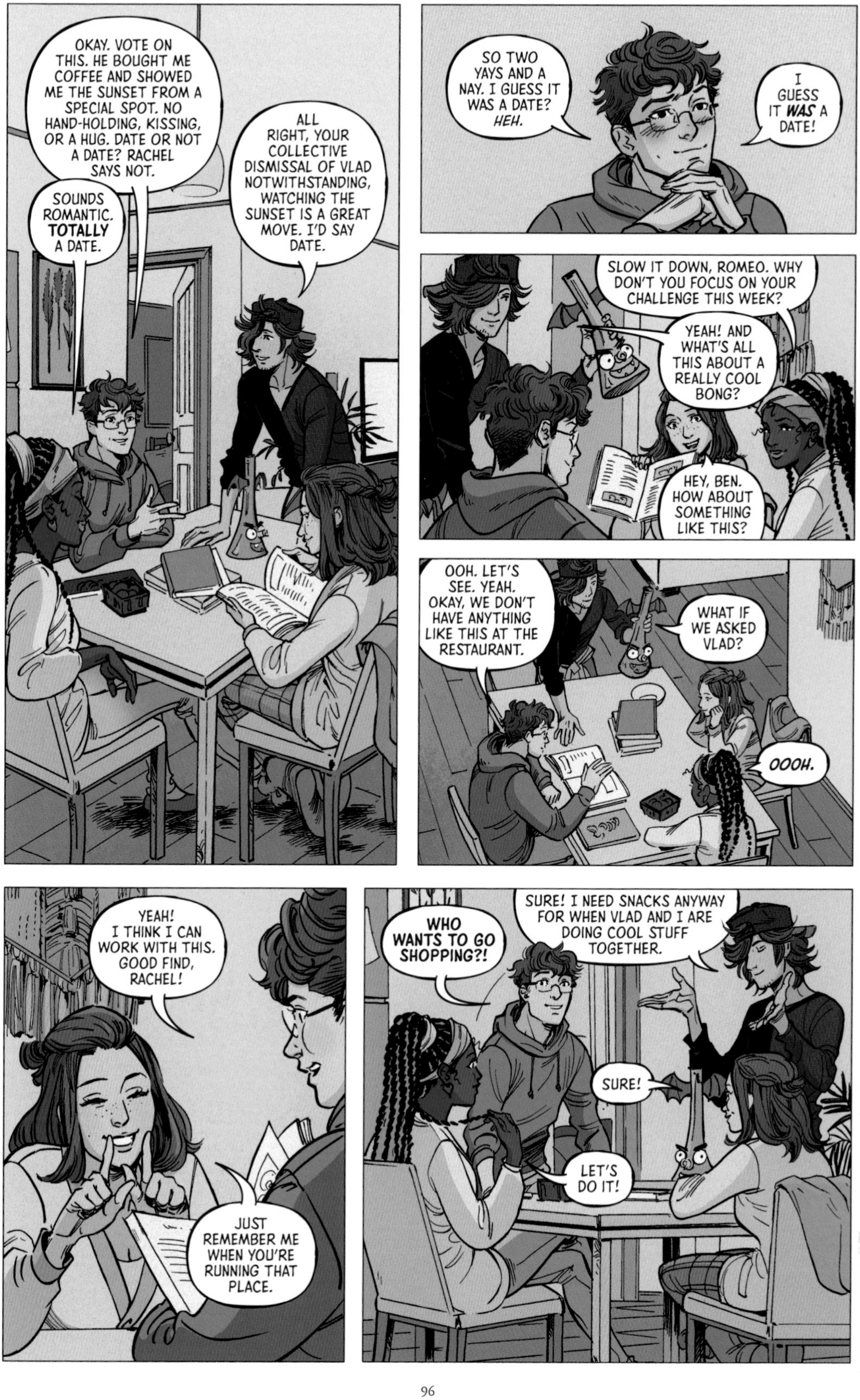
OKAY. VOTE ON THIS. HE BOUGHT ME COFFEE AND SHOWED ME THE SUNSET FROM A SPECIAL SPOT. NO HAND-HOLDING, KISSING, OR A HUG. DATE OR NOT A DATE? RACHEL SAYS NOT.
SOUNDS ROMANTIC. **TOTALLY** A DATE.
ALL RIGHT, YOUR COLLECTIVE DISMISSAL OF VLAD NOTWITHSTANDING, WATCHING THE SUNSET IS A GREAT MOVE. I'D SAY DATE.
SO TWO YAYS AND A NAY. I GUESS IT WAS A DATE? *HEH.*
I GUESS IT ***WAS*** A DATE!
SLOW IT DOWN, ROMEO. WHY DON'T YOU FOCUS ON YOUR CHALLENGE THIS WEEK?
YEAH! AND WHAT'S ALL THIS ABOUT A REALLY COOL BONG?
HEY, BEN. HOW ABOUT SOMETHING LIKE THIS?
OOH. LET'S SEE. YEAH. OKAY, WE DON'T HAVE ANYTHING LIKE THIS AT THE RESTAURANT.
WHAT IF WE ASKED VLAD?
OOOH.
YEAH! I THINK I CAN WORK WITH THIS. GOOD FIND, RACHEL!
JUST REMEMBER ME WHEN YOU'RE RUNNING THAT PLACE.
WHO WANTS TO GO SHOPPING?!
SURE! I NEED SNACKS ANYWAY FOR WHEN VLAD AND I ARE DOING COOL STUFF TOGETHER.
SURE!
LET'S DO IT!

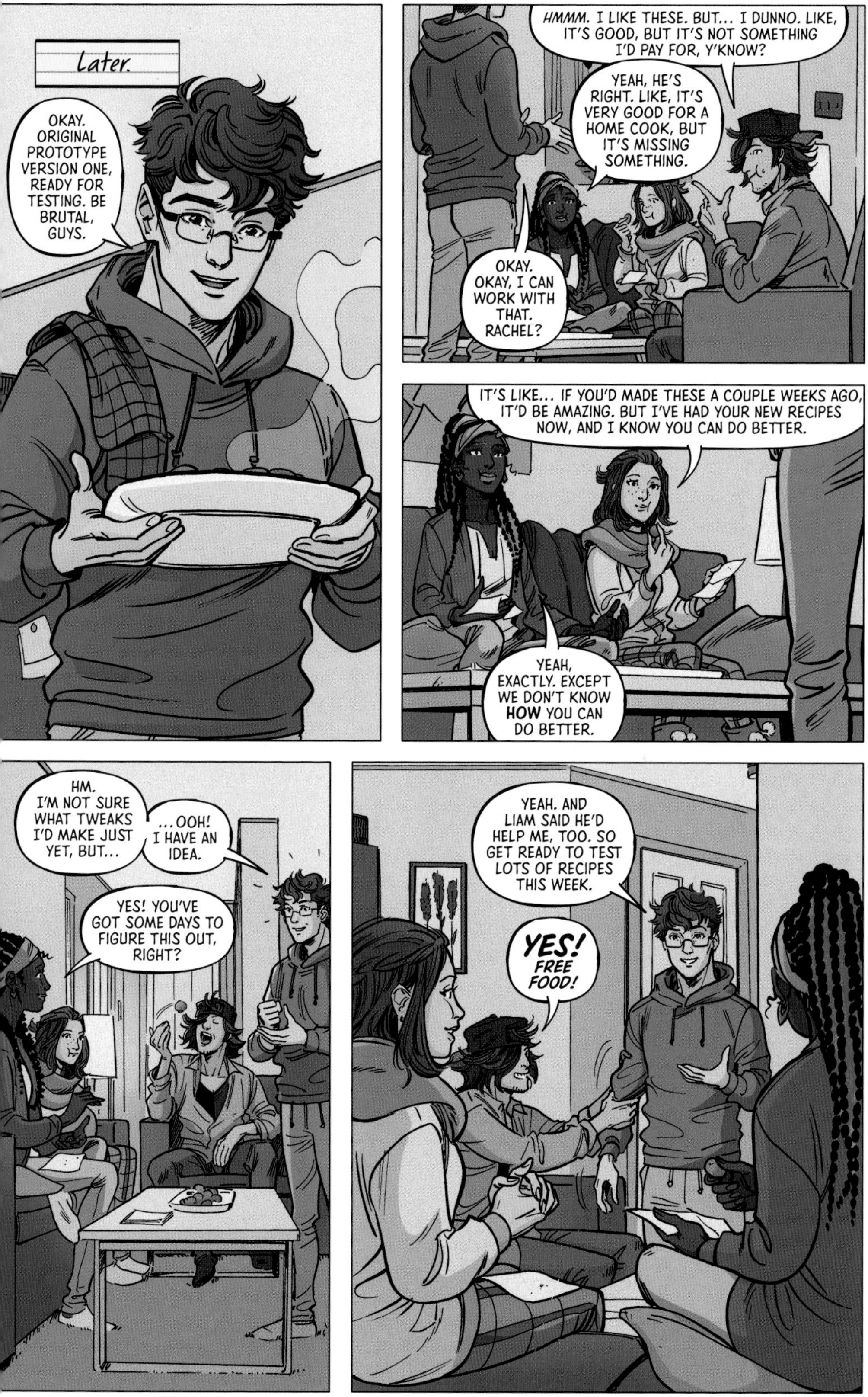

Later.
OKAY. ORIGINAL PROTOTYPE VERSION ONE, READY FOR TESTING. BE BRUTAL, GUYS.
HMMM. I LIKE THESE. BUT... I DUNNO. LIKE, IT'S GOOD, BUT IT'S NOT SOMETHING I'D PAY FOR, Y'KNOW?
YEAH, HE'S RIGHT. LIKE, IT'S VERY GOOD FOR A HOME COOK, BUT IT'S MISSING SOMETHING.
OKAY. OKAY, I CAN WORK WITH THAT. RACHEL?
IT'S LIKE... IF YOU'D MADE THESE A COUPLE WEEKS AGO, IT'D BE AMAZING. BUT I'VE HAD YOUR NEW RECIPES NOW, AND I KNOW YOU CAN DO BETTER.
YEAH, EXACTLY. EXCEPT WE DON'T KNOW **HOW** YOU CAN DO BETTER.
HM. I'M NOT SURE WHAT TWEAKS I'D MAKE JUST YET, BUT...
...OOH! I HAVE AN IDEA.
YES! YOU'VE GOT SOME DAYS TO FIGURE THIS OUT, RIGHT?
YEAH. AND LIAM SAID HE'D HELP ME, TOO. SO GET READY TO TEST LOTS OF RECIPES THIS WEEK.
YES! FREE FOOD!

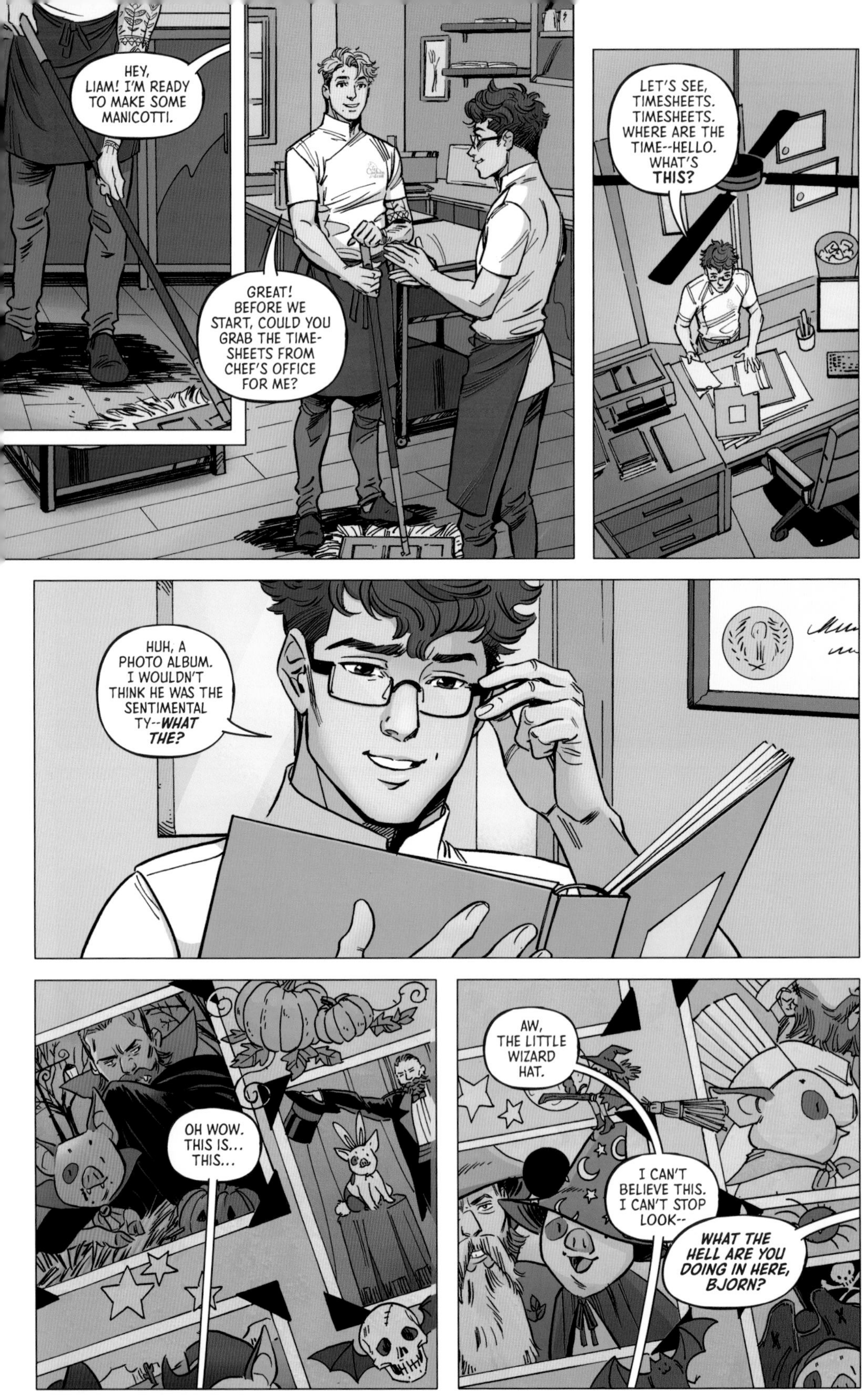
HEY, LIAM! I'M READY TO MAKE SOME MANICOTTI.
GREAT! BEFORE WE START, COULD YOU GRAB THE TIME-SHEETS FROM CHEF'S OFFICE FOR ME?
LET'S SEE, TIMESHEETS. TIMESHEETS. WHERE ARE THE TIME--HELLO. WHAT'S THIS?
HUH, A PHOTO ALBUM. I WOULDN'T THINK HE WAS THE SENTIMENTAL TY--WHAT THE?
OH WOW. THIS IS... THIS...
AW, THE LITTLE WIZARD HAT.
I CAN'T BELIEVE THIS. I CAN'T STOP LOOK--
WHAT THE HELL ARE YOU DOING IN HERE, BJORN?

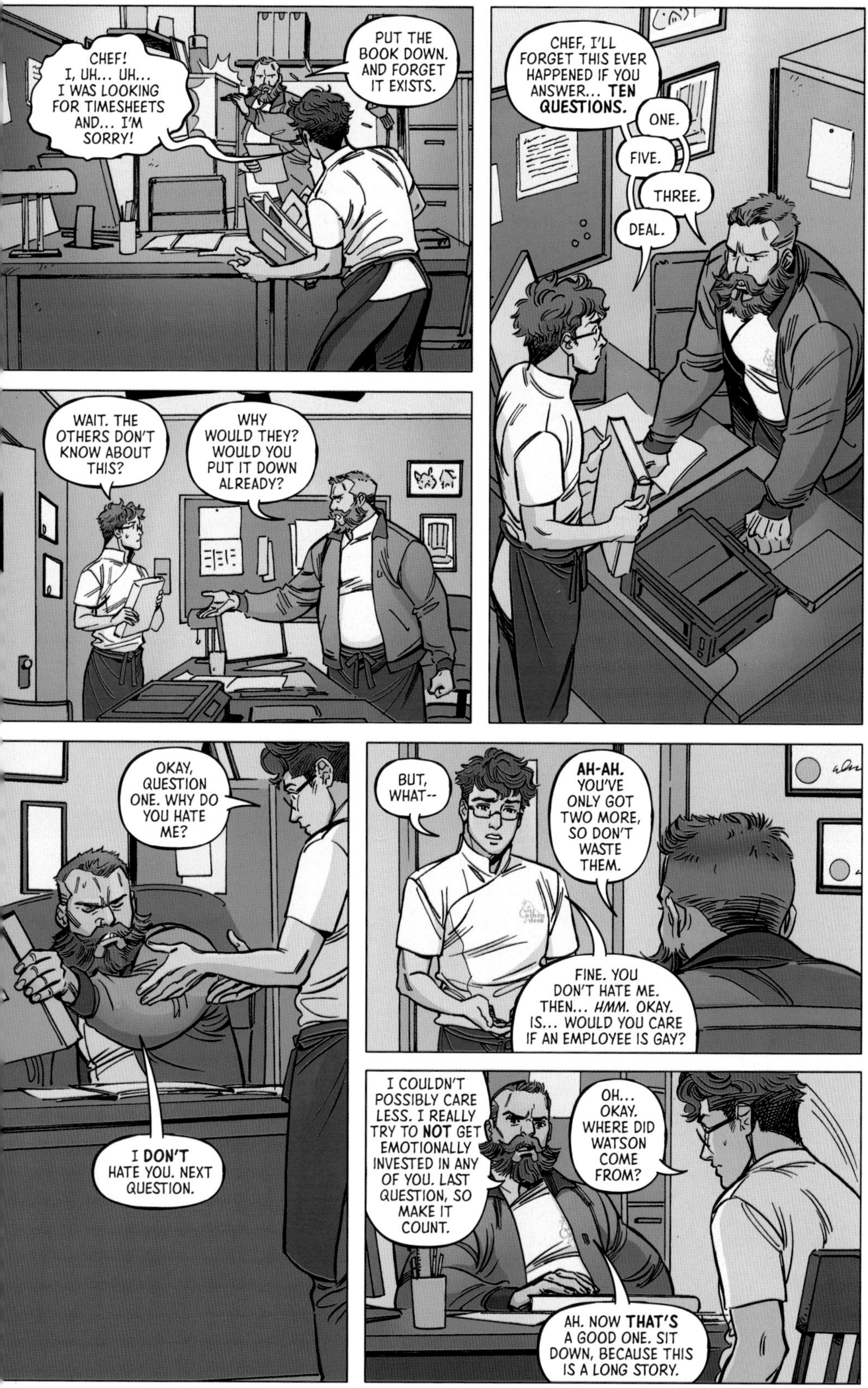
CHEF! I, UH... UH... I WAS LOOKING FOR TIMESHEETS AND... I'M SORRY!
PUT THE BOOK DOWN. AND FORGET IT EXISTS.
CHEF, I'LL FORGET THIS EVER HAPPENED IF YOU ANSWER... **TEN QUESTIONS.**
ONE.
FIVE.
THREE.
DEAL.
WAIT. THE OTHERS DON'T KNOW ABOUT THIS?
WHY WOULD THEY? WOULD YOU PUT IT DOWN ALREADY?
OKAY, QUESTION ONE. WHY DO YOU HATE ME?
I **DON'T** HATE YOU. NEXT QUESTION.
BUT, WHAT--
AH-AH. YOU'VE ONLY GOT TWO MORE, SO DON'T WASTE THEM.
FINE. YOU DON'T HATE ME. THEN... *HMM.* OKAY. IS... WOULD YOU CARE IF AN EMPLOYEE IS GAY?
I COULDN'T POSSIBLY CARE LESS. I REALLY TRY TO **NOT** GET EMOTIONALLY INVESTED IN ANY OF YOU. LAST QUESTION, SO MAKE IT COUNT.
OH... OKAY. WHERE DID WATSON COME FROM?
AH. NOW **THAT'S** A GOOD ONE. SIT DOWN, BECAUSE THIS IS A LONG STORY.

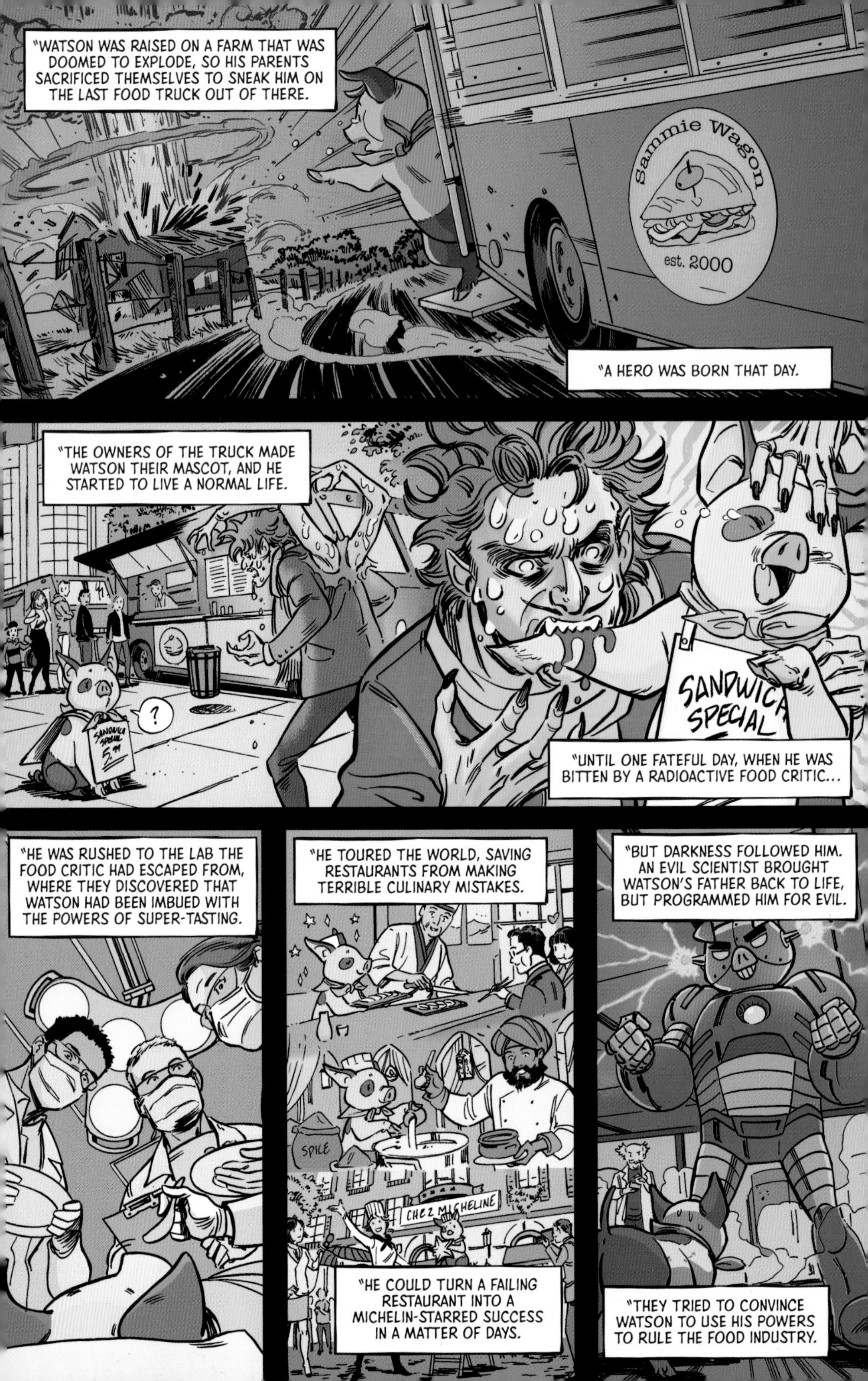
"WATSON WAS RAISED ON A FARM THAT WAS DOOMED TO EXPLODE, SO HIS PARENTS SACRIFICED THEMSELVES TO SNEAK HIM ON THE LAST FOOD TRUCK OUT OF THERE.
Sammie Wagon
est. 2000
"A HERO WAS BORN THAT DAY.
"THE OWNERS OF THE TRUCK MADE WATSON THEIR MASCOT, AND HE STARTED TO LIVE A NORMAL LIFE.
?
SANDWICH SPECIAL
"UNTIL ONE FATEFUL DAY, WHEN HE WAS BITTEN BY A RADIOACTIVE FOOD CRITIC...
"HE WAS RUSHED TO THE LAB THE FOOD CRITIC HAD ESCAPED FROM, WHERE THEY DISCOVERED THAT WATSON HAD BEEN IMBUED WITH THE POWERS OF SUPER-TASTING.
"HE TOURED THE WORLD, SAVING RESTAURANTS FROM MAKING TERRIBLE CULINARY MISTAKES.
SPICE
CHEZ MICHELINE
"HE COULD TURN A FAILING RESTAURANT INTO A MICHELIN-STARRED SUCCESS IN A MATTER OF DAYS.
"BUT DARKNESS FOLLOWED HIM. AN EVIL SCIENTIST BROUGHT WATSON'S FATHER BACK TO LIFE, BUT PROGRAMMED HIM FOR EVIL.
"THEY TRIED TO CONVINCE WATSON TO USE HIS POWERS TO RULE THE FOOD INDUSTRY.

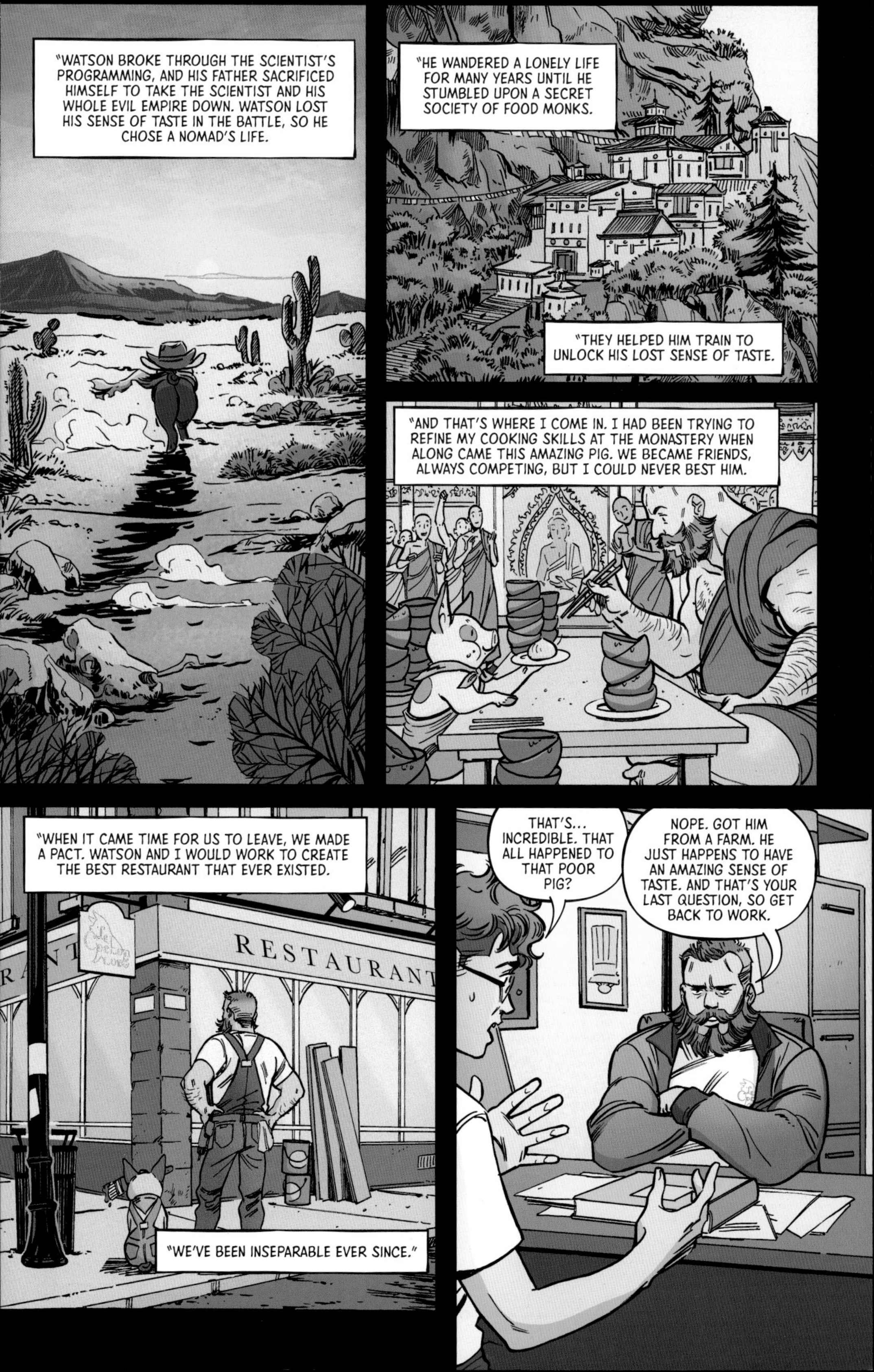
"WATSON BROKE THROUGH THE SCIENTIST'S PROGRAMMING, AND HIS FATHER SACRIFICED HIMSELF TO TAKE THE SCIENTIST AND HIS WHOLE EVIL EMPIRE DOWN. WATSON LOST HIS SENSE OF TASTE IN THE BATTLE, SO HE CHOSE A NOMAD'S LIFE.
"HE WANDERED A LONELY LIFE FOR MANY YEARS UNTIL HE STUMBLED UPON A SECRET SOCIETY OF FOOD MONKS.
"THEY HELPED HIM TRAIN TO UNLOCK HIS LOST SENSE OF TASTE.
"AND THAT'S WHERE I COME IN. I HAD BEEN TRYING TO REFINE MY COOKING SKILLS AT THE MONASTERY WHEN ALONG CAME THIS AMAZING PIG. WE BECAME FRIENDS, ALWAYS COMPETING, BUT I COULD NEVER BEST HIM.
"WHEN IT CAME TIME FOR US TO LEAVE, WE MADE A PACT. WATSON AND I WOULD WORK TO CREATE THE BEST RESTAURANT THAT EVER EXISTED.
RESTAURANT
"WE'VE BEEN INSEPARABLE EVER SINCE."
THAT'S... INCREDIBLE. THAT ALL HAPPENED TO THAT POOR PIG?
NOPE. GOT HIM FROM A FARM. HE JUST HAPPENS TO HAVE AN AMAZING SENSE OF TASTE. AND THAT'S YOUR LAST QUESTION, SO GET BACK TO WORK.

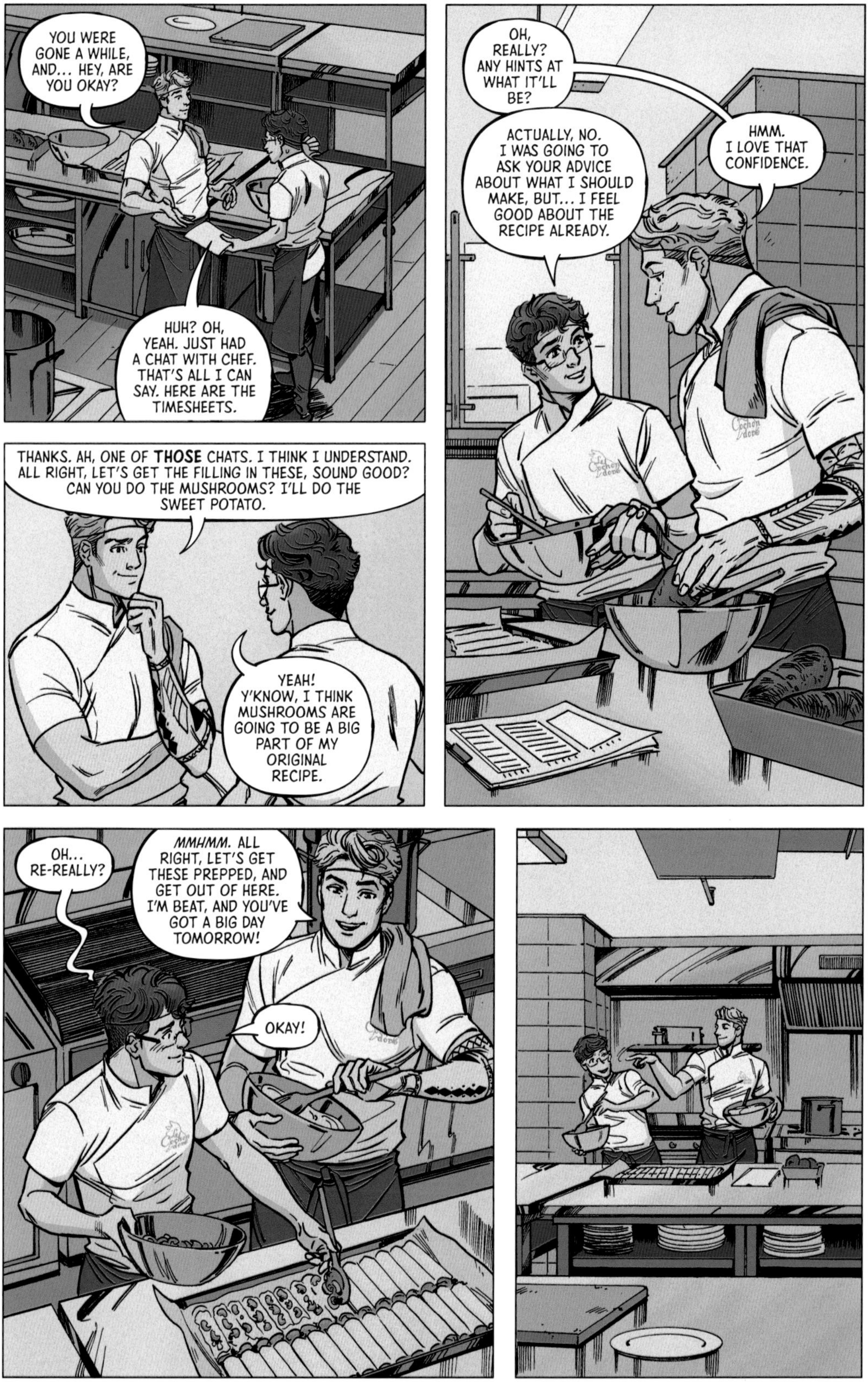
YOU WERE GONE A WHILE, AND... HEY, ARE YOU OKAY?
HUH? OH, YEAH. JUST HAD A CHAT WITH CHEF. THAT'S ALL I CAN SAY. HERE ARE THE TIMESHEETS.
THANKS. AH, ONE OF **THOSE** CHATS. I THINK I UNDERSTAND. ALL RIGHT, LET'S GET THE FILLING IN THESE, SOUND GOOD? CAN YOU DO THE MUSHROOMS? I'LL DO THE SWEET POTATO.
YEAH! Y'KNOW, I THINK MUSHROOMS ARE GOING TO BE A BIG PART OF MY ORIGINAL RECIPE.
OH, REALLY? ANY HINTS AT WHAT IT'LL BE?
ACTUALLY, NO. I WAS GOING TO ASK YOUR ADVICE ABOUT WHAT I SHOULD MAKE, BUT... I FEEL GOOD ABOUT THE RECIPE ALREADY.
HMM. I LOVE THAT CONFIDENCE.
OH... RE-REALLY?
MMHMM. ALL RIGHT, LET'S GET THESE PREPPED, AND GET OUT OF HERE. I'M BEAT, AND YOU'VE GOT A BIG DAY TOMORROW!
OKAY!

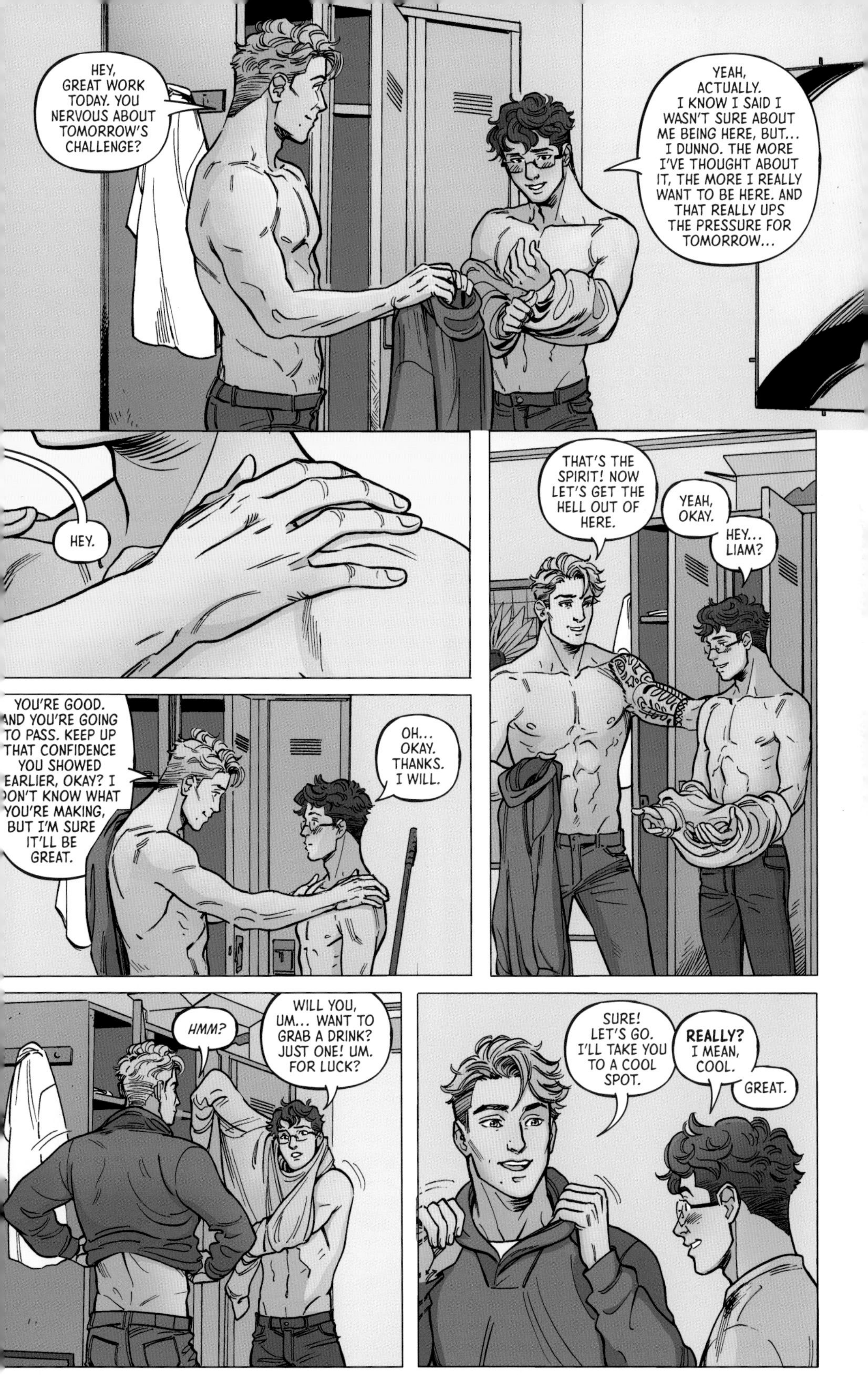
HEY, GREAT WORK TODAY. YOU NERVOUS ABOUT TOMORROW'S CHALLENGE?
YEAH, ACTUALLY. I KNOW I SAID I WASN'T SURE ABOUT ME BEING HERE, BUT... I DUNNO. THE MORE I'VE THOUGHT ABOUT IT, THE MORE I REALLY WANT TO BE HERE. AND THAT REALLY UPS THE PRESSURE FOR TOMORROW...
HEY.
YOU'RE GOOD. AND YOU'RE GOING TO PASS. KEEP UP THAT CONFIDENCE YOU SHOWED EARLIER, OKAY? I DON'T KNOW WHAT YOU'RE MAKING, BUT I'M SURE IT'LL BE GREAT.
OH... OKAY. THANKS. I WILL.
THAT'S THE SPIRIT! NOW LET'S GET THE HELL OUT OF HERE.
YEAH, OKAY.
HEY... LIAM?
HMM?
WILL YOU, UM... WANT TO GRAB A DRINK? JUST ONE! UM. FOR LUCK?
SURE! LET'S GO. I'LL TAKE YOU TO A COOL SPOT.
REALLY? I MEAN, COOL.
GREAT.

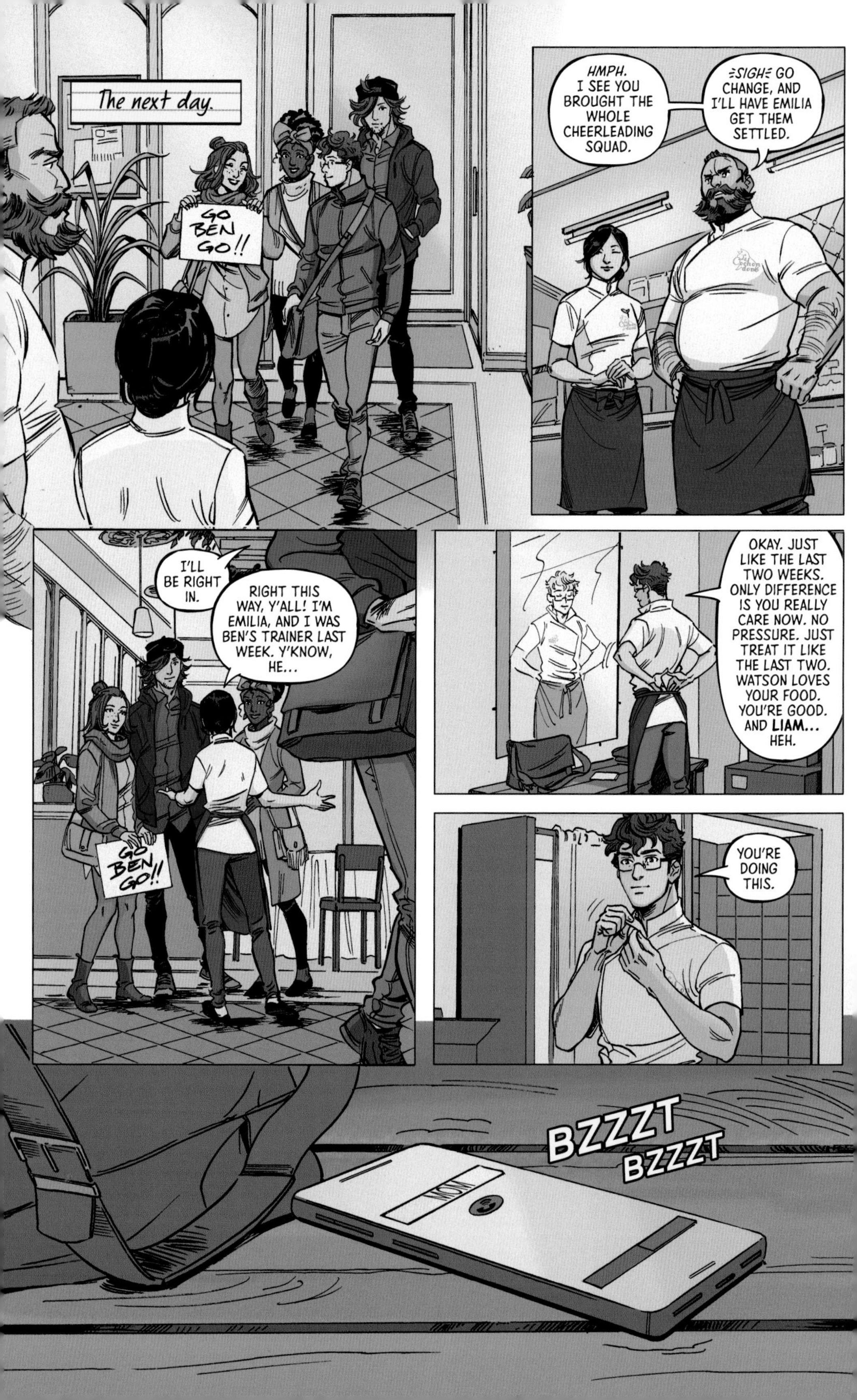
The next day.
GO BEN GO!!
HMPH. I SEE YOU BROUGHT THE WHOLE CHEERLEADING SQUAD.
=SIGH= GO CHANGE, AND I'LL HAVE EMILIA GET THEM SETTLED.
I'LL BE RIGHT IN.
RIGHT THIS WAY, Y'ALL! I'M EMILIA, AND I WAS BEN'S TRAINER LAST WEEK. Y'KNOW, HE...
GO BEN GO!!
OKAY. JUST LIKE THE LAST TWO WEEKS. ONLY DIFFERENCE IS YOU REALLY CARE NOW. NO PRESSURE. JUST TREAT IT LIKE THE LAST TWO. WATSON LOVES YOUR FOOD. YOU'RE GOOD. AND **LIAM...** HEH.
YOU'RE DOING THIS.
BZZZT BZZZT
MOM

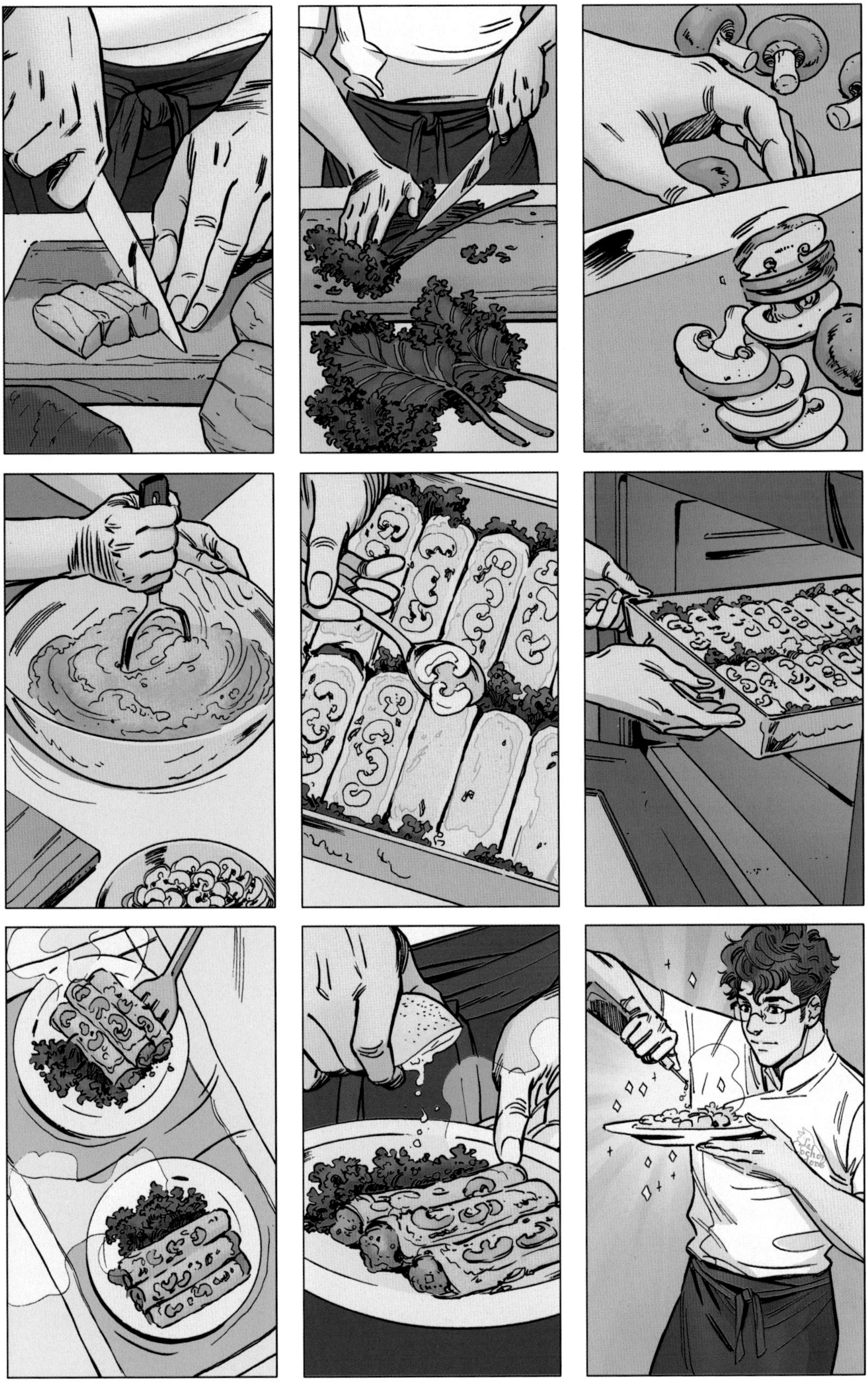

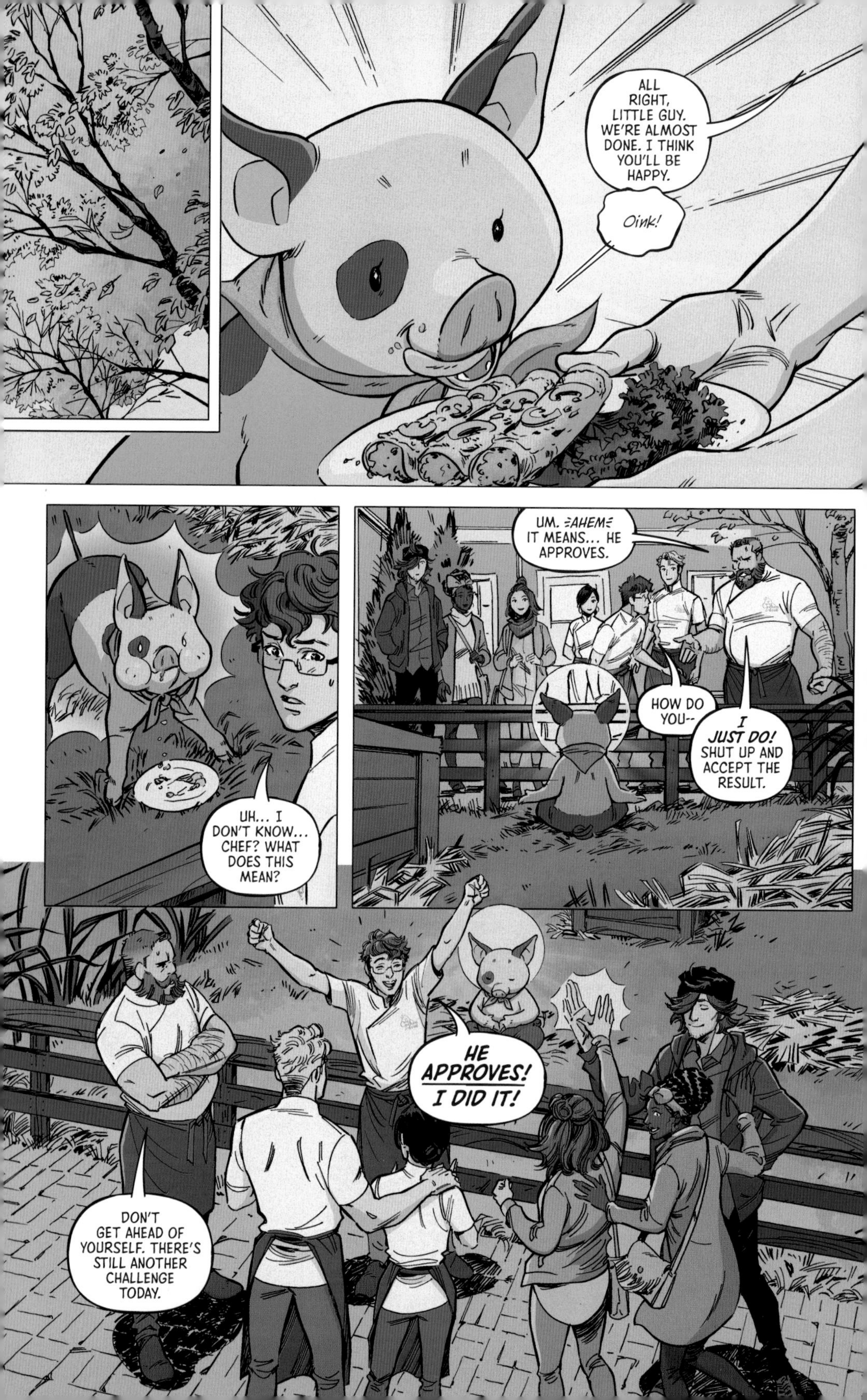
ALL RIGHT, LITTLE GUY. WE'RE ALMOST DONE. I THINK YOU'LL BE HAPPY.
Oink!
UH... I DON'T KNOW... CHEF? WHAT DOES THIS MEAN?
UM. AHEM IT MEANS... HE APPROVES.
HOW DO YOU--
I JUST DO! SHUT UP AND ACCEPT THE RESULT.
HE APPROVES! I DID IT!
DON'T GET AHEAD OF YOURSELF. THERE'S STILL ANOTHER CHALLENGE TODAY.

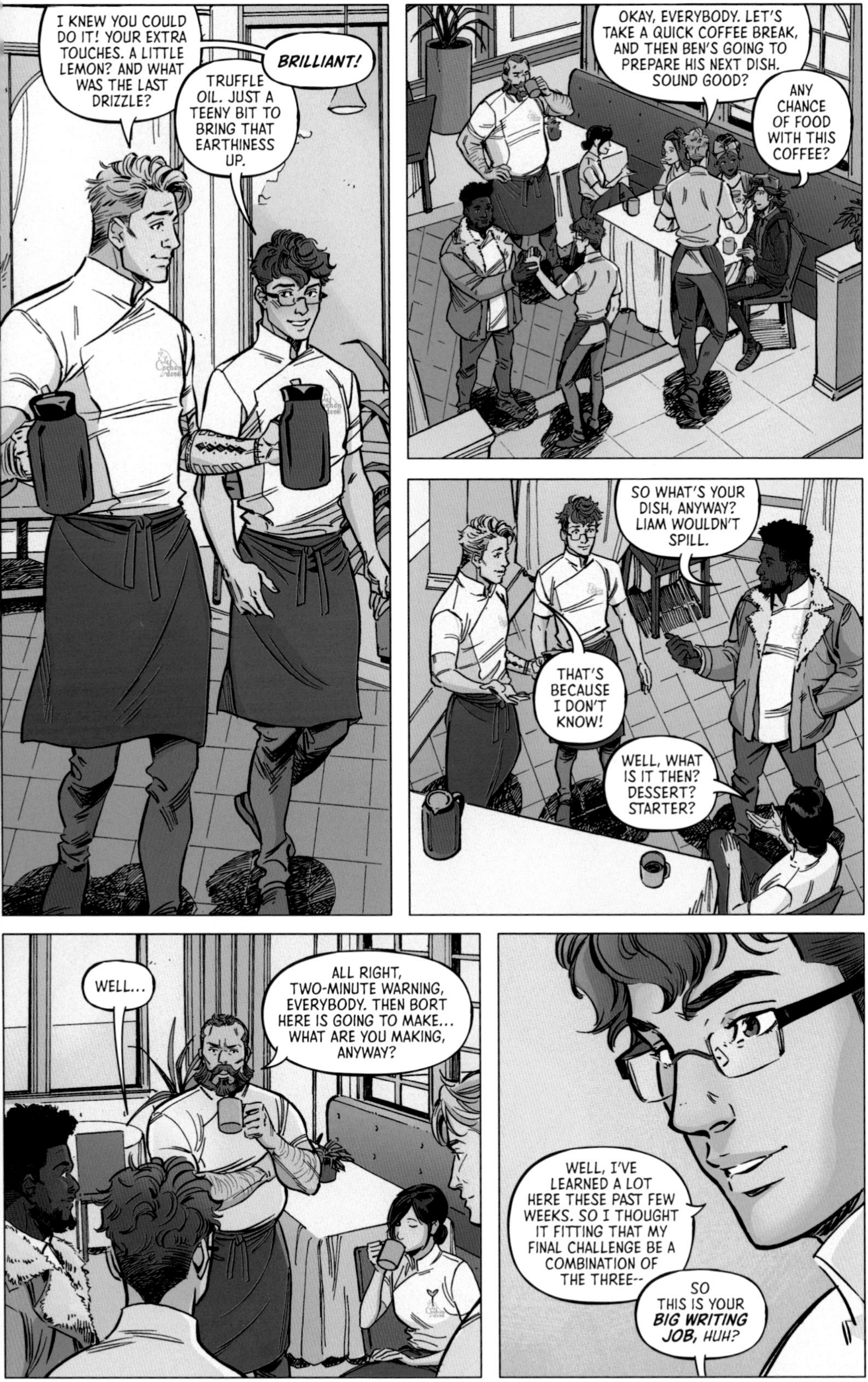
I KNEW YOU COULD DO IT! YOUR EXTRA TOUCHES. A LITTLE LEMON? AND WHAT WAS THE LAST DRIZZLE?
BRILLIANT!
TRUFFLE OIL. JUST A TEENY BIT TO BRING THAT EARTHINESS UP.
OKAY, EVERYBODY. LET'S TAKE A QUICK COFFEE BREAK, AND THEN BEN'S GOING TO PREPARE HIS NEXT DISH. SOUND GOOD?
ANY CHANCE OF FOOD WITH THIS COFFEE?
SO WHAT'S YOUR DISH, ANYWAY? LIAM WOULDN'T SPILL.
THAT'S BECAUSE I DON'T KNOW!
WELL, WHAT IS IT THEN? DESSERT? STARTER?
WELL...
ALL RIGHT, TWO-MINUTE WARNING, EVERYBODY. THEN BORT HERE IS GOING TO MAKE... WHAT ARE YOU MAKING, ANYWAY?
WELL, I'VE LEARNED A LOT HERE THESE PAST FEW WEEKS. SO I THOUGHT IT FITTING THAT MY FINAL CHALLENGE BE A COMBINATION OF THE THREE--
SO THIS IS YOUR BIG WRITING JOB, HUH?

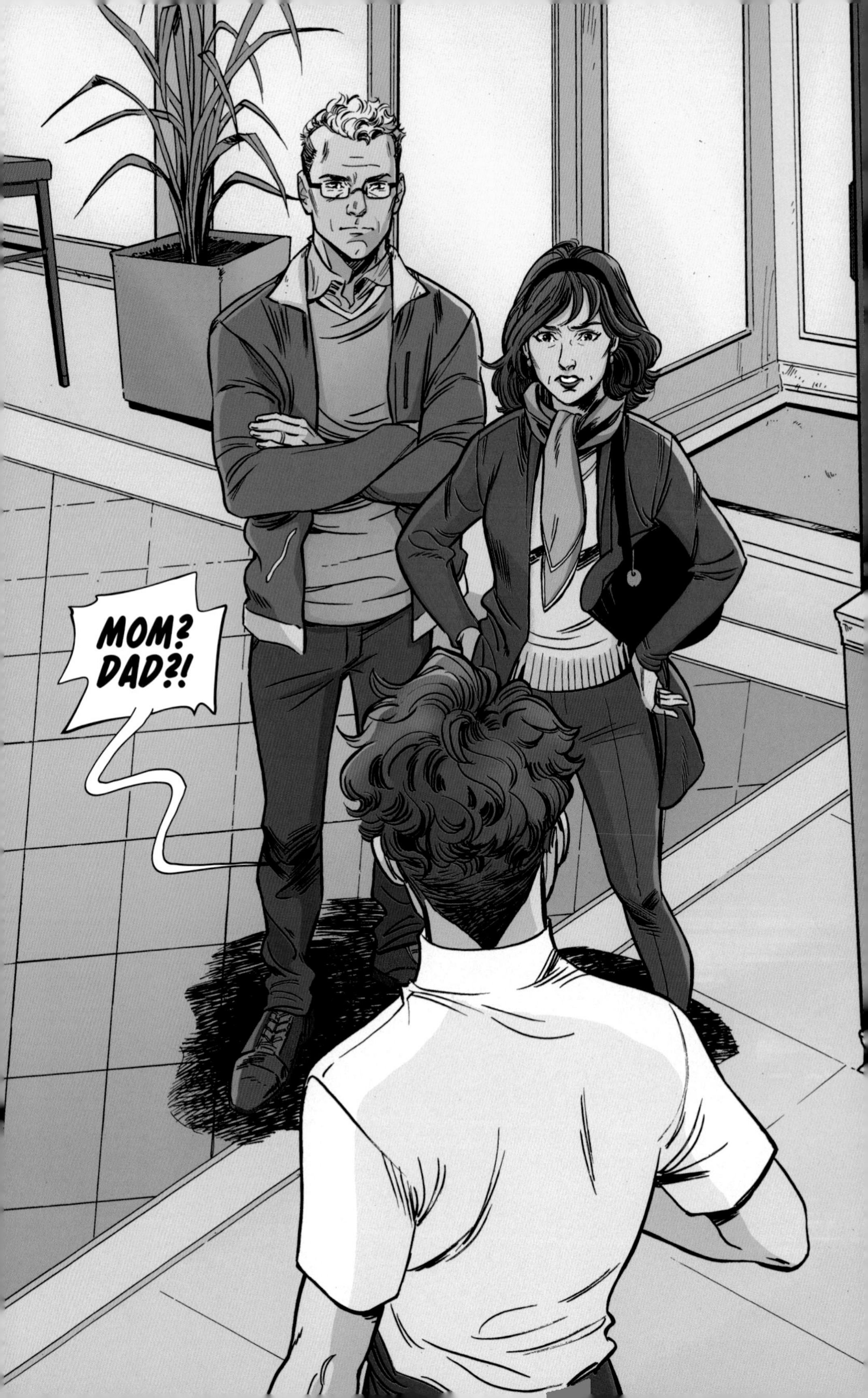
MOM? DAD?!

Chapter Five

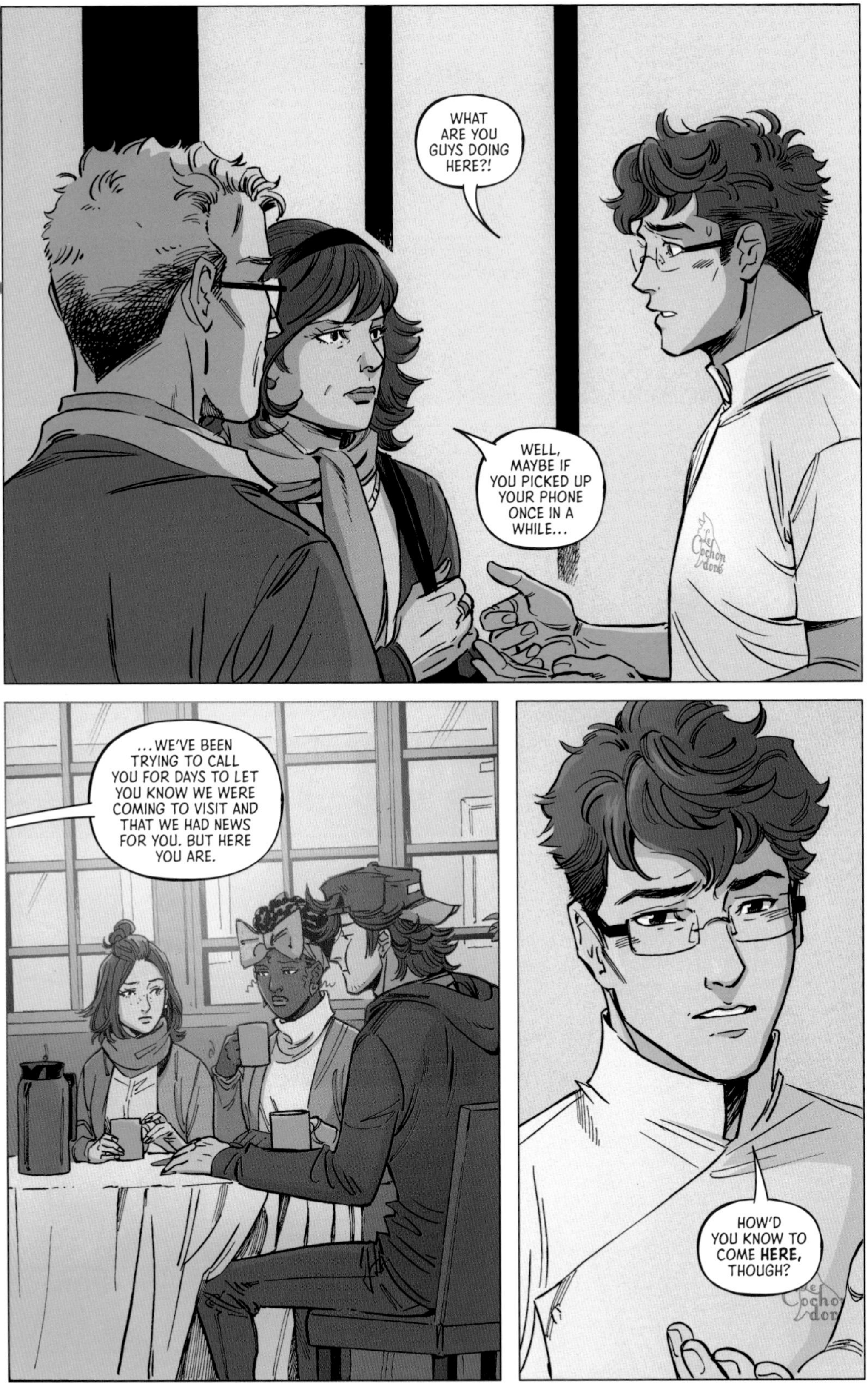
WHAT ARE YOU GUYS DOING HERE?!
WELL, MAYBE IF YOU PICKED UP YOUR PHONE ONCE IN A WHILE...
...WE'VE BEEN TRYING TO CALL YOU FOR DAYS TO LET YOU KNOW WE WERE COMING TO VISIT AND THAT WE HAD NEWS FOR YOU. BUT HERE YOU ARE.
HOW'D YOU KNOW TO COME **HERE,** THOUGH?

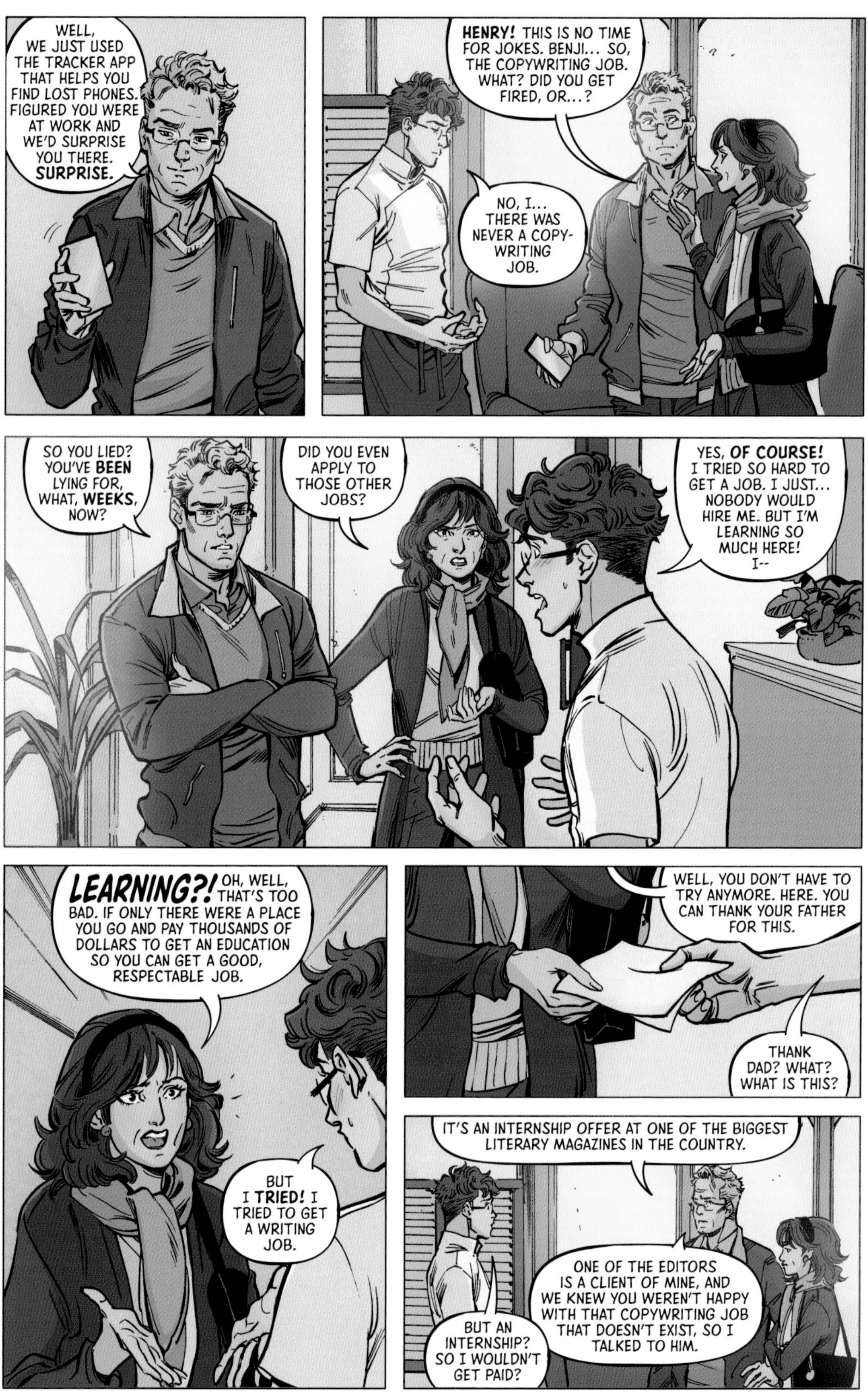
WELL, WE JUST USED THE TRACKER APP THAT HELPS YOU FIND LOST PHONES. FIGURED YOU WERE AT WORK AND WE'D SURPRISE YOU THERE. SURPRISE.
HENRY! THIS IS NO TIME FOR JOKES. BENJI... SO, THE COPYWRITING JOB. WHAT? DID YOU GET FIRED, OR...?
NO, I... THERE WAS NEVER A COPY-WRITING JOB.
SO YOU LIED? YOU'VE BEEN LYING FOR, WHAT, WEEKS, NOW?
DID YOU EVEN APPLY TO THOSE OTHER JOBS?
YES, OF COURSE! I TRIED SO HARD TO GET A JOB. I JUST... NOBODY WOULD HIRE ME. BUT I'M LEARNING SO MUCH HERE! I--
LEARNING?! OH, WELL, THAT'S TOO BAD. IF ONLY THERE WERE A PLACE YOU GO AND PAY THOUSANDS OF DOLLARS TO GET AN EDUCATION SO YOU CAN GET A GOOD, RESPECTABLE JOB.
BUT I TRIED! I TRIED TO GET A WRITING JOB.
WELL, YOU DON'T HAVE TO TRY ANYMORE. HERE. YOU CAN THANK YOUR FATHER FOR THIS.
THANK DAD? WHAT? WHAT IS THIS?
IT'S AN INTERNSHIP OFFER AT ONE OF THE BIGGEST LITERARY MAGAZINES IN THE COUNTRY.
ONE OF THE EDITORS IS A CLIENT OF MINE, AND WE KNEW YOU WEREN'T HAPPY WITH THAT COPYWRITING JOB THAT DOESN'T EXIST, SO I TALKED TO HIM.
BUT AN INTERNSHIP? SO I WOULDN'T GET PAID?

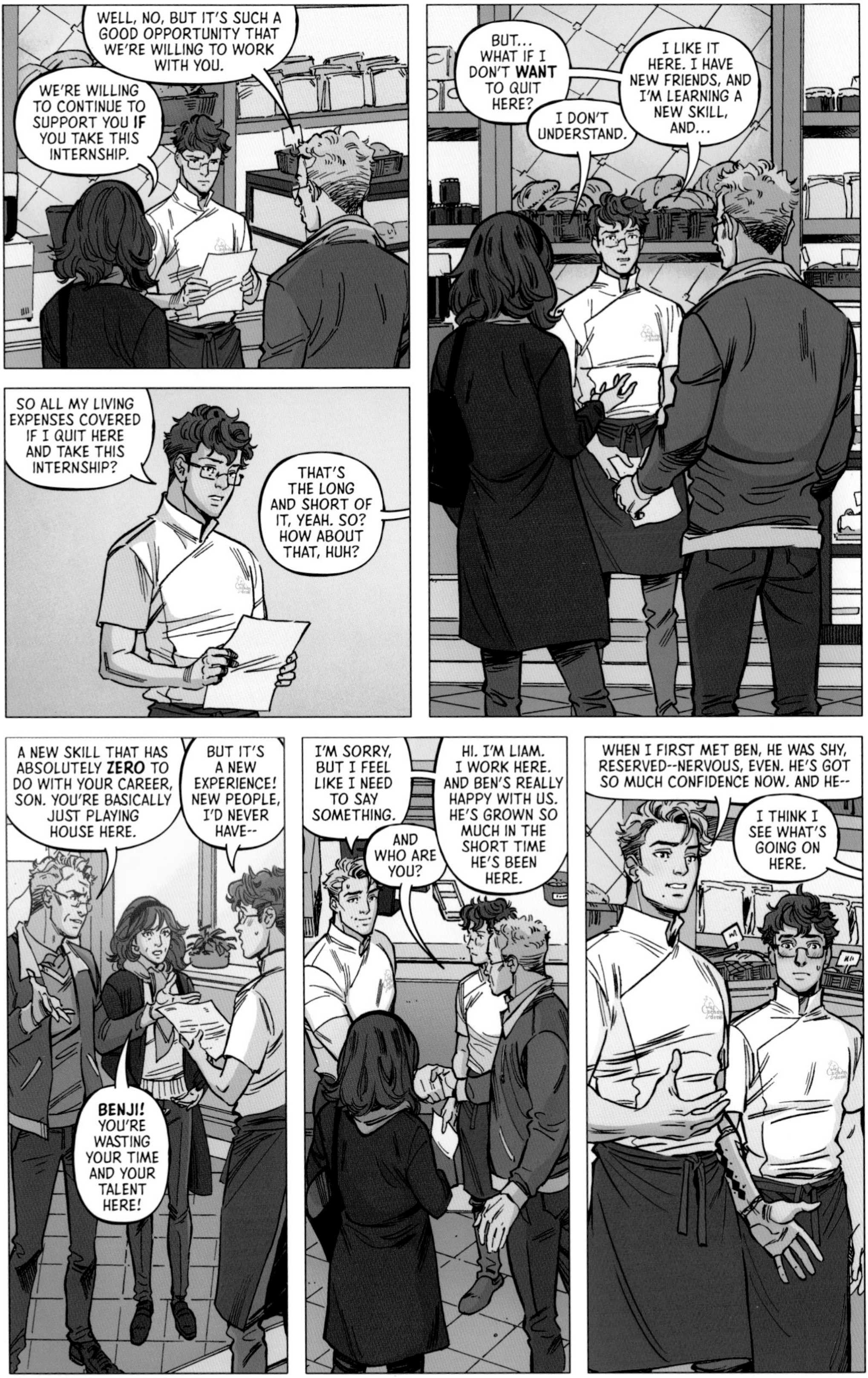
WELL, NO, BUT IT'S SUCH A GOOD OPPORTUNITY THAT WE'RE WILLING TO WORK WITH YOU.
WE'RE WILLING TO CONTINUE TO SUPPORT YOU **IF** YOU TAKE THIS INTERNSHIP.
BUT... WHAT IF I DON'T **WANT** TO QUIT HERE?
I LIKE IT HERE. I HAVE NEW FRIENDS, AND I'M LEARNING A NEW SKILL, AND...
I DON'T UNDERSTAND.
SO ALL MY LIVING EXPENSES COVERED IF I QUIT HERE AND TAKE THIS INTERNSHIP?
THAT'S THE LONG AND SHORT OF IT, YEAH. SO? HOW ABOUT THAT, HUH?
A NEW SKILL THAT HAS ABSOLUTELY **ZERO** TO DO WITH YOUR CAREER, SON. YOU'RE BASICALLY JUST PLAYING HOUSE HERE.
BUT IT'S A NEW EXPERIENCE! NEW PEOPLE, I'D NEVER HAVE--
BENJI! YOU'RE WASTING YOUR TIME AND YOUR TALENT HERE!
I'M SORRY, BUT I FEEL LIKE I NEED TO SAY SOMETHING.
AND WHO ARE YOU?
HI. I'M LIAM. I WORK HERE. AND BEN'S REALLY HAPPY WITH US. HE'S GROWN SO MUCH IN THE SHORT TIME HE'S BEEN HERE.
WHEN I FIRST MET BEN, HE WAS SHY, RESERVED--NERVOUS, EVEN. HE'S GOT SO MUCH CONFIDENCE NOW. AND HE--
I THINK I SEE WHAT'S GOING ON HERE.

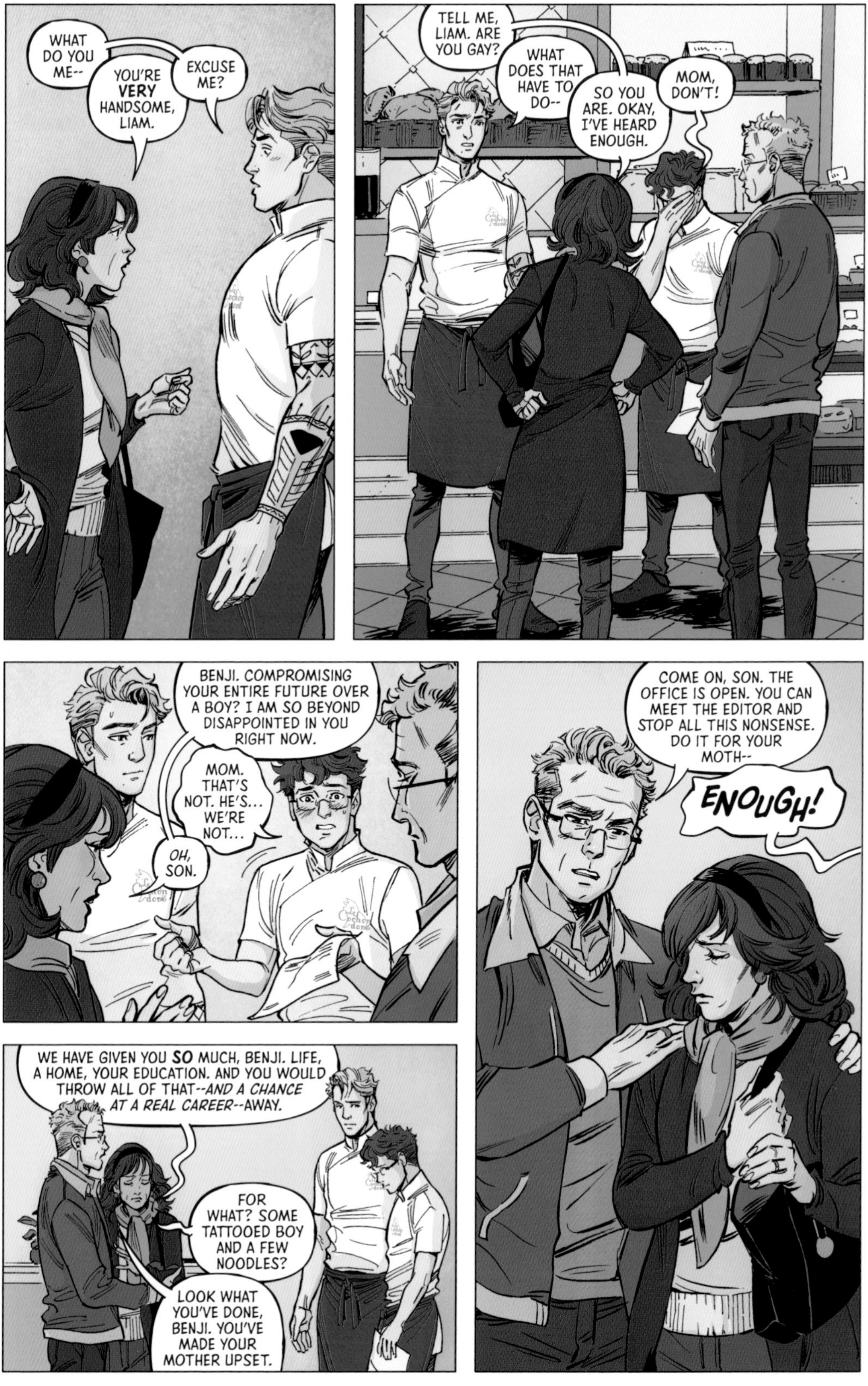
WHAT DO YOU ME--
YOU'RE **VERY** HANDSOME, LIAM.
EXCUSE ME?
TELL ME, LIAM. ARE YOU GAY?
WHAT DOES THAT HAVE TO DO--
SO YOU ARE. OKAY, I'VE HEARD ENOUGH.
MOM, DON'T!
BENJI. COMPROMISING YOUR ENTIRE FUTURE OVER A BOY? I AM SO BEYOND DISAPPOINTED IN YOU RIGHT NOW.
MOM. THAT'S NOT. HE'S... WE'RE NOT...
OH, SON.
WE HAVE GIVEN YOU **SO** MUCH, BENJI. LIFE, A HOME, YOUR EDUCATION. AND YOU WOULD THROW ALL OF THAT--*AND A CHANCE AT A REAL CAREER*--AWAY.
FOR WHAT? SOME TATTOOED BOY AND A FEW NOODLES?
LOOK WHAT YOU'VE DONE, BENJI. YOU'VE MADE YOUR MOTHER UPSET.
COME ON, SON. THE OFFICE IS OPEN. YOU CAN MEET THE EDITOR AND STOP ALL THIS NONSENSE. DO IT FOR YOUR MOTH--
ENOUGH!

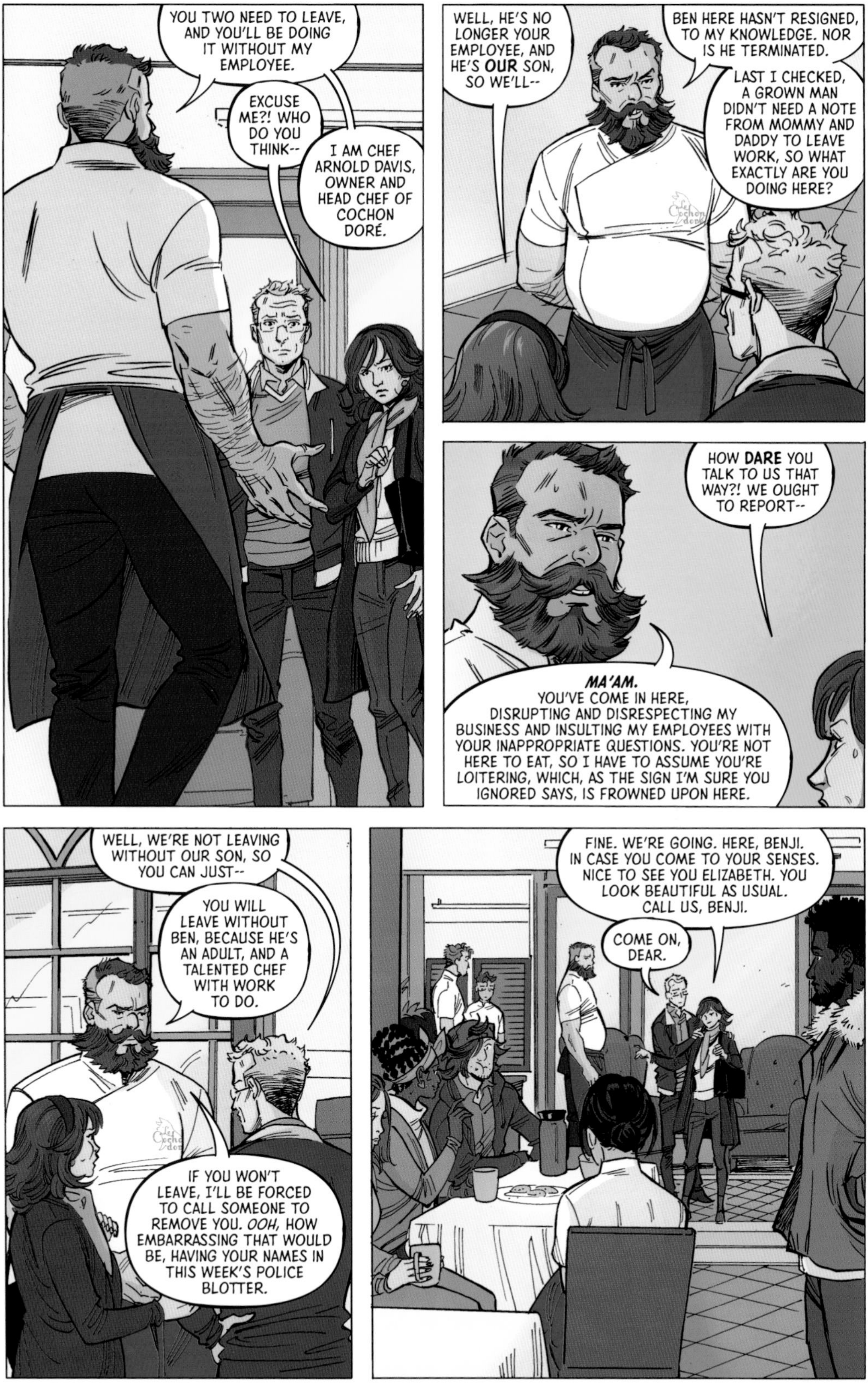
YOU TWO NEED TO LEAVE, AND YOU'LL BE DOING IT WITHOUT MY EMPLOYEE.
EXCUSE ME?! WHO DO YOU THINK--
I AM CHEF ARNOLD DAVIS, OWNER AND HEAD CHEF OF COCHON DORÉ.
WELL, HE'S NO LONGER YOUR EMPLOYEE, AND HE'S **OUR** SON, SO WE'LL--
BEN HERE HASN'T RESIGNED, TO MY KNOWLEDGE. NOR IS HE TERMINATED.
LAST I CHECKED, A GROWN MAN DIDN'T NEED A NOTE FROM MOMMY AND DADDY TO LEAVE WORK, SO WHAT EXACTLY ARE YOU DOING HERE?
HOW **DARE** YOU TALK TO US THAT WAY?! WE OUGHT TO REPORT--
MA'AM. YOU'VE COME IN HERE, DISRUPTING AND DISRESPECTING MY BUSINESS AND INSULTING MY EMPLOYEES WITH YOUR INAPPROPRIATE QUESTIONS. YOU'RE NOT HERE TO EAT, SO I HAVE TO ASSUME YOU'RE LOITERING, WHICH, AS THE SIGN I'M SURE YOU IGNORED SAYS, IS FROWNED UPON HERE.
WELL, WE'RE NOT LEAVING WITHOUT OUR SON, SO YOU CAN JUST--
YOU WILL LEAVE WITHOUT BEN, BECAUSE HE'S AN ADULT, AND A TALENTED CHEF WITH WORK TO DO.
IF YOU WON'T LEAVE, I'LL BE FORCED TO CALL SOMEONE TO REMOVE YOU. *OOH,* HOW EMBARRASSING THAT WOULD BE, HAVING YOUR NAMES IN THIS WEEK'S POLICE BLOTTER.
FINE. WE'RE GOING. HERE, BENJI. IN CASE YOU COME TO YOUR SENSES. NICE TO SEE YOU ELIZABETH. YOU LOOK BEAUTIFUL AS USUAL. CALL US, BENJI.
COME ON, DEAR.

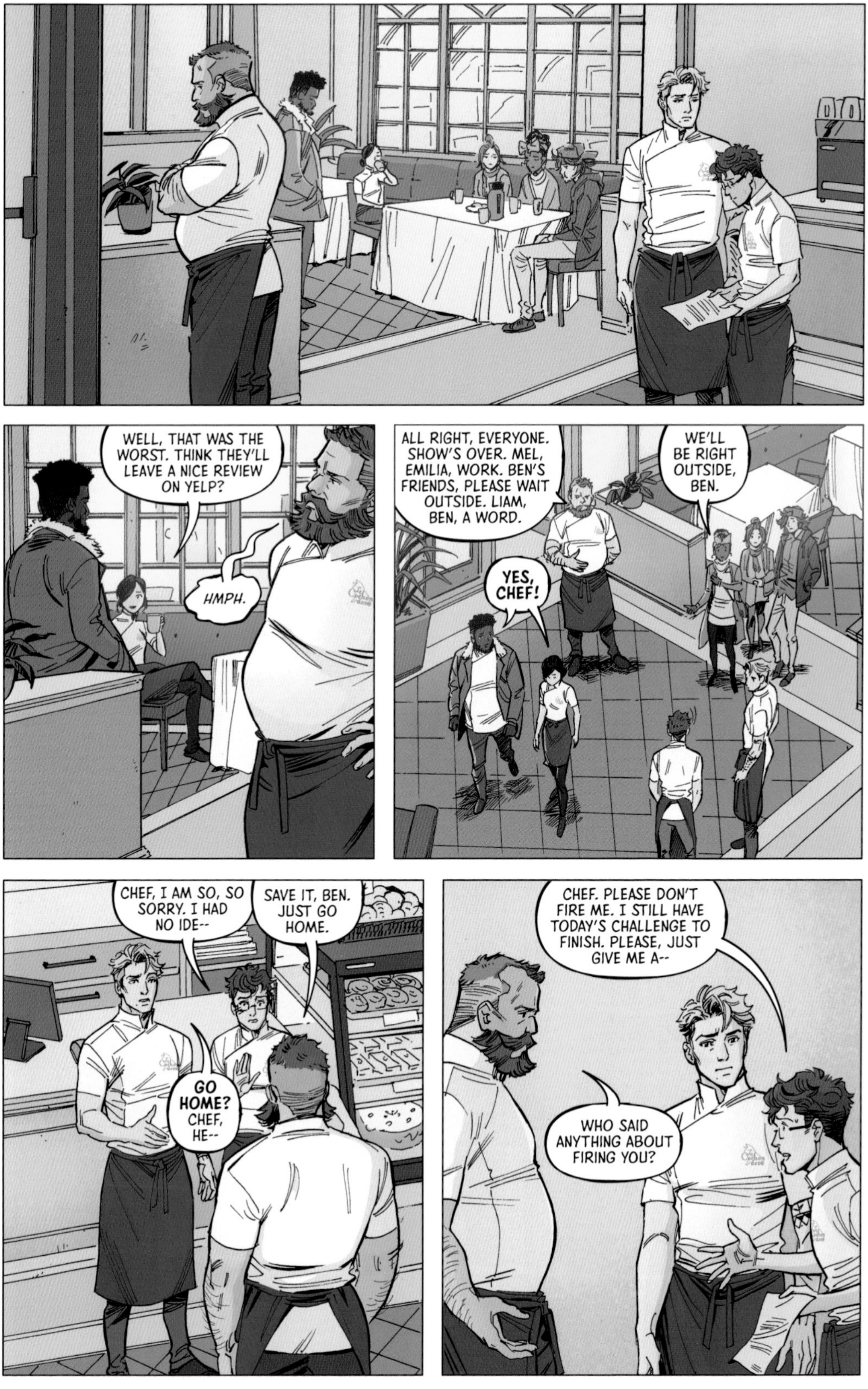
WELL, THAT WAS THE WORST. THINK THEY'LL LEAVE A NICE REVIEW ON YELP?
HMPH.
ALL RIGHT, EVERYONE. SHOW'S OVER. MEL, EMILIA, WORK. BEN'S FRIENDS, PLEASE WAIT OUTSIDE. LIAM, BEN, A WORD.
WE'LL BE RIGHT OUTSIDE, BEN.
YES, CHEF!
CHEF, I AM SO, SO SORRY. I HAD NO IDE--
SAVE IT, BEN. JUST GO HOME.
GO HOME? CHEF, HE--
CHEF. PLEASE DON'T FIRE ME. I STILL HAVE TODAY'S CHALLENGE TO FINISH. PLEASE, JUST GIVE ME A--
WHO SAID ANYTHING ABOUT FIRING YOU?

YOU'RE NOT FIRED, BEN. BUT YOU HAVE A LOT TO THINK ABOUT. TOO MUCH ON YOUR MIND TO COOK WELL TODAY.

I DON'T--

CHEF--

LET ME FINISH. I DON'T AGREE WITH WHAT YOUR PARENTS ARE DOING. BUT THEY HAVE GIVEN YOU AN OPTION, SOMETHING YOU SHOULD AT LEAST CONSIDER.

TAKE THE WEEKEND. WE'LL POSTPONE YOUR FINAL CHALLENGE UNTIL MONDAY. IF YOU DECIDE TO STAY WITH US, COME ON MONDAY AND COOK. IF NOT, WELL. DON'T COME BACK. UNDERSTOOD?

YES, CHEF.

LIAM. PAY HIM. BEN... GOOD LUCK.

YES, CHEF.

THANK YOU, CHEF.

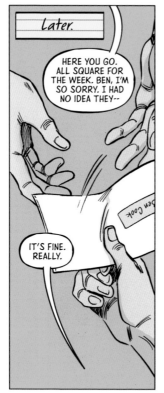

Later.

HERE YOU GO. ALL SQUARE FOR THE WEEK. BEN, I'M SO SORRY. I HAD NO IDEA THEY--

IT'S FINE. REALLY.

WAIT. BEFORE YOU GO, I JUST WANT YOU TO KNOW THAT I CA--

I'VE GOT TO GET GOING. SORRY, THEY'RE WAITING.

DAMN IT.

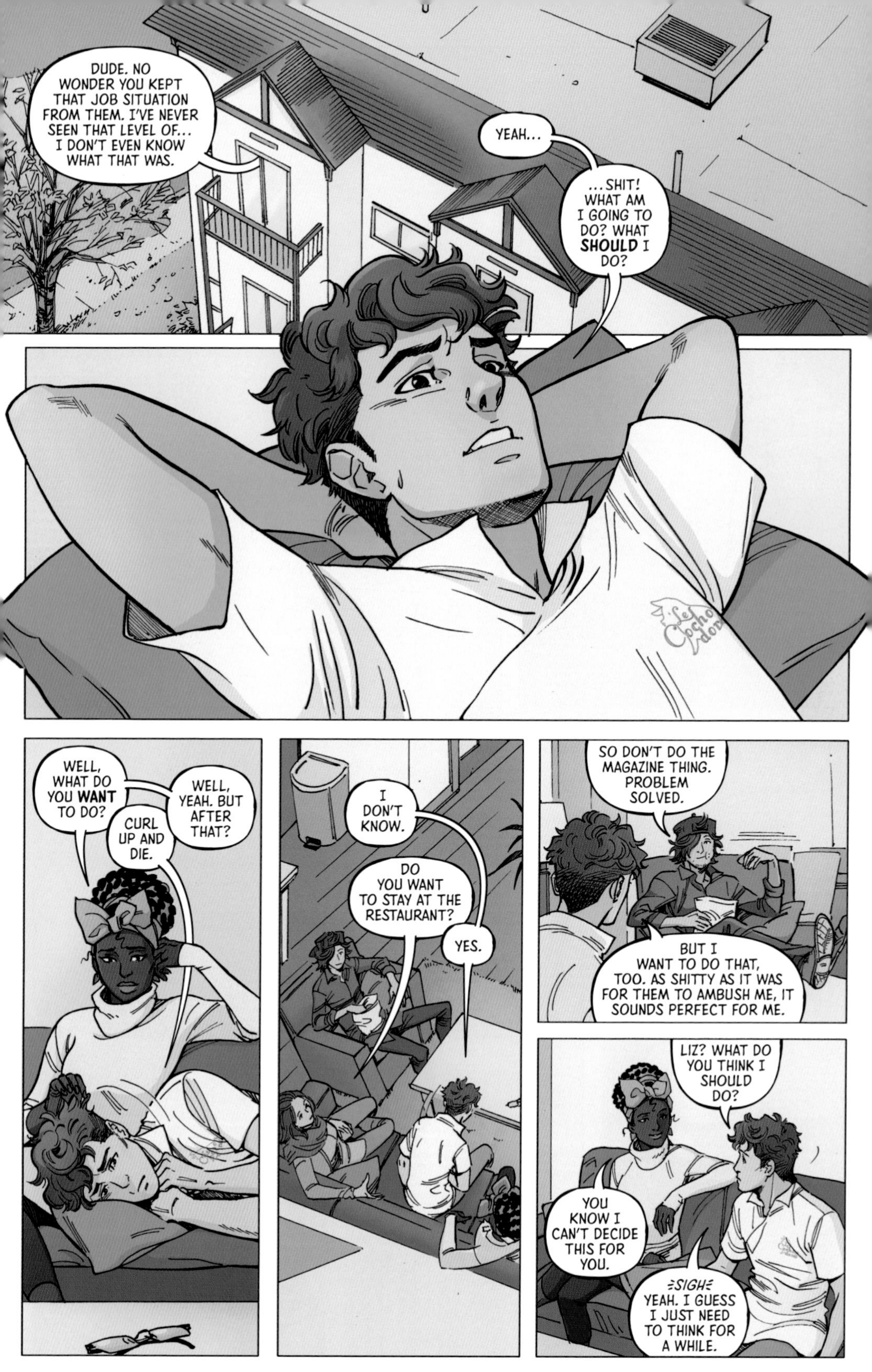
DUDE. NO WONDER YOU KEPT THAT JOB SITUATION FROM THEM. I'VE NEVER SEEN THAT LEVEL OF... I DON'T EVEN KNOW WHAT THAT WAS.
YEAH...
...SHIT! WHAT AM I GOING TO DO? WHAT SHOULD I DO?
WELL, WHAT DO YOU WANT TO DO?
CURL UP AND DIE.
WELL, YEAH. BUT AFTER THAT?
I DON'T KNOW.
DO YOU WANT TO STAY AT THE RESTAURANT?
YES.
SO DON'T DO THE MAGAZINE THING. PROBLEM SOLVED.
BUT I WANT TO DO THAT, TOO. AS SHITTY AS IT WAS FOR THEM TO AMBUSH ME, IT SOUNDS PERFECT FOR ME.
LIZ? WHAT DO YOU THINK I SHOULD DO?
YOU KNOW I CAN'T DECIDE THIS FOR YOU.
SIGH
YEAH. I GUESS I JUST NEED TO THINK FOR A WHILE.

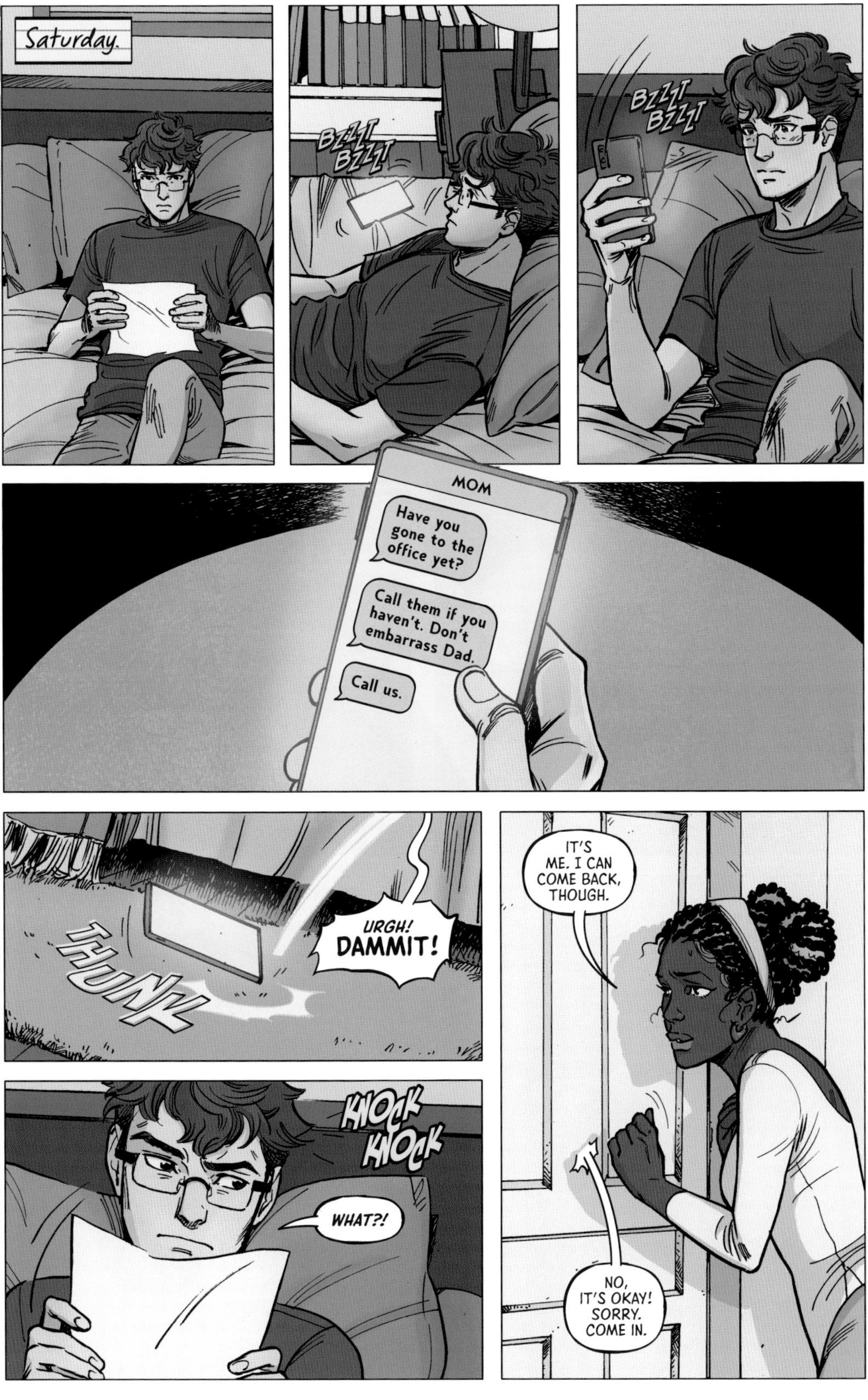
Saturday.
BZZZT BZZZT
BZZZT BZZZT
MOM
Have you gone to the office yet?
Call them if you haven't. Don't embarrass Dad.
Call us.
THUNK
URGH! DAMMIT!
KNOCK KNOCK
WHAT?!
IT'S ME. I CAN COME BACK, THOUGH.
NO, IT'S OKAY! SORRY. COME IN.

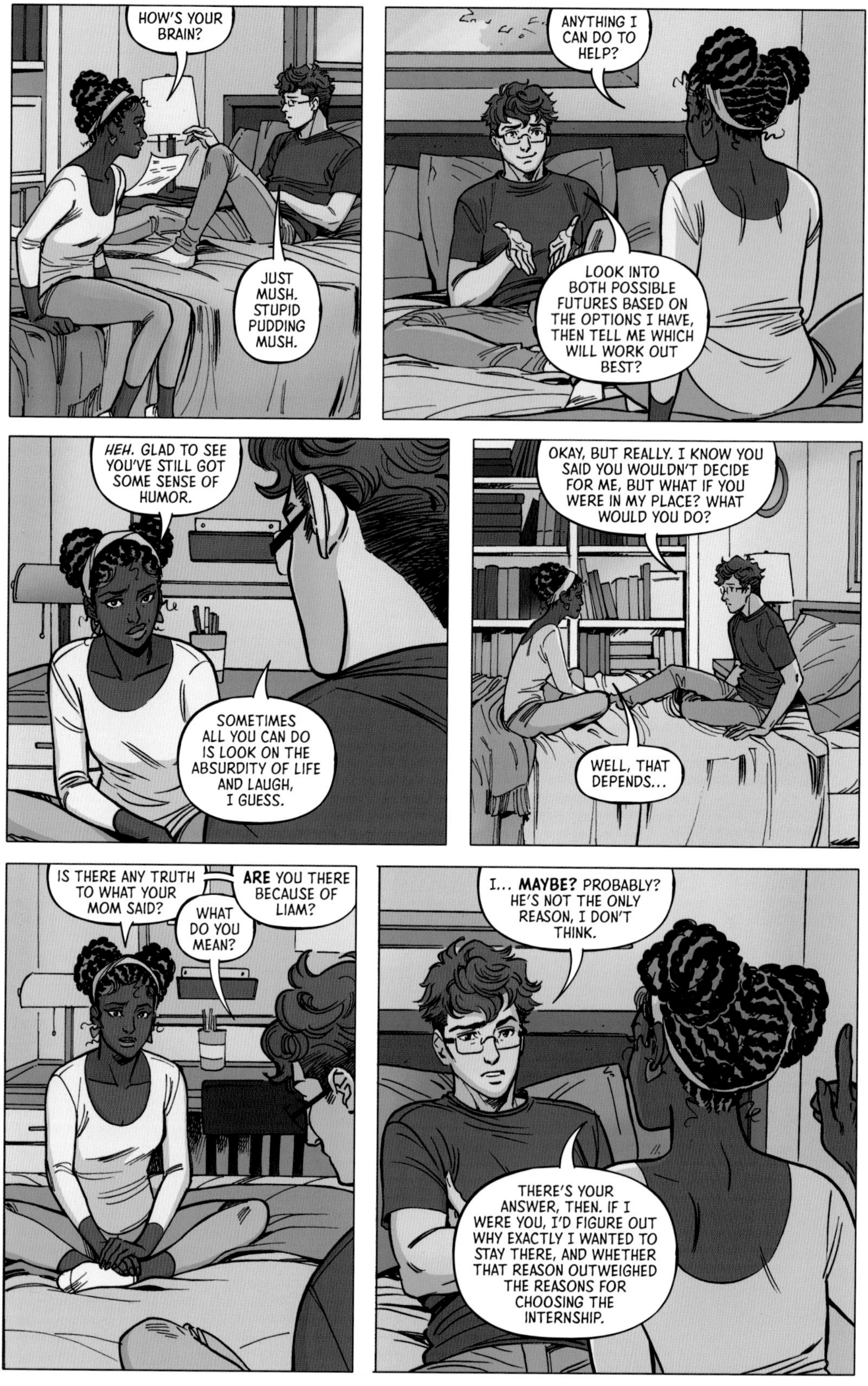
HOW'S YOUR BRAIN?
JUST MUSH. STUPID PUDDING MUSH.
ANYTHING I CAN DO TO HELP?
LOOK INTO BOTH POSSIBLE FUTURES BASED ON THE OPTIONS I HAVE, THEN TELL ME WHICH WILL WORK OUT BEST?
HEH. GLAD TO SEE YOU'VE STILL GOT SOME SENSE OF HUMOR.
SOMETIMES ALL YOU CAN DO IS LOOK ON THE ABSURDITY OF LIFE AND LAUGH, I GUESS.
OKAY, BUT REALLY. I KNOW YOU SAID YOU WOULDN'T DECIDE FOR ME, BUT WHAT IF YOU WERE IN MY PLACE? WHAT WOULD YOU DO?
WELL, THAT DEPENDS...
IS THERE ANY TRUTH TO WHAT YOUR MOM SAID?
ARE YOU THERE BECAUSE OF LIAM?
WHAT DO YOU MEAN?
I... **MAYBE?** PROBABLY? HE'S NOT THE ONLY REASON, I DON'T THINK.
THERE'S YOUR ANSWER, THEN. IF I WERE YOU, I'D FIGURE OUT WHY EXACTLY I WANTED TO STAY THERE, AND WHETHER THAT REASON OUTWEIGHED THE REASONS FOR CHOOSING THE INTERNSHIP.

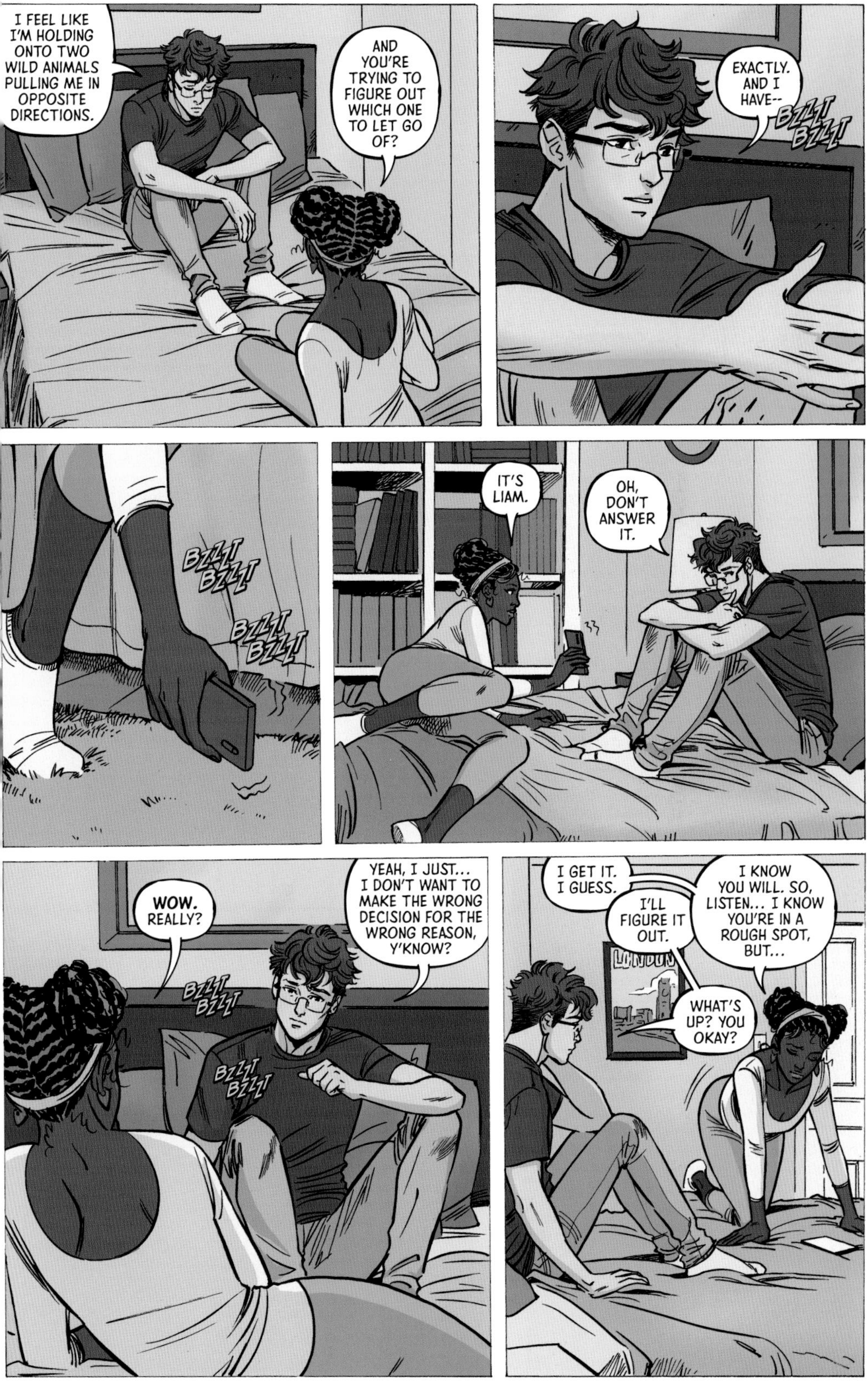

I FEEL LIKE I'M HOLDING ONTO TWO WILD ANIMALS PULLING ME IN OPPOSITE DIRECTIONS.
AND YOU'RE TRYING TO FIGURE OUT WHICH ONE TO LET GO OF?
EXACTLY. AND I HAVE--
BZZZT BZZZT
BZZZT BZZZT
BZZZT BZZZT
IT'S LIAM.
OH, DON'T ANSWER IT.
WOW. REALLY?
BZZZT BZZZT
YEAH, I JUST... I DON'T WANT TO MAKE THE WRONG DECISION FOR THE WRONG REASON, Y'KNOW?
BZZZT BZZZT
I GET IT. I GUESS.
I'LL FIGURE IT OUT.
I KNOW YOU WILL. SO, LISTEN... I KNOW YOU'RE IN A ROUGH SPOT, BUT...
LONDON
WHAT'S UP? YOU OKAY?

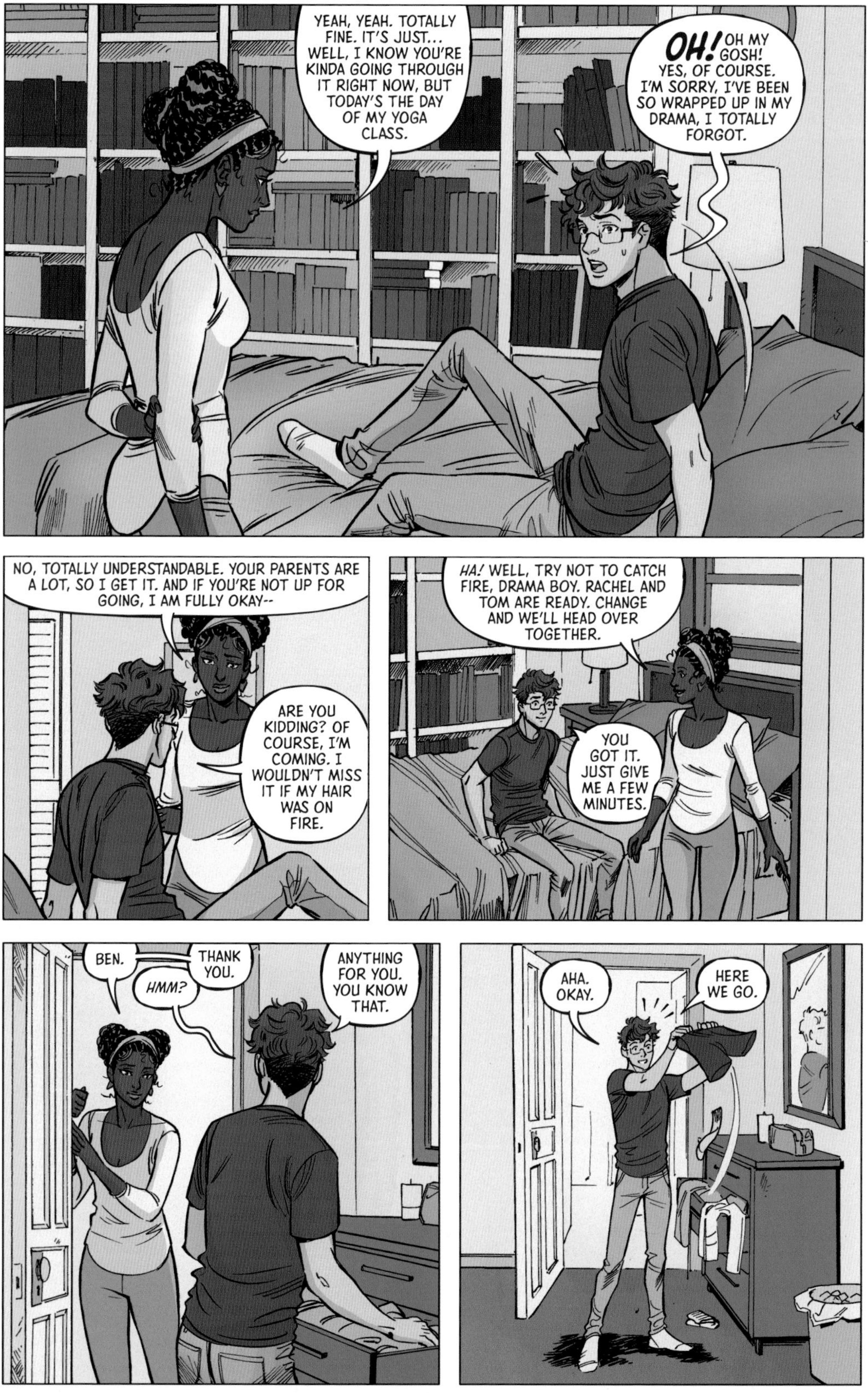

YEAH, YEAH. TOTALLY FINE. IT'S JUST... WELL, I KNOW YOU'RE KINDA GOING THROUGH IT RIGHT NOW, BUT TODAY'S THE DAY OF MY YOGA CLASS.
OH! OH MY GOSH! YES, OF COURSE. I'M SORRY, I'VE BEEN SO WRAPPED UP IN MY DRAMA, I TOTALLY FORGOT.
NO, TOTALLY UNDERSTANDABLE. YOUR PARENTS ARE A LOT, SO I GET IT. AND IF YOU'RE NOT UP FOR GOING, I AM FULLY OKAY--
ARE YOU KIDDING? OF COURSE, I'M COMING. I WOULDN'T MISS IT IF MY HAIR WAS ON FIRE.
HA! WELL, TRY NOT TO CATCH FIRE, DRAMA BOY. RACHEL AND TOM ARE READY. CHANGE AND WE'LL HEAD OVER TOGETHER.
YOU GOT IT. JUST GIVE ME A FEW MINUTES.
BEN.
HMM?
THANK YOU.
ANYTHING FOR YOU. YOU KNOW THAT.
AHA. OKAY.
HERE WE GO.

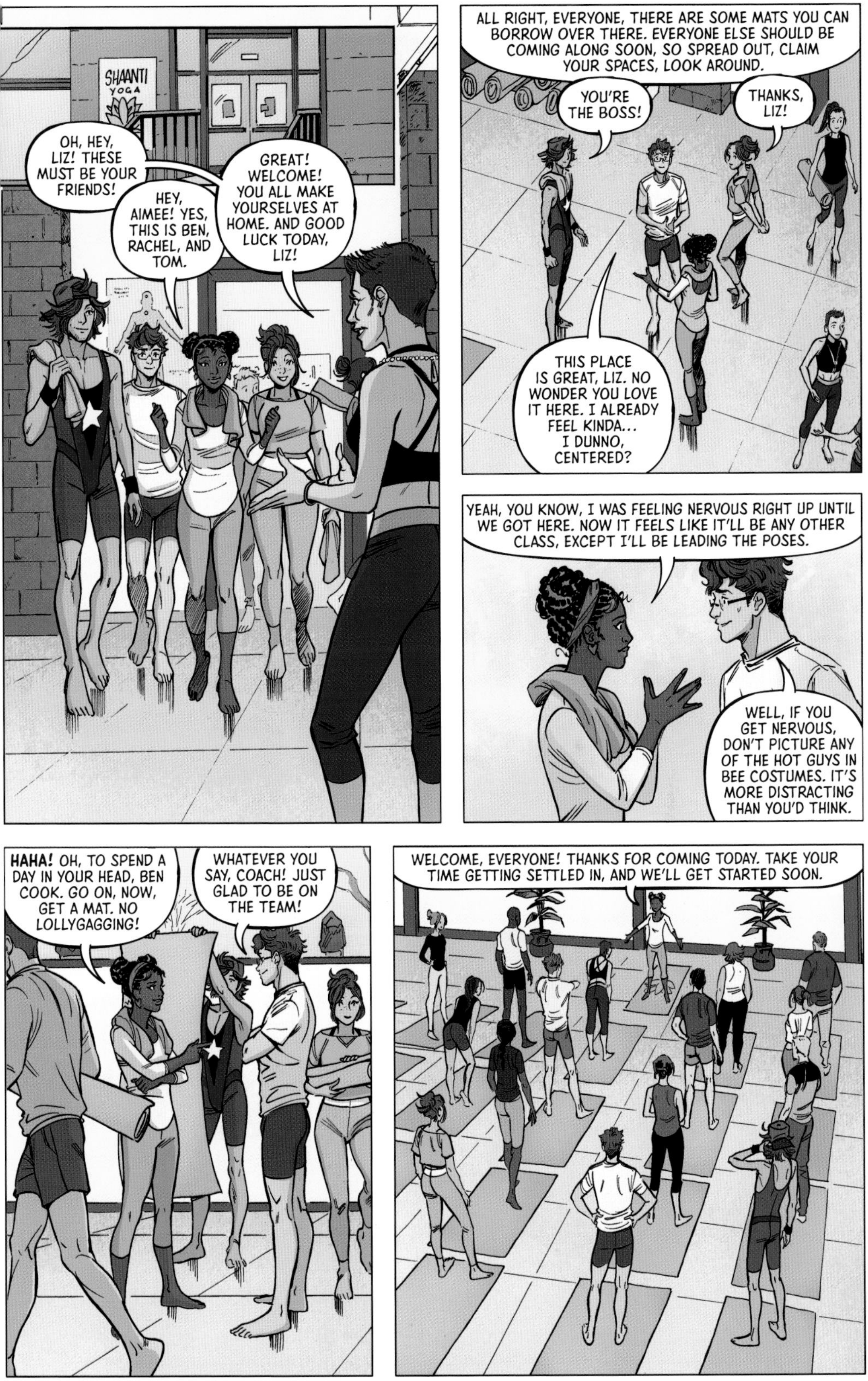
SHAANTI YOGA
OH, HEY, LIZ! THESE MUST BE YOUR FRIENDS!
HEY, AIMEE! YES, THIS IS BEN, RACHEL, AND TOM.
GREAT! WELCOME! YOU ALL MAKE YOURSELVES AT HOME. AND GOOD LUCK TODAY, LIZ!
ALL RIGHT, EVERYONE, THERE ARE SOME MATS YOU CAN BORROW OVER THERE. EVERYONE ELSE SHOULD BE COMING ALONG SOON, SO SPREAD OUT, CLAIM YOUR SPACES, LOOK AROUND.
YOU'RE THE BOSS!
THANKS, LIZ!
THIS PLACE IS GREAT, LIZ. NO WONDER YOU LOVE IT HERE. I ALREADY FEEL KINDA... I DUNNO, CENTERED?
YEAH, YOU KNOW, I WAS FEELING NERVOUS RIGHT UP UNTIL WE GOT HERE. NOW IT FEELS LIKE IT'LL BE ANY OTHER CLASS, EXCEPT I'LL BE LEADING THE POSES.
WELL, IF YOU GET NERVOUS, DON'T PICTURE ANY OF THE HOT GUYS IN BEE COSTUMES. IT'S MORE DISTRACTING THAN YOU'D THINK.
HAHA! OH, TO SPEND A DAY IN YOUR HEAD, BEN COOK. GO ON, NOW, GET A MAT. NO LOLLYGAGGING!
WHATEVER YOU SAY, COACH! JUST GLAD TO BE ON THE TEAM!
WELCOME, EVERYONE! THANKS FOR COMING TODAY. TAKE YOUR TIME GETTING SETTLED IN, AND WE'LL GET STARTED SOON.

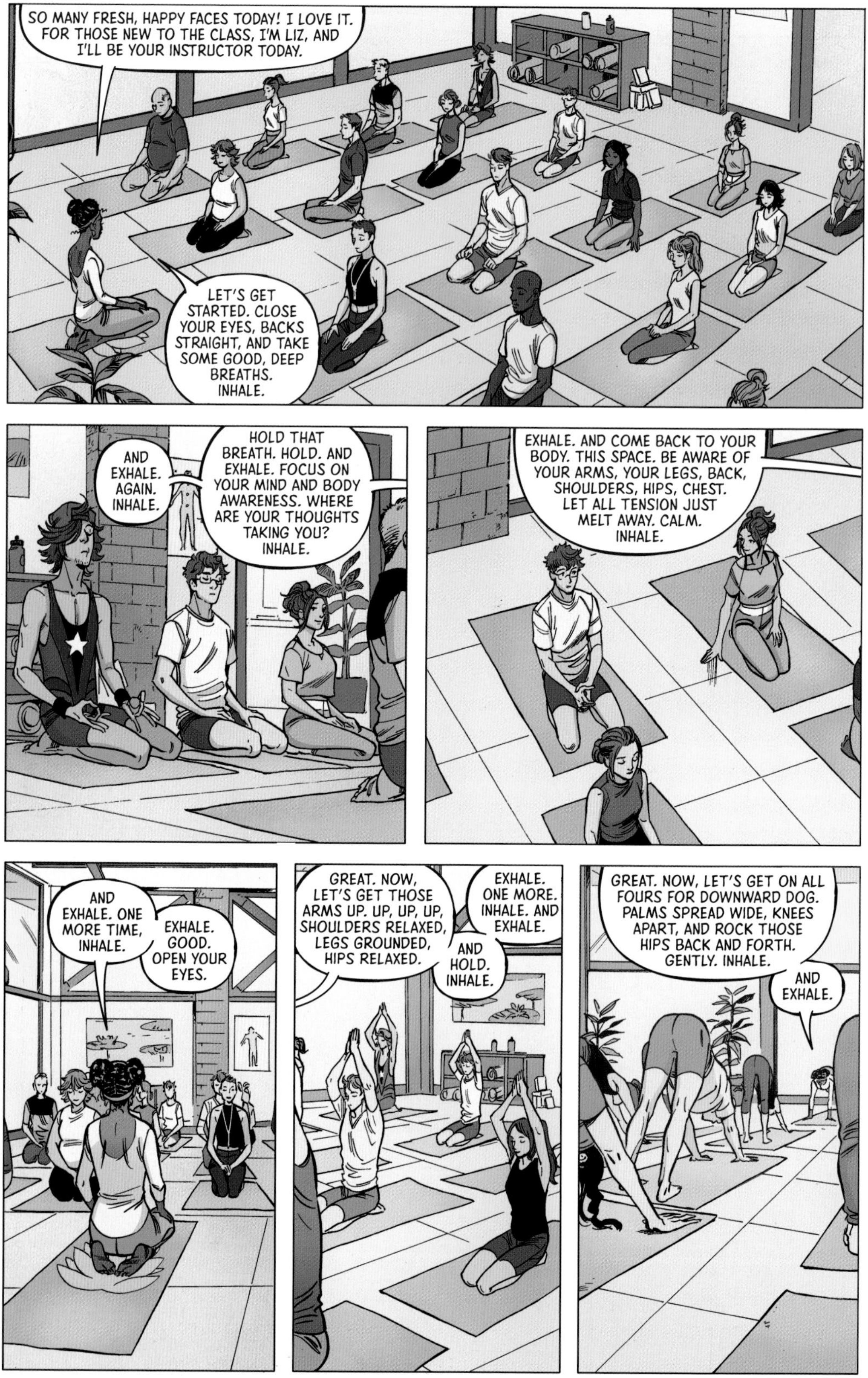

SO MANY FRESH, HAPPY FACES TODAY! I LOVE IT. FOR THOSE NEW TO THE CLASS, I'M LIZ, AND I'LL BE YOUR INSTRUCTOR TODAY.
LET'S GET STARTED. CLOSE YOUR EYES, BACKS STRAIGHT, AND TAKE SOME GOOD, DEEP BREATHS. INHALE.
AND EXHALE. AGAIN. INHALE.
HOLD THAT BREATH. HOLD. AND EXHALE. FOCUS ON YOUR MIND AND BODY AWARENESS. WHERE ARE YOUR THOUGHTS TAKING YOU? INHALE.
EXHALE. AND COME BACK TO YOUR BODY. THIS SPACE. BE AWARE OF YOUR ARMS, YOUR LEGS, BACK, SHOULDERS, HIPS, CHEST. LET ALL TENSION JUST MELT AWAY. CALM. INHALE.
AND EXHALE. ONE MORE TIME, INHALE.
EXHALE. GOOD. OPEN YOUR EYES.
GREAT. NOW, LET'S GET THOSE ARMS UP. UP, UP, UP, SHOULDERS RELAXED, LEGS GROUNDED, HIPS RELAXED.
AND HOLD. INHALE.
EXHALE. ONE MORE. INHALE. AND EXHALE.
GREAT. NOW, LET'S GET ON ALL FOURS FOR DOWNWARD DOG. PALMS SPREAD WIDE, KNEES APART, AND ROCK THOSE HIPS BACK AND FORTH. GENTLY. INHALE.
AND EXHALE.

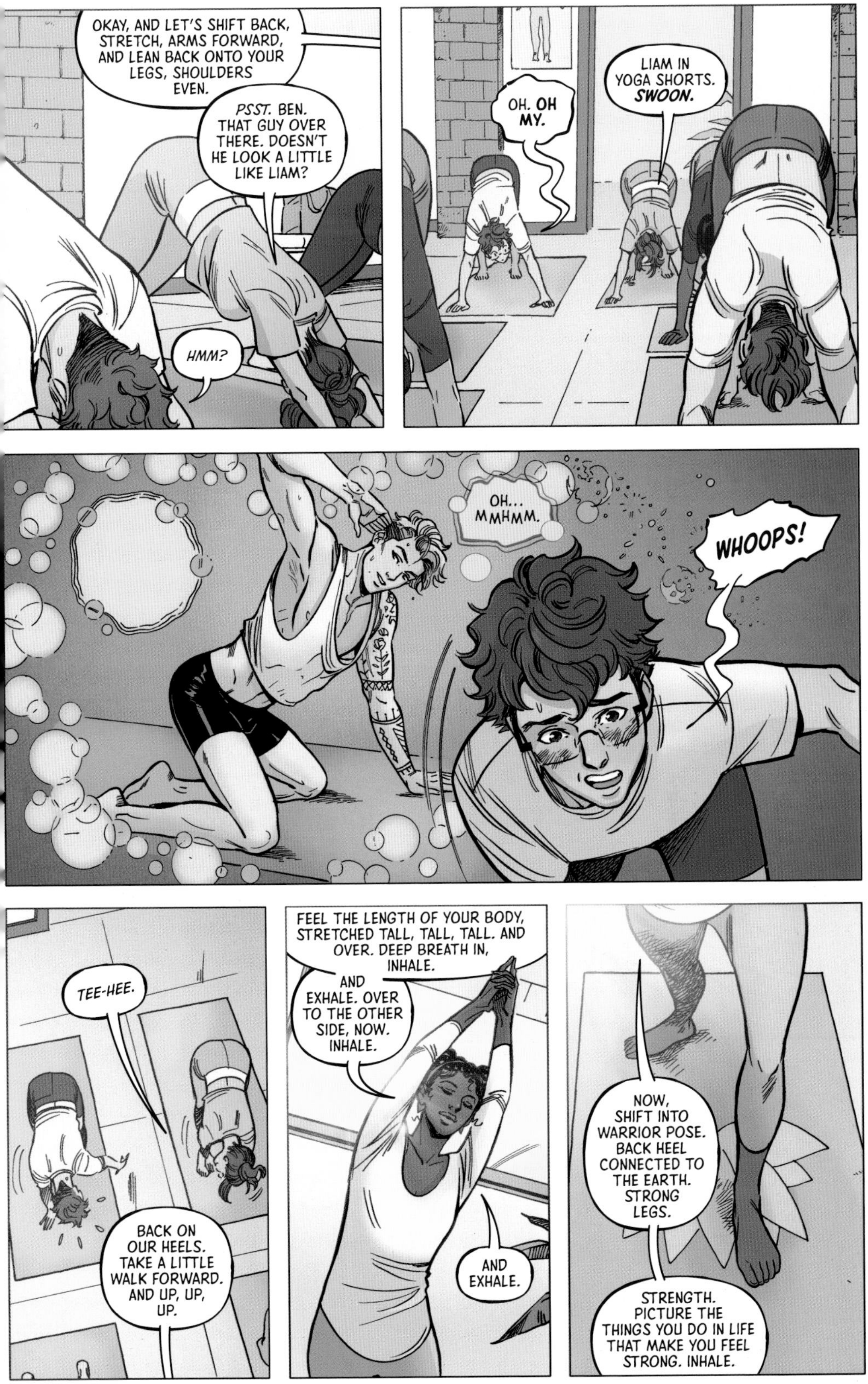
OKAY, AND LET'S SHIFT BACK, STRETCH, ARMS FORWARD, AND LEAN BACK ONTO YOUR LEGS, SHOULDERS EVEN.
PSST. BEN. THAT GUY OVER THERE. DOESN'T HE LOOK A LITTLE LIKE LIAM?
HMM?
OH. **OH MY.**
LIAM IN YOGA SHORTS. ***SWOON.***
OH... MMHMM.
WHOOPS!
TEE-HEE.
BACK ON OUR HEELS. TAKE A LITTLE WALK FORWARD. AND UP, UP, UP.
FEEL THE LENGTH OF YOUR BODY, STRETCHED TALL, TALL, TALL. AND OVER. DEEP BREATH IN, INHALE.
AND EXHALE. OVER TO THE OTHER SIDE, NOW. INHALE.
AND EXHALE.
NOW, SHIFT INTO WARRIOR POSE. BACK HEEL CONNECTED TO THE EARTH. STRONG LEGS.
STRENGTH. PICTURE THE THINGS YOU DO IN LIFE THAT MAKE YOU FEEL STRONG. INHALE.

EXHALE. FOR ME, IT'S THIS, BEING HERE, IN CONTROL OF MY OWN MIND AND BODY. DEEP BREATH, NOW, INHALE.

AND EXHALE. ARMS SLOWLY DOWN NOW.

HANDS ON YOUR HIPS. EMBRACE THAT STABILITY. FEET GROUNDED TO THE EARTH. INHALE.

AND EXHALE. FIND YOUR STRENGTH, NOW, INHALE.

AND EXHALE AS YOU TURN, LEGS SPREAD, HIPS STRONG. NOW, HEEL-TOE-HEEL-TOE TO BRING YOUR FEET TOGETHER, ARMS AT YOUR SIDE. INHALE. ARMS UP.

EXHALE. CHALLENGE YOUR STABILITY, NOW. THINK ABOUT WHAT MAKES YOU UNSURE AND PUSH IT AWAY AS YOU EXHALE.

IT'S OKAY IF YOU STUMBLE--JUST TAKE YOUR TIME AND FIND YOUR CENTER AGAIN. NOW HOLD. INHALE.

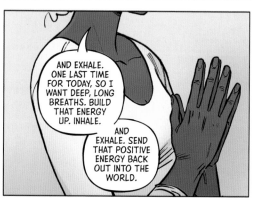

AND EXHALE. ONE LAST TIME FOR TODAY, SO I WANT DEEP, LONG BREATHS. BUILD THAT ENERGY UP. INHALE.

AND EXHALE. SEND THAT POSITIVE ENERGY BACK OUT INTO THE WORLD.

AND THAT'S OUR CLASS FOR TODAY. THANK YOU SO MUCH FOR JOINING US. NAMASTE.

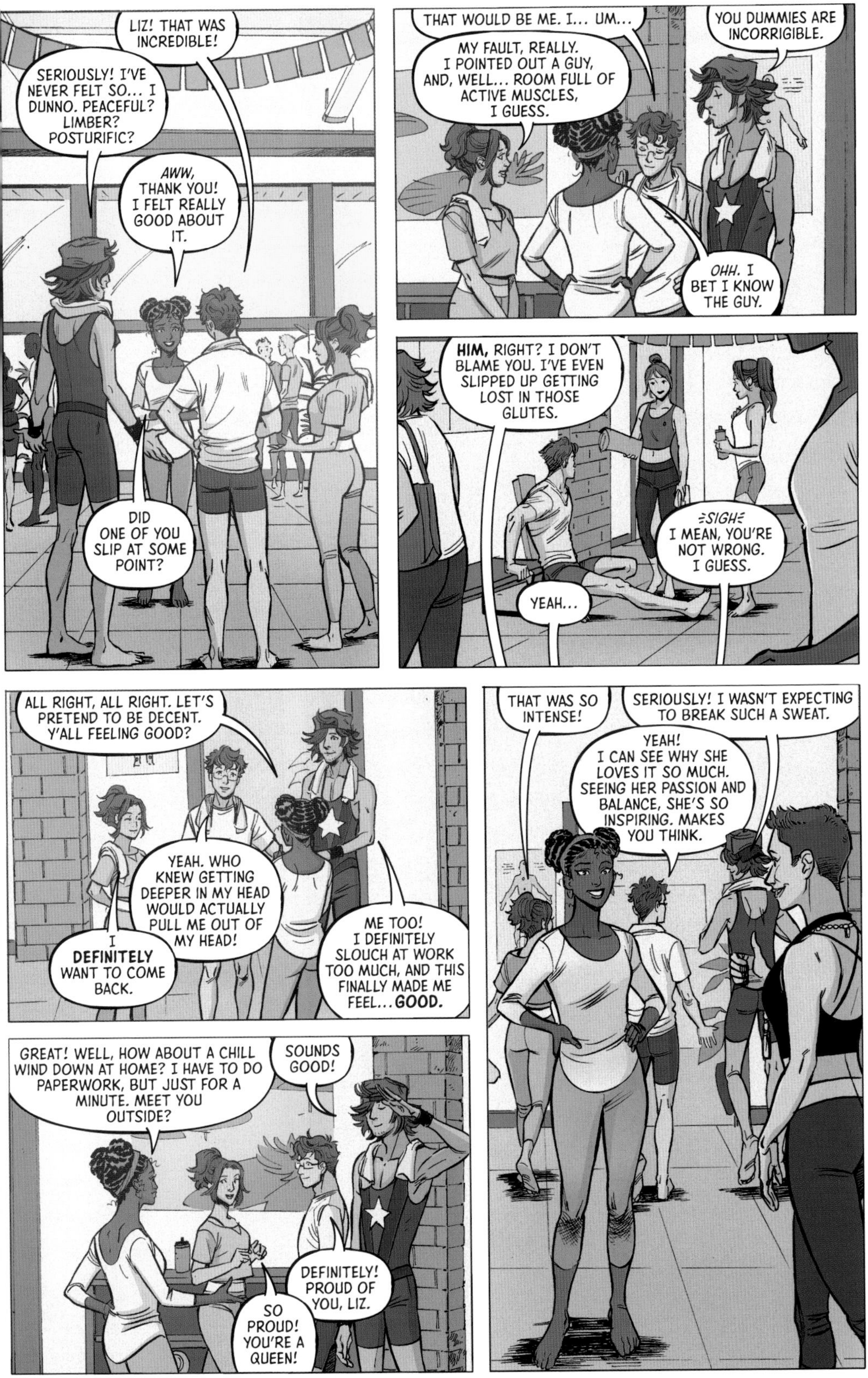
LIZ! THAT WAS INCREDIBLE!
SERIOUSLY! I'VE NEVER FELT SO... I DUNNO. PEACEFUL? LIMBER? POSTURIFIC?
AWW, THANK YOU! I FELT REALLY GOOD ABOUT IT.
DID ONE OF YOU SLIP AT SOME POINT?
THAT WOULD BE ME. I... UM...
MY FAULT, REALLY. I POINTED OUT A GUY, AND, WELL... ROOM FULL OF ACTIVE MUSCLES, I GUESS.
YOU DUMMIES ARE INCORRIGIBLE.
OHH. I BET I KNOW THE GUY.
HIM, RIGHT? I DON'T BLAME YOU. I'VE EVEN SLIPPED UP GETTING LOST IN THOSE GLUTES.
YEAH...
SIGH
I MEAN, YOU'RE NOT WRONG. I GUESS.
ALL RIGHT, ALL RIGHT. LET'S PRETEND TO BE DECENT. Y'ALL FEELING GOOD?
YEAH. WHO KNEW GETTING DEEPER IN MY HEAD WOULD ACTUALLY PULL ME OUT OF MY HEAD!
I DEFINITELY WANT TO COME BACK.
ME TOO! I DEFINITELY SLOUCH AT WORK TOO MUCH, AND THIS FINALLY MADE ME FEEL... GOOD.
GREAT! WELL, HOW ABOUT A CHILL WIND DOWN AT HOME? I HAVE TO DO PAPERWORK, BUT JUST FOR A MINUTE. MEET YOU OUTSIDE?
SOUNDS GOOD!
DEFINITELY! PROUD OF YOU, LIZ.
SO PROUD! YOU'RE A QUEEN!
THAT WAS SO INTENSE!
SERIOUSLY! I WASN'T EXPECTING TO BREAK SUCH A SWEAT.
YEAH! I CAN SEE WHY SHE LOVES IT SO MUCH. SEEING HER PASSION AND BALANCE, SHE'S SO INSPIRING. MAKES YOU THINK.

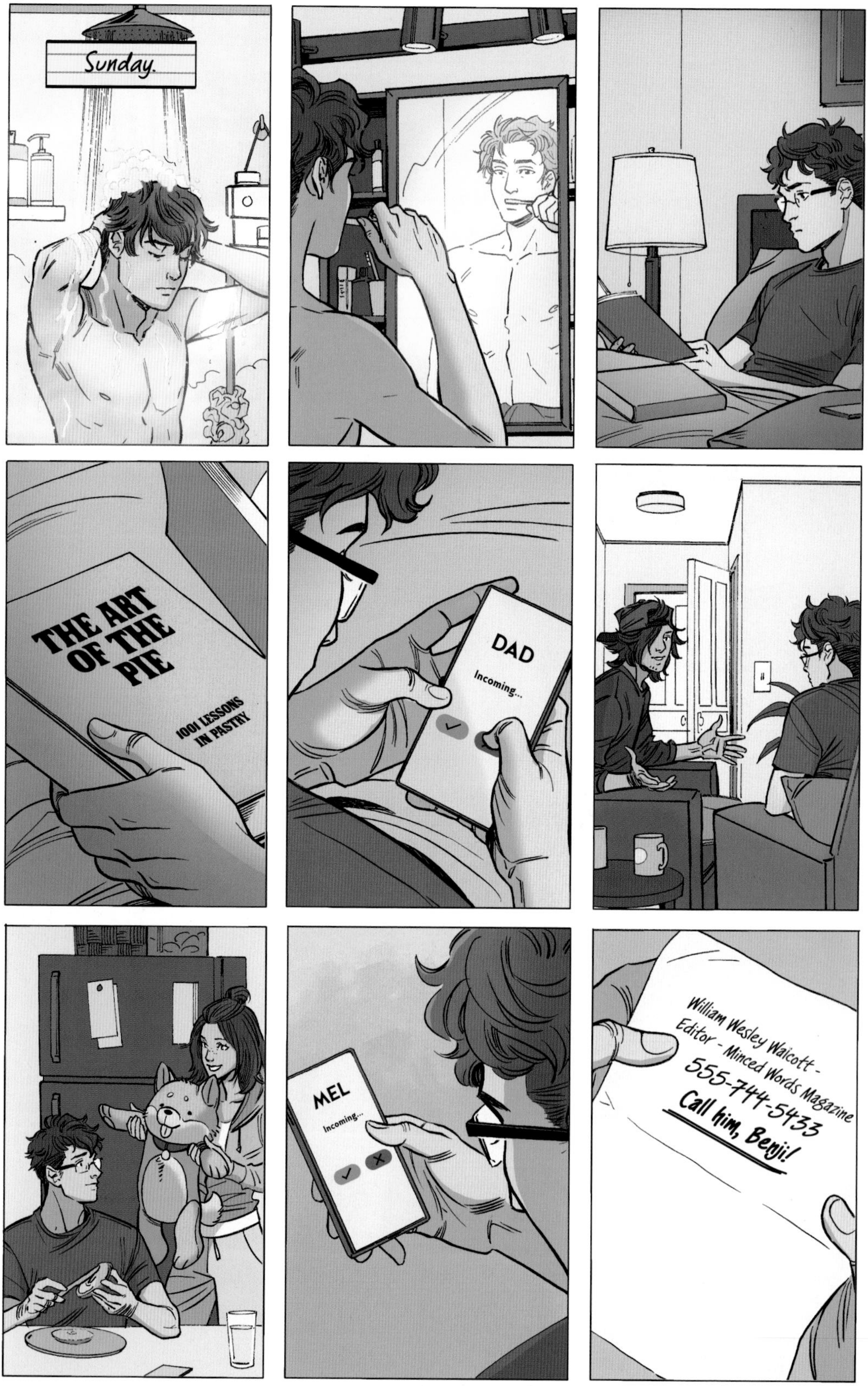
Sunday.
THE ART OF THE PIE
1001 LESSONS IN PASTRY
DAD
Incoming...
MEL
Incoming...
William Wesley Waicott -
Editor - Minced Words Magazine
555-744-5433
Call him, Benji!

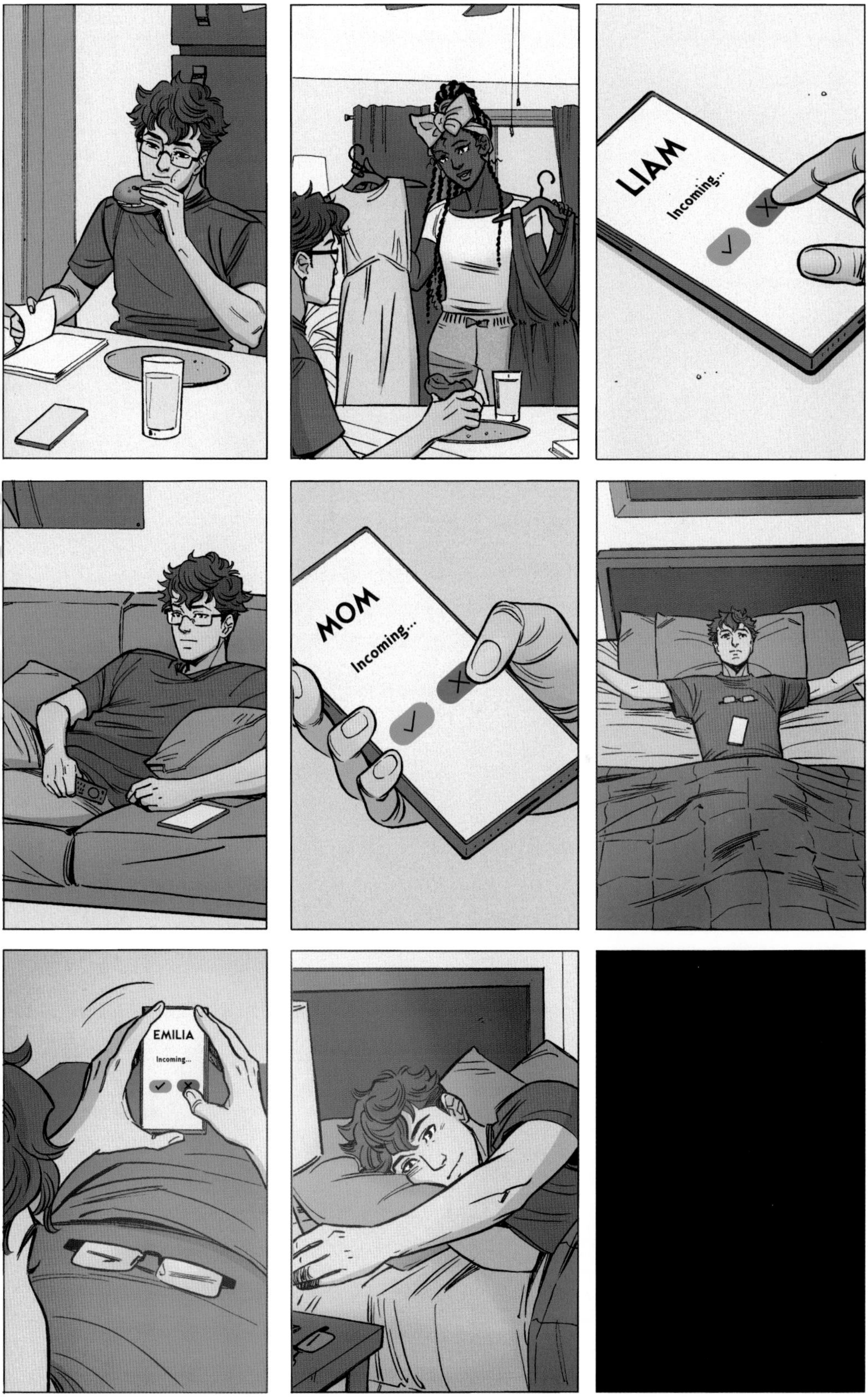
LIAM
Incoming...
MOM
Incoming...
EMILIA
Incoming...

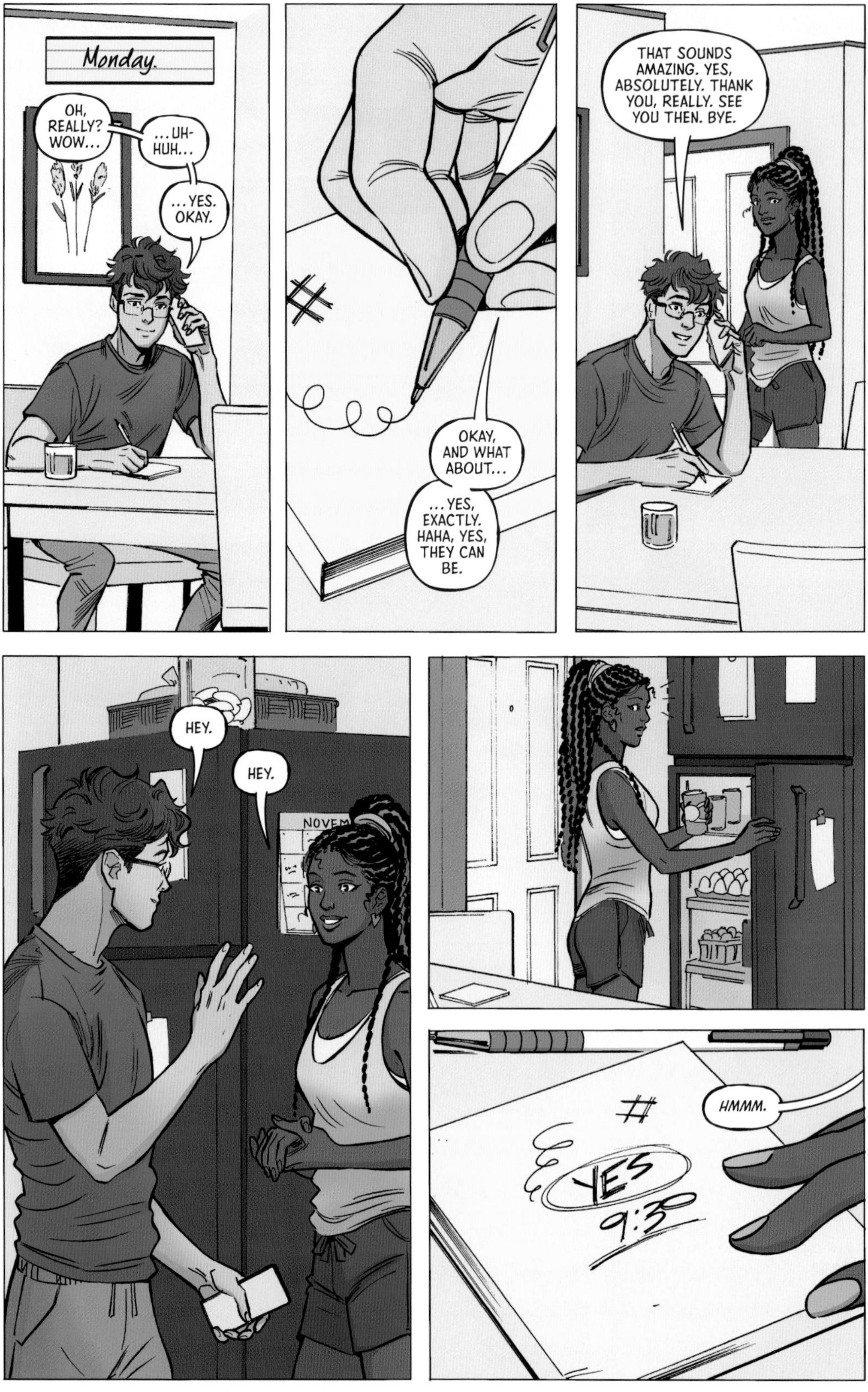
Monday.
OH, REALLY? WOW...
...UH-HUH...
...YES. OKAY.
OKAY, AND WHAT ABOUT...
...YES, EXACTLY. HAHA, YES, THEY CAN BE.
THAT SOUNDS AMAZING. YES, ABSOLUTELY. THANK YOU, REALLY. SEE YOU THEN. BYE.
HEY.
HEY.
HMMM.
YES
9:30

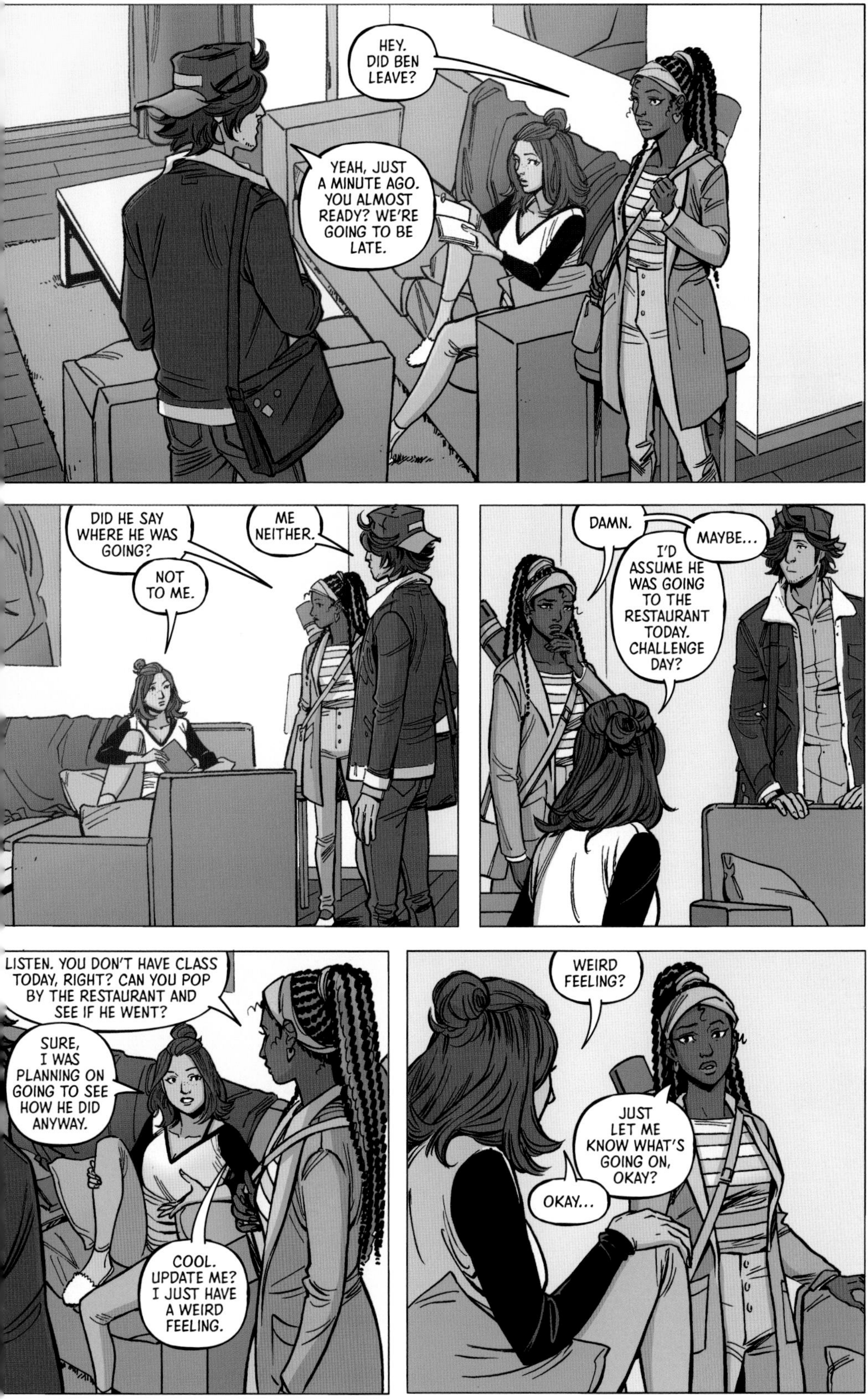
HEY. DID BEN LEAVE?
YEAH, JUST A MINUTE AGO. YOU ALMOST READY? WE'RE GOING TO BE LATE.
DID HE SAY WHERE HE WAS GOING?
NOT TO ME.
ME NEITHER.
DAMN.
MAYBE...
I'D ASSUME HE WAS GOING TO THE RESTAURANT TODAY. CHALLENGE DAY?
LISTEN. YOU DON'T HAVE CLASS TODAY, RIGHT? CAN YOU POP BY THE RESTAURANT AND SEE IF HE WENT?
SURE, I WAS PLANNING ON GOING TO SEE HOW HE DID ANYWAY.
COOL. UPDATE ME? I JUST HAVE A WEIRD FEELING.
WEIRD FEELING?
JUST LET ME KNOW WHAT'S GOING ON, OKAY?
OKAY...

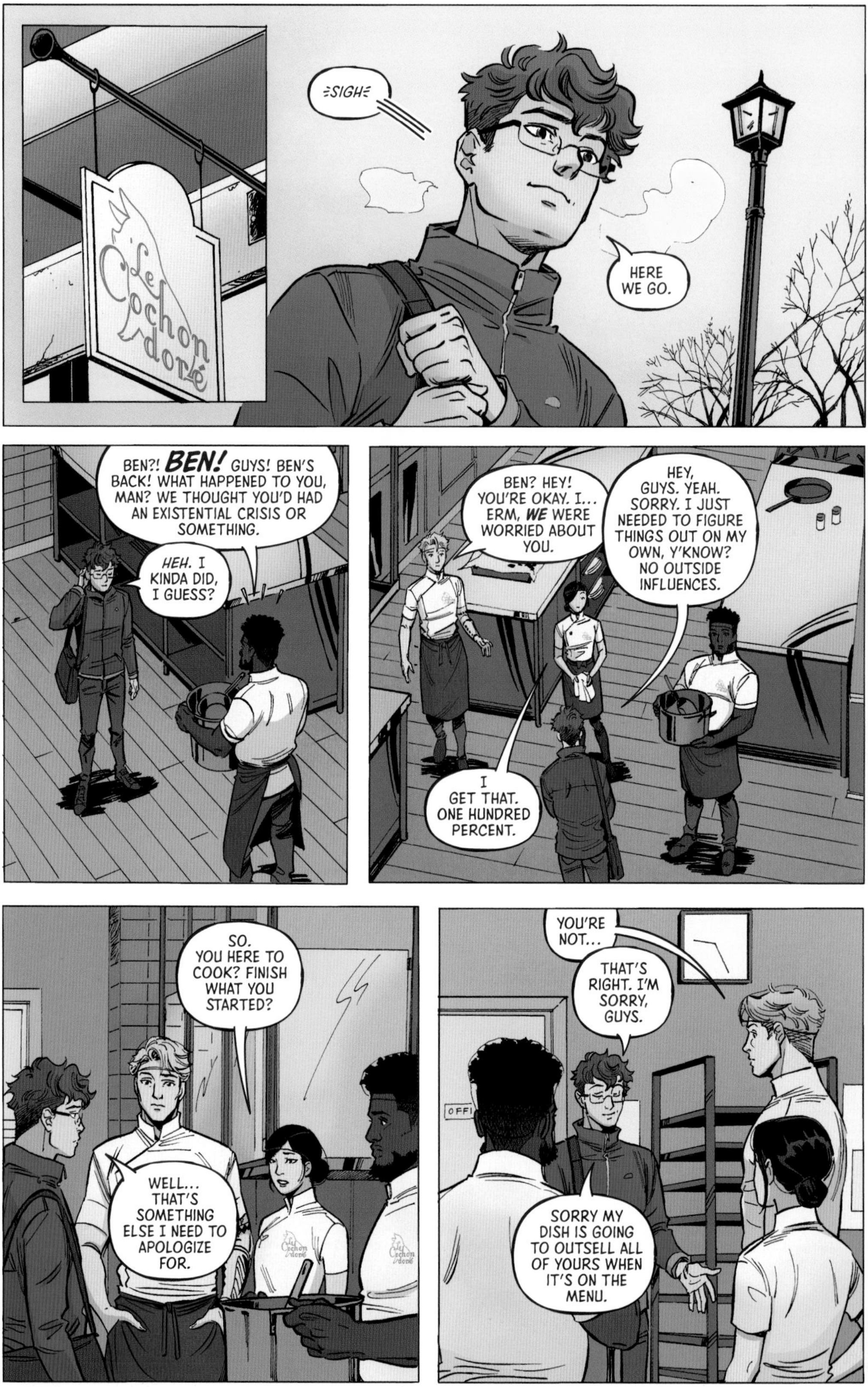
Le Cochon doré
=SIGH=
HERE WE GO.
BEN?! BEN! GUYS! BEN'S BACK! WHAT HAPPENED TO YOU, MAN? WE THOUGHT YOU'D HAD AN EXISTENTIAL CRISIS OR SOMETHING.
HEH. I KINDA DID, I GUESS?
BEN? HEY! YOU'RE OKAY. I... ERM, WE WERE WORRIED ABOUT YOU.
HEY, GUYS. YEAH. SORRY. I JUST NEEDED TO FIGURE THINGS OUT ON MY OWN, Y'KNOW? NO OUTSIDE INFLUENCES.
I GET THAT. ONE HUNDRED PERCENT.
SO. YOU HERE TO COOK? FINISH WHAT YOU STARTED?
WELL... THAT'S SOMETHING ELSE I NEED TO APOLOGIZE FOR.
YOU'RE NOT...
THAT'S RIGHT. I'M SORRY, GUYS.
SORRY MY DISH IS GOING TO OUTSELL ALL OF YOURS WHEN IT'S ON THE MENU.

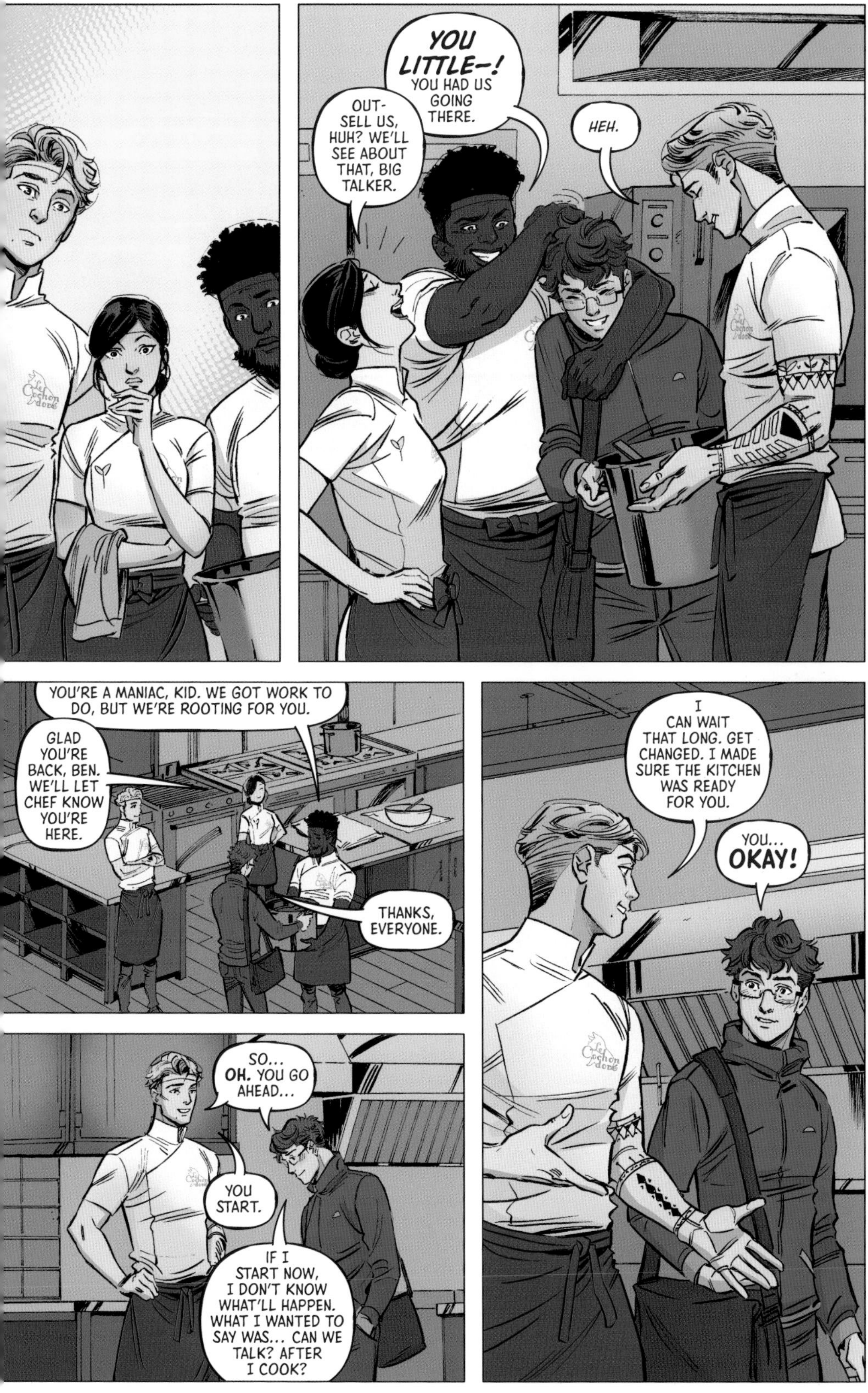
YOU LITTLE--! YOU HAD US GOING THERE.
OUT-SELL US, HUH? WE'LL SEE ABOUT THAT, BIG TALKER.
HEH.
YOU'RE A MANIAC, KID. WE GOT WORK TO DO, BUT WE'RE ROOTING FOR YOU.
GLAD YOU'RE BACK, BEN. WE'LL LET CHEF KNOW YOU'RE HERE.
THANKS, EVERYONE.
SO... OH. YOU GO AHEAD...
YOU START.
IF I START NOW, I DON'T KNOW WHAT'LL HAPPEN. WHAT I WANTED TO SAY WAS... CAN WE TALK? AFTER I COOK?
I CAN WAIT THAT LONG. GET CHANGED. I MADE SURE THE KITCHEN WAS READY FOR YOU.
YOU... OKAY!

HMPH. YOU CAME.

I DID.

GOOD. GO ON, THEN.

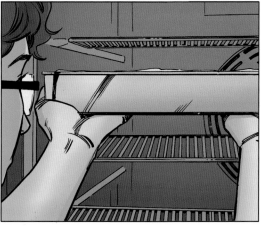

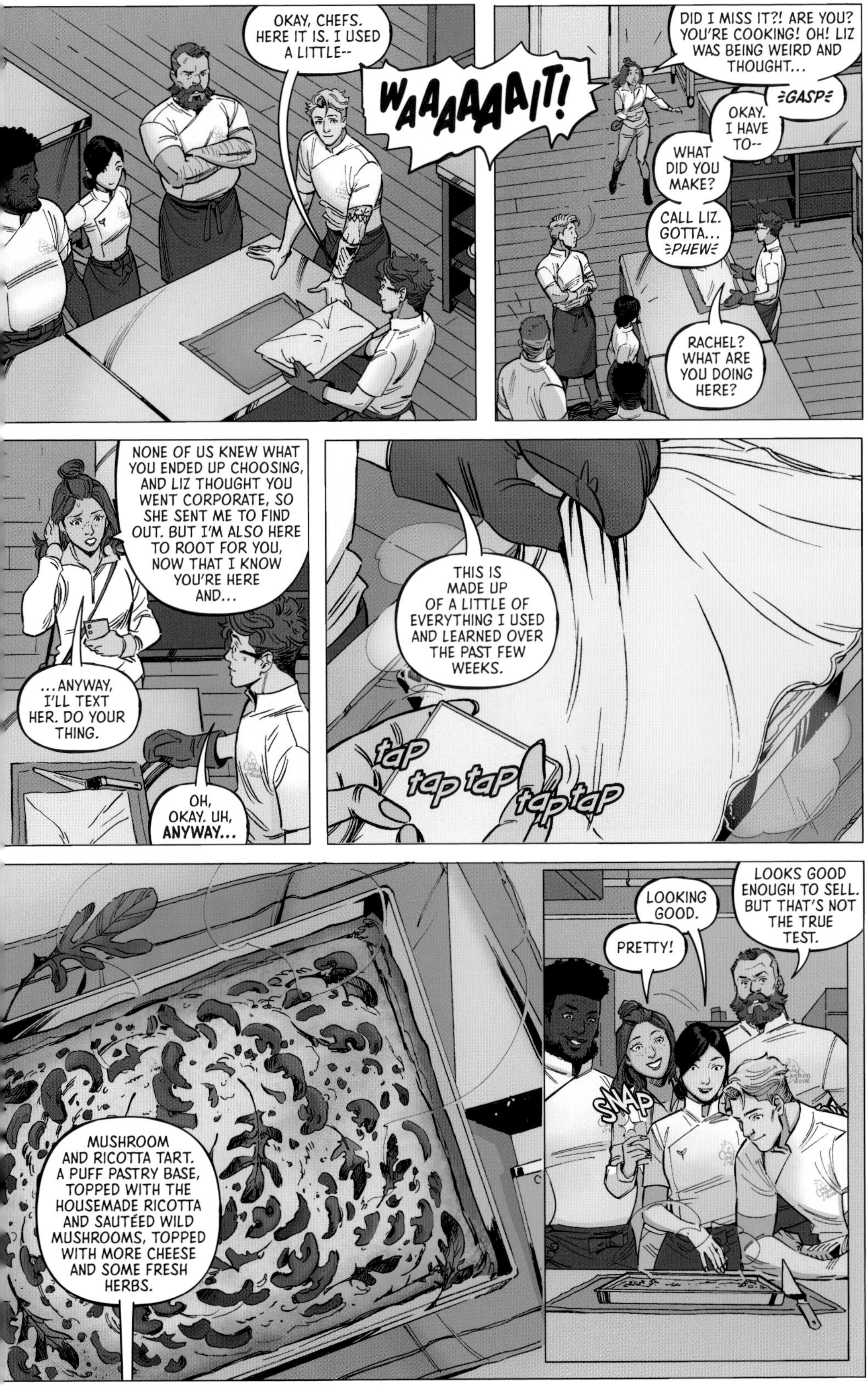
OKAY, CHEFS. HERE IT IS. I USED A LITTLE--
WAAAAAAIT!
DID I MISS IT?! ARE YOU? YOU'RE COOKING! OH! LIZ WAS BEING WEIRD AND THOUGHT...
GASP
OKAY. I HAVE TO--
WHAT DID YOU MAKE?
CALL LIZ. GOTTA... PHEW
RACHEL? WHAT ARE YOU DOING HERE?
NONE OF US KNEW WHAT YOU ENDED UP CHOOSING, AND LIZ THOUGHT YOU WENT CORPORATE, SO SHE SENT ME TO FIND OUT. BUT I'M ALSO HERE TO ROOT FOR YOU, NOW THAT I KNOW YOU'RE HERE AND...
...ANYWAY, I'LL TEXT HER. DO YOUR THING.
OH, OKAY. UH, **ANYWAY...**
THIS IS MADE UP OF A LITTLE OF EVERYTHING I USED AND LEARNED OVER THE PAST FEW WEEKS.
tap tap tap tap tap
MUSHROOM AND RICOTTA TART. A PUFF PASTRY BASE, TOPPED WITH THE HOUSEMADE RICOTTA AND SAUTÉED WILD MUSHROOMS, TOPPED WITH MORE CHEESE AND SOME FRESH HERBS.
LOOKING GOOD.
PRETTY!
LOOKS GOOD ENOUGH TO SELL. BUT THAT'S NOT THE TRUE TEST.
SNAP

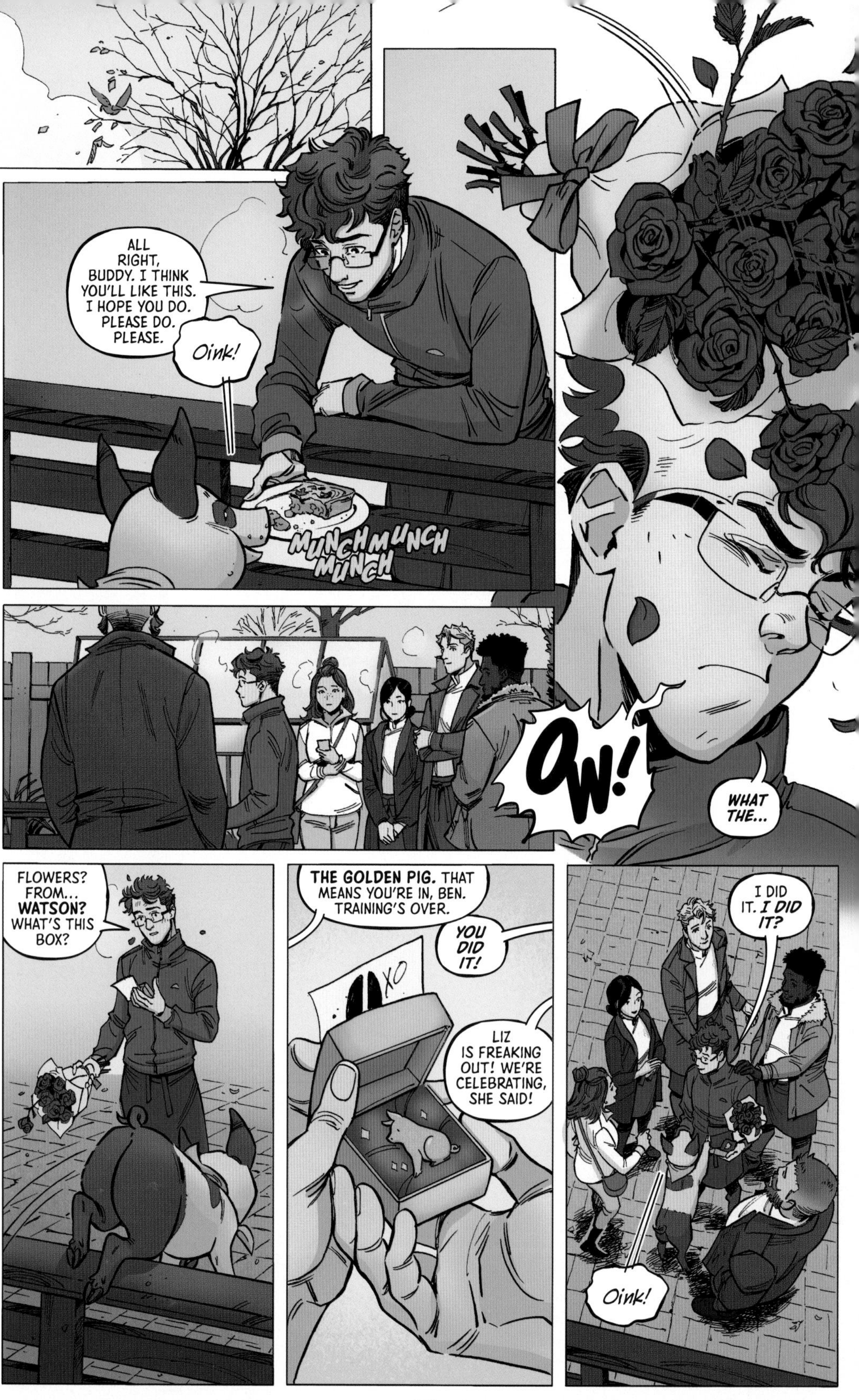
ALL RIGHT, BUDDY. I THINK YOU'LL LIKE THIS. I HOPE YOU DO. PLEASE DO. PLEASE.
Oink!
MUNCHMUNCH MUNCH
OW!
WHAT THE...
FLOWERS? FROM... WATSON? WHAT'S THIS BOX?
THE GOLDEN PIG. THAT MEANS YOU'RE IN, BEN. TRAINING'S OVER.
YOU DID IT!
XO
LIZ IS FREAKING OUT! WE'RE CELEBRATING, SHE SAID!
I DID IT. I DID IT?
Oink!

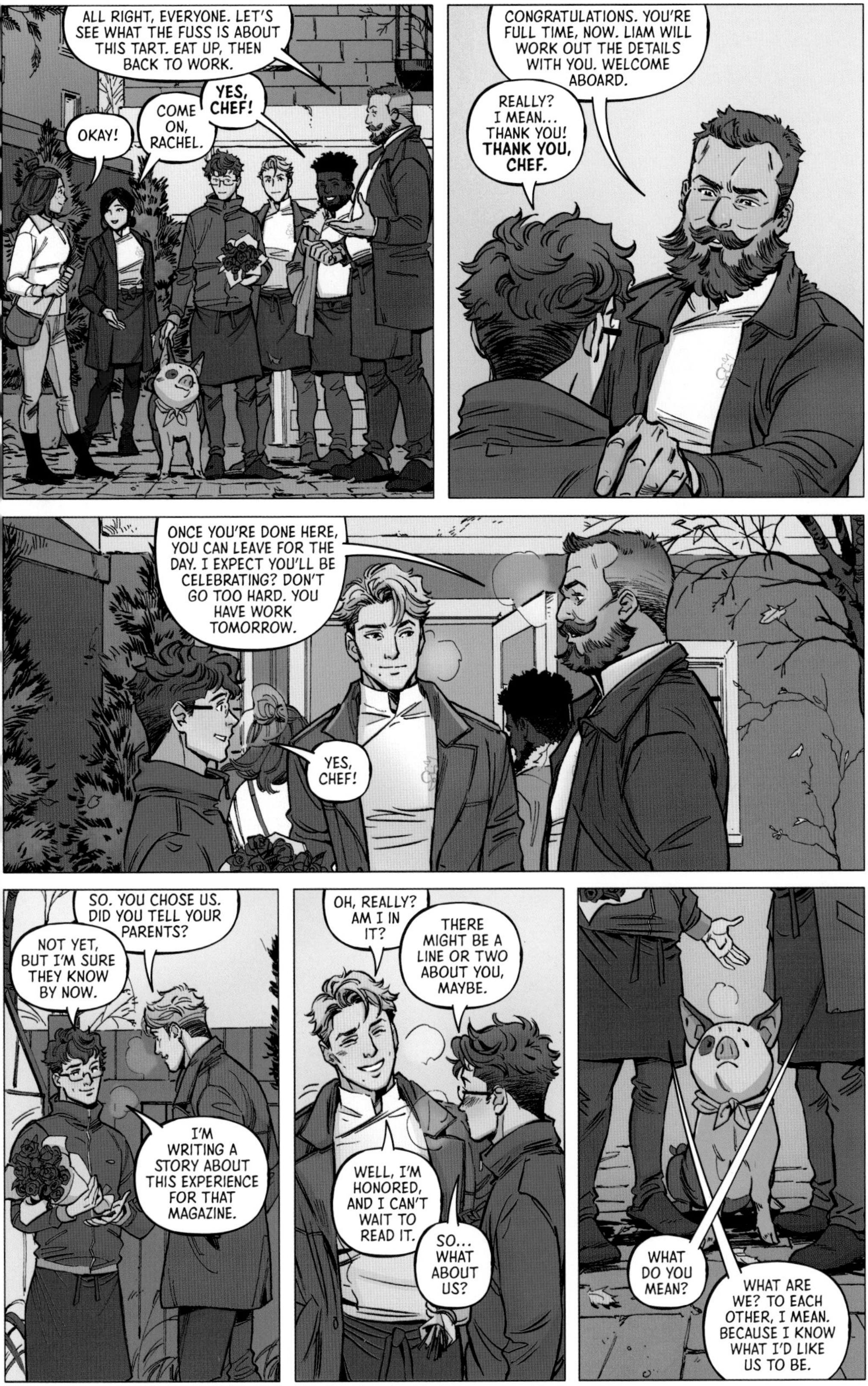
ALL RIGHT, EVERYONE. LET'S SEE WHAT THE FUSS IS ABOUT THIS TART. EAT UP, THEN BACK TO WORK.
YES, CHEF!
COME ON, RACHEL.
OKAY!
CONGRATULATIONS. YOU'RE FULL TIME, NOW. LIAM WILL WORK OUT THE DETAILS WITH YOU. WELCOME ABOARD.
REALLY? I MEAN... THANK YOU! THANK YOU, CHEF.
ONCE YOU'RE DONE HERE, YOU CAN LEAVE FOR THE DAY. I EXPECT YOU'LL BE CELEBRATING? DON'T GO TOO HARD. YOU HAVE WORK TOMORROW.
YES, CHEF!
SO. YOU CHOSE US. DID YOU TELL YOUR PARENTS?
NOT YET, BUT I'M SURE THEY KNOW BY NOW.
I'M WRITING A STORY ABOUT THIS EXPERIENCE FOR THAT MAGAZINE.
OH, REALLY? AM I IN IT?
THERE MIGHT BE A LINE OR TWO ABOUT YOU, MAYBE.
WELL, I'M HONORED, AND I CAN'T WAIT TO READ IT.
SO... WHAT ABOUT US?
WHAT DO YOU MEAN?
WHAT ARE WE? TO EACH OTHER, I MEAN. BECAUSE I KNOW WHAT I'D LIKE US TO BE.

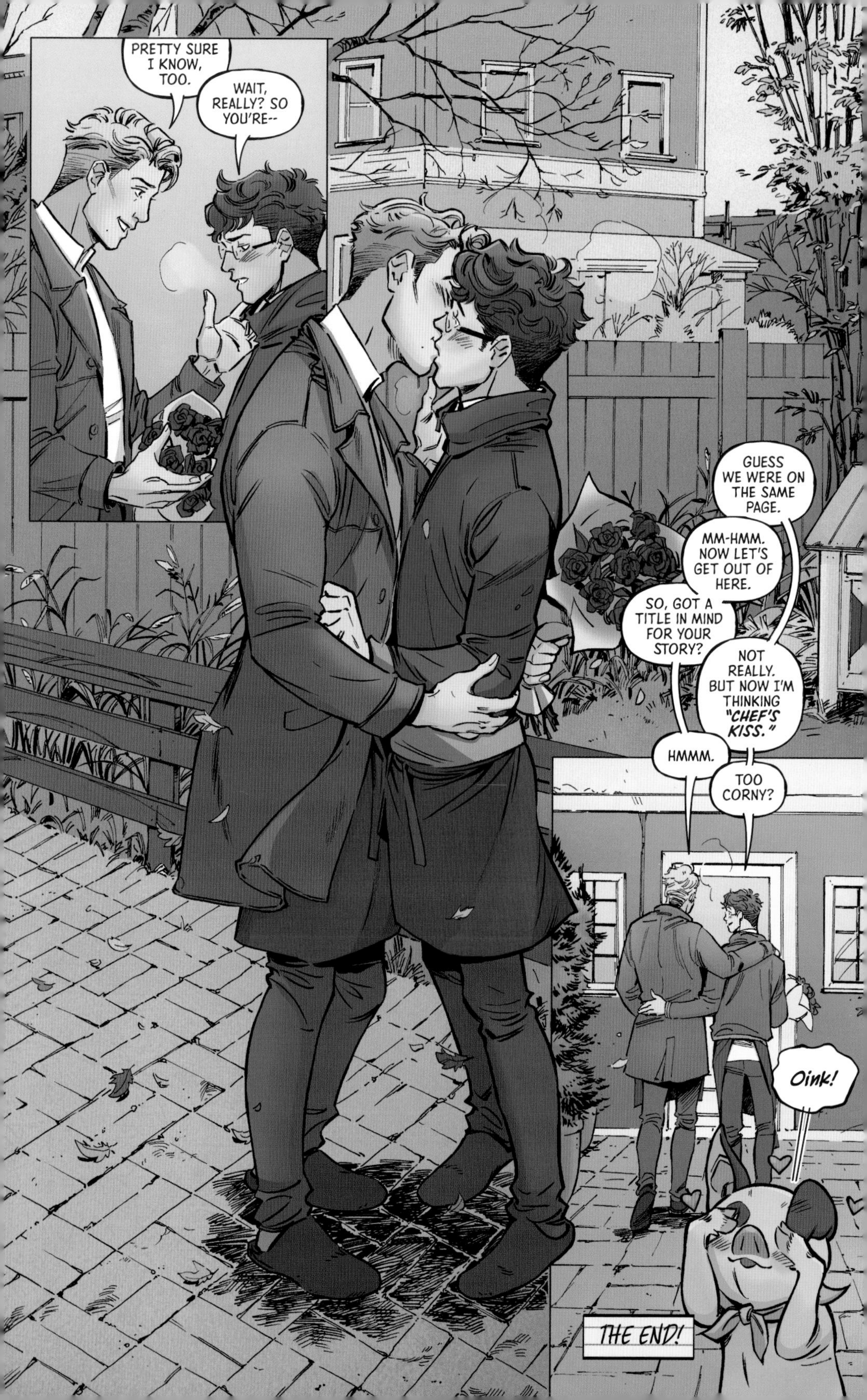
PRETTY SURE I KNOW, TOO.
WAIT, REALLY? SO YOU'RE--
GUESS WE WERE ON THE SAME PAGE.
MM-HMM. NOW LET'S GET OUT OF HERE.
SO, GOT A TITLE IN MIND FOR YOUR STORY?
NOT REALLY. BUT NOW I'M THINKING "CHEF'S KISS."
HMMM.
TOO CORNY?
Oink!
THE END!

Bonus Materials

Prelude to a (Chef's) Kiss!

A little peek into the various stages that brought *Chef's Kiss* to life...

Things always start with a script! To the right is a page of Jarrett's script, which then gets turned into line art from Danica (bottom left), which is then colored by Hank (bottom right) while it is being lettered by Hassan (page 96).

PAGE 82. Six panels.

PANEL 1. Ben is smiling. The others are curious, except Rachel. Tom gives up.

BEN:
Okay. Vote on this. He bought me coffee and showed me the sunset from a special spot. No hand holding, kissing, or a hug. Date, or not a date? Rachel says not.

LIZ:
Sounds romantic. Totally a date.

TOM:
Alright, your collective dismissal of Vlad notwithstanding, watching the sunset is a great move. I'd say date.

PANEL 2. Ben is swooning.

BEN:
So two yays and a nay. I guess it was a date? Heh. I guess it was a date!

PANEL 3. Liz is warning Ben. Tom is done with the conversation. Rachel points out the book.

LIZ:
Slow it down, Romeo. Why don't you focus on your challenge this week?

TOM:
Yeah! And what's all this about a great new bong?

RACHEL:
Hey, Ben. How about something like this?

PANEL 4. Ben takes the book from her. The others are gathered around him.

BEN:
Ooh. Let's see. Yeah. Okay, we don't have anything like this at the restaurant.

TOM:
What if we asked Vlad?

LIZ:
Oooh.

PANEL 5. Ben puts the book down to praise Rachel. She's beaming.

BEN:
Yeah! I think I can work with this. Good find, Rachel!

RACHEL:
Just remember me when you're running that place.

PANEL 6. Ben is excited. So are the others.

BEN:
Who wants to go shopping?!

TOM:
Sure! I need snacks anyway for when Vlad and I are doing cool stuff together.

RACHEL:
Sure!

LIZ:
Let's do it!

script

inks

colors

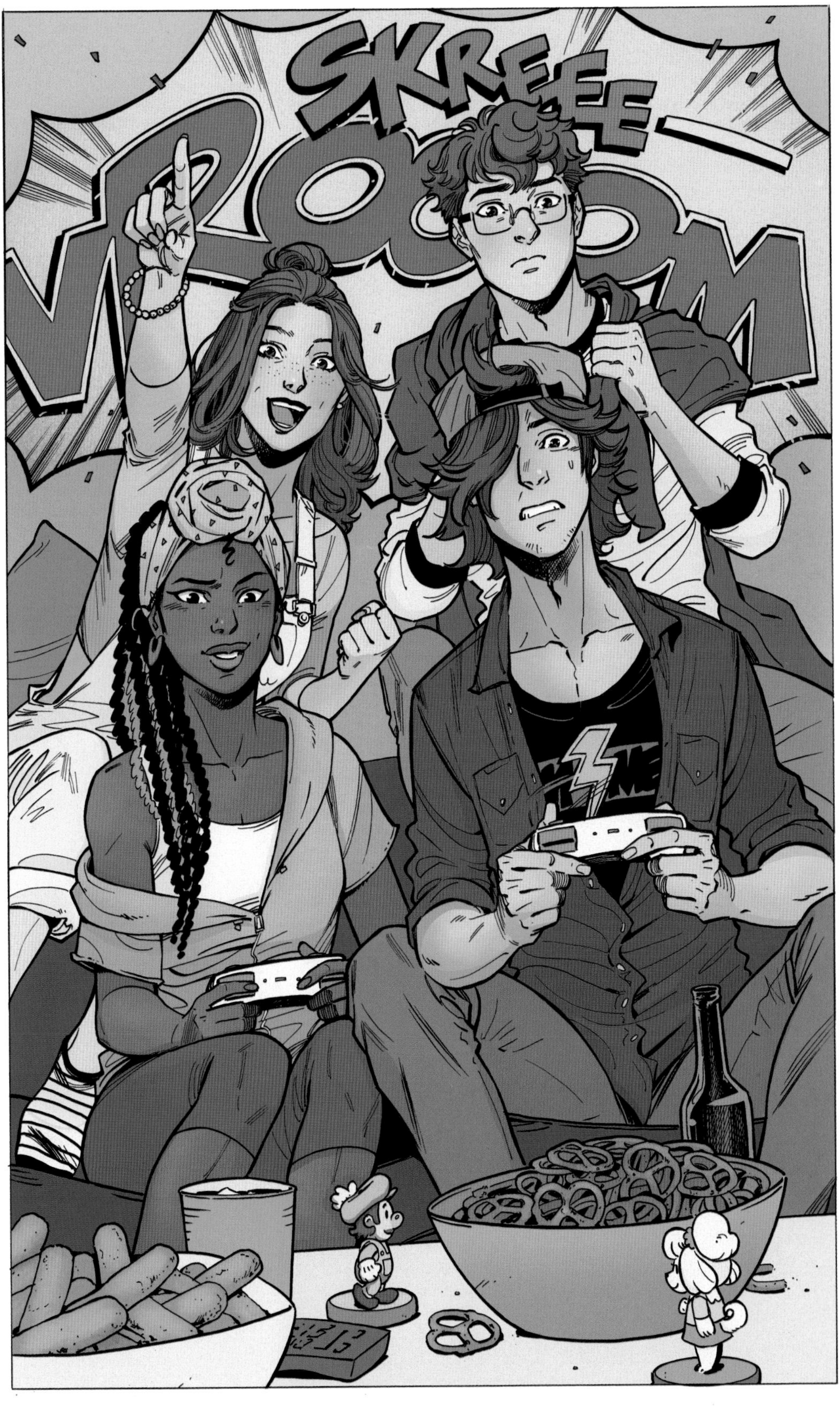
SKREEEE–
VROOOM

Bonus art by Danica Brine & colors by Hank Jones

- 1 package puff pastry, thawed according to package instructions
- 3 tbsp olive oil, divided
- 2 tbsp unsalted butter
- 24 oz mixed wild mushrooms, roughly chopped
- 2 cloves garlic, thinly sliced
- 1 tsp fresh thyme leaves
- 1 tbsp fresh parsley leaves, roughly chopped
- 1/2 cup ricotta
- 2 eggs
- 1 cup baby arugula
- 1 tbsp chives, finely chopped
- 1 lemon
- Parmesan cheese, to serve
- Kosher salt and freshly ground black pepper

Ben's Mushroom Ricotta Tart

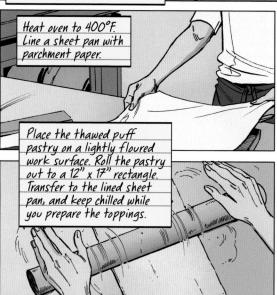

Heat oven to 400°F. Line a sheet pan with parchment paper.

Place the thawed puff pastry on a lightly floured work surface. Roll the pastry out to a 12" x 17" rectangle. Transfer to the lined sheet pan, and keep chilled while you prepare the toppings.

Melt 2 tbsp butter with 2 tbsp olive oil in a large skillet over medium-high heat until the butter is foaming.

Add mushrooms to the skillet, then season with 1 tsp salt and 1/2 tsp black pepper. Cook until moisture has evaporated and mushrooms are golden brown and slightly crispy, 10-15 minutes.

Add the garlic and 1 tsp thyme leaves to the skillet. Cook, stirring frequently, until fragrant, about 30-60 seconds. Remove from heat and let cool slightly.

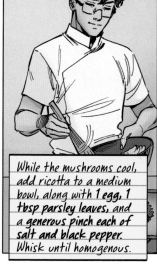

While the mushrooms cool, add ricotta to a medium bowl, along with 1 egg, 1 tbsp parsley leaves, and a generous pinch each of salt and black pepper. Whisk until homogenous.

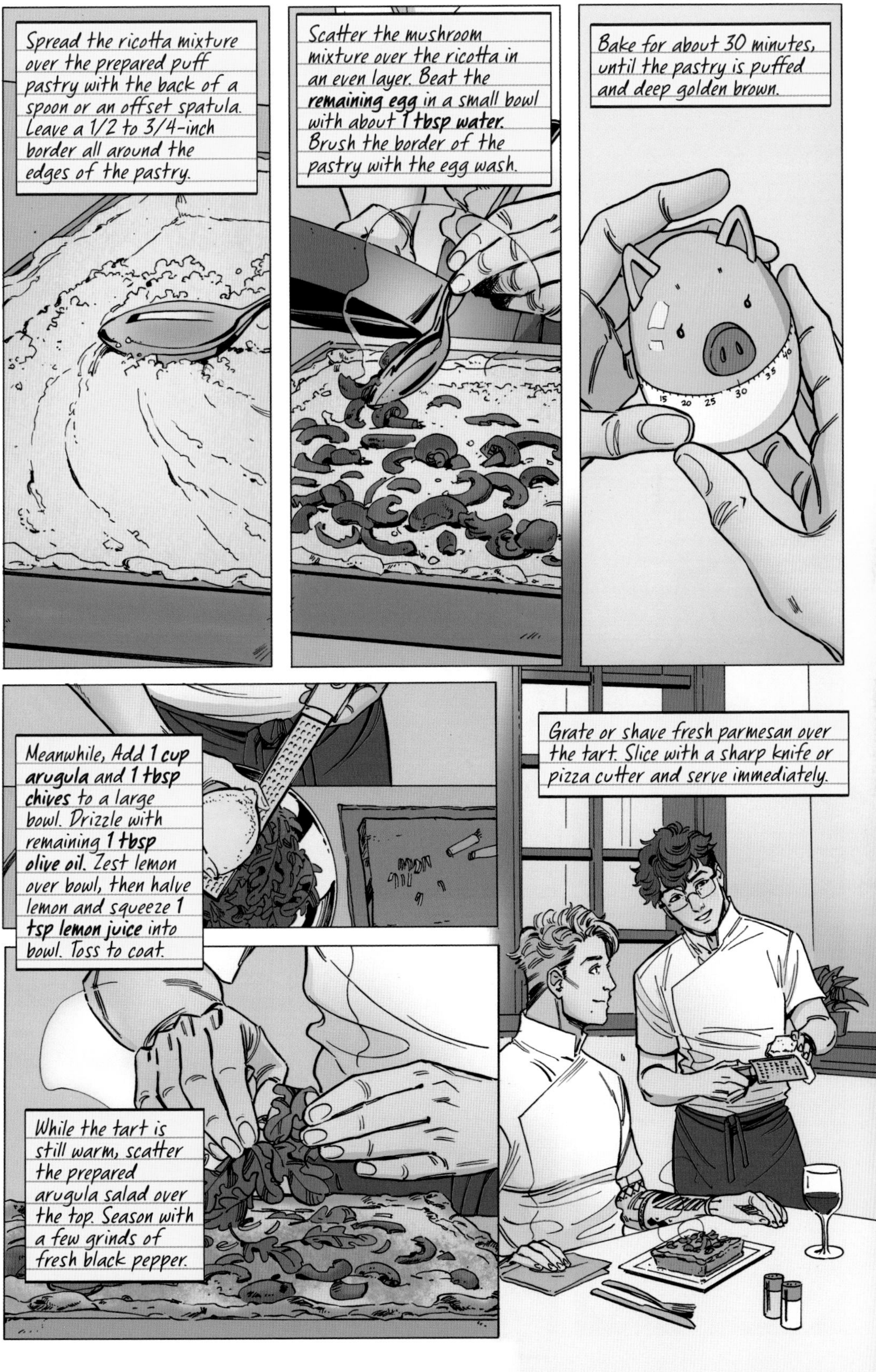
Spread the ricotta mixture over the prepared puff pastry with the back of a spoon or an offset spatula. Leave a 1/2 to 3/4-inch border all around the edges of the pastry.
Scatter the mushroom mixture over the ricotta in an even layer. Beat the remaining egg in a small bowl with about 1 tbsp water. Brush the border of the pastry with the egg wash.
Bake for about 30 minutes, until the pastry is puffed and deep golden brown.
15 20 25 30 35 40
Meanwhile, Add 1 cup arugula and 1 tbsp chives to a large bowl. Drizzle with remaining 1 tbsp olive oil. Zest lemon over bowl, then halve lemon and squeeze 1 tsp lemon juice into bowl. Toss to coat.
While the tart is still warm, scatter the prepared arugula salad over the top. Season with a few grinds of fresh black pepper.
Grate or shave fresh parmesan over the tart. Slice with a sharp knife or pizza cutter and serve immediately.

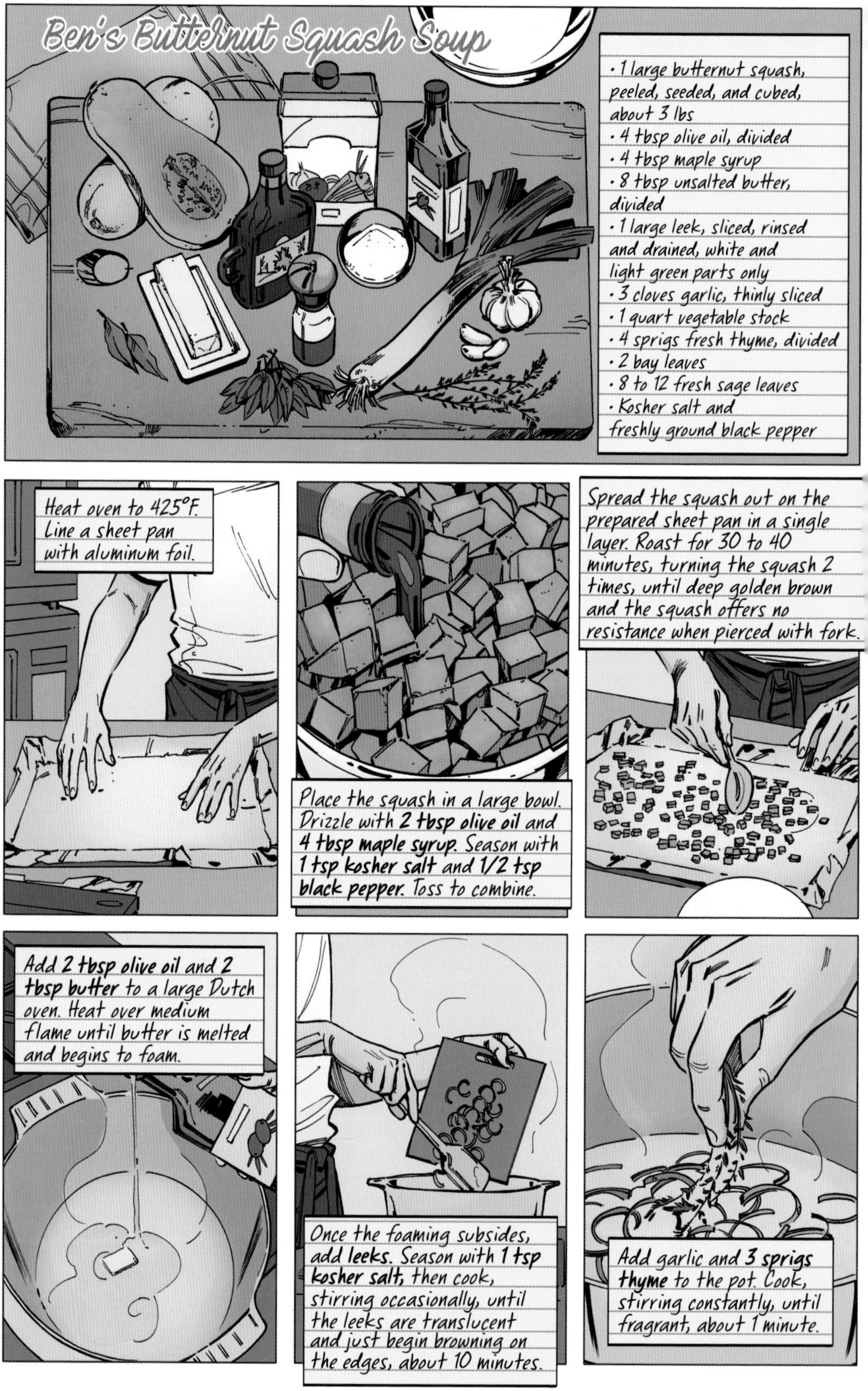
Ben's Butternut Squash Soup
• 1 large butternut squash, peeled, seeded, and cubed, about 3 lbs
• 4 tbsp olive oil, divided
• 4 tbsp maple syrup
• 8 tbsp unsalted butter, divided
• 1 large leek, sliced, rinsed and drained, white and light green parts only
• 3 cloves garlic, thinly sliced
• 1 quart vegetable stock
• 4 sprigs fresh thyme, divided
• 2 bay leaves
• 8 to 12 fresh sage leaves
• Kosher salt and freshly ground black pepper
Heat oven to 425°F. Line a sheet pan with aluminum foil.
Place the squash in a large bowl. Drizzle with **2 tbsp olive oil** and **4 tbsp maple syrup**. Season with **1 tsp kosher salt** and **1/2 tsp black pepper**. Toss to combine.
Spread the squash out on the prepared sheet pan in a single layer. Roast for 30 to 40 minutes, turning the squash 2 times, until deep golden brown and the squash offers no resistance when pierced with fork.
Add **2 tbsp olive oil** and **2 tbsp butter** to a large Dutch oven. Heat over medium flame until butter is melted and begins to foam.
Once the foaming subsides, add **leeks**. Season with **1 tsp kosher salt**, then cook, stirring occasionally, until the leeks are translucent and just begin browning on the edges, about 10 minutes.
Add garlic and **3 sprigs thyme** to the pot. Cook, stirring constantly, until fragrant, about 1 minute.

Add **roasted squash**, along with the **vegetable stock** and **bay leaves**, to the Dutch oven. Increase heat to medium high until boiling, then reduce to a simmer. Cook, uncovered, for 10 minutes.

Remove and discard the **bay leaves** and **thyme**. It's okay if the thyme leaves have fallen off the stems-- they'll blend up just fine.

Remove the Dutch oven from heat. Using an immersion blender, blend the soup until smooth. Taste for seasoning, add more salt and pepper to taste, then blend to combine, about 1 minute.

Melt the remaining **6 tbsp** butter in a small skillet over medium heat. Swirl the pan until butter is foaming, then add the remaining **1 sprig thyme**.

Once butter stops foaming and just turns golden brown, add **sage leaves**. Cook, swirling pan, until butter has darkened and sage is frizzled, about 15 to 20 seconds. Remove from heat.

Divide the soup evenly among four to six bowls. Garnish with **2 sage leaves** per bowl, and drizzle the browned butter in concentric circles around the leaves.

Enjoy!

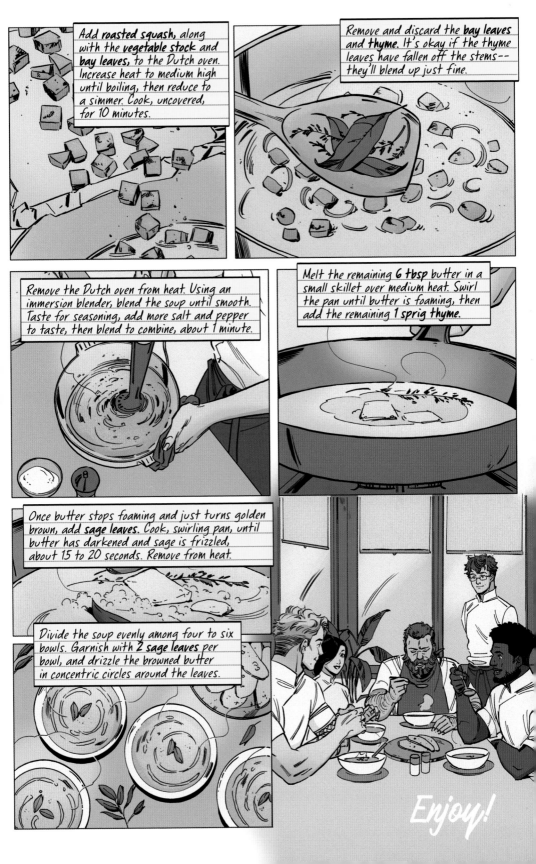

meet the *Chef's Kiss* characters!

Ben Cook

LOVES: His best friend Liz. The smell of vintage bookshops. Learning new skills. D&D. Tiki drinks. Confidence. Cooking for people he loves.

HATES: That magic isn't real. Feeling trapped. Family obligations. That he overthinks everything. Making the first move.

THEME SONG: "Butterflies" by Cub Sport

FUN FACT: Ben once created an entire D&D campaign specifically for Liz to help her get over an insufferable, guitar-playing ex. Playing a battle mage, she laid waste to Skye the Bard King and all his lands.

Liz Brooks

LOVES: Her best friend Ben. Meditation. The Squad. Sketching at aquariums. Sex-positivity. Fruit snacks. Her dad's BBQ. Sauvignon blanc.

HATES: Being wrong. Prudes. Body shaming. Bland food and boring people. Regressive politicians. Most rom-coms.

THEME SONG: "Like a Girl" by Lizzo

FUN FACT: Liz generally doesn't get competitive except when it comes to minigolf. She and Ben once got banned from a course when she climbed the windmill to proclaim her victory after a particularly heated match.

Tom Williams

LOVES: Summertime. Beer gardens. Solving problems. Living a minimal lifestyle. Lo-fi beats. Vibing. Anything sweet. Free food. His framily.

HATES: The word "framily," but not the concept. Sudden loud noises. Seasonal allergies. Karens, but who doesn't? Clutter. Bad vibes.

THEME SONG: "The Cult of Dionysus" by The Orion Experience

FUN FACT: The worst job Tom ever had was driving an ice cream truck, but only because they wouldn't let him eat the product while he was working. He earned enough to buy Vlad the Inhaler and immediately quit.

Rachel Defilippo

LOVES: When boys kiss boys. Yuri!!! on Ice. Haikyu!! Korean face masks. Candy. Harajuku fashion. Being held. Collecting plush. Hard cider.

HATES: Being bored. Thinking about the future. Not being herself. Being scolded. Bitter-flavored things. Her parents sometimes, but then she remembers that you shouldn't hate what you don't really know.

THEME SONG: "Gimme Chocolate" by Babymetal

FUN FACT: Rachel has held the record for most words written on the site that hosts her fan fiction for six straight years. Nobody else on the site comes close, and they probably never will.

Emilia Okamoto

LOVES: Her best friend Liam. Visiting her aunt in Osaka. Thunderstorms. Bullet trains. Perfectly cooked salmon, any cuisine. Horror movies. Whisky sours.

HATES: The lack of high-speed railways in the US. People that don't take care of their kitchen knives. Anyone who hurts her friends, especially when it's their own family members.

THEME SONG: "Girls in the Hood" by Megan Thee Stallion

FUN FACT: Emi's chef's knife has been in her family for four generations. She keeps it honed to a razor's edge at all times.

Mel Jackson

LOVES: Collecting old R&B and jazz records. The smell of rain. Thai iced tea. Cozy sweaters. His sound system. Going for long drives. Rural France in autumn. A good dark and stormy.

HATES: Stubbornness. Outdated cuisine. People that equate money with success.

THEME SONG: "What a Wonderful World" by Louis Armstrong

FUN FACT: Mel gets most of his vintage records from estate sales. It was at one of these sales where he discovered that vintage liquor is a Thing. A bottle of Gordon's Gin from the 1950s is his current favorite.

Chef Davis

LOVES: Minding his own business. When others mind their own business.

HATES: Busybodies. Gossip.

THEME SONG: "Shut Up" by The Black Eyed Peas

FUN FACT: If he hadn't become a chef, Davis wanted to be a professional dancer. Even now, he is shockingly light on his feet and graceful. He has a ballet routine that would bring you to tears, and he would appreciate you keeping that to yourself.

Liam Sommer

LOVES: His best friend Emi. Working up a good sweat. Cooking. Sitting in the sun with Watson. Whisky cocktails. Teaching.

HATES: Bullies. Corporate culture. Bigots. Confrontation on his own behalf. Sugary sodas.

THEME SONG: "Stand by Me" by Florence and the Machine

FUN FACT: Liam owns a hand-written recipe book that was left to him by his grandfather. It's his most treasured possession.

Watson

LOVES: Scritches behind the ears. Cuddling. Eating good food. *Charlotte's Web*. The movie *Babe*. The entire collected works of Akira Kurosawa, particularly *The Hidden Fortress*.

HATES: Food not made with love. Getting caught in the rain.

THEME SONG: "Happy" by Pharrell Williams

FUN FACT: Parts of his backstory, as told by Chef Davis, are true. But he'll never tell you which parts, mostly because he's a pig and can't speak in anything other than cute oinks.

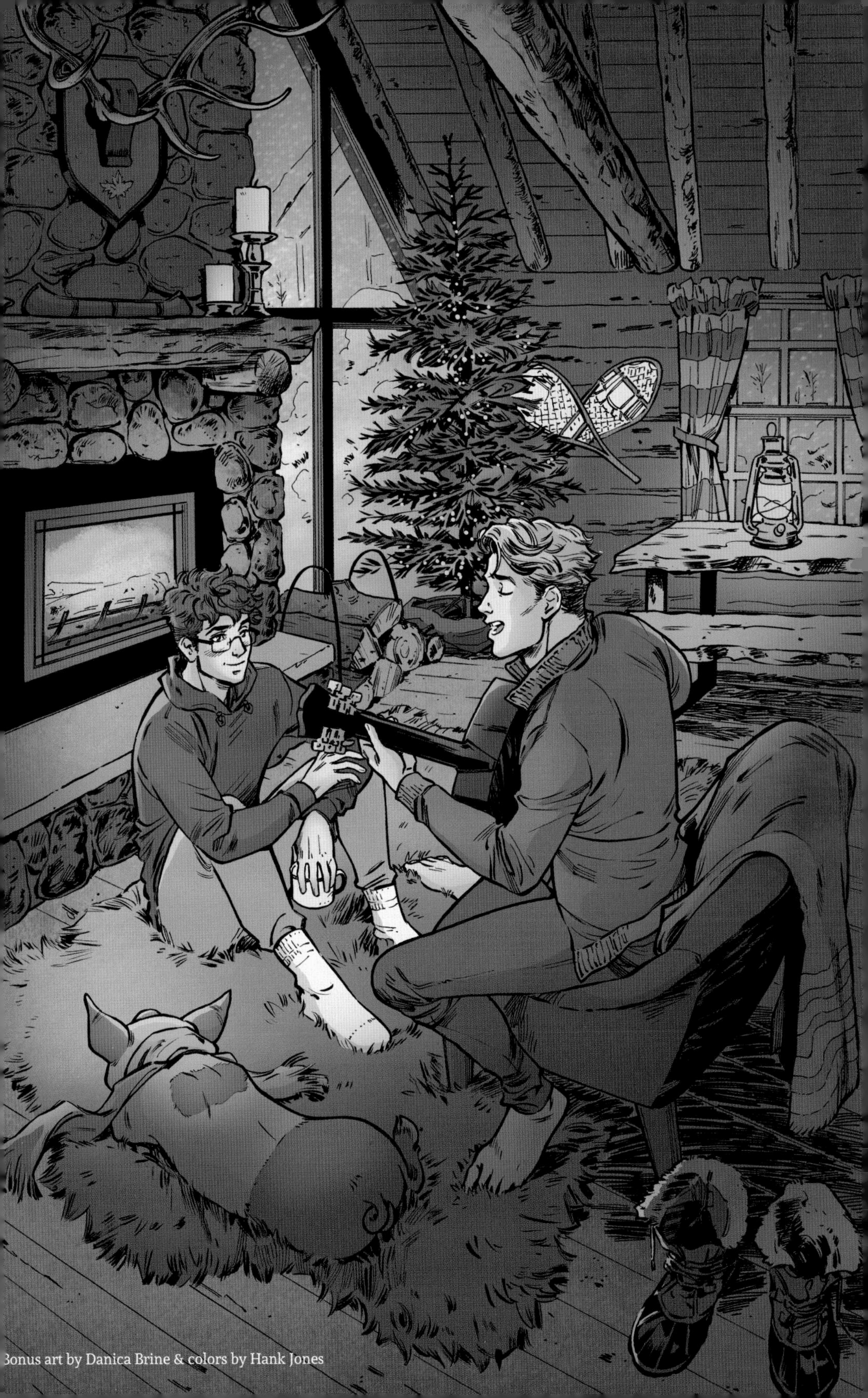

Bonus art by Danica Brine & colors by Hank Jones

Bonus art by Danica Brine
& colors by Hank Jones

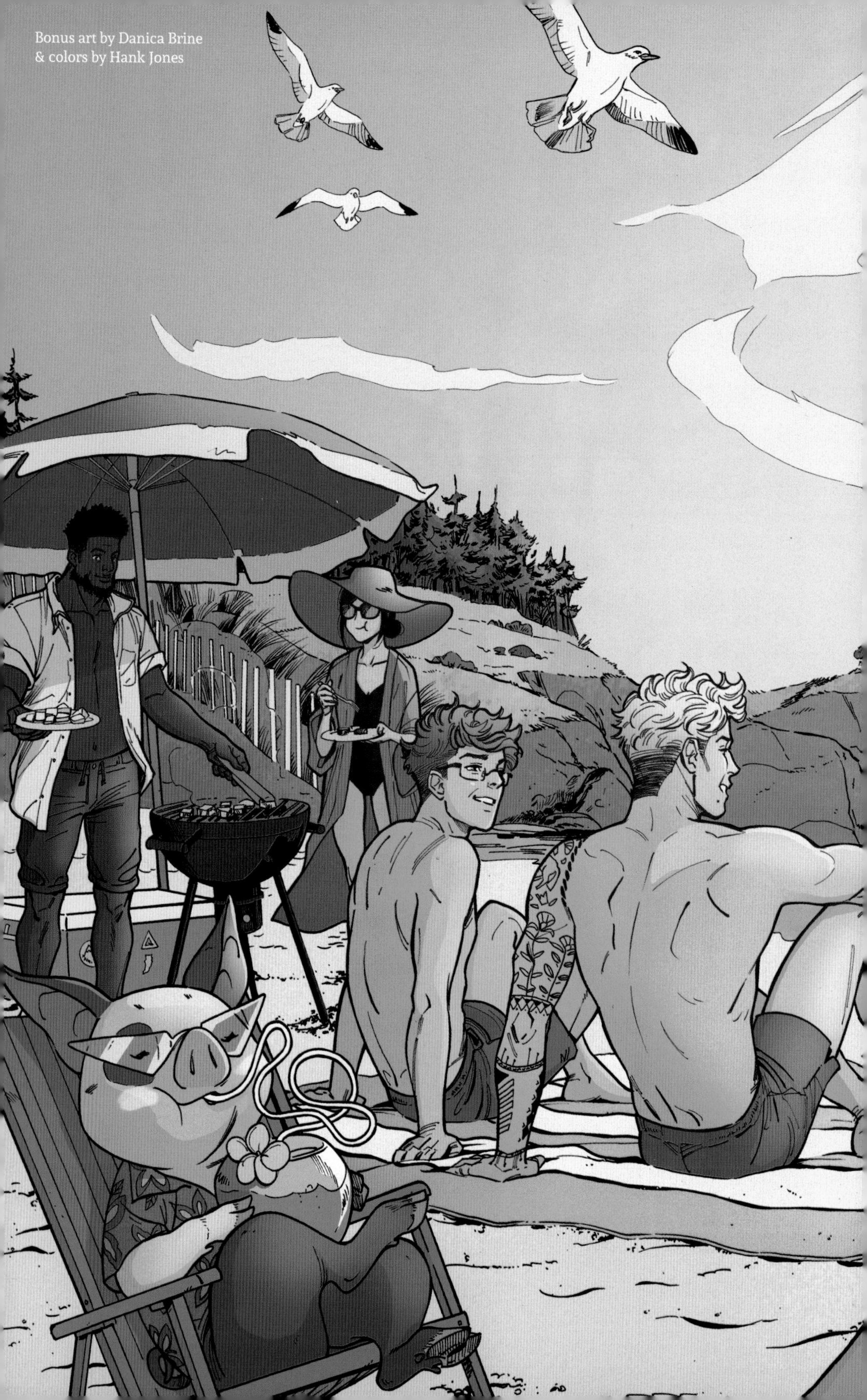

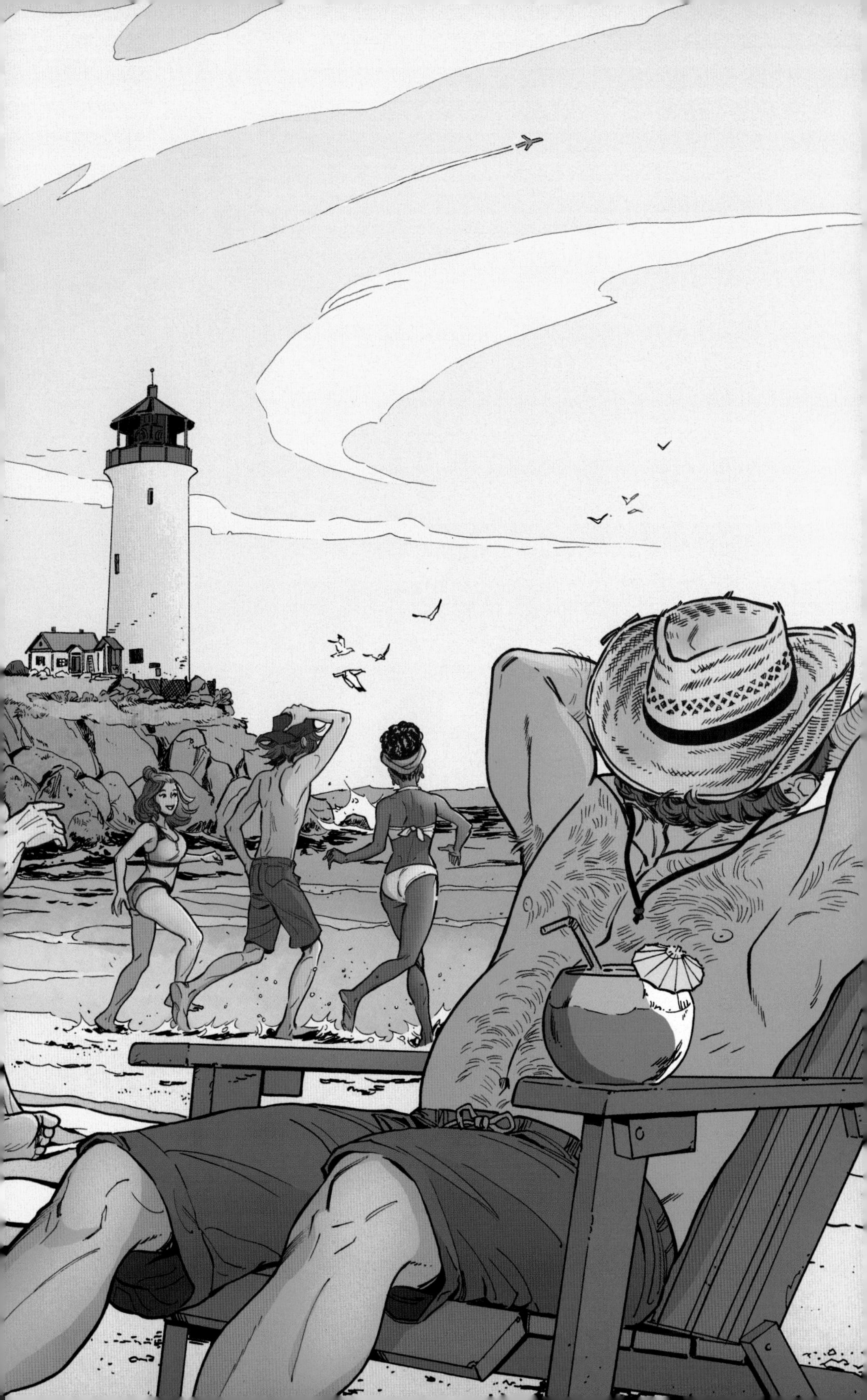

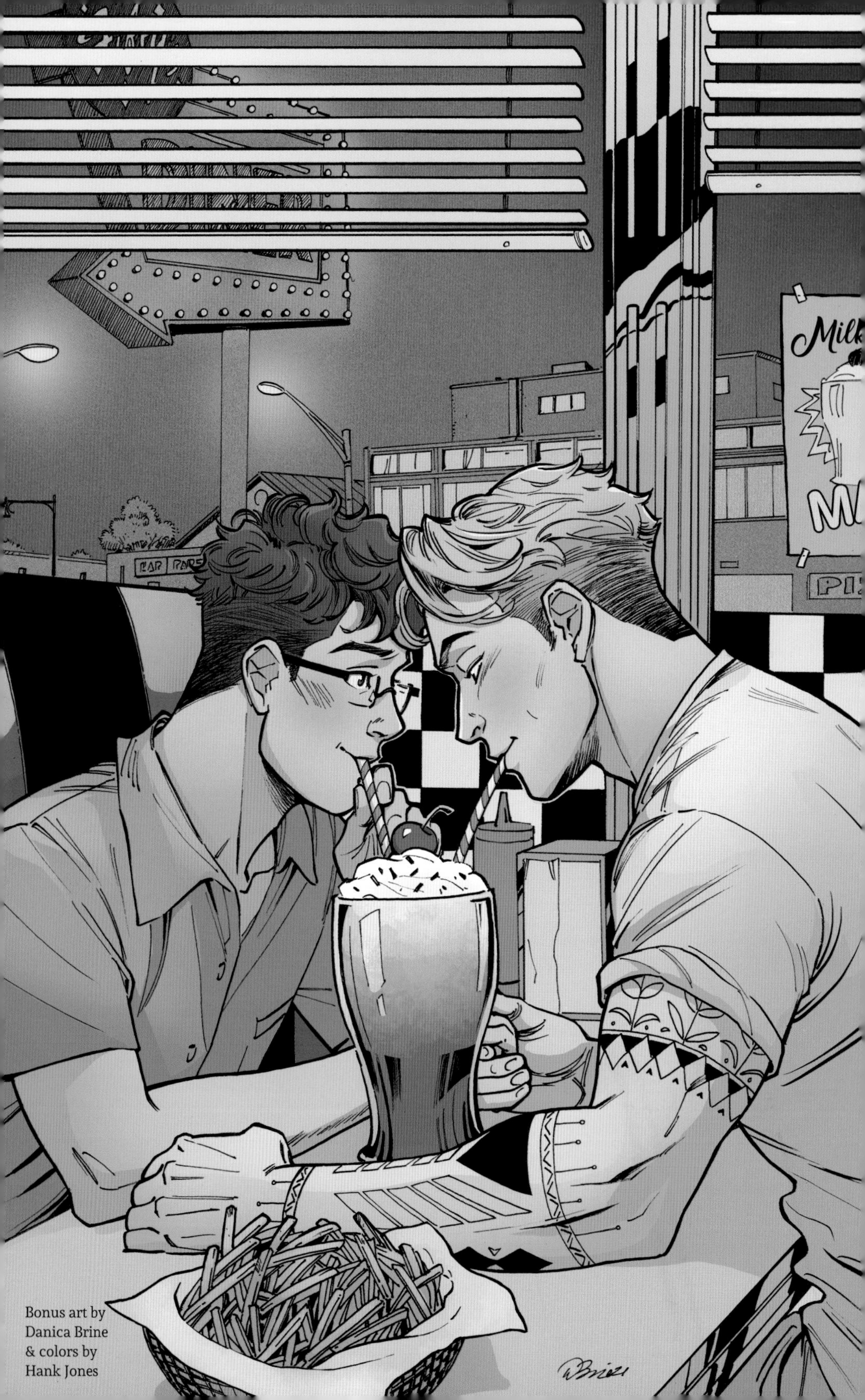

Bonus art by
Danica Brine
& colors by
Hank Jones

uest art by Kevin Wada

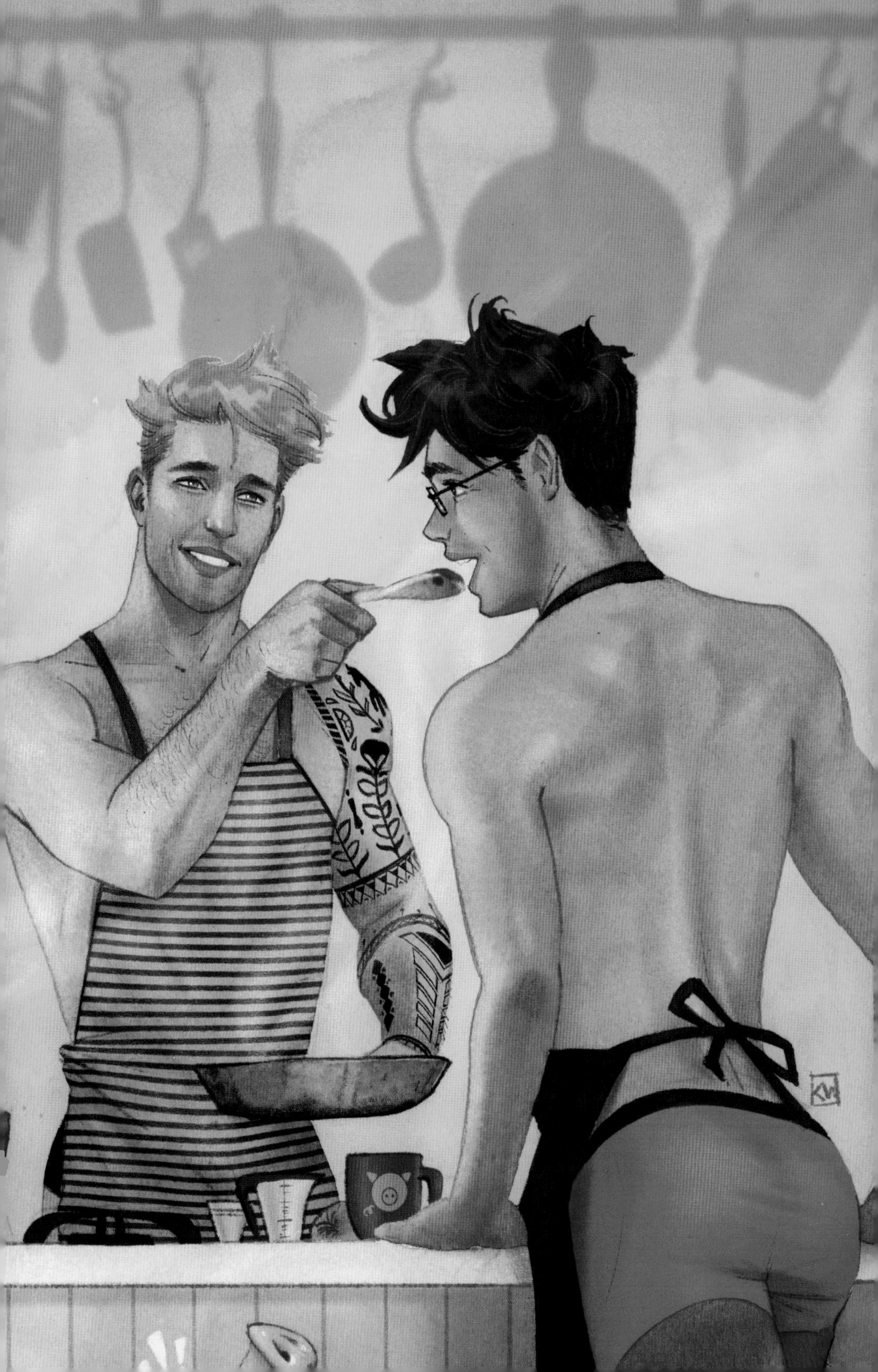

Guest art by Sara Richard

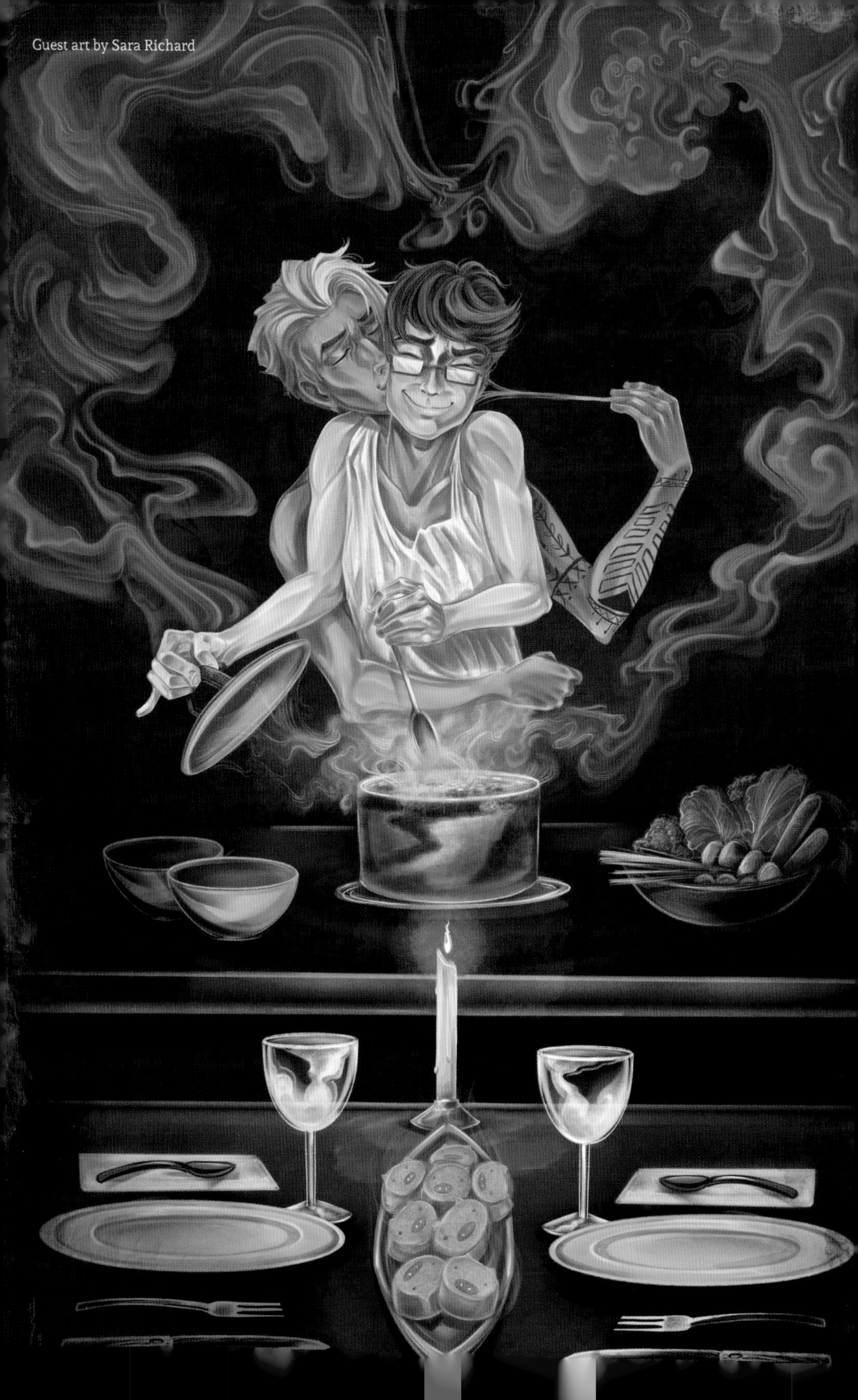

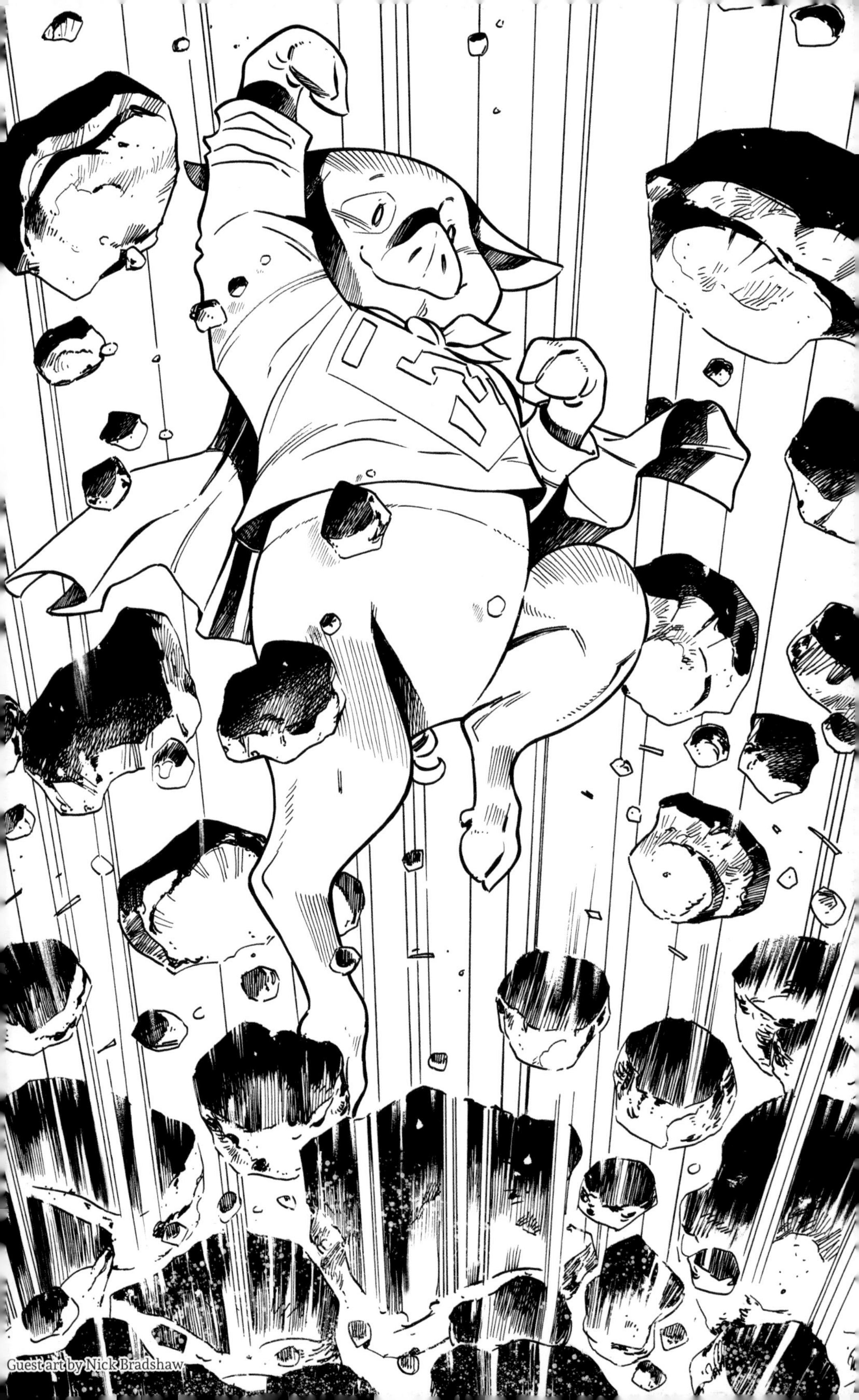
Guest art by Nick Bradshaw

Many, many thanks to everyone who supported me along the way:
Katie Cook, for reading every single draft of this thing, the constant encouragement, enthusiasm, and for shipping Ben and Liam as much as I do. John Layman, for the feedback, advice, and morning calls. Sara Richard, for cheering us on every step of the way. Emily Comerford, the Emi to my Liam. Bobby O'Neill, for laughing at my stupid jokes. Bob Shaw, for always believing in me. My Oni cheering squad: Brad, Amber, Michelle, and JLu. Our editors: Robin, Grace, and Sweet Sassy Cerasi, whose enthusiasm and gentle guidance kept this project fun. And, of course, Danica, Hank, and Hassan, who performed the forbidden alchemy needed to bring this book to life.

Jarrett Melendez

meet the Chef's Kiss creators!

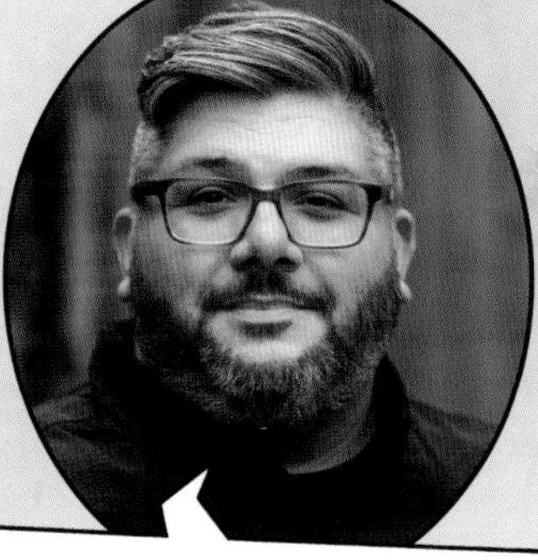

Jarrett Melendez grew up on the mean, deer-infested streets of Bucksport, Maine. A longtime fan of food and cooking, Jarrett has spent a lot of his time in kitchens, often as a paid professional! Jarrett is a regular contributor to Bon Appetit and Food52, and is the author of *The Comic Kitchen*, a fully illustrated, comic-style cookbook. When not cooking and writing about food, Jarrett usually writes comic books (like this one, *Chef's Kiss!*) and has contributed to the Ringo-nominated *All We Ever Wanted*, *Full Bleed*, and *Murder Hobo: Chaotic Neutral*. He is currently writing a graphic memoir for Oni Press. Jarrett lives in Somerville, Massachusetts, with his partner, Stuart, and their collection of Monokuro Boo plush pigs.

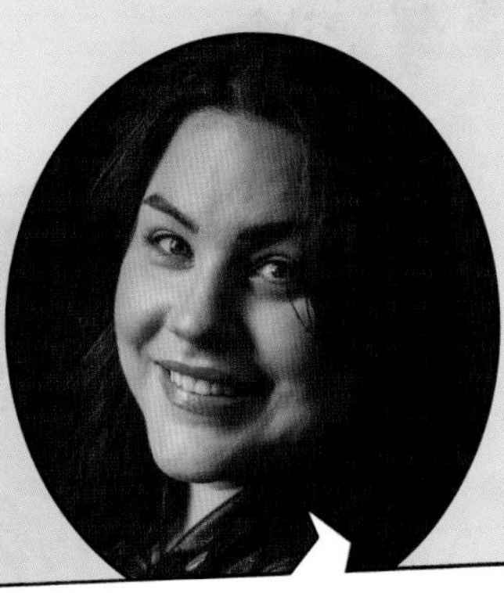

Danica Brine is walking sass in a leather jacket, forged in the icy lands of New Brunswick, Canada. From her waking hours to the moment she slumps over, asleep at her desk, Danica can be found with a drawing tool in her hands. Her work has been featured on the covers of *Wayward*, *Elephantmen*, *Exorsisters*, and *Doctor Who: The Thirteenth Doctor*. She's also contributed artwork to *All We Ever Wanted*, featured in the *New York Times* and *The Comic Kitchen*. When not working as a comic artist, she illustrates children's books for a Canadian French-language publisher. Danica lives in Moncton, New Brunswick, Canada, with her husband, Nick, and their shiba inu, Taro.

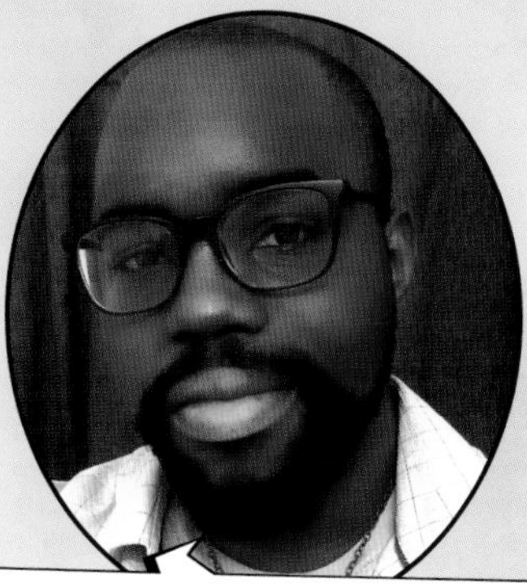

Hank Jones is a colorist based in Atlanta, Georgia. He loves comics, movies, and *really* loves video games. He also enjoys a nice cup of coffee during a rainy day.

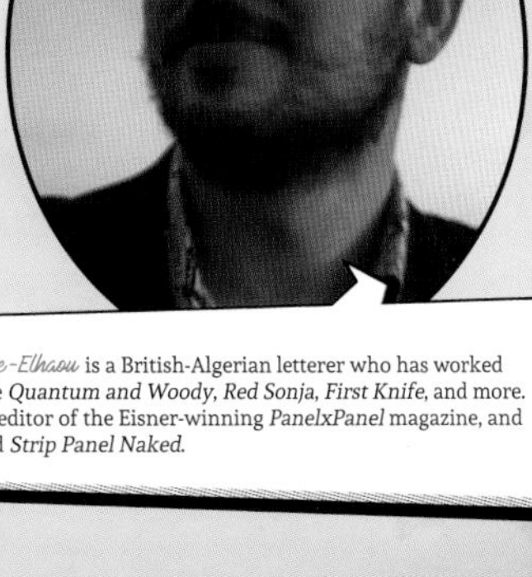

Hassan Otsmane-Elhaou is a British-Algerian letterer who has worked on comics like *Quantum and Woody*, *Red Sonja*, *First Knife*, and more. He's also the editor of the Eisner-winning *PanelxPanel* magazine, and voice behind *Strip Panel Naked*.

Mooncakes

By Suzanne Walker, Wendy Xu, and Joamette Gil

When teenage witch Nova's childhood friend, Tam, moves back to town, the two discover a sinister group plotting to harness Tam's werewolf powers for their own gain.

Hazards of Love

By Stan Stanley

Amparo's deal with the talking cat was simple: a drop of blood in order to become a better person. But when the cat steals their name and their body, becoming the "better person" they were promised, Amparo's spirit is imprisoned in a land of terrifying creatures known as Bright World. To return to the other side and see their true love again, Amparo must use every bit of cleverness to escape.

Martian Ghost Centaur

By Mat Heagerty and Steph Mided

Once a booming tourism destination, Southborough has lost most of its visitors ever since folks stopped believing their Sasquatch could be real. When a tech company starts buying up the town and pushing out all the people and places that make it special, a tenacious teen named Louie will do everything she can to save her town, including planning a bizarre, elaborate hoax.